The Real Horse Soldiers

Also by Timothy B. Smith:

The Decision Was Always My Own

Altogether Fitting and Proper

Grant Invades Tennessee

Shiloh: Conquer or Perish

The Mississippi Secession Convention

Rethinking Shiloh

Corinth 1862

James Z. George

Shiloh National Military Park - With Brian K. McCutchen

The Battle of Shiloh

Mississippi in the Civil War

A Chickamauga Memorial

The Golden Age of Battlefield Preservation

Shiloh and the Western Campaign of 1862 - With Edward Cunningham and Gary
D. Joiner

The Untold Story of Shiloh

Champion Hill

This Great Battlefield of Shiloh

The Real Horse Soldiers

*Benjamin Grierson's Epic 1863
Civil War Raid Through Mississippi*

Timothy B. Smith

Savas Beatie
California

Library of Congress Cataloging-in-Publication Data

Names: Smith, Timothy B., 1974- author.
Title: The Real Horse Soldiers: Benjamin Grierson's Epic 1863 Civil War Raid Through Mississippi / by Timothy B. Smith.
Description: El Dorado Hills, California: Savas Beatie [2018] |
Includes bibliographical references
Identifiers: LCCN 2018027431| ISBN: 9781611214284 (hardcover: alk. paper) |
ISBN: 9781611214291 (ebook)
Subjects: LCSH: Grierson's Cavalry Raid, 1863. |
United States—History—Civil War, 1861-1865—Cavalry operations.
Classification: LCC E475.23 .S55 2018 | DDC 973.7/33—dc23
LC record available at https://lccn.loc.gov/2018027431

Trade paperback ISBN-13: 978-1-61121-530-4

SB

Savas Beatie
989 Governor Drive, Suite 102
El Dorado Hills, CA 95762
916-941-6896
www.savasbeatie.com
sales@savasbeatie.com

Savas Beatie titles are available at special discounts for bulk purchases in the United States by corporations, institutions, and other organizations. For more details, contact us at the address or phone number above, by e-mail at sales@savasbeatie.com, or visit our website at www.savasbeatie.com for additional information.

Proudly printed in the United States of America

To God be the Glory

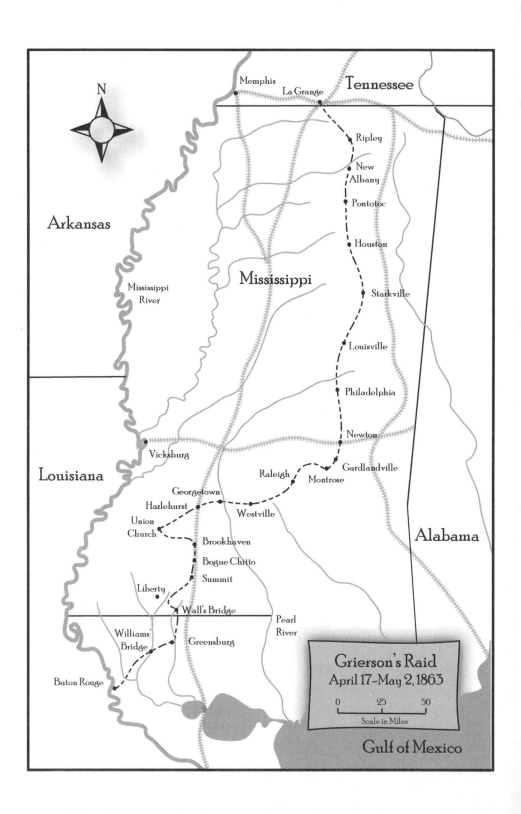

Grierson's Raid
April 17–May 2, 1863

0   25   50
Scale in Miles

Table of Contents

Table of Contents (continued)

List of Maps

List of Illustrations

List of Illustrations (continued)

Preface

The people of Brookhaven, Mississippi, would have raised their collective eyebrows had they known the name of the officer on the train passing through their little town. Some would have likely cursed his name and memory. The colonel had made a national name for himself decades earlier as a Union cavalry officer during the Civil War. Now, he commanded one of the nation's cavalry regiments stationed out west to keep the peace on the frontier.[1]

Most people riding the train would not have taken any notice of the sleepy little Mississippi railroad community, but this man did. He was as interested in Brookhaven as its citizens would have been in him. The two shared a history that forever bound them.[2]

Army officers routinely passed through Brookhaven, so the presence of one more would not have stirred much in the way of local interest. Colonel Benjamin H. Grierson of the 10th United States Cavalry, however, had a history not only with Brookhaven but with many other little towns along this stretch of the Illinois Central. Grierson had galloped through the region some 30 years earlier under quite different circumstances. As he put it, "Little did the citizens when passing to and from about the

---

1   Benjamin H. Grierson, *A Just and Righteous Cause: Benjamin H. Grierson's Civil War Memoir*, ed. Bruce J. Dinges and Shirley A. Leckie (Carbondale: Southern Illinois University Press, 2008), 168.

2   Ibid., 168.

streets suspect that the modest-looking individual who sat in the sleeper quietly gazing at the place was the man who had created such a stir in their midst so long ago."[3]

The town's calm demeanor stood in stark contrast to the scene he had witnessed back in 1863 when he rode through as an enemy raider. Grierson was in the middle of his famous ride through Mississippi that long-ago April, a bold, successful expedition that made him a household name north and south of the Mason-Dixon Line. In fact, he had torn up sections of the railroad he was now riding on and damaged the infrastructure at Brookhaven and other nearby towns. This time he was passing through from south to north rather than the other way around, peering through a foggy train window instead of from atop his warhorse. Yet "the scenes . . . were brought vividly to mind," Grierson recalled, "as were also those at other stations enacted nearly thirty-five years ago—by my command."[4]

One can only wonder about the emotions Grierson felt as he made that trip northward from New Orleans. What did he feel as the train approached the town of Summit? Did he think of the destruction he had inflicted there, including a large train and the cache of rum his soldiers had found? The train rolled past Bogue Chitto, where his soldiers burned the depot. Did he look about to catch a glimpse of the new structure that replaced the one destroyed? Perhaps he pondered the new bridges over which the train chugged; he and his men had destroyed many of the original trestles in 1863.

Grierson remembered Brookhaven as the train pulled into the station. "There was much running and yelling as our cavalry dashed into the place," he wrote. His recollections would have included leading his men as they put out fires spreading from government stores to privately owned buildings. He would also have been interested in Bahala, just north of Brookhaven, where he sent a detachment to break the railroad. And beyond Bahala there was Hazlehurst, where his raiding column first reached the railroad, created major havoc, and sent a phony message by telegraph to a Confederate commander.[5]

3   Ibid.

4   Ibid.

5   Ibid.

Soon it was all over and the train steamed its way past the area he had shaken up so in 1863. All these towns, he reflected, "looked about as they did in 1863, leaving out the bustle and excitement then caused by the presence of the Federal cavalry." Grierson slipped back into his seat, the memories his short sojourn had conjured up along the railroad in southwest Mississippi once again fresh in his mind.[6]

Grierson's Raid still conjures up emotions, though not on the personal level Grierson experienced or those the people of Brookhaven would have felt had he stepped off that train. The raid is an adventurous and dynamic story of daring and bravery, the perfect backdrop for literature and film. Despite its prominence, the true story has never been fully told.

Many who have tried their hand at telling this wonderful tale have taken liberties with the truth. Novelist Harold Sinclair, in his 1956 book *The Horse Soldiers*, used the historic raid as its basis, but as novelists are wont to do, he made up conversations and events. Hollywood movies, notoriously weak when it comes to facts, have no qualms about using cinematic license to enhance a story. Such was the case with the 1959 motion picture *The Horse Soldiers,* starring John Wayne and William Holden, which was based on Sinclair's novel. Even when the raid was presented as a history monograph, Dee Brown, the award-winning author of *Bury My Heart at Wounded Knee* (1970), felt free to take liberty with the facts and sources in his 1954 *Grierson's Raid* in a manner no academic historian would allow. In fact, Neil L. York, a historian of the memory of the raid, surmised that Brown "was not above creating conversations and stretching inferences, practices which most professional historians avoid and look askance at when they see it in others. But Brown the storyteller has never been felt bound by traditional orthodoxies, nor has he been intimidated by the raised eyebrows of his academic critics." I held off reading Brown's book until I finished the manuscript for the present work so that only primary sources would guide my thoughts and analysis. I support York's statement that Brown played extremely loose and fast with the sources, making his book at points almost fiction itself.[7]

6   Ibid.

7   Neil Longley York, *Fiction as Fact: The Horse Soldiers and Popular Memory* (Kent, OH: Kent State University Press, 2001), 28; John Lee Mahin and Martin Rackin, "The Horse Soldiers or Grierson's Raid," *Civil War History* (June 1959), vol.

It is my contention that Grierson's Raid is so deep, so enticing, and so adventurous that no embellishment is necessary. Stephen Forbes, one of the raid's participants and later one of its historians, summed it up thusly: "A cavalry raid at its best is essentially a *game* of strategy and speed, with personal violence as an incidental complication. It is played according to more or less definite rules, not inconsistent, indeed, with the players' killing each other if the game cannot be won in any other way; but it is commonly a strenuous game, rather than a bloody one, intensely exciting, but not necessarily very dangerous."[8]

My aim in this book is threefold. The first is to tell a good story. While novels and hybrid books on the raid may display deeper character development and more conversation, the basic adventure story itself is enough to keep the reader's attention even when told strictly in a factual, academic manner. The second goal is to provide more social context to the raid than previous histories have done, with larger emphasis given to the soldiers in the saddle with Grierson and the inhabitants of Mississippi along the way who were affected by the raid. Finally, I seek to put the raid in the proper military context. Other accounts downplay, through a lack of attention, the larger context while focusing on the adventure itself. Without proper context, however, it is impossible to fully understand the real reasons for the raid and its true impact on the course of the Civil War.

5, no. 2, 183-87. For literature on the raid, see Dee Brown, *Grierson's Raid* (Urbana: University of Illinois Press, 1954); William H. Leckie and Shirley A. Leckie, *Unlikely Warriors: General Benjamin H. Grierson and His Family* (Norman: University of Oklahoma Press, 1984); Tom Lalicki, *Grierson's Raid: A Daring Cavalry Strike Through the Heart of the Confederacy* (New York: Farrar, Straus and Giroux, 2004); Mark Lardas, *Roughshod Through Dixie: Grierson's Raid 1863* (New York: Osprey, 2010); D. Alexander Brown, "Grierson's Raid, 'Most Brilliant' of the War," *Civil War Times Illustrated* (June 1965), vol. 3, no. 9, 4-11, 25-32; Bruce J. Dinges, "Grierson's Raid" *Civil War Times Illustrated* (February 1996), vol. 34, no. 6, 50-60, 62, 64; Bruce Jacob Dinges, "The Making of a Cavalryman: Benjamin H. Grierson and the Civil War Along the Mississippi, 1861-1865," PhD diss., Rice University, 1978; Elizabeth K. Oaks, "Benjamin H. Grierson: Reluctant Horse Soldier and Gentle Raider," MA thesis, Mississippi State University, 1981.

8   S. A. Forbes, "Grierson's Cavalry Raid," Address Before the Illinois State Historical Society, January 24, 1907, *Transactions of the Illinois State Historical Society* (Springfield, IL: Phillips Bros. State Printers, 1908), 102.

Essentially, Grierson's Raid had two major goals. One was destruction—the breaking of the important Southern Railroad of Mississippi at Newton Station. In that sense, it was not altogether different from many of the other cavalry raids of the war. The second objective, which added to its uniqueness when compared to other cavalry raids, was to divert attention away from what was transpiring west of the Mississippi River in Louisiana, where Ulysses S. Grant intended to cross the river below Vicksburg with the Army of the Tennessee to begin a land campaign to capture the Confederate citadel. As Grierson later explained, "My raid cannot be considered separately. It and Grant's Vicksburg Campaign was *one* grand military achievement," although he added that the raid was not planned down to the letter. "Definite orders were not possible," he continued, "as every movement depended on circumstances & contingencies." When considered with the other diversions underway at the same time (some to divert attention from Grierson, who was the main diversion for Grant), the complex but brilliant operation was not unlike a complicated football play in which the offense, with a player in motion, runs a fake trap, bootleg, reverse, flea-flicker, Hail Mary pump fake in order to run a draw up the middle. While Confederate attention was drawn all over the field by the fakes, diversions, and misdirections, Grant ran the ball right up the middle and scored a touchdown at Vicksburg.[9]

Grierson, as part of this major trick play, managed to inflict a substantial amount of damage and divert attention away from Grant. For five critical days in April 1863, exactly when Grant was preparing and crossing the river, Grierson had the almost complete attention of the Confederate commander, John C. Pemberton. The hapless enemy commander was looking east and south for the elusive raider rather than west, where the main threat to Vicksburg's existence waited. A study of Pemberton's messages during those five days reveals that 95.7 percent were concerned with Grierson's activities rather than Grant's. Pemberton's biographer, Michael B. Ballard, concludes that a dazed Pemberton was reacting to the tangible threat he could see rather than the rumored one

---

9   Terrence J. Winschel, *Triumph and Defeat: The Vicksburg Campaign* (Mason City, IA: Savas Publishing Company, 1999), 36; T. W. Lippincott to S. A. Forbes, December 20, 1908 and February 20, 1909, in Stephen A. Forbes Papers, University of Illinois, hereafter cited as UI; T. W. Lippincott, "Grierson's Raid," n.d., in Stephen A. Forbes Papers, UI. For a discussion of mounted raids, see Edward G. Longacre, *Mounted Raids of the Civil War* (New York: A. S. Barnes, 1975).

across the mighty river. The real irony was that Grierson posed little actual threat; Grant was the one who could and did doom Vicksburg. In doing so, he also doomed the Confederacy.[10]

Grierson's Raid can be compared to the famous Doolittle Raid of World War II. The raid on Japan by American army bombers flown from an aircraft carrier deck did little lasting physical damage, but the psychological impact was significant. Grierson's drive through the heart of Mississippi had a similar effect on the people of that state and the Confederate high command. The 1942 diversion was so important that it solidified key Japanese leaders' views on operations against Midway, diverting attention away from other ongoing efforts in the South Pacific.[11]

It is fitting, then, that such a story receives wide recognition, even in fiction and film. But there has long been a need for a comprehensive factual study. One Federal general involved in the planning wrote of the desire to be remembered: "We did it not for the laurels we might win, but I hope these will be planted on our graves when we are dead & gone, by a grateful posterity." I hope I have done that in this book.[12]

---

10 U.S. War Department, *War of the Rebellion: A Compilation of the Official Records of the Union and Confederate Armies*, 128 vols. (Washington, DC: U.S. Government Printing Office, 1880-1901), Series 1, vol. 24, pt. 3, 781-800, hereafter cited (all citations being Series 1 unless otherwise noted) as *OR*; Michael B. Ballard, *Pemberton: A Biography* (Jackson: University Press of Mississippi, 1991), 139.

11 For the Doolittle Raid, see James M. Scott, *Target Tokyo: Jimmy Doolittle and the Raid That Avenged Pearl Harbor* (New York: W. W. Norton & Company, 2015).

12 W. S. Smith to S. A. Forbes, November 25, 1908, in Stephen A. Forbes Papers, UI.

Prologue

From the ironclad *Benton,* Ulysses S. Grant gazed across the Mississippi River through the early morning haze toward the distant shore. Along with Adm. David Dixon Porter, he was among the first Union soldiers preparing to land in Mississippi at the small burned-out village of Bruinsburg. Grant hoped his men could walk ashore and form a bridgehead. If the enemy were present, it was going to be a hard day. For Grant, everything was at stake, and not just this isolated operation. He had already tried and failed several times to put his army on the dry ground east of the river in order to capture Vicksburg. This attempt was the most difficult and dangerous, and there was no Plan B. If this gamble failed, Grant would be boxed into a situation from which he would be hard pressed to recover.[1]

The date was April 30, 1863, the same day President Abraham Lincoln had set aside a month earlier as "a day of national humiliation, fasting, and prayer." Lincoln believed the United States had "been the recipients of the choicest bounties of Heaven; we have been preserved these many years in peace and prosperity; we have grown in numbers, wealth, and power as no other nation has ever grown. But we have forgotten God."[2]

---

1 Edwin C. Bearss, *The Vicksburg Campaign*, 3 vols. (Dayton, OH: Morningside, 1985), vol. 2, 318.

2 Abraham Lincoln: "Proclamation 97—Appointing a Day of National Humiliation, Fasting, and Prayer," March 30, 1863, at Gerhard Peters and John T. Woolley, *The American Presidency Project*, http://www.presidency.ucsb.edu/ws/?pid=69891.

To rectify this omission, Lincoln declared: "I do hereby request all the people to abstain on that day from their ordinary secular pursuits, and to unite at their several places of public worship and their respective homes in keeping the day holy to the Lord and devoted to the humble discharge of the religious duties proper to that solemn occasion." Grant and his soldiers deep in Dixie could not "abstain . . . from their ordinary secular pursuits," despite the secular and unholy nature of fighting and killing. If they thought of Lincoln's proclamation that day, they would have been more than happy to have the prayers of millions of citizens turned in their direction. Their efforts would go a long way in determining whether there would be a united nation for God to continue to bless.[3]

Grant and his men needed all the divine intervention they could get that day, for they were about to undertake a massive operation that almost defied human agency and planning. Grant was managing what was, up to that time, the largest potentially opposed waterborne landing in American history until World War II.[4]

*   *   *

The crossing to Bruinsburg was the culmination of a long list of failures in Grant's attempt to reach Vicksburg. Since October 1862 he had been trying to get to the city that was the last major blocking point to Union control of the Mississippi River. Capturing Vicksburg had been considered as early as 1861, when Gen. Winfield Scott had fashioned his famous Anaconda Plan. Most rolled their eyes at Scott's idea, which would take months and likely years to implement. By late 1862, however, most people had come to realize that Scott's timing was not that far off. The concerted effort to reach Vicksburg, starting in the fall of 1862, solidified that realization when Grant spent several months unsuccessfully trying to reach the hill city, much less capture it.[5]

Grant began his movement south in late October 1862 with high hopes. He moved his divisions along the Mississippi Central Railroad through

---

3   Ibid.

4   Warren E. Grabau, *Ninety-Eight Days: A Geographer's View of the Vicksburg Campaign* (Knoxville: University of Tennessee Press, 2000), 148-49.

5   James M. McPherson, *Battle Cry of Freedom: The Civil War Era* (New York: Oxford University Press, 1988), 333-35.

Holly Springs and Oxford, where William T. Sherman joined him with other troops from Memphis. Grant decided to make a two-front advance by sending Sherman back to Memphis and down the Mississippi River to hopefully capture Vicksburg while the Confederates were concentrating on Grant in north Mississippi. The Confederates did not fall for the trick, and they turned Grant back with cavalry raids in his rear against his supply base at Holly Springs. In late December, Sherman's effort was met and thrown back at Chickasaw Bayou, just north of Vicksburg.[6]

When the new year brought a flooded river and tributaries, Grant turned to roundabout waterborne operations in an effort to bypass Vicksburg or the defenses Sherman had found so daunting in December. In Louisiana, Grant tried to dig a canal across a bend in the river near Vicksburg so his vessels could pass without coming under the Confederate guns. The effort failed, as did a wide-ranging route through Lake Providence. Two efforts east of the Mississippi River offered more promise. Engineers cut a levee and flooded the delta region, giving the Federals access to the spider web of rivers and bayous. Failure soon followed because the Confederates blocked the Yazoo Pass expedition at Fort Pemberton near Greenwood. A similar effort at Steele's Bayou also ended in failure and almost cost the navy several gunboats stuck in the narrow waterways of the delta.[7]

Between October 1862 and April 1863, the Federals attempted six different major efforts, plus several side operations, to reach Vicksburg. The geography of the region, Confederate resistance, and internal squabbling defeated them all and left Grant in a quandary. His six failed attempts had led him farther south, down the Mississippi River, until he was within sight of the city he could not reach. What to do next?[8]

The difficult geography and Confederate resistance concerned Grant, but the political factors swirling around his failures were even more troubling. Some of his officers, including his closest friend Sherman, counseled taking the army back up the Mississippi River and restarting the campaign from Memphis. "I was putting myself in a position voluntarily which an enemy would be glad to maneuver a year—or a

---

6   Bearss, *The Vicksburg Campaign*, vol. 1, 21-230.

7   Ibid., 421-596.

8   For a concise overview of Grant's attempts, see William L. Shea and Terrence J. Winschel, *Vicksburg Is the Key: The Struggle for the Mississippi River* (Lincoln: University of Nebraska Press, 2003).

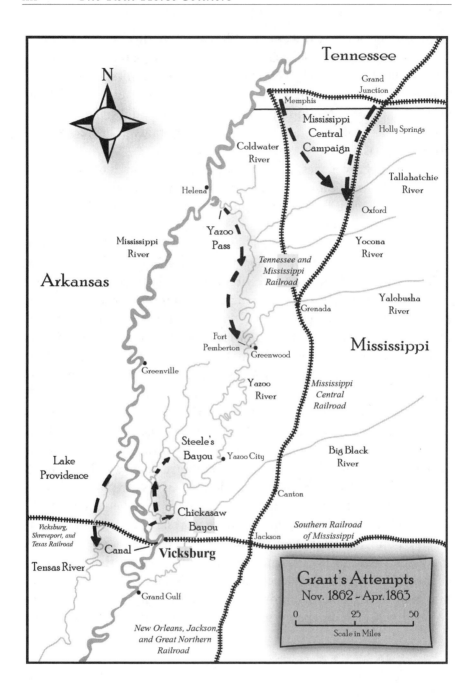

N

Tennessee

Grand
Junction

Memphis

Mississippi
Central
Campaign

Holly Springs

Coldwater
River

Tallahatchie
River

Helena

Yazoo
Pass

Oxford

Mississippi
River

Yocona
River

Arkansas

Tennessee and
Mississippi
Railroad

Yalobusha
River

Grenada

Fort
Pemberton
Greenwood

Mississippi

Greenville

Yazoo
River

Mississippi
Central
Railroad

Steele's
Bayou
Yazoo City

Big Black
River

Lake
Providence

Canton

Vicksburg,
Shreveport, and
Texas Railroad

Chickasaw
Bayou
Jackson

Southern Railroad
of Mississippi

Canal
Vicksburg

Tensas River

Grand Gulf

Grant's Attempts
Nov. 1862 ~ Apr. 1863

0   25   50

Scale in Miles

New Orleans, Jackson,
and Great Northern
Railroad

long time—to get me in," Grant remembered Sherman arguing. Grant, however, was determined to press forward, because the political fallout of a move backward would be disastrous, tantamount to an outright battlefield defeat. Grant would be admitting defeat, and the politicians and newspapermen who were already tiring of the slow campaign would have a field day. Grant had no choice; he had to move forward.[9]

Newspapermen could adversely sway public opinion, but the politicians held Grant's career in their hands. Some of Grant's generals had already begun undermining him, falsely reporting he was drinking again. Some politicians were only too eager to listen. More important, President Lincoln was growing more irritated by the day. General in chief Henry W. Halleck in Washington informed Grant, "The President . . . seems to be rather impatient about matters on the Mississippi." He then added, "You are too well advised of the anxiety of the Government for your success, and its disappointment at the delay, to render it necessary to urge upon you the importance of early action." Fortunately, Lincoln was not yet ready to make any changes, telling a friend who called for Grant's removal, "No, I rather like the man, and I think I will try him a little longer." But Grant was well aware that his time was about up.[10]

Without the military ability to attack up the steep bluffs directly at Vicksburg or the political ability to turn north and start a fresh campaign all over, Grant did the only thing he could and kept moving south. He decided he would send his Army of the Tennessee south, past Vicksburg, and across the Mississippi River below the city. Unlike his earlier approaches, Grant could then maneuver and advance toward Vicksburg on dry, level land. It was a huge gamble, but by that point a fairly easy decision. Much like being surrounded, Grant had no other reasonable choice.[11]

9   OR, 24, pt. 3, 179-80, 201; William T. Sherman, *Memoirs of General William T. Sherman: Written by Himself*, 2 vols. (New York: D. Appleton and Co., 1875), vol. 1, 315; Ulysses S. Grant, *Personal Memoirs of U.S. Grant*, 2 vols. (New York: Charles L. Webster and Co., 1885), vol. 1, 542-43; Brooks D. Simpson, *Ulysses S. Grant: Triumph over Adversity, 1822-1865* (Boston: Houghton Mifflin, 2000), 174.

10   OR, 24, pt. 3, 134; 24, pt. 1, 25, 28-29; Adam Badeau, *Military History of Ulysses S. Grant, From April, 1861, to April, 1865*, 2 vols. (New York: D. Appleton & Co., 1881), vol. 1, 180; Albert D. Richardson, *A Personal History of Ulysses S. Grant* (Hartford, CT: American Publishing Company, 1868), 290, 299.

11   Timothy B. Smith, *"The Decision Was Always My Own": Ulysses S. Grant and the Vicksburg Campaign* (Carbondale: Southern Illinois University Press, 2018), 80-85.

Even with the realization that it had to be done, Grant's seventh attempt was fraught with danger. His army would be south of Vicksburg, cut off from his supply chain except by a roundabout and long route over the bayous and creeks west of the river. Supplying the army would be a slow and tedious process. Once they had steamed south past Vicksburg's batteries, the navy gunboats could not return upriver, because the strong current would leave them nearly stationary in front of the Confederate guns. Most important, once he was downriver, Grant had to find a way to cross it and establish a bridgehead. If the Confederates deduced his intentions, they would be waiting for him in strength and make the crossing difficult and perhaps impossible.[12]

Thus Grant found himself, on Lincoln's day of fasting and prayer, about to cross the mighty river and invade Mississippi once more. In a sense his effort was akin to the oft-repeated story of the old Mississippi woman who left a prayer meeting in her town as it was about to be invaded by Union soldiers. She headed out on the road toward the enemy with a simple fire poker amid the jeers of her fellow citizens who asked what she could do with so little. She simply responded, "Sometimes you have to put feets to your prayers!"

*   *   *

Grant put "feets" to the many prayers lifted up that day and made his tremendous gamble less of a long shot through a series of feints and diversions in progress or just recently ended, some hundreds of miles away in different states. If these combined feints tricked the Confederate high command in Mississippi to take its collective eye off his crossing, getting into Mississippi would be much easier. Intelligence indicated that something must have worked: The enemy was nowhere to be seen across the river as the first Federals stormed ashore in Mississippi.

While two of his corps under John A. McClernand and James B. McPherson had been making the risky move south through Louisiana in preparation for the dangerous river crossing, Sherman's corps was making two major feints, one directly north of Vicksburg and the other farther north on the Mississippi River near Greenville. At the same time,

---

12 Michael B. Ballard, *Vicksburg: The Campaign That Opened the Mississippi* (Chapel Hill: University of North Carolina Press, 2004), 191-93.

another of Grant's corps commanders, Stephen A. Hurlbut, was launching infantry and cavalry raids out of Memphis and West Tennessee to pin down Confederate attention in northwestern Mississippi. Other divisions under Hurlbut coordinated with Abel Streight's famous "Mule March" from the Army of the Cumberland in Middle Tennessee and performed similar service against watchful Confederates in northeastern Mississippi.[13]

Hurlbut's most notable, damaging, and famous diversion that April, however, was a cavalry raid south and between two other shallow feints, one each into northwest and northeast Mississippi. The raid was conducted by a lone Union cavalry brigade, and it drove directly between the two thrusts, and, more importantly, directly between the pursuing Confederate commands in north Mississippi whose focus was now to the northwest and northeast. As Hurlbut incisively observed, "If this movement [Streight's raid] goes on, it will materially aid my contemplated cavalry dash on the railroad below, for it will draw off their cavalry force into Alabama, and leave my field clear."[14]

The intent of the raid was not just to penetrate the northern tier of Mississippi counties, as the others did, but to continue south to tear the heart out of Confederate Mississippi and destroy the most important rail line supplying Vicksburg. The raid's overarching strategic objective was to act as a large moving diversion for Grant's crossing. "I desire to time so as to co-operate with what I suppose to be your plan," Hurlbut wrote Grant, "to land below Vicksburg, on [the] south side of Black river." Hurlbut also hoped this raid would move Confederate garrisons defending Vicksburg and the all-important crossing points of the Mississippi River toward the east, allowing Grant a free hand to land his army and march inland.[15]

If all went according to plan, the deep raid led by an artsy music teacher from Jacksonville, Illinois, would be the most defining factor of Grant's attempt to reach and capture Vicksburg. At the least, if it was successful, the raid would be the most spectacular performance of musician Benjamin Grierson's career.

---

13 For the diversions, see Bearss, *The Vicksburg Campaign*, vol. 2, 107-253.

14 *OR*, 23, pt. 2, 214.

15 Ibid.

CHAPTER ONE

The Plan

Benjamin Grierson walked into XVI Corps commander Stephen A. Hurlbut's headquarters in Memphis, Tennessee, and was astonished at what he learned. Major General Ulysses S. Grant, Hurlbut's superior, wanted to make a bold move to focus Confederate attention away from the Mississippi River. This, in turn, would make it easier to push the Union Army of the Tennessee from Louisiana across the river into Mississippi and form a powerful beachhead below Vicksburg. Hurlbut, wrote Grierson, envisioned a mounted "expedition southward into Mississippi." As he would soon learn, however, this was no ordinary expedition, like countless others he had conducted over the past year or so. Rather, this was a much deeper, much bolder, and by extension, much more dangerous raid all the way down to the Southern Railroad of Mississippi, the main rail line connecting Vicksburg with the outside world. The weight of the operation began to sink in, Grierson remembered, when Hurlbut handed him "some maps and other papers giving information of the country over which the contemplated march would probably be made."[1]

The idea that would ultimately develop into Grierson's Raid, the most successful of the many diversions, was born out of Grant's necessity to get his army to Vicksburg so he could defeat the Confederates there and

---

1   Benjamin H. Grierson, *A Just and Righteous Cause: Benjamin H. Grierson's Civil War Memoir,* ed. Bruce J. Dinges and Shirley A. Leckie (Carbondale: Southern Illinois University Press, 2008), 134.

Ulysses S. Grant. Major General Ulysses S. Grant needed help in his advance on Vicksburg and realized what a cavalry raid in the enemy's rear might accomplish. It was he who first suggested the plan, and Grant strongly advised that Grierson lead it. *Library of Congress*

break their lock on the mighty river. His many efforts to date included digging what became known as "Grant's Canal" across the De Soto Peninsula, the Lake Providence operation, and the early stages of the Yazoo Pass operation. While still seeking a way to get around Vicksburg to the west, Grant also began contemplating additional efforts east of the Mississippi River, including a cavalry raid that would damage Confederate supply and communications east of the Confederate stronghold. While it was not anything like what would eventually develop and would never be conducted in the form originally envisioned, the idea germinated in

Grant's mind to use cavalry deep in the Confederate rear to break up their logistics system.[2]

Initially, Grant wanted to launch a cavalry raid south out of West Tennessee to break up the Mississippi Central Railroad, which ran north to south through the center of the state to Jackson. "If practicable," Grant wrote Hurlbut in Memphis on February 9, 1863, "I would like to have a Cavalry expedition penetrate as far South as possible on the Miss Central RR to destroy it." Grant was beginning to think seriously of using cavalry deep in Mississippi. About the same time, one of Hurlbut's commanders at Corinth, Charles S. Hamilton, under whom Grierson served, was thinking much the same thing. In all likelihood, the general idea came out of the January transfer of Confederate cavalry commander Earl Van Dorn's 5,000 mounted troops east to the Army of Tennessee. The "movement of Van Dorn's clears our front of all cavalry. . . . It is the time to strike," Hamilton insisted.[3]

Although Hamilton's idea was never reported to Grant, the latter soon expressed an even bolder plan. Grant knew the Southern Railroad of Mississippi—which ran across the state east from Vicksburg to Jackson and thence to Meridian—provided most of Vicksburg's supplies. He followed his earlier note to Hurlbut with a more detailed plan on February 13. A raid might "cut the rail-road East of Jackson Miss," explained Grant, who went on to include several caveats. "The *undertaking* would be a hazardous one but it would pay well if carried out," he lectured Hurlbut. "I do not direct that this shall be done but leave it for a volunteer enterprise." Proving he had been giving the idea more thought than his few words indicated, Grant informed the Memphis commander that he also had a man in mind to lead the effort: "It seems to me that Grierson with about 500 picked men might succeed in making his way South."[4]

Hurlbut, who once described the city of Memphis as having "more iniquity in it than any place since Sodom," jumped on Grant's

---

2   *OR* 24, pt. 3, 45; Stephen A. Forbes, "Grierson's Cavalry Raid: Eastern Mississippi Invaded," 1937, Vicksburg National Military Park, 1.

3   *OR* 24, pt. 3, 45; John Y. Simon, ed., *The Papers of Ulysses S. Grant*. 32 vols. to date. (Carbondale: Southern Illinois University Press, 1967-present), 7:307; Forbes, "Grierson's Cavalry Raid," 101; T. W. Lippincott to S. A. Forbes, December 20, 1908, in Stephen A. Forbes Papers, U of Illinois.

4   Simon, *PUSG*, vol. 7:317.

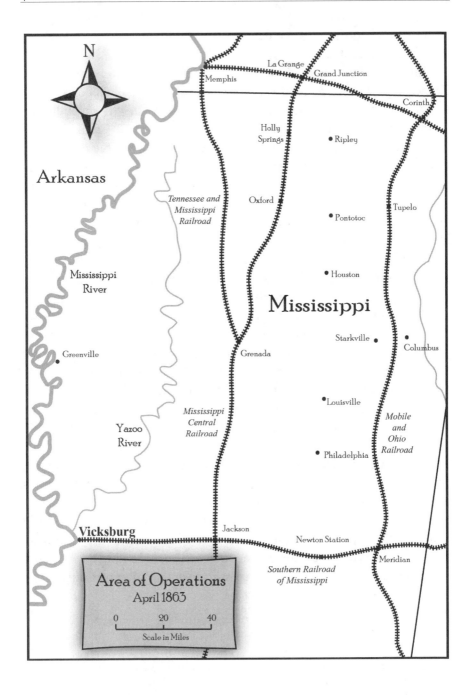

N

Arkansas

Mississippi
River

La Grange
Memphis
Grand Junction
Corinth

Holly
Springs
Ripley

*Tennessee and
Mississippi
Railroad*
Oxford
Tupelo
Pontotoc

Houston

Mississippi

Greenville
Grenada
Starkville
Columbus

*Mississippi
Central
Railroad*
Louisville

*Mobile
and
Ohio
Railroad*

Yazoo
River
Philadelphia

Vicksburg
Jackson
Newton Station
Meridian

Area of Operations
April 1863

0   20   40

Scale in Miles

*Southern Railroad
of Mississippi*

recommendation and began planning an elaborate raid on the Southern Railroad east of Jackson. The prewar politician whose rank stemmed more from his friendship with Abraham Lincoln than to any particular military prowess or experience, however, missed much of Grant's purpose. Hurlbut considered hitting the Big Black River Bridge well west of Jackson between that city and Vicksburg, a move one veteran later noted "would have concentrated Pemberton's army just where Grant did not want it." As excited as he was about the plan, Hurlbut was loathe to lose Grierson, preferring instead another colonel and another regiment for the dangerous raid. According to one Illinois trooper, Hurlbut wanted to "send other troops and another commander *to be captured.*" Hurlbut, like Hamilton, realized the move of Confederate cavalry from north Mississippi east toward Middle Tennessee presented the perfect opportunity for a thrust south because it "will remove nearly all cavalry from my front." Instead of the full grand raid, however, he ordered Grierson to take his brigade south across the Tallahatchie River to the Yalobusha River, "cut the wires, destroy bridges and demonstrate in that neighborhood." At the same time, Hurlbut planned to send a smaller cavalry force under Col. Albert Lee down through Holly Springs to make a wide sweep to Panola and Hernando, nearer to Memphis. While all this commotion was taking place, Col. Edward Hatch of the 2nd Iowa Cavalry, part of Hamilton's command, would push forward "night and day toward the main road between Meridian and Vicksburg, if possible to destroy the bridge across Pearl River, in rear of Jackson, and do as much damage as possible on that line." Hurlbut, who was not blind to the danger of such an operation, admitted the raid "appears perilous. But I think it can be done and done with safety." Allowing for adaptability, Hurlbut also wrote that Hatch's troopers would return "by the best course they can make." The thrusts, Hurlbut informed Grant, "may relieve you somewhat at Vicksburg."[5]

Grierson returned from Memphis to La Grange, Tennessee, the next day to begin preparing for his part in the plan. He immediately had his men paid and sent much of his own money home. Requests for clothing and equipment, however, were delayed. Worse, the February weather was awful and the hospitals were rapidly filling with sick men. "Under

5   *OR* 24, pt. 3, 58; T. W. Lippincott to S. A. Forbes, April 7, 1907, and December 20, 1908.

all the circumstances," Grierson explained, "I came about as near having the blues as I wished to, and a trifle nearer, and earnestly hoped that it would dry or freeze up, or that the sun would shine long enough to drive dull care away." Orders arrived for him on February 14 to "hold my whole effective force in readiness for a long and dangerous trip." Three days later, "eight tons of quartermaster stores" arrived for the troops. It appeared as though the raiders would finally be off.[6]

Hamilton, however, concerned by the prospect of failure, called off Colonel Hatch's participation "on account of intelligence received here." The loss of the 2nd Iowa Cavalry effectively canceled the entire operation. The "intelligence" was culled from a report by a Federal scout who had ventured as far south as Jackson. According to the reconnaissance, Confederate infantry was camped near the city, several hundred more were at Meridian, and, most concerning, a brigade of Confederate cavalry was at Grenada and a regiment at Okolona. Hamilton, who commanded a portion of the forces at Corinth, was concerned that a Union cavalry regiment sweeping down between the Confederate cavalry positions in north Mississippi would easily alert enemy troops farther south. If that occurred, there would be little chance of their riding out of the closing net of gray troops. The news disappointed Grierson, who viewed it within a larger context of Union high command favoritism. He long believed Hamilton favored Colonel Hatch and other commanders over him. "General Hamilton apparently hoped by a little delay to get me out of the way," Grierson concluded.[7]

Hurlbut, who was anything but pleased by Hamilton's decision, informed Grant that since Hamilton was holding his troops back, "I have considered it prudent, under this information, to withhold the cavalry dash." The frustrated Grant responded, "I was a good deal disappointed that Genl Hamilton should have countermanded the order of the expedition which you had fitted out for the purpose of cutting the road east from Vicksburg[,] particularly on such flimsy grounds. We do not expect the Miss Central and Mobile and Ohio road to be left entirely unprotected and the number of troops shown to be there by Genl Dodge['s] dispatch

6   Grierson, *A Just and Righteous Cause*, 135-36.

7   *OR* 24, pt. 3, 62-63; Grierson, *A Just and Righteous Cause*, 136; Charles S. Hamilton to B. H. Grierson, February 20, 1863, in Benjamin H. Grierson Papers, ALPL.

is as few as could be expected at any time." The manner in which "you had the expedition fitted out I think it must have succeeded," concluded the general, who demonstrated his iron determination to press on when he added, "I wish you would try it again unless your information is such that you would deem it an act of folly to send them."[8]

In hindsight, Hamilton's decision to call off the raid proved fortuitous to Union arms. Regardless of his reasons not to participate, his decision delayed the operation to a time when it would have the most desirable effect. Grant later admitted as much and noted that heavy rains and bad weather had inundated the area the cavalry was to have ridden through. "I regret that the expedition you had fitted out was not permitted to go," he wrote Hurlbut on March 9, "the weather, however, has been intolerably bad ever since that it might have failed."[9]

*   *   *

The plan for a major cavalry raid into Mississippi continued to simmer during the weeks that followed. Hurlbut addressed problems that existed between Grierson and Hamilton and set the groundwork for Grierson's full involvement by transferring that officer out of Hamilton's sphere of authority and directly into his own. Grant, meanwhile, continued to chew on the general idea of a large-scale cavalry thrust. In early March, after weeks of rain and bad weather, he sent Hurlbut a new plan. The Yazoo Pass effort was fully underway by this time, and contrary to what Grant later wrote in his memoirs, he was enthusiastic at the time about its success. "I had made so much calculation upon the expedition down Yazoo Pass . . . that I have made really but little calculation upon reaching Vicksburg by any other than Haynes' Bluff," he wrote Maj. Gen. William T. Sherman, who led one of Grant's army corps. Another indication was his presumed success in reaching Yazoo City, which he envisioned as a jumping-off point for at least a portion of this new cavalry raid: "My plan is to have the cavalry force you command cooperate with the cavalry it is in contemplation to start from some point on the Yazoo, either Yazoo City or Liverpool." A cavalry raid from any location along the lower Yazoo between Fort Pemberton at Greenwood and Haynes' Bluff near

8   Simon, *PUSG*, vol. 7, 364; *OR* 24, pt. 3, 62.

9   Grierson, *A Just and Righteous Cause*, 137; Simon, *PUSG*, vol. 7, 407.

William T. Sherman. Major General William T. Sherman was a staunch Grierson supporter and pushed for his promotion. His scout's report gave Grierson much-needed information about the area he would soon raid. *Library of Congress*

the mouth of the river could only have been possible if the Federals had success at one end or the other. Grant presumed the success would come from the north via the Yazoo Pass. He would be sorely disappointed.[10]

Grant's latest plan informed Hurlbut that he wanted multiple cavalry raids conducted at the same time. One would leave from La Grange,

10   *OR* 24, pt. 3, 126-27; Simon, *PUSG*, vol. 7, 406-7.

Tennessee, and cross the Tallahatchie River near New Albany, destroying the bridge there before moving "East of South so as to head Black River, or strike it where it can be crossed." At the same time, a force from the Yazoo River would ride south to destroy the Mississippi Central Railroad bridge over the Big Black River at Canton, while a third cavalry force would ride due east toward the Mobile and Ohio Railroad to threaten that line. "In reality," Grant explained, the purpose of all these forays was "to cover a[nother] move." While these three cavalry commands were riding across north Mississippi, a small contingent would branch off from the northernmost force and dash south. The others were simply to cover "a select portion of the Cavalry which will go South, and attempt to cut the Railroad east of Jackson." Grant believed the plan offered large dividends. "It is hoped by these moves of large forces of cavalry to cover the smaller party sufficiently to insure their success in reaching the [rail]road east of Jackson, and to do what they are sent for and return to the main body."[11]

By this time it was mid-March, and Grant's efforts in the Yazoo Pass were not producing the desired results (and Admiral David D. Porter had not yet mentioned the Steele's Bayou possibility to him). By this time Grant was thinking in larger terms. He hoped for success on the Yazoo Pass route, but if that failed, he was determined to move south of Vicksburg through Louisiana and approach the enemy stronghold from that direction. In that case, a cavalry raid east of Jackson would make even more sense. "I received notice that day [March 15] to hold my entire command in readiness for speedy and heavy service on which we were to be sent by order of General Grant," Grierson reported.[12]

As his operations in the bayous continued to flounder, however, Grant put several caveats on the plan he had described to Hurlbut. First, he wanted to see how the Yazoo Pass affair would turn out, which in turn would determine whether he would need to move his army south through Louisiana. "The date when the expedition should start will depend on movements here," he told Hurlbut. "You will be informed of the exact time for them to start." Digging down into the details of the raid, Grant ordered that "no vehicles should be taken along except ambulances, and they should have an extra pair of horses each." The troopers, he added,

11   Simon, *PUSG*, vol. 7, 406-7.

12   OR 24, pt. 3, 112, 119; Grierson, *A Just and Righteous Cause*, 138.

"should be instructed to keep well together, and let marauding alone for once and thereby better secure success." Last and perhaps most important, Grant once again recommended who he thought was the best officer for the dangerous job. "I look upon Grierson as being much better qualified to command this expedition than either Colonel Lee or Colonel John K. Mizner." Still, he left the decision to Hurlbut's discretion: "I do not dictate, however, who shall be sent."[13]

*   *   *

Hurlbut, who could read as well as anyone and better than most, understood Grant's intention and began working on the new plan with Grierson as its leader. Nothing was yet set in stone, and many aspects would change before the raid began, including some of its various commanders. Hamilton would resign on April 13 over a nasty controversy regarding rank. Grierson was glad of it. "General Hamilton was the most disagreeable man I had served under," he exclaimed. "He lacked many things which I had been taught to believe were essential to a gentleman. He was tyrannical, dogmatic, and repulsive in his manner and seemed to arrogate to himself the assumption of being one of the great men of the age." His place was assumed by William "Sooy" Smith, a graduate of West Point and a brigadier general who led a division at La Grange. Grierson found Smith to be "a very intelligent and agreeable gentleman." Smith, however, could do no more with the current situation than Grant, Hurlbut, or Hamilton. He complained of the Confederates having the initiative in raiding the Memphis and Charleston Railroad he was tasked with guarding, noting that "their cavalry was better mounted (on better bred horses) than ours and they generally got a day or two start of us when we pursued them." More disconcerting was the painfully obvious conclusion that no Federal cavalry was going to depart from any points on the Yazoo River remotely close to Yazoo City because Grant's Yazoo Pass operation was about to be deemed a waste of time and resources.[14]

Still, Hurlbut and Smith sifted through ways to cover their bases and take the fight to the enemy at the same time. Smith argued for taking the

13   Simon, *PUSG*, vol. 7, 407.

14   W. S. Smith to S. A. Forbes, May 4, 1907 and November 25, 1908, in Stephen A. Forbes Papers, UI; Grierson, *A Just and Righteous Cause,* 138-39; *OR* 24, pt. 1, 27.

William Sooy Smith. Brigadier General William Sooy Smith was the division commander tasked with sending Grierson south. He later tried to take much of the credit for its success. *Library of Congress*

initiative and "let[ting] them [Confederate cavalry] do the chasing instead of pursuing them" and "letting them have the fun of doing the chasing." Hurlbut and Smith (both later claimed to have come up with the initial idea) concocted a firm plan by which Smith could get everything he needed done. To carry it out, Hurlbut called upon Grant for more cavalry. "I absolutely need another regiment of cavalry at once," he urged.[15]

In order to hammer out the details of the plan, Hurlbut called both Grierson and division commander Smith to Memphis in late March for another planning session. Smith later claimed that by this time he had convinced Grierson of the need for the raid, writing "I got Grierson full of the idea of doing this and took him with me to Memphis." Smith went on to describe the cavalryman as "just the man to do it successfully, and that he could not have a better command for the purpose." Grierson later disputed Smith's claim of origination. "H - - - we made that raid ourselves, don't let anybody steal credit for it that belongs to us." The generals and the colonel agreed on many details at Memphis, including the supporting movements by Smith and Hurlbut from Memphis and La Grange designed to better allow Grierson, as Smith termed it, to "get the

15 W. S. Smith to S. A. Forbes, May 4, 1907 and November 25, 1908; Grierson, *A Just and Righteous Cause,* 138-39; *OR* 24, pt. 1, 27.

start of any cavalry force that might be sent to oppose him." What was to be done after damaging the Southern Railroad of Mississippi, however, quickly became the most contentious issue of the meeting. According to Sooy Smith, both he and Grierson advocated riding toward Baton Rouge, Louisiana, but Hurlbut would have none of it. The Memphis commander argued the cavalry column should turn around and return north to Tennessee. If true, Hurlbut was worried about such a long ride to Louisiana and the risk of losing much or perhaps all of his cavalry, some of his best regiments, and one of his finest cavalry commanders.[16]

According to Smith, he and Grierson were "sorely puzzled" at Hurlbut's insistence on returning the way they had come. Smith was so convinced his plan was the best that he took matters into his own hands. Once he returned to La Grange, he received Hurlbut's final orders "late in an evening. I slept little that night and in the morning sent for Grierson and told him to get ready for the raid as soon as possible." Smith recalled that Grierson "asked me which plan had been adopted and I told him he was to go to Baton Rouge" and that he would have "discretionary powers." Grierson knew better than to believe he would have full discretion on such an important decision. Smith later admitted Hurlbut's orders were to himself, not Grierson, and he would have the discretion to order the cavalryman where to ride. The division leader acknowledged that he "would take the responsibility" and that Grierson was not even "supposed to know what it [Hurlbut's order] was." If the raid was successful, there would be no questions asked. If it failed, Smith added, "I would take the consequences and should probably be cashiered for disobedience of orders." Grierson was ready and willing to make the hazardous raid, replying to Smith "in his falsetto voice . . . 'I'll do it.'"[17]

Hurlbut's most recent plan, which he communicated to Grant on April 1, was to send cavalry out from three locations: Corinth, Mississippi,

---

16 W. S. Smith to S. A. Forbes, November 10, 1905, May 4, 1907, and November 25, 1908, Stephen A. Forbes Papers, UI; William Sooy Smith, "The Mississippi Raid," *Military Essays and Recollections, Essays and Papers Read Before the Illinois Commandery,* 4 vols. (Chicago: Order of the Commandery, 1907), vol. 4, 380; Forbes, "Grierson's Cavalry Raid," 108, 123-24.

17 W. S. Smith to S. A. Forbes, November 10, 1905, May 4, 1907, and November 25, 1908; Smith, "Mississippi Raid," 380; Forbes, "Grierson's Cavalry Raid," 108, 123-24; T. W. Lippincott to S. A. Forbes, February 20, 1908.

and La Grange and Memphis, Tennessee. He hoped that raiding from three points across such a wide expanse would create an opening in the Confederate defenses of north Mississippi along the Tallahatchie River. The force from Corinth would sweep south toward Pontotoc. At the same time, the force from Memphis would occupy the Confederates in northwest Mississippi while an infantry brigade operated around Holly Springs. With the center cleared and the Confederates looking in two different directions, three cavalry regiments under Grierson would ride south out of La Grange along the Pontotoc Ridge. Once past the Tallahatchie River and the Confederate defensive cordon, one of Grierson's regiments would split off to the east and damage the Mobile and Ohio Railroad around Okolona while another regiment rode west to damage the Mississippi Central around Oxford. Success on these fronts would disrupt rail traffic in the northern part of the state, but it would also keep Confederate eyes off the third regiment, which Grierson would lead himself. This command would continue south and hit the Southern Railroad of Mississippi. Hurlbut also mentioned Meridian or Selma, Alabama, as targets, although he noted that "to break the Chunkey River or Pearl River Bridge [in Mississippi] would be my object."[18]

"I heartily approve of the move you propose," wrote back Grant two days after receiving Hurlbut's plans. In order to facilitate it, he sent more cavalry for Hurlbut's use. Grant gave additional approval four days later when Hurlbut sent Col. Albert Lee of the 7th Kansas Cavalry to Grant's headquarters to talk over the impending operation. Grant was fully agreeable, writing Hurlbut on April 10 that "the movements spoken of previously and now in your letter of the 7th, brought by Gen Lee you may make."[19]

The plan remained fluid and Hurlbut continued working to refine it, especially as other factors cropped up. Grenville Dodge, who was under Hurlbut's jurisdiction at Corinth, had been corresponding with officers from the Army of the Cumberland in Middle Tennessee about joint operations. Together they worked out a plan for Dodge to support a cavalry raid through north Alabama. That suited Hurlbut's plans just as well as the minor cavalry dash from Corinth and could possibly draw larger Confederate units eastward, farther away from Grierson's route.

18 *OR* 24, pt. 1, 27.

19 Simon, *PUSG*, vol. 8, 6, 41.

Grierson, meanwhile, bade his time scouting, raiding, and worrying over whether he would be promoted to brigadier general.[20]

By April 10, and with Grant's permission in hand, Hurlbut was ready to put his preliminary plans in motion and told his subordinates to prepare for the operation. He issued orders that day to Sooy Smith, who was tasked with overseeing the plans and sending Grierson southward. "The time for our projected cavalry movement is rapidly approaching," Hurlbut informed Smith. The evolving plan now included three parts. The first two consisted of Federal operations out of Corinth and Memphis. The cavalry force from Corinth would move east to cooperate with mounted infantry from William S. Rosecrans's Army of the Cumberland. Together, they would attack the Western and Atlantic Railroad running south from Chattanooga to Atlanta, the main Confederate supply route to the army in Middle Tennessee. Dodge (at Corinth) would also send infantry east into northern Alabama to help pull Confederate defenders out of northeastern Mississippi. At the same time, Hurlbut would personally direct forces out of the Memphis area to attract Confederate attention in northwest Mississippi. Once all this was in motion, Grierson would drive south from La Grange. "As soon as this movement is inaugurated, and the attention of the enemy drawn to that part of our line," Hurlbut explained, Grierson's three cavalry regiments would ride south with the same basic plan as before—one would split off to the east and one to the west to strike different railroads while Grierson's regiment continued south to hit the Southern Railroad. All three commands would be involved in "cutting . . . the roads, destroying the wires, burning provisions, and doing all the mischief they can," but only Grierson's regiment would continue deep into Mississippi, "breaking the east and west road thoroughly, and sweeping back by Alabama."[21]

Hurlbut informed Smith about the need to coordinate these widespread movements, adding that "final instructions as to the course, &c., will reach you in time." It would indeed take good timing to pull off the complex operation in a manner that coordinated with Grant's crossing of the Mississippi River. A possible hiccup was already in the mix, however, because Rosecrans's force was not yet in position to cooperate from Middle Tennessee. For the time being, everything was on hold.

---

20 Grierson, *A Just and Righteous Cause*, 138, 140.

21 *OR* 24, pt. 3, 185; Grierson, *A Just and Righteous Cause*, 138, 140.

Hurlbut ordered that the delay be used to prepare the horses and men. He wanted the cavalry in "the best order possible, both by grooming and care and by rest and feed. Let no exertion be spared in this matter," adding, "let the horses be all carefully shod."[22]

Everyone involved had high hopes for the success of the operation, including Hurlbut. "As this, if accomplished, will be a great thing," he wrote, ending his orders, "I am specially desirous that nothing interfere with the proper execution so far as the means in our power will admit."[23]

If Ulysses S. Grant had learned anything from the previous six failed attempts to reach Vicksburg, it was to think in large geographical terms. He put that philosophy into action when he began implementing the plan that would eventually result in his Army of the Tennessee crossing the Mississippi River. Orders went out authorizing the series of feints across the state of Mississippi and, in some cases, in other states as well. When considered as one, the operation was enormous, complex, and delicately interconnected. And so the Union juggernaut stirred itself into motion, slowly at first before gaining speed as a half-dozen feints peppered their way into history during April 1863.

*   *   *

Grant's farsighted use of various feints, demonstrations, and ruses to increase his chances of successfully shifting his army across the Mississippi River with as little enemy opposition as possible demonstrated a more modern handle on operational strategy than many students fully grasp. In fact, it follows in many respects the nine principles of war developed by the United States Army around 1900. Grant and company had it figured out decades earlier, even if they did not specifically say so in as many words.[24]

Even a rudimentary look at the principles reveals Grant's forward thinking. According to the modern army doctrinal manual, "seizing the initiative compels an enemy to react. Commanders use initiative to impose their will on an enemy or adversary or to control a situation." All of Grant's proposed operations were *offensive* in nature. He also used the

---

22 *OR* 24, pt. 3, 185.

23 Ibid., 185.

24 Terrence J. Winschel, *Triumph and Defeat: The Vicksburg Campaign,* 2 vols. (New York: Savas Beatie, 2006), vol. 2, 34.

principle of *economy of force*, which the manual described as follows: "Commanders allocate only the minimum combat power necessary to shaping and sustaining operations so they can mass combat power for the decisive operation." Grant's use of *maneuver* was likewise exemplary, with the modern field manual describing exactly what the general had done decades before: "Maneuver concentrates and disperses combat power to keep the enemy at a disadvantage. It achieves results that would otherwise be more costly. Effective maneuver keeps enemy forces off balance by making them confront new problems and new dangers faster than they can counter them." Grant used other principles spelled out in the army manual, including mass, unity of command, simplicity, and objective.[25]

When Grant sent General Sherman to feint in different places along the Mississippi River, he was maneuvering and using economy of force and the offensive to force the enemy to defend many points at once, none of which involved the true area of emphasis where Grant had massed most of his command. Similarly, the raids across northern Mississippi that pinned Confederate infantry and cavalry in specific geographical areas, or drew them away from the main area of movement, achieved the same thing. When Benjamin Grierson rode south on the morning of April 17, 1863, he was a part of a major coordinated plan of maneuver, economy of force, and offensive intended to cause Confederate heads to swivel helplessly in an effort to figure out what was happening. "No one knew my plans any more than they did those of Gen. Grant," wrote Grierson, "nor did either of us have predetermined (or definitely detailed) plans before starting on our hazardous undertakings. [But] the two movements, though widely separate at the time, were in conjunction. . . . I simply knew from previous conversation with the general, and afterwards by letter from an officer of high rank and in close relations with him, of his general contemplated movements."[26]

When Grant moved south through Louisiana below Vicksburg, two of his four corps marched with him: the XIII under Maj. Gen. John A. McClernand and the XVII under Maj. Gen. James B. McPherson. Two additional corps remained behind, at least temporarily, north of Vicksburg.

25 *Field Manual 3-0: Operations* (Washington, DC: Department of the Army, 2008), A1-A2.

26 B. H. Grierson to T. W. Lippincott, March 13, 1886, in Benjamin H. Grierson Papers, ALPL.

One of them, the XVI Corps under Hurlbut, was spread across West Tennessee and north Mississippi to garrison Memphis, Corinth, and the railroad running between those cities. None of these troops would be involved in the initial crossing of the Mississippi River or the land campaign necessary to reach Vicksburg, but they would perform the lion's share of the diversions that would make it easier for Grant to achieve his objectives. Grant intended something different for the XV Corps north of Vicksburg under William T. Sherman.[27]

Sherman was Grant's most trusted corps commander, and the latter left the former's corps above Vicksburg at Young's Point and Milliken's Bend so it could act independently as the need arose. Sherman's role involved making two major feints to help take Confederate eyes off Grant's movement across the river farther south. Once across on Mississippi soil, Grant intended to have Sherman rejoin him as soon as possible. Ironically, Grant's trusted subordinate and friend was not in full agreement with his latest operational plan. That did not stop Sherman from giving Grant his full support, however, even if he did not agree with what was about to take place. "I confess I don't like this roundabout project," he explained, "but we must support Grant in whatever he undertakes."[28]

The pair of feints Sherman was tasked with included an advance up the Yazoo River, just as he had done in late December 1862. His goal was to convince the Confederates he was going to attack up the steep bluffs he had found impossible to take the first time. In April 1863, however, there was an opportunity of another sort. "It may possibly happen that the enemy may so weaken his forces about Vicksburg and Haynes' Bluff as to make the latter vulnerable, particularly with a fall of water to give an extended landing," Grant wrote Sherman. However, he did not order an actual attack. Grant was well aware of the public pounding Sherman had taken months earlier after his bloody repulse at Chickasaw Bayou, and he realized that sending him back to the same place to repeat the rebuff a second time would be a public relations

27 For Hurlbut, see Jeffrey N. Lash, *A Politician Turned General: The Civil War Career of Stephen Augustus Hurlbut* (Kent, OH: Kent State University Press, 2003).

28 *OR* 24, pt. 3, 179-80, 201; William T. Sherman, *Memoirs of General William T. Sherman: Written by Himself.* 2 vols. (New York: D. Appleton and Co., 1875), vol. 1, 315; Ulysses S. Grant, *Personal Memoirs of U.S. Grant*, 2 vols. (New York: Charles L. Webster and Co., 1885), vol. 1, 542-43; Brooks D. Simpson, *Ulysses S. Grant: Triumph over Adversity, 1822-1865* (Boston: Houghton Mifflin Company, 2000), 174.

and political disaster for both of them. Sensitive to Sherman's prickly personality, Grant informed his corps commander that he should make the feint only "if you think it advisable."[29]

Sherman was more than happy to oblige—even if it meant another tactical defeat. He understood that his role was a necessity, part of a larger plan, and he would fully carry it out however Grant intended. "We will make as strong a demonstration as possible," he confirmed. "The troops will all understand the purpose, and will not be hurt by the repulse. The people of the country must find out the truth as they best can; it is none of their business. You are engaged in a hazardous enterprise, and, for good reasons, wish to divert attention; that is sufficient to me, and it shall be done." That was quite a statement given that Sherman was less than enthusiastic about Grant's operation in the first place.[30]

His concerns notwithstanding, Sherman planned his part well and waited until Grant approached the actual crossing point later in April before moving. Meanwhile, another division of his corps was just finishing a similar feint almost a 100 miles to the north. Sherman had sent Frederick Steele and his division northward to Greenville, Mississippi, in mid-April, where Steele landed and marched inland, crossing Black Bayou and tramping on to Deer Creek. "My command has just returned to this place," Steele reported to Sherman from Greenville, "having pursued the rebels . . . about 43 miles down Deer Creek." Confederates in the area offered a semblance of a defense, but Steele's column quickly pushed them back as he advanced along Deer Creek to a plantation owned by Confederate Maj. Gen. Samuel G. French.[31]

The effects of Steele's effort rippled across the region. Confederate commanders in the area flooded the delta with troops in a desperate effort to stop the advance. One infantry brigade moved north from the Vicksburg area while another moved west from the Greenwood garrison. "The enemy is in force," wrote a Confederate division commander, who added that the area needed infantry, artillery, and cavalry and "very

---

29 *OR* 24, pt. 3, 231, 240; John F. Marszalek, "'A Full Share of All the Credit': Sherman and Grant to the Fall of Vicksburg," in Steven E. Woodworth, ed., *Grant's Lieutenants: From Cairo to Vicksburg* (Lawrence: University Press of Kansas, 2001), 18.

30 *OR* 24, pt. 3, 242-43.

31 Ibid., 502-3.

much the latter." There was little that could be done to stop Steele, who fought small skirmishes and caused as much commotion as possible as he advanced south. When he decided he had done enough and driven as deep as prudence allowed, he turned his column about and returned to Greenville loaded with the supplies his men had not destroyed. Slaves from nearby plantations followed the Unionists, realizing this expedition might offer their only access to freedom.[32]

Sherman's dual diversions along the Mississippi River, one under Steele and the other still yet to set off, would give the Confederate high command plenty to think about. The Rebel brass had seen these types of operations before in some of Grant's previous attempts to reach Vicksburg, and their scrambling to parry them had generated some success. John Pemberton, the Confederate commander at Vicksburg, had no way of knowing these were mere feints—small parts of a much larger operational plan. As a result, he believed the efforts to confront and repulse Steele's expedition had been successful. He had no idea Grant was only toying with him while he orchestrated the real effort below the citadel that would spell the doom of Vicksburg.

*   *   *

Sherman's diversions were intended to last only until he could disengage at each point and move swiftly south to join the other two corps of the Army of the Tennessee below Vicksburg. This was not the case with the other corps in West Tennessee and north Mississippi. Grant never intended to have General Hurlbut's XVI Corps make the crossing or join in the fight for the city. Rather, Hurlbut was tasked with holding the line from Memphis to Corinth. But just because they were garrison troops holding a leg while the other three corps flayed the Confederate main body did not mean they would not play a major role in the larger operational scheme. In fact, Hurlbut's contribution was vital, because it provided the major feints Grant needed to take Confederate eyes off the potential crossing point and the army marching through Louisiana to get there.[33]

---

32   Ibid., 502-4.

33   Timothy B. Smith, *The Decision Was Always My Own: Ulysses S. Grant and the Vicksburg Campaign* (Carbondale: Southern Illinois University Press, 2018), 80-101.

Hurlbut had four basic movements underway just before or during Grant's crossing, each designed to tie up most of the Confederates in northern Mississippi and, in combination with Sherman's efforts, force Pemberton to focus in exactly the opposite direction from where Grant would cross the river. "The cavalry dash I desire to time so as to co-operate with what I suppose to be your plan," Hurlbut wrote Grant, "to land below Vicksburg, on [the] south side of Black River, silencing the Grand Gulf batteries. By cutting the road, I shall, as I think, materially aid in the movement, as well as by shoving the heads of infantry columns as low as the Tallahatchie."[34]

Most of the diversion required would come from Hurlbut's XVI Corps. Accordingly, he dispatched several raids into northwestern Mississippi from his Memphis headquarters, intended to operate together for larger effect, "making a strong diversion in his [Grierson's] favor," recalled General Smith. Two raids left the Memphis area in the middle part of April. Colonel George E. Bryant of the 12th Wisconsin marched with three regiments of infantry and an artillery battery, later joined by cavalry, and moved across Nonconnah Creek toward Hernando. There the command broke up a Confederate camp and skirmished with enemy forces. Bryant's column pressed on to the Coldwater River but met firm resistance there and did not press the issue. Still, he gathered numerous prisoners as well as horses and mules, arms, and a large stash of supplies. "In killed and wounded," Bryant reported, "I know the enemy has suffered more than we have, and the captures, at least, are clear profit."[35]

A second raid, a cavalry force under William Sooy Smith himself, probed south at the same time toward Holly Springs and the Tallahatchie River. Smith rode from La Grange through Holly Springs, Sardis, and Senatobia before making his way back north. He never met up with Bryant, as Hurlbut intended, but he did come away with prisoners, horses, and other supplies. Hurlbut admitted to Grant that the efforts did not achieve everything he had hoped they might. After noting the failure of the columns to link up, he added that "the expedition against [the enemy] . . . suffered the misfortune of most combined movements."

---

34 *OR* 23, pt. 2, 214; Bearss, *The Vicksburg Campaign*, vol. 2, 129-31.

35 W. S. Smith to S. A. Forbes, May 4, 1907; *OR* 24, pt. 3, 557-59; Edwin Levings to Parent, April 25, 1863, in Edwin D. Levings Papers, University of Wisconsin-River Falls.

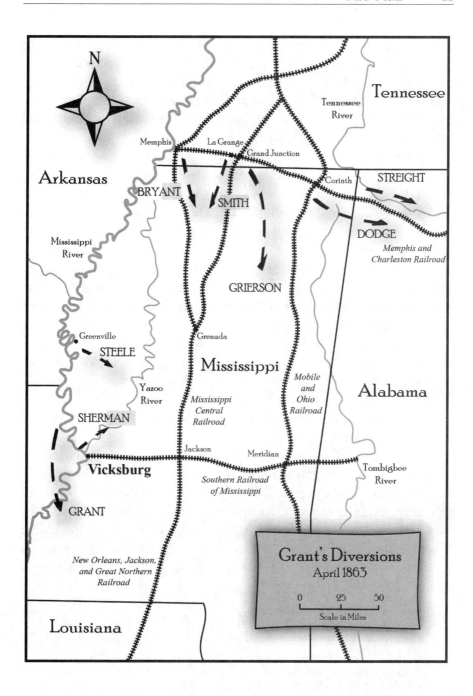

N

Tennessee River

Tennessee

Memphis   La Grange
Grand Junction

Arkansas

BRYANT
Corinth   STREIGHT

SMITH

Mississippi River

DODGE
Memphis and
Charleston Railroad

GRIERSON

Greenville
STEELE

Grenada

Mississippi

Yazoo
River

Mississippi
Central
Railroad

Mobile
and
Ohio
Railroad

Alabama

SHERMAN

Jackson   Meridian

Tombigbee
River

Vicksburg

GRANT

Southern Railroad
of Mississippi

New Orleans, Jackson,
and Great Northern
Railroad

Grant's Diversions
April 1863

0   25   50

Scale in Miles

Louisiana

Nevertheless, the joint raids into northwestern Mississippi effectively pinned down much of the Confederate force in that area under district commander Gen. James R. Chalmers. The Southern commander regularly informed Pemberton of the enemy advance, writing "can you give me more cavalry?" and "unless I get help, I must fall back to Panola, and that gives up the provision region."[36]

Hurlbut utilized much of his force nailing down the Confederates in northwestern Mississippi, but he did not ignore the enemy garrisoning the northeastern portion of the state. As noted, his commander there, Grenville Dodge, coordinated his efforts with neighboring department commander Rosecrans. The Union command situation in the Western Theater in April 1863 was a divided affair, unlike what it had been earlier in the war when Henry W. Halleck had been in charge of the entire theater. After being called to Washington D.C. at Lincoln's behest to serve as general-in-chief of the Union armies, Halleck refused to leave anyone to command in his place. Perhaps he believed no single officer could handle the job he was leaving, but whatever the reason, he broke the theater apart—which was precisely the opposite of what he had argued so vehemently for when he was seeking the command in early 1862. As a result, in early 1863 the Western Theater was cut up into different departments, most notably Grant's in the Mississippi Valley and Rosecrans's in Middle Tennessee.[37]

Dodge, one of Grant's subordinates, was more than willing to coordinate with Rosecrans, especially when a joint raid would aid both. In mid-April, Dodge marched from Corinth across north Mississippi into north Alabama to provide a firm location from which to launch this raid. Colonel Abel D. Streight, who had mounted his men on mules, led the expedition. The famous "Mule March," as it became known, was a developing disaster in many ways, not the least of which revolved around the ornery mules themselves.[38]

36 OR 24, pt. 3, 554-55, 562-63; Andrew Brown, "The First Mississippi Partisan Rangers, C.S.A.," *Civil War History* (December 1955), vol. 1, no. 4, 384.

37 Bearss, *The Vicksburg Campaign*, vol. 2, 129-31. For Halleck, see John F. Marszalek, *Commander of All Lincoln's Armies: A Life of General Henry W. Halleck* (Cambridge, MA: Belknap Press of Harvard University Press, 2004).

38 For Streight's Raid, see Bearss, *The Vicksburg Campaign*, vol. 2, 129-77 and Edwin C. Bearss, "Colonel Streight Drives for the Western and Atlantic Railroad," *Alabama Historical Quarterly* (Summer 1964), vol. 26, 133-86.

Hurlbut could not have been happier. The effort peeled away from the tri-state area a large Confederate cavalry force under Nathan Bedford Forrest and gained the attention of Confederate commanders in northeastern Mississippi. Even Confederate theater commander Joseph E. Johnston focused on the raid, which meant fewer Confederates were watching the main Union effort under Grant in Louisiana. Grierson's raid, which had yet to begin, was about to sow even more confusion within the Confederate ranks by plunging straight into the yawning gap created by the efforts of Smith, Bryant, and Streight.[39]

*   *   *

Final instructions for Grierson arrived when Hurlbut informed Smith on April 15 to be prepared to send the musician-turned-officer and his men south two days later. "I wish them to start sharply at or before daylight on Friday morning, moving by the best route for Pontotoc," ordered Hurlbut. "Rapidity is the necessity of this special duty." Once at Pontotoc, the former plan was resurrected, calling for one of the three regiments to ride east and another west, leaving Grierson to continue riding south with the remaining regiment. The two side regiments were to "destroy wires, &c., and use up as much of the track as they can, and do it thoroughly; break up all provision depots they can find, burn tanks, and do all the damage possible; gather all the horses they can manage, and return by the best route they can select."[40]

The noisy clatter to the east and west was intended as little more than a sideshow, however, for the main effort rested with Grierson. "The strongest and best mounted command," Hurlbut continued, "will proceed with all possible speed, making direct for the Jackson and Meridian road, and break it up, either at the Chunkey Bridge or some other stream, cutting wires and destroying track in every direction, as far as they can reach." Hurlbut also wanted other things accomplished if within reach, including "that they may be able to strike Jackson or Columbus." He also asked that an attempt be made, if possible, to hit Canton's rail facilities. "In all these cases they and their horses must live on the country, and horses, of course, will be taken wherever advantageous," he explained,

---

39   *OR* 23, pt. 2, 214.

40   Ibid., pt. 3, 197.

Stephen A. Hurlbut. As commander of the XVI Corps with his headquarters in Memphis, Tennessee, Major General Stephen A. Hurlbut oversaw the preparation and launch of Grierson's raid. *Library of Congress*

stipulating that "they should start with oats in the nosebags, and with four days' provisions, cautioned when they set out to make them last."[41]

The entire series of diversions was moving along rather well given the difficulty of coordinating such far-flung events, but one problem remained. Grant had made it clear from the start that he wanted Grierson in command of the main raid, but the former music teacher was in Illinois on a leave of absence granted earlier that month when the unfolding plan was still in development. Hurlbut informed Sooy Smith that he had "telegraphed for Grierson to return at once, and [I] expect him before Wednesday." The afternoon of April 16 came and went and Grierson had yet to return. It was just hours before the command was set to leave at daylight the next morning. "If Grierson does not arrive in time," commanded Hurlbut, "Hatch, who is [the] ranking officer in fact, will take command." He added that "the force sent down on the long dash will be selected without reference to regiments, unless Grierson returns, when he had best take his own." Hurlbut felt the need to "explain to the officers that as much credit and usefulness belongs to those who take the flank as the others."[42]

*   *   *

41 Ibid.

42 Ibid., 185, 197.

Daniel Ruggles. Brigadier General Daniel Ruggles, who had made a name for himself at Shiloh, commanded the northernmost district in Mississippi, through which Grierson first rode. Ruggles's lethargic response allowed Grierson to continue south without much hindrance. *Photographic History of the Civil War*

Unbeknownst to the Confederates, Grant was planning a perfect storm. With diversion after diversion masking the main thrust, they would be hard pressed to discover and adapt to what was happening in time to do much of anything about it. Worse, the route proposed for the Union raiders happened to be along the boundary line of two districts within General Pemberton's Department of Mississippi and East Louisiana. To the east in Mississippi, Brig. Gen. Daniel Ruggles commanded the area around Columbus, Mississippi, north to the Tallahatchie River. His main point of concern was the vital Mobile and Ohio Railroad. To the west was the district under Brigadier General Chalmers, whose line ran from the Tallahatchie River south and encompassed the Mississippi Central Railroad. Neither administrative region was properly manned, and both commanders had to depend upon Mississippi state militia units, none of which were well organized, properly armed, or even interested in serious fighting. Galloping Union cavalry bent on creating havoc along the fault line between these two districts would make organizing and coordinating an effort to stop it nearly impossible. And there was precious little in the history of either Chalmers or Ruggles that promised that such a thing was likely to occur.[43]

---

43 Warren E. Grabau, *Ninety-Eight Days: A Geographer's View of the Vicksburg Campaign* (Knoxville: University of Tennessee Press, 2000), 112.

The other Federal diversions made proper coordination even more difficult. These were diversions for Grierson's raid, which in turn was the main diversion for Grant's overall advance on Vicksburg. With Chalmers's hands full trying to deal with Sooy Smith's and Bryant's marches, it fell to Ruggles to defend the seam running down the center of the state. He had pitifully few troops to do so. Only two regular cavalry regiments, Lt. Col. Clark Barteau's 2nd Tennessee and Lt. Col. James Cunningham's 2nd Alabama, along with a newly organized Mississippi militia cavalry regiment and two cavalry battalions, were at his disposal. Cunningham's Alabama cavalry regiment was farther south while Barteau manned his headquarters at Verona, nearer to Tupelo, to be in proximity to his dispersed Tennessee companies watching the approaches to the district across the Tallahatchie River.[44]

Fortunately for the Federals, Ruggles was not focused on watching the fault line between the districts. Dodge's eastward movement had caught his attention, but he had not yet sent any troops to assist those chasing Streight's mule-mounted raiders. Confederate attention was split, focusing on the flanks, with no one watching the center. And that is exactly where Hurlbut intended for Grierson to ride—if the colonel returned in time.

---

44 Ibid., 116-17.

CHAPTER TWO

The Leader

While generations of Lees had long dwelled in Virginia by the time of the Civil War, and Ulysses S. Grant traced his ancestors back to early New England, Benjamin Grierson had no such American lineage. His family's arrival in America was much more recent, but that did not prevent him from obtaining success in this newfound country of opportunity.[1]

Grierson's family was Scots-Irish, his mother and father hailing from Dublin, Ireland. His grandfather commanded cavalry in the Irish Catholic Rebellion of 1798, and his father Robert worked as a bookkeeper in Ireland, but opportunities were limited and the family ambitious for a better life. After a trip to the New World in 1810 as a logbook chronicler and navigator on a sailing ship, Robert determined to take his family there for good. The journey, Grierson later concluded, was "no doubt the main cause of his subsequent emigration to this country." In 1818, Robert booked passage on a ship bound for New York. The vessel, blown off course and damaged, was fortunate to have made it to Bermuda. It was months before the family, including Robert, his two young daughters, and his pregnant wife Mary, who was less than enthusiastic about moving to America, arrived in New York. She gave birth to a third child soon after they arrived, but the infant boy died just a few months later. Hardships

---

1   T. W. Lippincott, "Genl. B. H. Grierson, Biography and Sketch of the Famous Raid," n.d., in Stephen A. Forbes Papers, UI. For Grierson himself, see Dinges, "The Making of a Cavalryman."

Benjamin H. Grierson. Colonel Benjamin H. Grierson rose to national fame with his epic cavalry raid through Mississippi. Just a couple of years prior he had been a business failure deep in debt, but the raid almost single-handedly made him a national hero and helped launch a long and successful career in the United States Army. *Randy Beck*

aside, Robert was determined to become a merchant and, after a short stop at Philadelphia, set out for Pittsburgh, Pennsylvania. There, in western Pennsylvania, Robert opened a small store, and the Griersons immersed themselves in the American way of life.[2]

The family lived in the same building Robert kept his thriving store and made shoes. Mary, however, was still unhappy, leaving Grierson to later speculate, "It probably appeared to her as if she had been journeying to the end of the rainbow for much less than the fabulous pot of gold." The couple welcomed more children, another son and their third daughter. On July 8, 1826, yet another boy was born. This one they named Benjamin Henry.[3]

The Grierson store was successful, but the lure of the westward movement called. After selling the business, the Griersons moved northwest into the Ohio country to Youngstown. Benjamin was only three, but he made the journey well. The family enjoyed the slower pace of life in the frontier village, and Robert made good on his endeavors, opening a store and making money in real estate.[4]

The family grew into a middle-class existence in Youngstown. They enjoyed literature, theater, and especially music, which Robert and Mary instilled in Benjamin at an early age. Mary was the soul of the family, a caring, religious, warm woman. Robert, on the other hand, was a stern patriarch, a good provider with a tendency toward rage some called the "Grierson temper." Benjamin so hated his father's temper that he developed a lifelong tendency of avoiding confrontation in any way possible. As the boys grew, Benjamin's older brother, John, developed into a hard worker while Benjamin gravitated toward play. His father once chastised young Benjamin, who recalled him saying that "he would rather have one boy like John to work than a ten-acre lot full of such boys as myself." Many years later, Benjamin fondly remembered a pond in the middle of town where the boys sailed their boats in the summer and skated in the winter. "Were it possible," he admitted later, "gladly

---

2   Grierson, *A Just and Righteous Cause*, 11-12; Leckie and Leckie, *Unlikely Warriors*, 3-4.

3   Grierson, *A Just and Righteous Cause*, 13; William H Leckie and Shirley A. Leckie, *Unlikely Warriors: General Benjamin Grierson and His Family* (Norman: University of Oklahoma Press, 1984), 6-7.

4   Leckie and Leckie, *Unlikely Warriors*, 6-7.

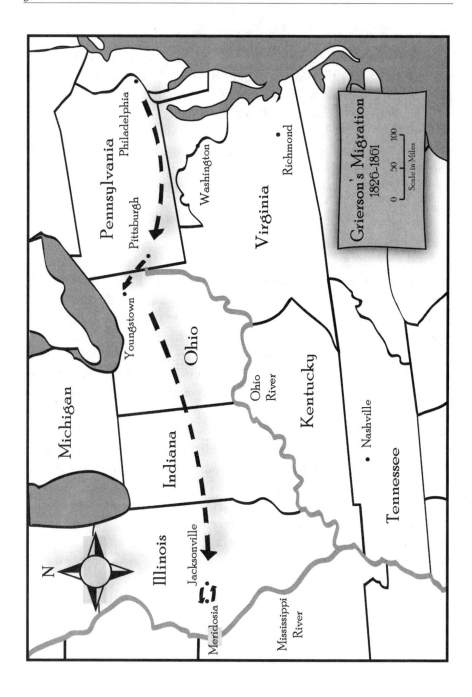

Grierson's Migration
1826-1861

0   50   100
Scale in Miles

would I be placed back to live in reality those happy and memorable boyhood days."[5]

Not all memories were as pleasant. It was in Youngstown that the eight-year-old lad suffered a terrible injury. Against her better judgment, Mary allowed her young son to accompany the older males on a day of work in the countryside to clear land for farming. Benjamin convinced his mother to allow him to go despite the free-flowing alcohol that usually attended such events. The trouble started when the boy's horse bolted, but young Grierson managed to hold on to the runaway beast by the neck, which he seemed to find great fun: "I kept my position quite well for a time and was enjoying the ride hugely, laughingly chirping at the horse." Once the horse stopped and he dismounted, however, the spooked animal kicked the boy "with full force, striking me squarely in the face." The kick opened a large gash, temporarily blinded him, and knocked him unconscious. He remained in a coma for days. Fortunately, he came out of the coma and recovered his sight. "The skill of the doctors, good nursing, and the prayers of my dear mother finally brought me through to health again," he explained. The only noticeable result was a scar on his face that he covered with a thick beard as soon as he was able to grow one. Some blamed his brother for the accident, but Grierson took full responsibility, writing that "the calamity was brought upon myself by my reckless desire for a free and unencumbered ride on that wild horse." Some historians claim Grierson developed a strong fear of horses from the incident, an assertion others dispute and have been unable to verify. Either way, the boy who would grow up to be one of the greatest cavalrymen produced in the Civil War experienced a singularly significant childhood event involving a horse.[6]

While a teenager, Grierson made the acquaintance of Alice Kirk, whose similar Irish heritage drew the two together. She was an artful young lady with a similar love for music, but her most obvious trait was her deep religiosity inherited from her strict father. The two were almost inseparable during their teenage years, but her father was not predisposed to young Grierson because of what he thought were bad habits. His attention

---

5   Grierson, *A Just and Righteous Cause*, 15, 23; Leckie and Leckie, *Unlikely Warriors*, 8, 10.

6   Brown, *Grierson's Raid*, 23; Grierson, *A Just and Righteous Cause*, 16-17, 374n1; Leckie and Leckie, *Unlikely Warriors*, 10-11.

to music did not bode well for a livelihood, but most of all, he was not very religious. After an episode in which Grierson innocently climbed the trellis to Alice's porch to talk to her and her aunt (by invitation of the aunt), Kirk admonished him at the store where he worked and gave "me a talking to on account of my injudicious action." Alice's father was so concerned that he sent his daughter away to school for three years.[7]

Alice was back home by 1848, but the renewed relationship hit another snag. When it came time to consider marriage, Alice refused because Grierson was not a man of faith. She tried to discuss his vices, but Benjamin, who had already made it a habit to avoid confrontations whenever possible, refused to listen. She endured several months of inner turmoil, the desire to marry the man she loved battling against her concern it was not God's will that she marry him. That fact that Grierson refused to attend church, drank alcohol, and chewed tobacco did not help.[8]

The crisis came in 1849 when the Griersons made yet another westward move, this time all the way to Jacksonville in west-central Illinois, a new land teeming with possibility. There, Grierson's father would once more set up a successful store. Alice decided not to accompany Benjamin, and the decision broke both of their hearts. An opportunity to teach school in Springfield, however, moved Alice west soon thereafter and brought the two together again. Realizing the only man she would ever truly love was so nearby, Alice finally consented to marry him. The pair exchanged wedding vows on September 24, 1854. Alice's father, an elder in their church, was still not convinced but performed the wedding. Her father, Grierson observed, was by that time "older and perhaps wiser" and "regained his former friendship for me." Looking back years later, he would fondly recall, "I cannot see how we could have been made more happy than during the early days of our married life."[9]

Alice, however, was not as happy as she thought she would be, especially with a little one on the way just a couple of months after the wedding. Grierson continued his occasional drinking, chewing, and pool playing—habits that did not bode well for the future. The main trouble

---

7   Grierson, *A Just and Righteous Cause*, 25; Leckie and Leckie, *Unlikely Warriors*, 16.

8   Leckie and Leckie, *Unlikely Warriors*, 17.

9   Grierson, *A Just and Righteous Cause*, 28; Leckie and Leckie, *Unlikely Warriors*, 18-20, 25, 27.

Alice Grierson and Sons. Alice was Grierson's rock, and together they produced two sons. Colonel Grierson was playing with the boys in his hallway when orders arrived to return to camp and lead the raid. *Fort Davis National Historic Site*

the coupled faced, however, was financial. They initially had no choice but to live with his parents, never a good thing for mutual bonding, while he settled into business life as a merchant like his father.[10]

When an opportunity developed to go into business just a few miles west of Jacksonville with a partner, Grierson had to borrow money to do so. Alice's prosperous father was not inclined to make a loan to his son-in-law, but he did so anyway, and Grierson and his partner opened a small store in Meredosia. Unfortunately, the Panic of 1857 hit soon thereafter, and the store lost money because buyers could not pay the high prices. The new merchants had to extend credit if they wanted to move any inventory, and that resulted in mounting bad debts. "Instead of restricting our business when so many were breaking up," Grierson later admitted, "we extended it too widely and sold largely on credit." The arrival of a second child deepened Grierson's financial troubles. Even worse, the boy died just two years later, a tragedy that sent both parents into a deep gloom amid all the other troubles they had to bear. Fortunately, a third child took away some of the heartache.[11]

The Griersons' burdens, financial and otherwise, arrived as the nation experienced the worst political crisis of its young life. When the Southern states began to secede in 1860, Grierson's store collapsed and both partners lost everything, including their homes. Without any income, Benjamin, Alice, and the children had no choice but to return to Jacksonville and move back in with Benjamin's parents. Alice had been more than happy to leave that difficult situation years earlier, but now they had two young children and no viable way to feed them. The larger family, however, was not doing much better, because one of Grierson's sisters had died and his mother had suffered a massive stroke.[12]

The stress was nearly unbearable, both on the Grierson family and on the nation they had adopted as their own.

*   *   *

10 Grierson, *A Just and Righteous Cause*, 28; Leckie and Leckie, *Unlikely Warriors*, 28.

11 Grierson, *A Just and Righteous Cause*, 30; Leckie and Leckie, *Unlikely Warriors*, 30, 36, 39, 43.

12 Grierson, *A Just and Righteous Cause*, 30; Leckie and Leckie, *Unlikely Warriors*, 38, 45-46.

In the midst of all the turmoil, Grierson found outlets to keep his mind occupied. One was politics. He supported the antislavery crusade and John C. Fremont in 1856, describing himself as the "only man in the town and precinct who openly declared himself a Republican." When a Democrat announced at a gathering there was not a man in town who would dare admit he was Republican, Grierson challenged the assertion and gave a short speech followed by his own "Hip, Hip, Hurrah!" The cheer, he later wrote with some bemusement, was "given with a will by myself alone, to the astonishment of the unterrified Democrats present." Warned he would be assaulted if he went to the polls and voted Republican, Grierson armed himself and went anyway. Instead of violence, he convinced several others to vote Republican in the heavily Democratic precinct. Despite the titled political landscape, Grierson made good political friends. The Griersons welcomed an Illinois lawyer named Abraham Lincoln into their home to spend the night while he traversed the state amid the Lincoln-Douglas debates. Two years later, Grierson avidly supported Lincoln in the presidential election of 1860. Even more fortunate for Benjamin was the fact that Jacksonville native and good friend Richard Yates was elected governor of Illinois.[13]

In addition to politics, Grierson loved the arts. From an early age his mother imbued within him a passion for theater, novels, and poetry, but the music she loved so much took flame in his soul even as a youngster, and the Irish ballads she sang to him made a special impression. "From my earliest remembrance, I had a great love and talent for music," he explained. At first he displayed his talent by singing and whistling, and his father humored him by borrowing a flute from an Ohio neighbor. Soon the boy was in the habit of memorizing songs and practicing them until he had them mastered. He worked with Isaac White, a local Youngstown music professor, at his school and progressed from the flute to other instruments, including guitar, clarinet, piano, and violin. "I was so infatuated with music that I could think of but little else," he admitted, "being unwilling to give up playing the flute even to eat or sleep." By the age of 13, locals banded together to buy him a fine clarinet of his

13   Grierson, *A Just and Righteous Cause*, 31-32; Leckie and Leckie, *Unlikely Warriors*, 35, 42.

own, and he joined the Youngstown school band. He also took part in providing music at campaign events for William Henry Harrison.[14]

The infamous youthful horse accident also played a role in Grierson's musical development. "There was not one person excepting my mother who believed that I could possibly live," he recalled. His recovery required sequestration in a dark room for several months because his mother was worried the blindness would return if he did not do so. He had ample time on his hands during those months, which his mother and sisters filled with singing and music. The impact was significant, and he used the occasion to prime his imagination and art sensitivity.[15]

By the time Grierson entered the workforce as a merchant clerk, he was giving music lessons and repairing instruments. He even learned to play a strange one-of-a-kind device—a large wooden box with keys and a bell "shaped somewhat like a bassoon, but different. The music I got out of it was astonishing." His love for music played a large role in his courtship of Alice, who loved it as much as he did. The pair often performed duets and wrote lyrics. He combined his two loves, he later explained, by opening the window of his bedroom and pointing his clarinet in the direction of her mansion and playing the tunes "I knew she most admired. Of course, my warm feelings towards her enabled me to execute with precision and give that kind of expression so essential to the proper rendering of music." When Grierson wrote and even conducted his own creations, Alice beamed with pride. Later, when the Griersons moved to Illinois, he conducted the state capital's Springfield Band. In Illinois, he merged his passions and wrote songs for campaigns, including Lincoln's 1860 run for the presidency.[16]

Unfortunately, there was little money to be made as a band leader or composer, especially in rural Illinois. With the financial collapse and political crisis, Grierson found himself without a home, deep in debt, and

14 Grierson, *A Just and Righteous Cause*, 19-20; Leckie and Leckie, *Unlikely Warriors*, 8, 12.

15 Grierson, *A Just and Righteous Cause*, 17; Leckie and Leckie, *Unlikely Warriors*, 11, 34.

16 Grierson, *A Just and Righteous Cause*, 20-21, 25; Leckie and Leckie, *Unlikely Warriors*, 12, 16, 21, 24, 29-30, 41. For Grierson's compositions, see his papers in ALPL and Benjamin Henry Grierson Vertical File, Gettysburg College.

having several mouths to feed. What he had no way of knowing was that the most unique opportunity of his life was heading in his direction.[17]

*   *   *

The age-old question of whether important events shape the man or the man influences events was on full display during the Civil War. Many prominent examples offer themselves, two of the most conspicuous being Abraham Lincoln and Ulysses S. Grant. Benjamin H. Grierson would follow this Illinois pattern.

In 1860 Lincoln was an out-of-work politician. He had recently lost a senate race and was vilified, mocked, and denounced even as he ran for president. Today he is widely considered one of our best and most influential presidents. Would that have been the case if the country had avoided a civil war? Likewise, Grant was a failure at almost everything he had attempted before the Civil War. The conflict completely remade the man, provided his niche for success, and elevated him to be one of the most popular Americans of his time. It also secured for him the presidency in 1868.[18]

Benjamin Grierson experienced a similar elevation in his life status, albeit on a distinctly more modest level. He had failed in business, was deep in debt, his marriage was suffering, and he had been reduced to living with and being provided for by his family. He was a foundering man in need of a boost and a direction change. The Civil War provided the change he needed. The peaceful music teacher who had endured a frightful experience with a horse during his early years would become one of the most prominent cavalry commanders of his age.[19]

Grierson had some military experience prior to the war. When he lived in Ohio, he joined that state's militia and served in a cavalry regiment (not surprisingly) as a bugler. The militia was little more than a drinking club, and the men elected "well-known drunkards" as officers and the muster was "a good deal of fun," Grierson admitted. "I little thought

---

17 Leckie and Leckie, *Unlikely Warriors*, 46.

18 For Lincoln, see David Herbert Donald, *Lincoln* (New York: Simon & Shuster, 1995). For Grant, Ronald C. White, *American Ulysses: A Life of Ulysses S. Grant* (New York: Random House, 2016).

19 Grierson, *A Just and Righteous Cause*, 33.

that the time would ever come when I could be called upon to serve in earnest." He was serving as "trumpeter" for the company when it was assigned to a militia regiment and one of his father's associates was named its commander. "We continued five years in that position," he added, "and received certificates for services thus rendered."[20]

Nothing about playing at war prepared him for the real thing when North and South split apart. "Of course," he admitted, "the knowledge and experience gained by service with the Ohio militia was not essentially beneficial in aiding me to command successfully in serious warfare." Being a firm Republican with strong abolitionist and Unionist sentiments, Grierson supported fellow Illinoisan Lincoln in the spring of 1861 and even talked of joining the service. His desperate financial situation and desperately ill mother, however, coupled with Alice's opposition to enlistment (mainly because of her concern for how army life would further corrupt her already nonpious husband) stalled such a move. When his mother survived another stroke and stabilized, however, Grierson helped organize a local company from Jacksonville that would eventually become part of the 10th Illinois Infantry. "I immediately did all in my power to sustain the right and to hasten the enrollment and organization of troops," he confirmed. While he was weighing his options and balancing his familial concerns, the company's ranks filled. Other companies were being raised around Jacksonville, and one of them was destined to become part of the 6th Illinois Cavalry.[21]

When the heavy unease broke into open war in April 1861, Grierson prepared to take part and began reading widely about tactics. He received his break when his friend and Jacksonville native Governor Yates called him to Springfield to deliver dispatches. Yates sent Grierson to Benjamin Prentiss at Cairo, Illinois, with a pouch of papers, including a general's commission. The appreciative Prentiss offered Grierson a spot on his staff, a kindness "thankfully received and accepted." Unfortunately, it was an unpaid volunteer position, but it held some promise. Alice was

---

20 Ibid., 37-38; Leckie and Leckie, *Unlikely Warriors*, 17. Some claim Grierson received an appointment to West Point but turned it down. See Brown, *Grierson's Raid*, 25. Grierson's biographer, Bruce Dinges, researched the question and found no evidence of such an appointment. See Dinges, "The Making of a Cavalryman," 54-55n32.

21 Grierson, *A Just and Righteous Cause*, 36, 38; Leckie and Leckie, *Unlikely Warriors*, 47-48.

Governor Richard Yates. Jacksonville, Illinois, native and Grierson friend Governor Richard Yates changed Grierson's fortunes when he appointed him as major in the 6th Illinois Cavalry. *Courtesy of Steve Hicks*

less than thrilled because now she would have to take care of his ailing mother as well as the two active boys all by herself. It is doubtful whether his letter trying to explain his decision—"I must (to be true to myself & country) stand not idly by in this hour of time"—influenced his wife.[22]

Grierson stuck with Prentiss during his command tenure at Cairo and later in Missouri. A hoped-for elevation in permanent rank and pay, however, never came. My service, he later complained, was "still unpaid for and unrecognized officially on the Army Register." Alice's continued disapproval of his course of action did not help, and Grierson began to despair over his limited options. "Do not be troubled about sending money at present, I have still five dollars left," she wrote him with obvious sarcasm. Fortunately for Grierson his brother John repeatedly bailed him out, but the sibling wrote Alice that her husband "had a screw loose in his bump of order."[23]

22 Grierson, *A Just and Righteous Cause*, 37; Leckie and Leckie, *Unlikely Warriors*, 48.

23 Grierson, *A Just and Righteous Cause*, 38, 41, 52, 54-56; Leckie and Leckie, *Unlikely Warriors*, 50, 52, 54, 56.

Grierson's increasingly unhappy connection with Prentiss reached a head when Prentiss lost a rank dispute with Ulysses S. Grant. Grierson stood with his friend Prentiss but grew embarrassed when he "became very violent and abusive" toward Grant. Grierson took his concerns to Governor Yates, who promised the young staffer that he would find him a secure spot as soon as possible. Months ebbed by with no change, however, and Grierson became more despondent over what he described as "the unsatisfactory condition of my private affairs." A personal visit to Springfield did not improve his official position, but it did allow him to spend time with Alice and the boys.[24]

Grierson's career took a significant upswing when Yates finally came through and appointed him a major in the 6th Illinois Cavalry. The cavalry regiment had three battalions, two of which already had commanding majors. If he accepted, Grierson would be junior to the other two officers. Several officers had already refused the post because of that fact, although several captains in the regiment wanted the job. Grierson accepted with high hopes and reported to Camp Yates with his own horse and equipment. Unfortunately, his high expectations were quickly dashed. Illinois and the federal government were having a hard time supplying the large number of recruits needed to wage the growing war, and the regiment spent months without either horses or weapons. Discipline within the 6th Illinois was almost nonexistent, as were supplies and pay, which would not be forthcoming until the regiment mustered into federal service. Most of the problems centered around the regiment's political colonel, Thomas M. Cavanaugh, who was absent much of the time and devoid of any leadership abilities, and his carousing adjutant son, who also hampered efficiency and morale. Grierson's own spirit suffered accordingly: "It was no wonder that I was disgusted with soldiering where it was all work and no pay."[25]

Rather than acquiesce to what was transpiring, Grierson set out to make sure his four-company battalion was the best in the regiment. Initially his men resisted all his efforts to instill discipline, including some of the captains who had wanted his job. "My patience, energy, and ability

24 Grierson, *A Just and Righteous Cause*, 38, 41, 52, 54-56; Leckie and Leckie, *Unlikely Warriors*, 50, 52, 54, 56.

25 Grierson, *A Just and Righteous Cause*, 57; Leckie and Leckie, *Unlikely Warriors*, 57, 59, 61; Benjamin H. Grierson, Compiled Service Record, NARA.

were soon thoroughly tested," he later admitted. It became so bad that
Grierson thought to "quit and go home, where if I was obliged to starve,
I possibly might have the satisfaction of dying in my wife's arms."[26]

Eventually, his firm but fair hand and balanced approach convinced
the recruits he was working for them, not against them. Still, shaping
them into soldiers was a difficult task. At one point Grierson informed
his unhappy subordinates, if "it was found that I was not a suitable
person for the position, I would surrender it to anyone else for whom
the officers and men might signify their preference." When he offered
to leave, the men would not hear of it. Even more gratifying, the man
leading the support was Capt. Reuben Loomis, who had earlier wanted
the position for himself. When whispers within the regiment emerged
against Colonel Cavanaugh, some of the men wanted Grierson to replace
him. The conflict-immune Grierson would have none of it. Some of
the soldiers even produced a petition for Governor Yates, but Grierson
refused to join the mutiny. The lack of news reaching the camp also
disheartened Grierson, who later joked, "We might as well have been
on top of the Rocky Mountains." When news did arrive, however, it
was usually unwelcome. A letter informed him that his mother had had
another stroke and was once again at the point of death. Leave was
granted, and Grierson made a quick trip to Jacksonville.[27]

Despite these and other problems, Grierson soon had his battalion
in fighting shape. He drilled the men constantly, and classes for officers
taught tactics and drill. Morale rose. After delivering a speech that "quite
astonished myself as well as the soldiers," he recalled, "I received three
cheers from the entire battalion." His frequent musical renditions at parties
and hotels also drew praise from the men and officers. Unfortunately for
the 6th Illinois, however, the majors at the head of the other two battalions
were not as diligent, and their commands suffered accordingly. Rather
than training the men themselves, they depended on a hired drillmaster,
who "spent his time in guzzling beer at the sutler's and talking loudly
about what great things he expected to accomplish."[28]

26 Grierson, *A Just and Righteous Cause*, 62-65, 67; Leckie and Leckie, *Unlikely Warriors*, 60-61.

27 Grierson, *A Just and Righteous Cause*, 62-65, 67; Leckie and Leckie, *Unlikely Warriors*, 60-61.

28 Grierson, *A Just and Righteous Cause*, 65-67.

The regiment was mustered into federal service at Camp Butler on November 19, 1861, and was sent south without having been issued weapons. Grierson's four companies traveled to Smithland, Kentucky, on the Ohio River at the mouth of the Cumberland River. Grierson was relieved that he and his men were finally on the move and away "from the deplorable regimental entanglements." For a time he found himself the ranking officer there, but that ended when the battalion rejoined the rest of the regiment at Paducah. Grierson pleaded with anyone who would listen that his troopers needed weapons, including Paducah commander William T. Sherman and army commander U. S. Grant. Unfortunately, no arms were available. Grierson's private efforts to obtain them also failed, although he eventually managed to find 150 Sharps carbines that had somehow escaped the attention of others.[29]

Grierson's career soon took another upswing. In April 1862 most of the officers in the regiment petitioned for Colonel Cavanaugh's removal and Grierson's promotion—especially after an embarrassing regimental review during which only Grierson's battalion displayed any martial ability. Cavanaugh saw the writing on the wall and left in disgrace. His "conduct had rendered him totally unfit for the position," wrote a disgusted Grierson, and his acts "bore marked evidence of insanity." On April 13, Grierson was called aboard a steamboat to see his old friend Governor Yates, where, "much to my surprise, [I] came off soon after colonel of the 6th Illinois Cavalry, with my commission in my pocket received without any effort on my part." Yates introduced Grierson to his guests as "a very young colonel, just five minutes old." His was a swift rise for such a novice cavalryman, but Grierson had already demonstrated significant ability and had, in fact, expended substantial efforts to get his command in shape.[30]

Some "thought me a rather common-looking colonel," explained Grierson, but department commander Henry Halleck told him he "looked active and wiry enough to make a good cavalryman." The new colonel was determined to uphold discipline and re-instill order in the entire regiment. After a bold confrontation with rogue captains from the other pair of battalions who did not like being corralled after acting so long

---

29 Ibid., 72-73, 75, 80; Leckie and Leckie, *Unlikely Warriors*, 66-67.

30 Grierson, *A Just and Righteous Cause*, 68; Leckie and Leckie, *Unlikely Warriors*, 67-69, 71-72, 77, 79.

with complete freedom, Grierson worked the 6th Illinois Cavalry into a cohesive and effective command. His role was made somewhat easier when weapons finally arrived to properly arm his troopers. [31]

The higher rank brought with it an increase in monthly pay to $253, which helped Alice warm a bit to life in the army. She still pestered her husband about his morality, especially cigar smoking, which "spoiled" his kisses, and advised him to attend religious services in the camp. Grierson demurred to the latter suggestion by countering that the chaplain was boring. Alice visited him on occasion, despite the fact that the regiment was moving farther south with the larger army. Eventually the regiment moved to Memphis, Tennessee, where Grierson took in as much music and theater as possible. Once he became convinced he would be stationed there for some time, Alice and the boys moved from Illinois to join him. Their sojourn in Tennessee was short and they returned to Jacksonville when Grierson and his command were transferred east to La Grange, Tennessee. [32]

Grierson received a chance to test his own abilities and those of his well-trained 6th Illinois Cavalry during the summer, fall, and winter months of 1862. The operations consisted of several small raids into northern Mississippi against Confederate cavalry. The fighting was mostly skirmishing, but it was still dangerous. During one affair, several bullets ripped through his coat and pants, and one passed between his fingers but did not break the skin. His horse, Old Barber, was wounded but survived. On another occasion, he informed Alice, "a carbine ball passed just over my right ear so close as to cause the ear and head to be swollen and painful for a few days." The fighting increased Grierson's confidence in his commanders in general and in General Sherman in particular, who presented the colonel with a captured silver-plated weapon in recognition of his good work. On occasion, he commanded a cavalry brigade consisting of his own regiment and the 7th Illinois Cavalry and 2nd Iowa Cavalry. Other officers, junior in rank, also led the brigade at times, but the nonconfrontational Grierson raised no objections. Grierson hoped his extra efforts would secure a brigadier general's star,

31 Grierson, *A Just and Righteous Cause*, 62, 68, 82; Leckie and Leckie, *Unlikely Warriors*, 67-69, 71-72, 77.

32 Grierson, *A Just and Righteous Cause*, 62, 68, 82; Leckie and Leckie, *Unlikely Warriors*, 67-69, 71-72, 77.

but months passed without promotion. During this period, his mother finally succumbed to her health issues, but that October he received his wish to have his brother John appointed as the quartermaster of his regiment. The Grierson boys were together once again.[33]

By this time, Grierson had made a name for himself, and both Sherman and Grant were impressed with him. His reports recounted daring mounted affairs, including one surprise attack on a Confederate camp ("If we had fallen from the skies, they could not have been more surprised"). Because of my "constant and active scouting, the country from forty to fifty miles around Memphis was kept well scoured," he concluded, "and no rebel organization could be formed within that distance and remain." After one of Grierson's successful raids, Sherman teased the enemy by sending whiskey and a note that "Colonel Grierson had returned to Memphis and that he would soon be sent again to pay his respects to the Confederate forces." Grant recommended Grierson for additional responsibilities and urged his promotion to brigadier general as early as February 1863. Unfortunately, when he wrote this to President Lincoln, Grant mistakenly attached Grierson to the 6th Missouri Cavalry rather than the 6th Illinois.[34]

By the time Grant began contemplating a cavalry raid deep into Mississippi to inflict damage and divert attention away from his Vicksburg operations, he was well familiar with Grierson and confident he was the right man for the job. Sherman, who had also been pushing for Grierson's promotion to brigadier general, agreed. "I certainly wish your promotion if you want it," he wrote the regimental commander. "Grant speaks in the highest terms of you and ratifies all I wrote him of you," he continued, adding that "you have the goodwill of your late and present commander." Sherman confided to Grant that Grierson "is the best Cavalry officer I have yet had."[35]

Despite Sherman's lobbying on Grierson's behalf, no promotion arrived. Homesick and upset and with the planning for the raid having

---

33 Grierson, *A Just and Righteous Cause*, 102, 107-8, 118; Leckie and Leckie, *Unlikely Warriors*, 71-76.

34 Grierson, *A Just and Righteous Cause*; Leckie and Leckie, *Unlikely Warriors*, 83; Simon, *PUSG*, vol. 7, 301-2.

35 William T. Sherman to B. H. Grierson, February 9, 1863, in William T. Sherman Letters, MDAH; Simon, *PUSG*, vol. 6, 409.

stalled, Grierson took the opportunity in early April to leave on a furlough and traveled back to Jacksonville to see Alice and the boys. General Hurlbut realized the cavalryman needed rest and sent him with orders to Springfield as a "bearer of dispatches." As Grierson later wrote, "Of course it did not take long to get ready for my departure on such a welcome mission." He first traveled to Memphis by train to pay his respects to Hurlbut, who sprang from his desk chair and clasped both of Grierson's hands while whispering, "God Bless, Grierson. Go home at once. I'll give you all the time possible and telegraph you when to return." Unable to speak, the emotional colonel encircled his arms around the general's waist "and gave him in return a genuine hug, which I dare say he never forgot," adding, "There were two pair of moist eyes in that room before I left on my mission of love."[36]

Grierson arrived in Jacksonville on April 6 to the delight of his family. "That visit home was one of the most enjoyable experiences of my life," he confessed long after the war. "It was an oasis of love in the midst of a desert of doubt, darkness, and uncertainty." It was also an opportunity to inform Alice of the dangerous mission upon which he would soon embark.[37]

*   *   *

Grierson arrived on the national scene at a time when cavalry doctrine was undergoing great change. In some ways, his unorthodoxy as a commander was less a product of that change and more a cause of it. The changing role of cavalry would become evident in the American Civil War, and Grierson would play a significant role in bringing it about.[38]

36 William T. Sherman to B. H. Grierson, February 9, 1863; Grierson, *A Just and Righteous Cause*, 109, 112-13; Leckie and Leckie, *Unlikely Warriors*, 83; S. A. Hurlbut to B. H. Grierson, April 3, 1863, Benjamin H. Grierson Papers, ALPL.

37 Grierson, *A Just and Righteous Cause*, 144.

38 For Union cavalry in the Civil War, see Albert G. Brackett, *History of the United States Cavalry, From the Formation of the Federal Government to the 1st of June, 1863. To Which Is Added a List of All of the Cavalry Regiments, with the Names of Their Commanders, Which Have Been in the United States Service Since the Breaking Out of the Rebellion* (New York: Harper and Brothers, 1865) and Stephen Z. Starr, *The Union Cavalry in the Civil War*, 3 vols. (Baton Rouge: Louisiana State University Press, 1979-85).

Through much of history, cavalry had been used as offensive shock troops, riding into battle at the critical moment when the infantry and artillery had the enemy on the run. The thought of thundering horses and shooting or slashing riders was disconcerting to fleeing soldiers already in a state of fright and confusion. Napoleon was a master of this tactic and used mounted troops to finish off a nearly beaten enemy, spread chaos among the routed soldiers, and help bring about final victory on the battlefield—Field Marshal Jaochim Murat's timely attack at Jena in 1806 being a prime example.[39]

American cavalry theory and tactics, however, little resembled those glorious days of Napoleon. The United States military opted for a hybrid formation of dragoons or mounted cavalry rather than pure infantry or cavalry. Moreover, the tactics taught by Denis Hart Mahan at West Point did not emphasize the saber attack. Instead, American theory called for cavalry to screen the army, escort general officers, perform scouting and reconnaissance, and deliver messages. Before the Civil War and during its early months, cavalry rarely engaged in pitched battle, which led to the common slogan, "Who ever saw a dead cavalryman?"[40]

When cavalry did engage in combat during the early years of the Civil War, it was usually in ways Napoleon would not have recognized. Cavalry charges, for example, were uncommon during the war, especially against infantry and artillery. More often, horse soldiers were employed on an army's flanks or as army-wide file closers to keep stragglers from melting away to the rear. Only rarely were cavalry units turned loose at the critical moment in a pitched battle to turn an enemy retreat into a rout. The use of large numbers of cavalry in battle came later, during the latter part of the war when cavalry doctrine had advanced and mounted troopers moved quickly to a particular part of a battlefield to fight dismounted as infantry. Under this circumstance, one of every four troopers remained in the rear to hold the horses, leaving only three of

39 David G. Chandler, *The Campaigns of Napoleon: The Mind and Method of History's Greatest Soldier* (New York: Scribner, 1966) 486; Paddy Griffith, *Battle Tactics of the Civil War* (New Haven: Yale University Press, 1987), 180; Grady McWhiney and Perry D. Jamieson, *Attack and Die: Civil War Military Tactics and the Southern Heritage* (Tuscaloosa: University of Alabama Press, 1982), 126.

40 Griffith, *Battle Tactics of the Civil War*, 181; McWhiney and Jamieson, *Attack and Die*, 133.

his companions to fight on the battle line. As a result, this tactic reduced the effective fighting strength by one-fourth.[41]

One reason cavalry was used rarely as shock troops early in the war was that cavalry doctrine divided the mounted troops among infantry components, either on the brigade or division level. It was not until early 1862 that the Union military devised a system of brigades for cavalry; the development of divisions and corps took even longer to implement. (Confederates arrived at this organizational structure before the Federals.) The net effect dispersed cavalry to the brigade or division level and spread it across the battlefield, especially on the flanks. Likewise, the chain of command within which these units operated was similarly divided, leaving each brigade or division commander with authority over his own specific body of cavalry. This made it nearly impossible to mass horsemen and send them into action at a critical time of a battle because there was no one with the authority or ability to implement its use in that manner.[42]

As a result, the U.S. Army used cavalry to perform other tasks. When an army was in camp (which was the majority of the time, as battles were infrequent affairs), cavalry screened its front, scouted, and garrisoned nearby locales. However, another major development was emerging, and it was in this arena Benjamin Grierson would make his most solid contribution to the evolving cavalry doctrine.[43]

Early in the Civil War, commanders on both sides began to realize that mounted troops under effective leaders could operate far behind enemy lines to disrupt supply lines, communications, and even the nerves of opposing commanders. The Civil War is full of examples, from Jeb Stuart's rides around the Union Army of the Potomac to Earl Van Dorn's and Nathan Bedford Forrest's successful raids on Grant's supply lines during the Mississippi Central campaign. As the war moved on, larger raids took place, some successful and others not. It became obvious, however, that raiding was now a key element of the cavalry's work, and Grierson stood on the cusp of broad change as he prepared to conduct his raid through much of Mississippi in April 1863—an especially ironic

41 McWhiney and Jamieson, *Attack and Die*, 126, 133, 135.

42 Griffith, *Battle Tactics of the Civil War*, 182; Jack Coggins, *Arms and Equipment of the Civil War* (New York: Fairfax Press, 1983), 48.

43 Griffith, *Battle Tactics of the Civil War*, 183; McWhiney and Jamieson, *Attack and Die*, 139.

situation for a music teacher some historians have described as being afraid of horses.[44]

*   *   *

Despite all the detailed planning for the major cavalry raid into Mississippi, a major sticking point remained. The general layout of the route was clear, the identity of the units that would participate was confirmed, and the hoped-for effect of the raid and related operations envisioned. The man Hurlbut, Smith, and Grant tapped to lead the raid, however, was at home in Illinois. If Grierson was going to command it, he would have to get back to Tennessee by the time the cavalry moved out on April 17, the morning Hurlbut had confirmed the raid would begin.[45]

Grierson needed the rest his furlough provided and he enjoyed it. He spent quality time with Alice and did not want to leave, basking as he did in the light of family and fatherhood in his familiar and comfortable surroundings in Illinois. Still, duty called. The thought of his departure was even less appealing with the knowledge that, when he returned to Tennessee, he would leave on a more dangerous mission than any he had thus far experienced. Exactly what crossed his mind we shall never know, but he likely tossed about the various scenarios that could happen to him and how they would affect his family. Would he make it back or would he be captured in the enemy's heartland? Worse would be an injury or wound that altered his lifestyle forever or an amputation that would end his musical passion. Almost unthinkable was the possibility of death and its implications for Alice and the children.[46]

When Grierson left on his furlough, he had no idea whether or when he might be called back to Tennessee. Hurlbut was steadily working at

44 For more on raiding, see Longacre, *Mounted Raids of the Civil War*, and Robert B. Mackey, *The Uncivil War: Irregular Warfare in the Upper South, 1861-1865* (Norman: University of Oklahoma Press, 2004). Not all historians have viewed this major development in the use of cavalry as a positive one. One writer charged that this duty often "became little more than a license to roam off into the enemy's rear areas searching for plunder and glory." The example of Stuart's rides around the Union army and the command confusion another attempt produced during the Gettysburg campaign are often cited as proof. See, for example, Griffith, *Battle Tactics of the Civil War*, 183-84.

45 *OR* 24, pt. 3, 196.

46 Grierson, *A Just and Righteous Cause*, 144.

his Memphis headquarters, making plans and coordinating the effort with not only Grant at Vicksburg but with Rosecrans in Middle Tennessee. Any chance of success required the components to work in unison. By mid-April, Grant was moving his army south through Louisiana on his seventh attempt to reach Vicksburg. It was a major and risky undertaking and there was no going back. Similarly, Rosecrans and his subordinates had worked out the Streight mule raid, which would leave Nashville, circle south into northern Alabama, and work its way east toward Georgia. The only missing piece was Grierson's presence.[47]

On April 13, just four days before the main Mississippi raid was set to begin, Hurlbut sent a short message to Jacksonville, Illinois, by telegraph: "Return immediately. By command of General Hurlbut." Grierson recalled, "While I was romping helter-skelter about the hall, like a big boy, with Charlie and Robert, all in high glee, their mother looking on approvingly, there came a rap on the front door, which was opened by Mrs. Grierson as a boy handed her a telegram." Alice turned and handed the note to her husband, saying, "Ben, here are your orders." The clear meaning of the seven-word order was not lost on Grierson. He had already informed Alice of the danger, which was "so desperate that it was not ordered, but only accepted as a volunteer service." He later mused wistfully, "Our parting may be imagined but cannot be fully realized by any person not placed in a similar situation."[48]

Grierson left Jacksonville by train and made his way to St. Louis. Once at the Mississippi River, he hopped a steamboat and by the afternoon of April 16 was in Memphis, where he met with a now considerably more nervous Hurlbut. Grierson did not have time to visit Governor Yates, who was in town, because Hurlbut had a special train waiting to take him to La Grange. The colonel took a brief moment to write a note to Alice, letting her know he was leaving on "the expedition I spoke to you about" and not to worry as he would "be gone probably three weeks & perhaps longer—possibly not so long. . . . But you must not be alarmed should you not hear from me inside of a month." Then, either to calm her nerves or in a piece of writing that revealed his own fear, he added, "I have a faith and hope that I will return O.K. and you must pray for

47 *OR* 24, pt. 3, 196.

48 S. A. Hurlbut to B. H. Grierson, April 13, 1863; Grierson, *A Just and Righteous Cause*, 144-45.

my safe return and the success of the expedition. I will endeavor to do so myself and will not neglect to use all due caution."[49]

With his brigade already prepared for the movement scheduled to begin the next morning, Grierson grilled Hurlbut about the route he was to take, Grant's location, the intentions of his superiors, and numerous other details. "I learned as nearly as possible the condition of affairs as to the whereabouts of General Grant and his army, the probable operations of our troops for the future, and all that could be given me as to the whereabouts and movements of the rebel forces," he confirmed. Hurlbut also relayed Grant's best wishes and emphasized again that, because of its extremely hazardous nature, the mission was voluntary. The meeting ended with Hurlbut wishing him well. "I parted with General Hurlbut with much feeling, but a most determined will to do my whole duty to accomplish the desired object."[50]

Grierson traveled east by train to La Grange, where he arrived around sundown on April 16 and went straight into a meeting with Sooy Smith, whom, Grierson recalled, was "very glad to see me." Smith passed along the latest information as well as "every possible aid and some additional verbal instructions, together with some important papers covering information in regard to movements of the enemy." By this time the sun had set, but Grierson still had much to do. The home he had just left, however, was still very much on his mind. He took a moment to write once more to Alice, telling her to "be cheerful and happy and may God in his goodness bless and care for you and all at home and guard and protect me while away and bring me safely back to you . . . kiss and hug the boys for me."[51]

The raid was set to begin in just a few hours.

49 B. H. Grierson to Alice, April 1863, in Benjamin H. Grierson Papers, ALPL.

50 Ibid.; Grierson, *A Just and Righteous Cause*, 144-45.

51 B. H. Grierson to Alice, April 1863; Grierson, *A Just and Righteous Cause*, 145; John Grierson to Alice, April 17, 1863.

CHAPTER THREE

The Brigade

Many ties bind Illinois and Mississippi. Some of the railroads developed in the Magnolia State in the 1850s were chartered in Illinois with plans to connect them with northern lines to facilitate travel and transportation of goods easily between the states and their respective regions. Decades later Illinoisans would be interested in proposed national parks, especially Vicksburg in Mississippi. One of Illinois's favored sons, Abraham Lincoln, visited Mississippi earlier in life while traveling down the river bearing its name, and the presidential library of another one of Illinois's favorite sons, Ulysses S. Grant, resides at Mississippi State University.[1]

The Civil War connection between the two states was even stronger. More Illinois troops fought in the Union Army of the Tennessee at Vicksburg than troops from any other state. Grant, who was living in Galena, Illinois, and working in his father's store when the war began, became a colonel in the 21st Illinois before rising to command all the Union armies. And, of course, there was the Mississippi River. Despite the southern state being its namesake, it could just as well have been named the Illinois River, because the entire western boundary of the northern state bordered the waterway from Galena in the north to Cairo in the south. Illinoisans had just as much at stake when Mississippi and Louisiana seceded as Mississippi did, and they were not about to let

---

1 For the Ulysses S. Grant Presidential Library, see http://www.usgrantlibrary.org/.

the pathway to so much prosperity be controlled by the seceding states. They volunteered in droves, following the call of a favorite son who was now president of the United States.[2]

As fate would have it, the main commands tasked with performing one of the most daring and lively feats of the war were Illinois units: the 6th and 7th Cavalry regiments and Battery K of the 1st Illinois Artillery. The raiding column would be joined briefly by an Iowa cavalry regiment (the 2nd), with the entire brigade under the command of Illinois resident Benjamin Grierson, whose superior was Illinois corps commander Stephen Hurlbut in an army led by Illinois native Grant. The rather unique situation was not lost on one Illinois trooper who concluded, "I doubt not that it will be conceded that the history of this Mississippi campaign may properly enough be called a legitimate part of the history of this State."[3]

*   *   *

Given its fast-paced nature, the planned raid had to be carried out by horse soldiers. As noted earlier, cavalry usage was undergoing rapid change during the Civil War, moving away from European-style operations and taking on a unique American twist. Economics played a major role in this change because cavalry was expensive, and thus much harder to raise, organize, train, and maintain than infantry or artillery, and money in the Union army was at a premium.[4]

The expense came from the extra cost of horses and their equipment, and the federal government was picky about what it wanted in a good horse. One advertisement called for animals "not less than fifteen hands high, between five and nine years of age, of dark colors, well broken to the saddle, compactly built, and free from all defects. No mares will be received." Early in the war, noted Grierson, General Sherman "was somewhat inclined to undervalue the service of the cavalry and, in a general way, looked upon it as more expensive than useful." In the infantry or even the artillery, the tools of war primarily included inanimate objects that cost much less than a horse. One historian quipped that a horse

2   For Illinois in the Civil War, see Victor Hicken, *Illinois in the Civil War* (Urbana: University of Illinois Press, 1966).

3   Forbes, "Grierson's Cavalry Raid," 99.

4   Griffith, *Battle Tactics of the Civil War*, 181.

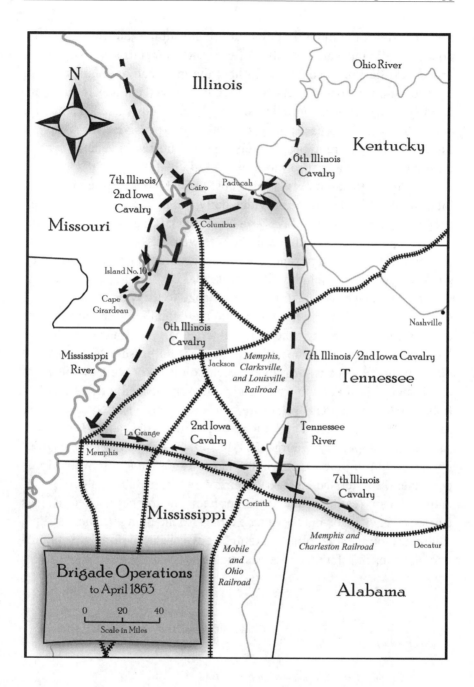

Ohio River

Illinois

Kentucky

N

6th Illinois
Cavalry

7th Illinois/
2nd Iowa
Cavalry

Cairo   Paducah

Missouri

Columbus

Island No. 10

Cape
Girardeau

Nashville

6th Illinois
Cavalry

Mississippi
River

Jackson   *Memphis,
Clarksville,
and Louisville
Railroad*

7th Illinois/2nd Iowa Cavalry

Tennessee

2nd Iowa
Cavalry

La Grange

Memphis

Tennessee
River

7th Illinois
Cavalry

Mississippi

Corinth

*Mobile
and
Ohio
Railroad*

*Memphis and
Charleston Railroad*   Decatur

Alabama

Brigade Operations
to April 1863

0   20   40

Scale in Miles

cost "ten times the monthly pay of a private soldier and five times the price of a rifle musket." Infantry officers and their staff required horses, and the artillery needed horses to haul the guns and ammunition. The transportation system of every branch required draft animals to function. Cavalry, however, was more demanding. Every soldier needed a mount, and at $100 to $150 each, horses were very expensive. One historian estimated there were approximately 825,000 horses in federal service during the war, at a cost of more than $124,000,000.[5]

Caring for the animals was also costly. Each horse also consumed a lot of food, which had to be provided daily. Supplying the oats and grain needed to keep horses healthy was a huge undertaking. Medical care was also demanding. Their vulnerable hooves were susceptible to cracking, infections, inflammations, and other maladies. Improper shoeing created a host of problems, including lameness. Making sure hooves were kept in excellent shape was of utmost importance to a cavalryman.[6]

Recruits, particularly those not intimately familiar with horses, were in for a rude awakening when they entered service. Caring for horses required an unusual amount of equipment, from brushes to combs and blankets, to feed bags carried by each soldier—as well as the large anvils and specialized tools needed by blacksmiths and farriers that had to be carried in wagons. To ensure comfort for both horse and trooper, saddles had to fit well. The Union army utilized the famed McClellan saddle, developed by George B. McClellan after observing cavalry operations during the Crimean War in the 1850s. In addition to all this equipment, soldiers had to carry their own gear, including a gun, saber, eating utensils, canteen, and any other items the trooper needed. Horses carried a heavy load, and they made quite a sound doing it. The "rattling, jingling, jerking, scrabbling, cursing, I never heard before," exclaimed one observer in reference to a passing cavalry column.[7]

5   Grierson, *A Just and Righteous Cause*, 110; Brown, *Grierson's Raid*, 38; Griffith, *Battle Tactics of the Civil War*, 181; Coggins, *Arms and Equipment of the Civil War*, 52.

6   Coggins, *Arms and Equipment of the Civil War*, 53.

7   Ibid.; David S. Heidler and Jeanne T. Heidler, eds., *Encyclopedia of the American Civil War: A Political, Social, and Military History*, 5 vols. (Santa Barbara, CA: ABC-CLIO, 2000), vol. 1, 379.

A cavalryman soon learned to put his main effort into what was most needed when it was needed. Simple things like combing the horse or making sure blankets were properly laid under the saddle were important. So was walking a horse at certain times instead of running them mercilessly. Watering was always necessary, especially when the animal was heavily used. These things and more were learned as the troopers gained experience in the field.[8]

In addition to the expense of equipping and maintaining cavalry, it also required significant training to be effective. Most recruits joined the army woefully lacking in the basic ideas of horse care, cavalry theory, or tactics. It took much longer to train a cavalry regiment for effective frontline service than an infantry unit, and it took longer for a cavalry regiment to achieve veteran status than it did infantry or artillery. Training raw soldiers to be cavalrymen was analogous to producing capable naval aviators in World War II; both required more time and work than was needed to train regular seamen or infantrymen.[9]

The organization of a cavalry regiment exemplified the need for more men, material, and supporting cast. A mounted regiment was larger than a corresponding infantry regiment by two companies (cavalry units had 12 companies while infantry had only 10). Prewar cavalry doctrine called for splitting companies or troops into two troop organizations. During the Civil War, cavalry regiments could be easily subdivided into three equal four-company battalions. Four companies of cavalry was a substantial body.[10]

The desire to have battalions operate independently also required more officers. Cavalry and infantry regiments each had a commanding colonel and a lieutenant colonel as second in command, but the former had three majors while the latter had only one. In theory this was so a major could command each of the three battalions while the two higher officers commanded the whole, even if separated. In practice, the colonel or lieutenant colonel usually commanded one of the battalions himself or he would command a combination of two of the three battalions. The need to care for the horses also required more support positions

8   Coggins, *Arms and Equipment of the Civil War*, 53; Brown, *Grierson's Raid*, 17.

9   Griffith, *Battle Tactics of the Civil War*, 182.

10   Coggins, *Arms and Equipment of the Civil War*, 48.

A Union Cavalryman. Sergeant James Carnes in 1862, a typical Union cavalryman during the early years of the Civil War. Carnes died in August 1862 and thus did not participate in the raid. *Randy Beck*

beyond the standard adjutants, quartermasters, and similar positions in an infantry command. A cavalry regiment, for example, required its own blacksmith, saddler, and farrier, complete with a traveling forge, so any problems with the horses, particularly with horseshoes, could be alleviated quickly and without returning to a garrison.[11]

Some historians have found fault with army commanders who did not use such an expensive arm in the way the Europeans did—to attack the enemy at the critical moment in a battle. While there may be some merit in their position, American commanders learned to use cavalry more efficiently as the war progressed. By 1864 both sides operated large corps of cavalry. The Union's success with cavalry helped turn the tide of several battles. Philip Sheridan's operations late in the war against the Confederate left flank at Petersburg, for example, are prime examples. In the western theater, large late-war raids such as those conducted by James Harrison Wilson and Benjamin Grierson were also very effective.[12]

Mounted units normally traveled in columns similar to infantry, in fours if the roads could handle it, but in twos if the roads were not yet standardized or modernized, which was often the case in the more frontier-oriented west. A cavalry unit could cover as much as thirty miles a day without severely taxing the men or their mounts through a combination of walking, trotting, and, if necessary in the midst of a crisis or need, galloping.[13]

A cavalry column on the move was quite impressive. A regiment in a column of fours, for instance (not including the large number of support vehicles hauling the forge and quartermaster wagons), stretched out as far as a mile. A regiment moving in a column of twos was significantly longer. The clanking of metal on metal, the cacophony of voices, the rumbling of hooves, and the drifting smell of leather and horse sweat added to the splendid display. Finally, a cavalry column, even in a slow trot, much less at a gallop, suggested both the power and the great potential of cavalry at war.[14]

---

11 Heidler and Heidler, *Encyclopedia of the American Civil War*, vol. 1, 378; Coggins, *Arms and Equipment of the Civil War*, 48.

12 Griffith, *Battle Tactics of the Civil War*, 183.

13 Coggins, *Arms and Equipment of the Civil War*, 51.

14 Griffith, *Battle Tactics of the Civil War*, 181; Coggins, *Arms and Equipment of the Civil War*, 51.

*   *   *

Benjamin Grierson led a brigade of three cavalry regiments in April 1863. "I found it much pleasanter to have command of a brigade than only a regiment," he later explained, "as it removed me from the everlasting noise and confusion of horses, mules, and soldiers." He also quipped that "'there is no rest for the wicked,' and I often wondered if the cavalryman did not belong to that class." The only drawback, at least as he saw it, was that, "although exercising a brigadier general's command, I was not a general, yet [I was] obliged to perform the work without being able to draw the pay of that grade."[15]

The key unit in the brigade was Grierson's own 6th Illinois Cavalry. General Hurlbut, while organizing the raid, explained that "the force sent down on the long dash will be selected without reference to regiments, unless Grierson returns, when he had best take his own." Grierson, of course, returned in time to lead the raid, and his regiment was naturally a main staple of his attention. The 6th Illinois was a well-organized and veteran outfit, having been in service nearly a year and a half by that time, and about a year of it under Grierson's watchful eye. The 6th Illinois began as individual companies created by Lincoln's call for troops. Most of the members of the regiment hailed from the extreme southern portion of the state, the same vicinity from which many Illinoisans left to join the Confederacy. In fact, Lincoln worried about the southern counties of Illinois, Indiana, and Ohio and how they might behave because they were more economically tied to the economy of the Ohio and Mississippi Rivers than to the railroad network of northern Illinois. As a result, Lincoln appointed numerous so-called political generals from the southern counties of Illinois (a region dubbed as Little Egypt), most notably politicians John A. McClernand and John A. Logan.[16]

A full 10 counties in Little Egypt, including four Ohio River counties and two bordering the Mississippi River, sent men to serve in the 6th Illinois Cavalry. These included Massac, Gallatin, and Pope Counties

---

15 Grierson, *A Just and Righteous Cause*, 129, 133.

16 *OR* 24, pt. 3, 185, 197. For McClernand, see Richard L. Kiper, *Major General John Alexander McClernand: Politician in Uniform* (Kent, OH: Kent State University Press, 1999). For Logan, see James Pickett Jones, *Black Jack: John A. Logan and Southern Illinois in the Civil War Era* (Carbondale: Southern Illinois University Press, 1995).

along the Ohio River; Alexander County (which included the river town of Cairo) at the tip of the state, where the Ohio joined the Mississippi River; Union County farther north on the Mississippi; and farther inland but still in the southern cone of the state, Johnson, Saline, Hamilton, Edwards, and Richland Counties. The regiment was so heavily populated with men from southern Illinois that the warm-under-the-collar Republican Grierson once referred to it as "my Egyptian Democratic regiment."[17]

Only three other counties across the rest of the state—Cass, Morgan, and LaSalle—provided men for the unit. Cass and Morgan were in the west-central portion of the state, the latter boasting Grierson's home at Jacksonville. Men from both counties comprised Company C, which was thus tied more closely to Grierson. LaSalle was in northern Illinois and sent part of Company B.[18]

In terms of raw numbers, most of the men hailed from Pope County on the Ohio River (parts of Companies A, B, and G) and Hamilton County (Companies D, H, and part of K). Saline and Gallatin Counties each sent parts of Companies F, K, and L while the other counties split a company, as in the case of Alexander and Union splitting Company M, Edwards and Richland Company E, and Morgan and Cass Company C. Perry County fully recruited Company I.[19]

The companies came together at Camp Butler in Springfield in November 1861, where they were given their numerical designation. The governor appointed Thomas H. Cavanaugh as its original colonel, John Olney as lieutenant colonel, and Grierson as one of the majors. The regiment moved to Shawneetown on the Ohio River near the Illinois-Indiana border a few days later and stayed there until the battles of Forts Henry and Donelson in February 1862. The need for more mounted troops to cover the newly acquired portions of the Confederacy pulled the Illinois troopers south, first to Paducah and then to Columbus, Kentucky, the main bastion on the Mississippi River that was finally in Union hands.

17 ILGenWeb Project, "6th Illinois Cavalry Regiment," 1997, https://civilwar.illinoisgenweb.org/reg_html/cav_006.html; Grierson, *A Just and Righteous Cause*, 85.

18 ILGenWeb Project, "6th Illinois Cavalry Regiment," 1997, https://civilwar.illinoisgenweb.org/reg_html/cav_006.html.

19 Ibid.

A good illustration of the need to defend this territory was the fact that the regiment was split so it could garrison several places at once.[20]

Garrisoning needs increased as the Federals occupied more land. Five of the 6th Illinois companies were sent to the Memphis area, five to the vicinity around Trenton, Tennessee, and two remained in the rear to garrison and operate out of Paducah. Few Confederate regulars were that far north, but the Illinois troopers were kept busy combating guerrillas who were harassing the Federals' transportation and logistical network. Casualties were light, with only two killed, six wounded, and one captured during this period.[21]

More important to the regiment was the change in command in the spring of 1862. Grierson jumped from major to colonel when the incompetent Cavanaugh resigned on March 28. Captain Reuben Loomis, who had earlier wanted Grierson's position as major, became the regiment's lieutenant colonel. He remained one of Grierson's solid supporters and often commanded the regiment when Grierson had to command the brigade. The regiment also went through numerous majors after Grierson left that position.[22]

After what Grierson described as "repeated applications to General Grant and Sherman," the regiment's companies were once again combined in the fall of 1862 at Memphis. The Illinois troopers were destined for a new kind of service because a new kind of commander was now in charge of the Army of the Tennessee. Henry Halleck (quite the Jominian in that he was more inclined to disperse, garrison, and protect conquered territory rather than unite his forces to move forward and conquer more objectives) had been called to Washington. His transfer left Grant in charge in West Tennessee. By that October, Grant had been elevated to departmental level and given more flexibility in how he conducted operations. Unlike Halleck, Grant was more Clausewitzian in matters of war and favored moving forward and attacking the enemy rather than holding large amounts of territory and key places. He used his new command opportunities to begin an advance against the Confederate stronghold at Vicksburg that

20   J. N. Reece, *Report of the Adjutant General of the State of Illinois*, 9 vols. (Springfield, IL: Journal Company, 1900-1902), vol. 8, 3, 50; "History of Sixth Cavalry," n.d., J. W. Vance Papers, CHM.

21   Reece, *Report of the Adjutant General of the State of Illinois*, vol. 8, 50.

22   Ibid., vol. 8, 3.

November. That offensive would come to be known as the Mississippi Central campaign, named after the rail line running south toward Grenada. Grant established a forward base at Holly Springs as he moved south along the railroad with about 40,000 men, hoping Confederate Gen. John Pemberton would move out of Vicksburg and meet him around Grenada. General Sherman, before being detached and sent down the river to what would become known as Chickasaw Bayou, moved south from Memphis with more divisions along the Mississippi and Tennessee Railroad to join Grant. Grierson's 6th Illinois Cavalry led Sherman's move out of Memphis, confronting the enemy at the Tallahatchie River before moving south to College Hill and Oxford to unite with Grant. Grierson enjoyed serving under Sherman and noted wryly that the Ohioan "did not intend to permit the grass to grow under the feet of the cavalry horses, or to let their riders suffer for want of suitable exercise."[23]

Twin Confederate cavalry raids that December under Nathan Bedford Forrest and Earl Van Dorn, however, shook up the entire department and ended Grant's first attempt to take Vicksburg. On December 11, Forrest led a raid into West Tennessee, disrupting Union communications while skillfully eluding Union pursuers. Van Dorn, meanwhile, left Grenada on December 17, rode around Grant's command, and sacked Holly Springs behind the Union lines, destroying tons of supplies and capturing 1,500 men. Grierson's position in north Mississippi precluded any viable attempt to catch Forrest in northwest Tennessee, but Grant sent the 6th Illinois after Van Dorn. For seven days Grierson led his troopers on the chase, but they were never able to catch the elusive Southerner. Nevertheless, Grierson displayed great skill in the pursuit as well as true leadership qualities. Unfortunately, other cavalry commanders, such as John K. Mizner and Albert Lee, did not.[24]

By January 1863 the enemy raids ended and Grant began to plan another way to get to Vicksburg. His attempts to take the bastion along roundabout routes through the maze of creeks, bayous, and swamps in the delta on both sides of the Mississippi River also proved unsuccessful. Cavalry played only a small role in those operations, the waterlogged

---

23   William T. Sherman to Benjamin H. Grierson, December 9, 1862; Grierson, *A Just and Righteous Cause*, 98-99.

24   Grierson, *A Just and Righteous Cause*, 123, 125, 128; Reece, *Report of the Adjutant General of the State of Illinois*, vol. 8, 50.

Reuben Loomis. Lieutenant Colonel Reuben
Loomis commanded the 6th Illinois Cavalry,
Grierson's own regiment, on the raid because
Grierson led the brigade. Loomis performed
steadily despite a bad case of hemorrhoids.
Martyrs and Heroes

terrain precluding much mounted effort. Instead, most of the Federal
cavalry was held in West Tennessee and used to either raid into Mississippi
or repulse enemy probes. The main objects of importance were the
Memphis and Charleston Railroad and the other major lines running
through the region. Grierson and company saw plenty of action during
the first months of 1863 while based at the cavalry depot at La Grange,
Tennessee, where Grierson commanded the brigade and Lieutenant
Colonel Loomis led the 6th Illinois.[25]

By the eve of the April 1863 raid, the 6th Illinois regiment numbered
around 500 effectives, which 37-year-old Lieutenant Colonel Loomis kept
under his careful eye. Like many others, Loomis arrived in Illinois from
points farther east—in his case via Ohio after leaving his birth state of
Massachusetts. In Perry County, Illinois, he became a prosperous farmer
and recruited a cavalry company when the war broke out. Loomis rose
through the ranks to major and then lieutenant colonel, often commanding
the regiment, as he was in April 1863 when Grierson commanded the
brigade.[26]

25 Reece, *Report of the Adjutant General of the State of Illinois*, vol. 8, 50, 102.

26 R. W. Surby, *Grierson Raids, and Hatch's Sixty-Four Days March, with Biographical
Sketches, also the Life and Adventures of Chickasaw, the Scout* (Chicago: Rounds

By April 1863 the regiment had been involved in numerous raids, patrols, and its share of combat. The extensive resumption of operations and warming weather, however, exhausted the men and weakened the horses. "This big sand hill is not a very cool place," grumbled trooper James Cole. "The horses of our regiment are mostly all run down [and] we are turning over a lot today, preparing for hard work again." Rations were monotonous, continued the trooper, who observed that he and his comrades "are living on hard tack and sow belley. We get bakers bread a part of the time. Hard crackers & sow belley will thou be ever near & dear to me." Despite their plight, Loomis's command maintained good morale and was ready for action.[27]

Grierson was very proud of his regiment as he prepared to lead his Illinois troopers on the raid into Mississippi on April 17. He knew he would also probably need to depend upon them heavily during the coming days. After all, he had made them into what they were, and he was not about to let his best regiment go to waste.

*   *   *

On paper, at least, the 7th Illinois Cavalry seemed to have much in common with its sister regiment. Both it and the 6th Illinois Cavalry hailed from the same state, both were brigaded together under Grierson, and both would follow him deep into Mississippi. But that is where their similarities ended.[28]

Most of the men in the 6th Illinois Cavalry came from the southern counties, but the men of the 7th came from all over the state. A few southern counties sent men to the regiment, including Randolph on the Mississippi River and White County farther east. Gallatin and Edwards Counties, which had also sent men to the 6th Illinois Cavalry, provided men for the 7th. In central Illinois a group of eastern counties (including Macon, Shelby, Fayette, and Edgar), together with a few western counties (Knox, McDonough, and Fulton) provided men. An additional slate of northern counties also had sons in the regiment. These included Carroll,

and James, 1865), 20; James Barnet, *The Martyrs and Heroes of Illinois in the Great Rebellion: Biographical Sketches* (Chicago: J. Barnet, 1865), 79-81.

27   James Cole to Cousin, April 7, 1863, in James M. Cole Papers, ALPL.

28   Reece, *Report of the Adjutant General of the State of Illinois*, vol. 8, 102.

Ogle, Lee, and LaSalle, the latter having also provided riders for Grierson's 6th Illinois. Many counties sent only partial companies, although Edgar, Knox, Fayette, Shelby, Macon, McDonough, and Randolph fielded entire companies for the regiment. Only two counties, Knox and White, sent men to more than one company.[29]

Like its sister regiment, the 7th Illinois Cavalry was mustered into service at Camp Butler in October 1861. Colonel William Pitt Kellogg was its original commander, although he missed some of the early training because he was on detached duty in the west. Much of the initial training was overseen by Lt. Col. Edward Prince of Quincy, Illinois. An assortment of majors came and went throughout the early months, but the Midwest farmers and artisans quickly learned their equestrian trade. "My horse pleases me well," professed one of the 7th Illinois men, "and is learning to follow me like a dog."[30]

Like Grierson's regiment, the 7th Illinois Cavalry was split in two, with four companies sent to the Cairo area. After a brief concentration of the entire regiment there on Christmas Day 1861, 8 of the regiment's 12 companies were shipped in January 1862 across the Mississippi River to Cape Girardeau, Missouri. The 7th Illinois spent most of its time keeping marauding Confederate guerrillas away from the Federal garrisons, "scouting the country, giving protection to Union citizens and running out the rebels."[31]

Major campaigns took form as the weather warmed in the spring of 1862. The 7th Illinois once again concentrated at Cape Girardeau as part of Maj. Gen. John Pope's newly created Army of the Mississippi. Pope was preparing for a combined army-navy advance against New Madrid and Island No. 10, two Confederate defensive positions 60 miles below Columbus, Kentucky, guarding the Mississippi River. While most of the fighting was conducted by the navy, the 7th Illinois provided important support scouting and covering supply lines and leading the advance

---

29 ILGenWeb Project, "6th Illinois Cavalry Regiment," 1997, https://civilwar. illinoisgenweb.org/reg_html/cav_007.html.

30 Reece, *Report of the Adjutant General of the State of Illinois*, vol. 8, 53, 102; Brown, *Grierson's Raid*, 11.

31 Reece, *Report of the Adjutant General of the State of Illinois*, vol. 8, 102; T. M. Eddy, *The Patriotism of Illinois: A Record of the Civil and Military History of the State in the War for the Union*, 2 vols. (Chicago: Clarke & Co., 1865-86), vol. 2, 622-23.

of the army against New Madrid, where it captured a battery of steel breech-loading guns. When the operation ended with the fall of Island No. 10 in early April, Pope and his command were ordered east to the Tennessee River to join with two other armies led by General Halleck, who was preparing an advance from Pittsburg Landing to Corinth, Mississippi. The grueling drive on Corinth included the laborious task of corduroying roads in preparation for the advance and fighting the Rebels. The 7th Illinois's Maj. Zenas Aplington was shot through the head and killed on May 8.[32]

Significant changes greeted the regiment after the fall of Corinth. Colonel Kellogg resigned immediately after the campaign ended, leaving the post to the next in command, Edward Prince. Prince was a seasoned officer, if only in his late 20s, and had experienced his own share of problems, including a combat wound and an arrest courtesy of Kellogg. His new lieutenant colonel, William D. Blackburn, was just 25. Horatio C. Nelson, an ironically named subordinate tasked with leading horse soldiers, replaced the late Major Aplington.[33]

More change was on the way. Once Halleck captured Corinth at the end of May, he dispersed his huge army in various directions. The 7th Illinois Cavalry ended up in northern Alabama, guarding a 40-mile stretch of the Memphis and Charleston Railroad from Tuscumbia, Alabama, east to where the line crossed the Tennessee River at Decatur. When the line was abandoned later that fall, the regiment returned to the Corinth area, where it lost 40 men killed or wounded in the battles of Iuka and Corinth in early October.[34]

Late in the fall of 1862 Grant prepared to move south toward Vicksburg. The 7th Illinois skirmished heavily with enemy cavalry as Grant advanced toward Grenada. The Illinois troopers also took part in the raid on the Mobile and Ohio Railroad in mid-December that helped break the line near Okolona, Mississippi, and was instrumental in alerting Grant to Van

32 Reece, *Report of the Adjutant General of the State of Illinois*, vol. 8, 102; Eddy, *The Patriotism of Illinois*, vol. 2, 622. For letters from a 7th Illinois Cavalry trooper, see William H. Dennis Letters, Ellen Waddle McCoy Papers, Southeast Missouri State University.

33 Reece, *Report of the Adjutant General of the State of Illinois*, vol. 8, 53; Edward Prince, Compiled Service Record, NARA.

34 Reece, *Report of the Adjutant General of the State of Illinois*, vol. 8, 102.

Edward Prince. Colonel Edward Prince was commander of the 7th Illinois Cavalry and was a solid, if somewhat excitable, sounding board for Grierson on the raid. They would later have a falling out over Prince's jealousy of Grierson's fame. *Randy Beck*

Dorn's raid toward Holly Springs. Confederate cavalry were discovered crossing behind their path near Pontotoc, riding north instead of chasing the Federal cavalry. According to the 7th Illinois's official history, by the end of December it had "marched over 900 miles during the month of December, and being engaged with the enemy nearly every day to a greater or less extent."[35]

After the failure of Grant's Mississippi Central Railroad Campaign, the 7th Illinois Cavalry joined its sister regiment (the 6th) and the 2nd Iowa Cavalry at La Grange, Tennessee, in the brigade led by Benjamin Grierson. It "made frequent forages into West Tennessee," reported the regiment's historian, "relieving the rebel inhabitants of many fine horses and mules, which were abundant in that region." The troopers also broke up Confederate conscription attempts. The major Confederate nemesis operating in the area, Col. Robert V. Richardson, saw his camp invaded and his quartermaster captured. Richardson himself barely escaped with a wound to his leg.[36]

The 7th Illinois was a seasoned cavalry command with good officers and men by the time it was to ride into Mississippi with Grierson. The

35 Ibid.

36 Ibid., vol. 8, 102-3.

regiment numbered 542 effectives. Its commander, Col. Edward Prince, was an able though excitable field officer with broad experience on many fronts. As was the case with many others of his day, Prince had migrated west to Illinois from his 1832 birthplace in East Bloomfield, New York. For a time he lived in Grierson's hometown of Jacksonville before attaining a law degree and settling in Quincy. With the advent of the war, Prince became an expert drillmaster, which he parlayed into a commission from Governor Yates as lieutenant colonel of the regiment. By the time he ascended to the top position he was more than capable of handling that level of command—and was just what Grierson needed as he set out on this unique journey.[37]

*   *   *

Grierson's third regiment more than held its own in the brigade. In fact, the 2nd Iowa Cavalry was perhaps the most veteran of all three. It certainly was not afraid of a hard fight. As one Iowan put it in a letter home, "The Secesh up there [meaning back home], do they realize that the 2nd Iowa are just as ready to kill them as Southern rebels and if anything more so."[38]

The members of the 2nd Iowa Cavalry came from two parts of the Hawkeye State. As would be expected in this relatively new addition to the Union, the majority of the population was situated in the eastern swath, mostly along the Mississippi River. When the companies began forming during the first summer of the war, several counties sent men, including Des Moines, Muscatine, Scott, and Jackson Counties. Johnson and Delaware Counties, both inland counties, also sent companies. The other major county sources of manpower were in the north-central portion of the state, where Cerro Gordo, Franklin, Hamilton, Marshall,

---

37 Jonas Rawalt to Son, May 11, 1863, in Marguerite Rawalt Papers, ALPL; Surby, *Grierson Raids*, 13, 20.

38 Franklin Hammond to Sister, April 1863, in Franklin Hammond Collection, State Historical Society of Iowa. For the 2nd Iowa Cavalry, see Lyman B. Pierce, *History of the Second Iowa Cavalry; Containing a Detailed Account of Its Organization, Marches, and the Battles in Which It Has Participated; Also, a Complete Roster of Each Company* (Burlington, IA: Hawk-Eye Steam Book and Job Printing Establishment, 1865); A. B. Rush Letters, in State Historical Society of Iowa; and Stephen Z. Starr, "Hawkeyes on Horseback: The Second Iowa Volunteer Cavalry," *Civil War History* (September 1977), vol. 23, no. 3, 212-27.

and Polk (home of the state capital at Des Moines) also sent men to the regiment. Some counties raised and sent entire companies, such as Marshall and Polk, while others provided men to multiple companies, including Jackson and Muscatine. Scott County, on the Mississippi River at Davenport and Rock Island, sent men to nine different companies.[39]

The companies that would become the 2nd Iowa Cavalry were mustered into service at Davenport, Iowa, in September 1861. The Iowa governor appointed West Point graduate and career army officer Washington L. Elliott as the regiment's colonel. Unlike the inept Colonel Cavanaugh of the 6th Illinois Cavalry, Elliott introduced his troopers to rigid drill practice, and the 2nd regiment was soon one of the best-trained cavalry commands in the entire federal service. Its lieutenant colonel, Edward Hatch, was also an outstanding officer. The 30-year-old graduate of Norwich Military Academy in Vermont was a career officer, though he once found himself under arrest for swatting a soldier with the flat of his sword, cursing him, and tying up the unfortunate trooper by his hands. The majors were also solid. The regiment was a force to be reckoned with, especially with two of the three battalions armed with fast-shooting Colt revolving rifles.[40]

The 2nd Iowa left Davenport in December and moved to St. Louis's Benton Barracks, where it received additional training. It moved to the front in mid-February 1862, first to the Cairo area. Like the 7th Illinois Cavalry, the Iowans took part in the New Madrid and Island No. 10 operations under John Pope, fighting at times as separate battalions. Like the Illinoisans, they, too, made the long journey east to the Tennessee River and participated in the operations against Corinth, Mississippi, in the spring of 1862.[41]

The Iowans showed their mettle in numerous skirmishes outside Corinth, including a daring charge against an artillery battery. The troopers played a dramatic role at Farmington on May 9 after being ordered to

---

39 Iowa, Adjutant General's Office, *Roster and Record of Iowa Soldiers in the War of the Rebellion, Together with Historical Sketches of Volunteer Organizations, 1861-1866*, 6 vols. (Des Moines: Emory H. English and E. D. Chassell, 1908-11), vol. 4, 215; "2nd Regiment, Iowa Cavalry," FamilySearch, https://familysearch.org/wiki/en/2nd_Regiment_Iowa_Cavalry.

40 Adjutant General's Office, *Roster and Record of Iowa Soldiers in the War of the Rebellion*, vol. 4, 215, Pierce, *History of the Second Iowa Cavalry*, preface; Edward Hatch, Compiled Service Record, NARA.

41 A. A. Stuart, *Iowa Colonels and Regiments: Being a History of Iowa Regiments in the War of the Rebellion* (Des Moines: Mills & Co., 1865), 565-66; Adjutant General's Office, *Roster and Record of Iowa Soldiers in the War of the Rebellion*, vol. 4, 215-16.

charge the battery. They did so with gusto, disrupting Confederate plans and helping break the line in several places. The Iowans also made a dash into the Confederate rear in late May. Unbeknownst to the Federal high command, the Confederates were evacuating south along the Mobile and Ohio Railroad just as Colonel Elliott led his regiment, together with the 2nd Michigan Cavalry under Col. Philip Sheridan, to Booneville. There, the daring cavalrymen broke the line and disrupted a portion of the enemy retreat.[42]

This string of successes resulted in Elliot's promotion to brigadier general, and he served with General Pope as his cavalry commander thereafter. The regimental mantle of leadership fell to its lieutenant colonel, Edward Hatch, who was promoted to colonel of the 2nd Cavalry.[43]

While the 6th Illinois Cavalry operated farther in the rear and the 7th Illinois Cavalry guarded the railroad in Alabama, the 2nd Iowa spent the arduous summer and fall of 1862 camped mostly at Rienzi in a brigade led by Sheridan. The regiment was front and center in the actions around Iuka and Corinth in September and October. Occasionally, the Iowans found themselves in a brigade under Colonel Hatch, with Maj. Datus E. Coon commanding the regiment in Hatch's absence. The regiment also took part in Grant's initial advance into Mississippi in late 1862, although once that plan failed, it moved back to La Grange, Tennessee.[44]

At nearly 600 effectives, the 2nd Iowa Cavalry was the largest of Grierson's three regiments. Its able commander, Colonel Hatch, had been born in 1832 in Maine and had been a part of the steady progress of westward migration during the early days of Manifest Destiny. As was the custom, most Americans migrated laterally, the Griersons being a prime example. As a result, most New Englanders wound up in the northwestern or midwestern states. Hatch settled in Muscatine, Iowa, in the 1850s and went into the lumber business along the Mississippi River. When the war broke out, he volunteered and steadily rose in rank from major to lieutenant colonel and, finally, colonel of the regiment. Hatch was an able and steady counterpart to Grierson, if somewhat a

42 Timothy B. Smith, *Corinth 1862: Siege, Battle, Occupation* (Lawrence: University Press of Kansas, 2012), 41; Stuart, *Iowa Colonels and Regiments*, 566-67; Adjutant General's Office, *Roster and Record of Iowa Soldiers in the War of the Rebellion*, vol. 4, 217-18.

43 Stuart, *Iowa Colonels and Regiments*, 570-71.

44 Ibid., 571-72; Adjutant General's Office, *Roster and Record of Iowa Soldiers in the War of the Rebellion*, vol. 4, 221-22.

Edward Hatch. Grierson's senior commander on the raid was Colonel Edward Hatch of the 2nd Iowa Cavalry. He was not happy about playing a diversionary role for the raid, but Hatch performed his duties well. *Library of Congress*

competitor in the no-holds-barred rise of field officers during the Civil War. Grierson was more than willing to accept that sort of competition if it provided him with a seasoned colonel at the head of a seasoned regiment. And that is exactly what Hatch and his Iowans provided.[45]

*   *   *

The final unit in the roughly 1,700-man force Grierson was preparing to take southward on his raid was Battery K of the 1st Illinois Artillery. Commanded by Capt. Jason B. Smith, it was the most unique organization of the brigade. Many Illinois batteries had already gained something of a reputation by this point in the war, including the two Chicago light artillery batteries that had seen action at Fort Donelson and Waterhouse's, McAllister's, and Bouton's batteries of the same regiment that had fought at Shiloh. Smith's Battery K, organized out of Johnson and Pope Counties in southern Illinois, had mustered into service at Shawneetown in January 1862, but it had not yet had much of an opportunity to make a name for itself.[46]

---

45 Stuart, *Iowa Colonels and Regiments*, 571; Surby, *Grierson Raids*, 20.

46 Grierson, *A Just and Righteous Cause*, 146.

Smith was from Vienna, Illinois, and he was more than just an artilleryman in Uncle Sam's army; he was also a minister of the gospel in the Methodist Episcopal Church. Born in South Carolina in 1805, Smith was older than most Civil War soldiers. He migrated west at an early age, first to Kentucky and then to Illinois, where he worked as a blacksmith and served as a county judge in Johnson County. Smith gained some military experience in the 1830s during the Black Hawk War. His son, Jasper, served in the battery as a cannoneer.[47]

Although Smith was a pious man, he had no problem standing up for himself and his men. The members of the battery went to war with their own horses and initially organized as a cavalry company. Because they were not fully equipped, however, the paymaster refused to pay the men the mandatory 70 cents per diem for their horses. After squabbling over the issue, someone suggested making the company into an artillery unit with small mounted cannon that could be used with the horses the men had brought with them. Thus the company transitioned to artillery. A second paymaster, however, refused to pay the men for their horses because they were not cavalry mounts but artillery horses! Smith, righteously indignant at such treatment, fought hard for his men to get them every penny to which they were entitled.[48]

While most batteries had 6- or 12-pound field guns pulled by large draft horses, Smith's battery was armed with what he described as "2 Pound Mounted Cannon." The two-pound Woodruff guns were steel tubes weighing about 150 pounds each. The guns sat on small and poorly designed carriages that were easily damaged. The entire cannon-and-carriage combination was so light it could be pulled by only two horses, with two others hauling the limbers holding the small ammunition chests. Grierson's adjutant, Lt. Samuel Woodward, described them as "six very light field pieces" that shot "small round shot and canister." The lightness and mobility of these guns also limited their firepower. Grierson, however, did not need to pack a heavy punch, because he did not intend to do any

47 Mrs. P. T. Chapman, *A History of Johnson County, Illinois* (n.p.: Press of the Herron News, 1925), 62, 130, 478; Jasper F. Smith Obituary, February 14, 1930, *Verden* [OK] *News*; N. Dale Talkington, *A Time Remembered: The Verdan, Oklahoma Cemetery* (n.p.: n.p., 1999), 141; Reece, *Report of the Adjutant General of the State of Illinois*, vol. 8, 644-45, 664-65; Battery K, 1st Illinois Artillery Muster Roll, RG 94, E 57, NARA.

48 James B. Smith to Silas Noble, March 14, 1862 and General Strong, June 10, 1862, in James B. Smith, Compiled Service Record, NARA.

Woodruff Gun. The six guns of Captain Jason B. Smith's Battery K, 1st Illinois Light Artillery, provided Grierson with additional firepower at critical times. The battery was armed with small two-pound Woodruff guns, an example of which is on display in White Hall, Illinois. *Author*

fighting that would require a serious artillery presence. If he got into a tight spot, the small steel guns offered more firepower than dismounted cavalry could deliver, making Battery K of the 1st Illinois Artillery the perfect guns to accompany him on this raid.[49]

* * *

49 "From One of Grierson's Cavalry," *Union Monitor* (Litchfield, IL), June 5, 1863; S. L. Woodward, "Grierson's Raid, April 17th to May 2d, 1863," *Journal of the United States Cavalry Association* (April 1904), vol. 14, no. 52, 686. For armament, see Battery K, 1st Illinois Artillery Muster Roll, RG 94, E 57, NARA.

On April 16, with the march scheduled to begin the next morning, the companies on detached duty were ordered to concentrate. News that the hour had arrived electrified the men, with one admitting, "Considerable emotion could be perceived in and about the camps." Charles W. Whitsit, one of the 6th Illinois Cavalry's captains, was doubly excited because he had just received word that same day of his promotion to major.[50]

With their orders in hand, the troopers set about making sure everything was ready. Leather items like bridles and harnesses were double-checked and oiled, weapons cleaned, and personal items carefully packed for the long haul ahead. Horses were fed and rested as much as possible while blacksmiths finished last-minute work on the animals still needing shoes. Surgeons examined the men to determine who was fit for the long ride and who was not; only those well enough to see the ride through would set off in the morning. Quartermasters double-checked the food the men would carry, although the five days of bread, coffee, sugar, and salt would not be enough to last the entire raid; the troopers would have to fend for themselves once they ran out. One Illinoisan remembered the rations were issued "with the understanding they were to last ten [days]." Ordnance officers distributed enough ammunition so that the regiments carried anywhere from 70 to 100 rounds per man, depending on what type of weapon each carried. Brigade and regimental adjutants finished the necessary paperwork. Few other than Grierson himself knew the purpose, direction, or length of the raid or of the dangers involved. What was patently obvious was that this expedition was going to be different than other routine forays.[51]

Some of the troopers had just returned from operations, and their horses were worn down. According to Grierson's adjutant Woodward, the regiments "were so badly mounted that it was necessary to dismount the brigade wagon train and use the mules to complete the mount of one

50 H. R. Curtiss, diary, April 16, 1863, Wisconsin Historical Society; Pierce, *History of the Second Iowa Cavalry*, 48; Surby, *Grierson Raids*, 19; *History of Kossuth, Hancock and Winnebego Counties, Iowa* (Springfield, IL: Union Publishing Company, 1884), 845; Hoffman Atkinson to "Capt.," April 16, 1863, in Henry C. Forbes Papers, CHM; "The Late Major Whitsit," n.d., in Thomas W. Lippincott Papers, ALPL.

51 Surby, *Grierson Raids*, 20; Forbes, "Grierson's Cavalry Raid," 102; Grierson, *A Just and Righteous Cause*, 154; *OR* 24, pt. 1, 531; Daniel E. Robbins to Parents, May 5, 1863, in Daniel E. Robbins Letters, HC; Woodward, "Grierson's Raid," 686. For soldiers left behind, see Collier Family Papers, in Civil War Documents, USAMHI. For armament information, see the muster rolls for the 6th and 7th Illinois and 2nd Iowa cavalries, RG 94, E 57, NARA.

regiment." The 2nd Iowa had the most exhausted horses. Sick soldiers were necessarily left behind. Some, in hospitals as far away as Memphis, did their best to keep track of their regiments. "I hear the 2nd Iowa Cav have been out on a scout," one convalescent later wrote. Some healthy troopers, however, had to stay to guard and preserve the camp and everything that went along with it. "A wail went up from those who were necessarily left behind to guard the camp," admitted Woodward. One of those Grierson left in La Grange was his brother John, quartermaster of the regiment.[52]

Fortunately for Benjamin Grierson, his trusty adjutant helped him prepare for the complex raiding operation. Samuel Woodward was a native of New Jersey. Their relationship began early in the war when the young man asked Grierson for help against the secessionists in his adopted Paducah. There was little Grierson could officially do about the problem. When he recommended Woodward join the Union army, the man enlisted in the 6th Illinois Cavalry. Woodward worked first as a clerk and served Sherman in that capacity at Shiloh before being transferred to Grierson. On the eve of the raid, as time grew increasingly short, Woodward stalked the camp, overseeing the myriad details required by a raid of this magnitude. Thinking ahead, he threw together a few sandwiches "for the first day's luncheon, trusting to Providence from day to day for subsistence."[53]

Once he arrived in La Grange, Grierson felt just as rushed. "I had a busy night of it," he recalled, "and found myself too much engaged with official duties to gain time enough to write another note to Mrs. Grierson." Accordingly, he had his brother John write the note to Alice for him, including a description of how Grierson was "up nearly all night preparing." Grierson, added John, had asked him to remind Alice that he was leaving "on her lucky day (Friday)." In an effort to allay her fears, he clumsily added, "I fear for the result but know Benj is prudent and careful."[54]

---

52 Obadiah Ethelbert Baker, diary, April 20, 1863, in Obadiah Ethelbert Baker Papers, Huntington Library; Woodward, "Grierson's Raid," 686; George Rawlinson to Wife, April 1, 1863, in Rawlinson Family Papers, ALPL.

53 John Grierson to Alice, April 17, 1863; Woodward, "Grierson's Raid," 685-86; Grierson, *A Just and Righteous Cause*, 86, 145-46, 387n3; Leckie and Leckie, *Unlikely Warriors*, 84; Samuel L. Woodward, Compiled Service Record, NARA.

54 John Grierson to Alice, April 17, 1863; Woodward, "Grierson's Raid," 685-86; Grierson, *A Just and Righteous Cause*, 86, 145-46, 387n3; Leckie and Leckie, *Unlikely Warriors*, 84; Samuel L. Woodward, Compiled Service Record, NARA.

Samuel L. Woodward. Grierson's friend and confidant, Lieutenant Samuel L. Woodward, performed many of the clerical duties for Grierson and was present at most of the decision-making events on the raid. *Abraham Lincoln Presidential Library*

Grierson took only a few personal effects with him. One was his trusty Jew's harp to while away lonely times with the music that always soothed his soul. He also took his copy of Colton's pocket map of Mississippi, which "though small, is very correct." A compass finished out his personal effects.[55]

Significantly more important than these belongings was a scout's report, apparently provided by General Sherman, of the plantations, supplies, and resistance he could expect to meet along the proposed route. Grierson was familiar with the northern region of the state, having ridden across it numerous times in raids and counterraids. Once he dropped below the Oxford to Pontotoc to Tupelo line, however, he would be in unfamiliar territory. Grierson had little idea what he would find there; his handy map showed only the general direction he was to ride.[56]

The report prepared by the unnamed scout provided Grierson with good information and advice, most of which he would follow. Still, the

---

55 *OR* 24, pt. 1, 529; Leckie and Leckie, *Unlikely Warriors*, 84; York, *Fiction as Fact*, 148n27.

56 *OR* 24, pt. 1, 529; Leckie and Leckie, *Unlikely Warriors*, 84; Raid Instructions, n.d., William T. Sherman Letters, MDAH.

report, at least initially, must have given Grierson pause. The man had evidently been sent out from the Vicksburg region three months earlier in January 1863, so the information was quite dated. The report noted that the "best route" was to follow the Pontotoc Ridge south through Pontotoc and Houston and then a route from Starkville, Louisville, and Philadelphia to the Southern Railroad. The report also opined that the best way to damage the railroad was to destroy the numerous bridges over the Chunkey River just east of Newton Station. Apparently channeling the thinking of Generals Hurlbut and Smith, the scouting report also suggested the best way to accomplish this was for the column to divide, one section moving toward the Mobile and Ohio as far as Meridian, and the other riding eastward toward Kosciusko and Carthage, with the goal of meeting in Newton County.[57]

The scouting report also explained to Grierson how to escape any Confederate pursuers: "To return, the old Military road which passes near Decatur and leads North Eastward through Columbus may be taken to the latter place and thence as circumstances may determine to Tuscumbia Corinth or La Grange." The paper also included information on provisions. There would be "plenty of forage and provisions as far South as Macon in Noxubee County," it claimed, although they would be scarce below that toward Meridian. "Cattle hogs & fowls however will be found in abundance" all the way, and "soldiers need carry nothing but flour or meal and Salt." Abundant enemy stores, "mostly corn and bacon," had been collected at the various stations along the Mobile and Ohio Railroad. By "returning as suggested, the rich corn region about Columbus Aberdeen Okolona and Cotton Gin can be swept of Negroes and stock thus cutting off the most productive portion of Mississippi from the rebel resources."[58]

The valuable report also discussed Confederate defenses. Up to January 8, it explained, "no military guard was kept at Meridian, nor at any place on the Southern road East of Jackson." Grierson would also not have to worry much about the local citizens, because "the large majority of the people will be found of the poorer classes who by kind treatment can be made loyal. They are all heartily tired of the war and wish for nothing better than the old government." At that point the report read as if it had been written by Sherman himself: "The few rich among them

57 Raid Instructions, n.d., William T. Sherman Letters.

58 Ibid.

have made public sentiment heretofore and should be made to feel the horrors of the war they have brought on the county." In fact, read the report, the "common practice with the secession leaders on the advance of Federal troops" was to point out "Union men" and tell the Federals they were the leading secessionists, "that the spoliation might fall on them while their accusers would escape."[59]

While Grierson digested the report and his adjutant performed his final duties, the Federal troopers who would launch themselves into Mississippi remained generally optimistic. One Illinois man went so far as to assure his family that he would be safe. Just four days before departing, he wrote his sister, "You can all rest perfectly easy in regard to our safety here, as there is not an enemy in the vicinity, save a few tormenting guerillas, who bother us a great deal more than they hurt us." The wonderful weather made the festive feeling even better. "The weather is charming," an Illinois trooper wrote in mid-April. "Fruit trees have shed their blossoms, and the young fruit is beginning to be seen. The forests are putting on their verdant hues. Every natural prospect pleases. . . . We had, last night, an owl serenade," he continued, "occasionally these birds have their concerts. It is amusing in the extreme, to hear their refrains. Sometimes they seem to be on the [verge] of glee, and instantly, almost, they go from ha! ha! ha! To the most plaintive strains who! who! whoa!" As if an afterthought, the soldier remembered his lot and cause, adding, "But man is vile." Another Federal, wondering what the vast preparation portended, correctly surmised they were going to "play smash with the railroads."[60]

Grierson, who knew little more than the purpose of the raid, remained hopeful. "If the expedition is successful—it will be of great benefit to the service and will not set me back any," he explained to Alice. He also noted the possibility of helping Grant: "Other movements (of less extent) will take place from various points along the lines and my movements are to aid a greater movement which is to take place at a distant point or points."[61]

The grand scheme was coming together nicely, but the time to plan and prepare was over. All that was left was to perform flawlessly, something the musician Grierson was well accustomed to doing.

59 Ibid.

60 S. A. Forbes to Sister, April 13, 1863, in Stephen A. Forbes Papers, UI; "Army Correspondence," *Weekly Register* (Canton, IL), May 4, 1863.

61 "Army Correspondence," *Weekly Register* (Canton, IL), May 4, 1863; Surby, *Grierson Raids*, 20; B. H. Grierson to Alice, April 1863.

CHAPTER FOUR

The Start

Clanging accoutrements and clattering hooves broke the stillness on the early morning of Friday, April 17. After a night long on work and short on rest, Benjamin Grierson finally pushed his 1,700 men south out of La Grange, Tennessee. It was not yet 7:00 a.m. Years later, Grierson remembered the surreal nature of the commencement of the raid: "As the sun rose bright and clear and tinged with golden hues the tops of the trees and high ground in the vicinity of the town, and while a most refreshing breeze swept diagonally across the column, we moved southward into Mississippi." He and his trusted adjutant, Samuel Woodward, led the way, stopping only to talk once more with General Smith as the column passed out of town. "We shook hands cordially," Grierson explained, "and mounting my horse I rode away waving my hat and shouting, 'Once more, good-bye General.'"[1]

The three cavalry regiments were well on the way by the time the brigade commander and his staffer caught up, and an Illinois trooper also remarked on the same "gentle breeze from the south." Lieutenant Colonel Loomis led Grierson's own 6th Illinois Cavalry in the advance formed in a column of twos, followed by Colonel Prince and the troopers of the 7th Illinois Cavalry. Smith's battery was next in line, with Colonel Hatch's 2nd Iowa Cavalry bringing up the rear. Whether there was any jealousy of position passed unremarked, but no one would have been

---

1   John Grierson to Alice, April 17, 1863; Grierson, *A Just and Righteous Cause*, 146; Daniel E. Robbins to Parents, May 5, 1863.

surprised that Grierson's former regiment led the way. If anyone would have been perturbed about the order, it would have been Hatch, whose Iowans were choking on the dust at the end of the column. If Grierson had not returned on time, Hatch would have led the raid. Regardless of order, Grierson's command was a brigade of veteran troopers, and unbeknownst to most in the column, they would need all the experience they had, together with some good fortune, to make it through their difficult task. What they were tasked to do remained a mystery to the men in the ranks. "No person other than myself and Lieutenant S. L. Woodward, a.a.a [acting assistant adjutant] general of the brigade," explained the colonel, "knew the probable extent of the expedition on which we had started." They were embarking on "an expedition so mysterious that even the commanding officer did not know, beyond a certain objective, where it was going," wrote Woodward, "or when, if ever, it would return."[2]

The men were as ready as they would ever be, armed, as Capt. Henry Forbes of the 7th Illinois indicated, with "ammunition and a pocket full of salt." The troopers knew they were embarking on something quite different than the usual short raids, Forbes continued, even if they did not know all the details. The push out of La Grange with so many men and a battery of guns "meant to the Cavaliers a grand campaign, and there was no need of the bugle call on the morning of the 17th." Forbes elaborated on the cheerful feelings coursing through the ranks as the troopers rode out of town:

As the sun rose full and fine over a beautifully irregular eastern horizon, the command, not without abundant song and jollity, took the road leading southward from the village, through a lonely waste of little pineclad, sandy hills. Blithe and gay, going no one knew where or why—no one cared. The only things they did care for was that something should happen. Of course there were toil and danger, possibly disaster and death ahead; these were regular items in their soldier's bill of fare, and so, stretching itself slowly out, gleaming and deadly, like some huge glittering snake, the old Brigade slid off the sunlit hills into the cover of the Mississippi woods.[3]

*   *   *

2   Surby, *Grierson Raids*, 21; John S. C. Abbott, "Heroic Deeds of Heroic Men," *Harper's New Monthly Magazine* (February 1865), vol. 30, Issue 77, 273; Grierson, *A Just and Righteous Cause*, 146; Woodward, "Grierson's Raid," 685.

3   Henry C. Forbes, "Grierson's Raid," in Henry C. Forbes Papers, CHM, 5-6, copy in Henry C. Forbes Papers, UI.

By the time Grierson led his column southward, at least eight different components to the overall plan Grant had put in place were in motion or had just finished. Each worked in unison, different components of the same overall effort at different stages of advancement. The move closest to Vicksburg was the main effort, where Grant's Army of the Tennessee would cross the river with, hopefully, little or no opposition. Before that could happen, the various cavalry raids planned around it needed time to develop in order to maximize their strategic impact. The result was a staggered process of diversion that would eventually impact the war in five states, sometimes by plan and sometimes by accident.

One of the major feints was already over. As noted earlier, Frederick Steele had plunged into the Mississippi delta from Greenville in early April, battled both Confederates and the terrain, and returned to Greenville by April 10. Steele's continued presence there, as his division went into camp at Greenville, focused Confederate attention for a time on the Mississippi River and the northwestern portion of the state.[4]

On April 17, Generals Sherman and McClernand were gathering and repairing naval gunboats and transports damaged while passing the Vicksburg batteries the night before. At the same time, McClernand was shifting his corps south through Louisiana to position his command for the crossing that would occur in only a matter of days. McClernand's headquarters were below Vicksburg and in New Carthage by that date, and he was pressing forward toward Grand Gulf in expectation of the navy silencing the batteries there before going over.[5]

While McClernand moved, Grant prepared to implement Sherman's direct feint north of Vicksburg. He mentioned to Sherman on April 24 (one week after Grierson left La Grange) the possibility of moving on Haynes' Bluff, and he followed up that suggestion with a formal request on April 27. Most of Sherman's corps was already in the area at Milliken's Bend, so it would not be difficult to get his troops in position for the feint at the climactic moment when Grant intended to cross south of Vicksburg.[6]

---

4   *OR* 24, pt. 1, 501.

5   Ibid., pt. 3, 200-201; *OR* 24 pt. 1, 140-41.

6   *OR* 24, pt. 3, 231, 240.

Coordinating the longer raids and their supporting casts took more effort, and because they would take time to develop, an earlier start was necessary. General Hurlbut, from his headquarters in Memphis, was in charge of creating much of the chaos Grant hoped to spread across northern Mississippi. "Grierson's cavalry expedition started at daylight from La Grange," he informed Grant on April 17. "I do not expect to hear from him for fifteen or twenty days, unless from Southern papers." Even if Hurlbut learned much about Grierson's raid, he was not apt to say much about it except through official channels. The entire affair had been organized under wraps, which an Illinois trooper left behind at La Grange made clear when he wrote home, "The direction and number of the expedition are, for the present, contraband." Hurlbut continued: "These various movements along our length of line will, I hope, so distract their attention that Grierson's party will get a fair start and be well down to their destination before they can be resisted by adequate force. God speed him, for he has started gallantly on a long and perilous ride. I shall anxiously await intelligence of the result."[7]

The "various movements along our length of line" did not pass unnoticed. One of Grierson's men recalled how the Federals "swarmed out from the north, suddenly and almost simultaneously." Not long after Grierson rode south on April 17, Gen. Sooy Smith led the cavalry wing of the thrust from Grand Junction into northwestern Mississippi. Smith hoped to make it all the way south to the Tallahatchie River that day. The infantry component from Memphis under Colonel Bryant left that city the next day, April 18, marching south as well. Confederate commanders in the area quickly discovered these thrusts and scrambled to meet them.[8]

General Grenville Dodge at Corinth, Mississippi, meanwhile, was already two days into his advance east toward northern Alabama when Grierson moved from La Grange on April 17. Dodge was supposed to meet Abel Streight at Eastport on April 16, but Streight (whose brigade had to make the trip along the Tennessee River from Fort Henry on April 17) was delayed and would not reach the area until April 19. Once they combined, Dodge rode only far enough with Streight to get

---

7   "Army Correspondence," *Weekly Register* (Canton, IL), May 4, 1863; *OR* 24, pt. 3, 202.

8   *OR* 24, pt. 3, 203; *OR* 24, pt. 1, 557; Forbes, "Grierson's Cavalry Raid," 101.

that commander and his "wretchedly mounted, mainly on mules" men headed east.[9]

Seven different bodies of troops in five different major operations across four different states had either just concluded, were still on the move, or were gearing up to move when Grierson led his three regiments and artillery battery south into Mississippi on April 17. What was remarkable about this far-flung complex affair was that the opening moves worked to perfection. The activity east and west of Grierson, together with movement along the Mississippi River, created a corridor of unguarded terrain deep into Mississippi along the Pontotoc Ridge. The Confederate line in north Mississippi, wrote one Federal, was "completely pulled apart and piled up at its ends." That middle area was precisely the region Grierson intended to penetrate when he directed his troopers south from the high ground upon which La Grange sat, crossed the Wolf River, and slipped into Mississippi toward Ripley, the first significant town along the proposed route. The mounted thrust, wrote an officer, was "a nimble sword through an unguarded point, into the very vitals of the Confederate position."[10]

*   *   *

Seventeen hundred troopers was a large number of cavalrymen, especially for a raid intended to last more than a few days. Grierson's column of riders, "marching by twos," extended well over two miles, not counting the artillery. "A most cheerful spirit prevailed throughout the entire command," wrote Grierson, "and both officers and men had plainly observable on their manly countenances a stern and determined look which presaged devotion to duty and gave assurance of success." Grierson even waxed poetic about the horses carrying his men, observing how "the vigor of the soldiers was conveyed to the noble animals they rode, as they felt the pressure of the thighs of their riders, as gracefully they bore themselves and adapted their motion to that of their horses." As the Union column wound its way along the open road, "the invigorating

9   *OR* 23, pt. 1, 246, 286; *OR* 24, pt. 3, 777; Forbes, "Grierson's Cavalry Raid," 101. Confederate scouts reported "a large number of pack-mules" in the area, but they had no idea what it meant.

10   Forbes, "Grierson's Cavalry Raid," 102.

atmosphere and the buoyant spirits of the moving force plainly indicated the strength and power of the command, as fearlessly it entered upon an important expedition, the extent and destination of which was really not fully known to myself." A potentially significant problem arose when the leading 6th Illinois Cavalry took a wrong road and traveled part of the way on its own path. The wings rejoined soon thereafter with no harm done.[11]

Not long after they entered Mississippi, an Illinois trooper remembered coming across a young boy driving an ox wagon. He "looked rather seedy," thought Richard Surby, "and, unfortunately for him, wore a very good looking hat, which one of the boys took a fancy to and relieved him of, leaving the poor fellow looking rather sad." Grierson had ordered his troopers to leave the civilians alone, but it was impossible to control every man in the column. Colonel Prince rectified the situation when he "pulled out his pocket-book and gave him a two-dollar greenback, which seemed to please him very much."[12]

There was no way to keep such a large-scale movement secret for long. The Confederates and civilians in the area had seen columns of cavalry many times before, and though they may have cringed about having to endure another visit from the enemy, none would have divined the full significance of the expedition. If they gave it much thought at all, it was more likely the Federals were conducting yet another shallow raid into Mississippi, not a deep thrust into Confederate territory with important ramifications. Grierson would use these preconceived notions to his advantage.[13]

The Illinois colonel wanted his column to remain as inconspicuous as possible, but he also had to keep in mind how best to accomplish the goals set forth by Generals Hurlbut and Smith. Once well into Mississippi, the plan called for Grierson to send one of his three regiments east to damage the Mobile and Ohio Railroad between Tupelo and West Point and dispatch a second regiment west to damage the Mississippi Central. Both regiments would then make their way back to Tennessee as best they could, inflicting as much damage as possible while endeavoring

11 Ibid., 7; Grierson, *A Just and Righteous Cause*, 146-47; Surby, *Grierson Raids*, 23.

12 Surby, *Grierson Raids*, 23.

13 Woodward, "Grierson's Raid," 688.

to confuse the enemy as to their real purpose. Grierson's remaining regiment, meanwhile, would swiftly drive south in an effort to reach and seriously damage the Southern Railroad of Mississippi.[14]

First, however, Grierson had to get far enough into Mississippi to implement the plan. He marched rapidly the first day, his regiments in column and mostly riding on the same road. It did not take long to realize the 1,700-man column was far too long to travel on a single thoroughfare. His options were limited, however, so he continued on, riding southeast toward Ripley along the higher Pontotoc Ridge. This route provided a much easier ride than having to negotiate deep river valleys and their even deeper watercourses.[15]

Only a small party of Confederates were seen the entire first day, and Union pursuers captured three of them. The ride continued "without material interruption." In fact, it was rather pleasant, as the poetic Grierson later recalled: "The flowers of spring in all their freshness of beauty added to the fragrance and variety of the scenery which surrounded us as we went marching on into and through the domain of the South." Beautiful it may have been, but it was still a long day.[16]

Northeast Mississippi was well known for being lukewarm for the Confederacy to begin with, and several of the hill counties in that part of the state had voted for cooperationist delegates to the Mississippi Secession Convention. These men maintained their opposition to secession even when many other cooperationists from other counties changed sides for the sake of unity and voted to leave the Union. Tishomingo and Itawamba Counties in the northeast were the most opposed to secession, but others along the top tier or two of counties were less so. Tippah County, where Grierson was about to go into camp near Ripley,

---

14 *OR* 24, pt. 3, 197.

15 Ibid., pt. 1, 522.

16 Grierson, *A Just and Righteous Cause*, 147; *OR* 24, pt. 1, 522, 529; Woodward, "Grierson's Raid," 688; Dinges, "The Making of a Cavalryman," 370n48.

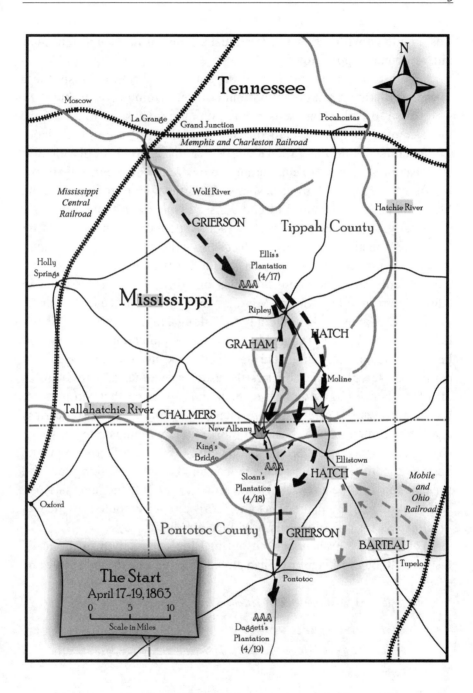

The Start
April 17–19, 1863

0   5   10
Scale in Miles

was populated with staunch secessionists. Thus far it had not translated into any major opposition.[17]

Union influence in this part of the state also weakened resistance. These northern counties were not under direct Union control, but they were close to Union garrisons positioned along the railroad. In effect, these counties, Tippah included, were something of a no-man's-land. Confederates along the Tallahatchie River to the south rarely entered the area unless they were conducting a quick raid, and they were always fearful of triggering a strong response from the Union troops along the Memphis and Charleston Railroad.[18] As a result, even though it was a potentially dangerous area for Grierson, especially with railroads on either side of him the enemy could use to concentrate troops to block his path, it proved an easy first day's ride for the brigade.[19]

The column made about 30 miles on April 17 before arriving in "the neighborhood of Ripley, Miss.," where Grierson decided to make camp on Dr. James B. Ellis's plantation along Tippah Creek near Shady Grove. Grierson liked to camp his men on large plantations or farms, and he had done so many times during other raids into the state. He often confronted the plantation owners themselves, who usually resisted his efforts to house large numbers of men and horses on their property. It was of little use to offer direct resistance, for one man was powerless against an armed Federal host, but most planters remonstrated anyway. Grierson always approached the main house the same way, riding up and demanding "the keys of the smokehouse and barns" and asking for food for his men and their horses. He intended to live off the land as much as he could, and the plantations and farms along his route provided an ideal means for refreshing his tired men and horses.[20]

The camping process played out at Ellis's plantation in the usual fashion, although Ellis himself had already moved east to Booneville and

---

17   Smith, *The Mississippi Secession Convention: Delegates and Deliberations in Politics and War, 1861-1865* (Jackson: University Press of Mississippi, 2014), 35, 79; Woodward, "Grierson's Raid," 688.

18   Smith, *Mississippi in the Civil War: The Home Front* (Mississippi Heritage Series), 114.

19   Forbes, "Grierson's Cavalry Raid," 103.

20   Grierson, *A Just and Righteous Cause*, 148; Surby, *Grierson Raids*, 28; Andrew Brown, *Story of Tippah County, Mississippi: The First Century* (Ripley, MS: Tippah County Historical and Genealogical Society, 1998), 42-43; 1850 Tippah County Population Census, NARA; Land Deed Index, Ripley Public Library; James B. Ellis Deeds, Tippah County Chancery Clerk Index.

was not present to offer any objection. Once on the property, Grierson scouted out the best location to bed down. According to Henry Forbes, "The best place for a cavalry bivouac is a woodland in which the forest shelter gives fuel and cover, and shrubberies, not too densely placed, afford hitching for the horses." By the time the bugler sounded the halt, the head of the column was on the bivouac site. "The leading company forms company front," Forbes related, "and the regiments mass in its rear in column of companies." Staff officers issued orders to throw out pickets and camp, and the order to break ranks followed.[21]

Once on their own, the men, desirous of being first at whatever goods they could find, "fly from the camp in every direction like the drops of water from a swiftly whirling wheel." Guards were posted to oversee the major sources of food, such as barns, chicken coops, or smokehouses. Once that task was completed on the Ellis plantation, the 6th Illinois Cavalry's commissary officer, William Pollard—the only such officer on the raid—doled out the food to the various companies. There was much to enjoy on places like this, and the men soon dispersed, "never forgetting their need, though they may sometimes forget their manners." Most looked for fodder and food "on the one case for his horse and his bed, in the other for his supper." Even the pickets left their stations, but Captain Forbes observed there was "no need for pickets during foraging time. The whole country is picketed for some miles in every direction."[22]

The first order of business after gathering food and wood was caring for the horses. A man's horse, observed Forbes, "is first stripped, rubbed, fed and fastened for the night." Equipment was checked and arranged so it could be utilized quickly if an emergency arose. Only after the horses were cared for did the troopers themselves eat, and by this time they were usually famished. "No prudent person," joked Forbes, "prefers to interfere with a trooper when he is getting supper." A trooper cooked his supper over a campfire, burning what had once been fence rails. The entire process was something of an art form: "A tin cup boils his coffee: a forked stick supported by a prop before the fire, broils his rasher of cured ham, or his steak of fresh pig, to a turn, and in the ashes he bakes

---

21 D. T. Herndon, ed., *Centennial History of Arkansas*, 3 vols. (Little Rock: S. J. Clarke Publishing Company, 1922), vol. 3, 533; Forbes, "Grierson's Raid," 7.

22 Surby, *Grierson Raids*, 29; Forbes, "Grierson's Raid," 7-8.

the ever-to-be remembered and never-to-be-surpassed hoe-cake. Feast fit for a king!"[23]

Once they had finished eating, the men enjoyed some downtime around their fires before falling asleep with a rubber blanket for a mattress and a saddle for a pillow. On cold or rainy nights the troopers devised better accommodations, such as a framework of sticks and limbs covered by their rubber blankets and situated close enough to the fire to heat the structure. Forbes recounted that "if he has ridden well and foraged fairly, he sleeps luxuriously as any Dives on his couch of eiderdown, and wakes haughty as a king."[24]

Sleep was cut short when the bugle sounded well before daylight, rousing the troopers from their slumber and into a "storm of busy preparation." The men ate what they could, rekindling the fires to do so. Horses fed on the soft bedding they had slept on the night before, and then they were saddled and made ready for the long ride ahead. With their bodies renewed and minds clear, the troopers mounted and moved out. Forbes remembered it all many years later with a longing fondness. All of this, he explained, gave a "stern significance to the splendid panorama, a hint of the coming march, of the sudden onset, the splendid charge, the possible death. Farewell the scene; we shall never see the like again."[25]

*   *   *

The Southern Railroad of Mississippi was still more than 150 miles to the south, and Grierson would need to move quickly to reach it. Yet significant difficulties awaited him. The column was about to transition out of no-man's-land in the upper tier of Mississippi counties into firmly held enemy territory. Scouts were already informing him that Confederate regimental-strength camps were situated somewhere to his front and on both his flanks. Just as important was the fact that the column was approaching the Tallahatchie River, the first of many serious terrain obstacles.[26]

Grierson and his troopers pushed deeper into Mississippi on April 18, with the 7th Illinois Cavalry in the lead. The brigade passed through

23   Forbes, "Grierson's Raid," 7-8.

24   Ibid., 8-9.

25   Ibid.

26   *OR* 24, pt. 1, 522.

Ripley around 8:30 a.m. without any fanfare or interruption. Judge Orlando Davis, one of Tippah County's Mississippi Secession Convention delegates, had little to say about the event, noting in his diary only that "they made no stop at Ripley, passed right on south." Approaching the Tallahatchie River with his single column strung out for two miles behind Grierson would have been foolhardy. Once beyond Ripley, he divided his command into three wings so he could move forward along a broad front. It was more likely than not that the Confederates would offer a defense along the river, much like General Pemberton's earlier stand the previous December when Grant was trying to move south. Grierson, explained Adjutant Woodward, wanted to show "an imposing front."[27]

The river's headwaters flowed from east of Grierson's column off the high ground of Pontotoc Ridge. Several tributaries ran down the slope and into the main river channel, which flowed in a westerly course through New Albany and thence north of Oxford and Panola before entering the delta in a wide valley just to the west. The Coldwater River joined it there, and the water made its way south to Greenwood, which was the route portions of Grant's army had taken during the earlier Yazoo Pass effort. At Greenwood, where Fort Pemberton had blocked Grant's thrust, the Tallahatchie joined the Yalobusha to form the Yazoo River. The Tallahatchie was not so imposing near its headwaters around New Albany, but it represented a major obstacle, especially if properly defended.[28]

Grierson divided his command into three groups and approached the river along a six-mile front. His idea was that if one of the three sections could get across the waterway, it would aid the others by outflanking the defenders. Grant crossed this same river five months earlier using the same tactic and launching a flanking movement with cavalry and infantry from the west and turning the Confederate defenses along the river, forcing the enemy to withdraw without much of a fight. Grierson proposed to do the same thing. He sent one battalion (four companies) of the 7th Illinois Cavalry along the main road to New Albany under Maj. John M. Graham. While Graham's force moved forward in an effort to keep any enemy at New Albany pinned down, a larger force consisting of the rest of the 7th Illinois Cavalry under Colonel Prince, together with

27 Surby, *Grierson Raids*, 23; Woodward, "Grierson's Raid," 688; Orlando Davis, diary, April 18, 1863, http://www.rootsweb.ancestry.com/~mscivilw/davis.htm.

28 Smith, "Victory At Any Cost: The Yazoo Pass Expedition." *Journal of Mississippi History*, vol. 67, no. 2 (Summer 2007), 147-66.

the entire 6th Illinois Cavalry under Lieutenant Colonel Loomis, crossed the river two miles east (upriver) at a ford. To make sure he could get a body of troops across, Grierson also sent Colonel Hatch and his Iowans farther east to Molino, which sat on the main channel in the middle of many tributaries that came together to form the river.[29]

None of the three Union groups met much resistance. As it turned out, the strongest body of troops in the center (most of the 6th and part of the 7th regiments) easily waded or swam across the river. Once on the far side, Grierson turned the column south and it rejoined the main Pontotoc road below New Albany. The Illinois troopers captured a few Confederates along the way, and, Colonel Prince recalled, the scouts "killed one rebel who persistently fired upon the advance."[30]

The other two columns met more opposition. On the far left, Colonel Hatch and the 2nd Iowa Cavalry skirmished with Col. J. F. Smith's partisan rangers around Ellistown. The state militia regiment was organizing at Chesterville just to the south, between Pontotoc and Tupelo, when news reached them that Federal troopers were approaching. The Mississippians quickly moved forward to meet them. Because they were not yet fully organized, the Confederates could only put a few hundred men into what evolved into a running skirmish, and Hatch easily pushed them aside. He did so with care, however, detached as he was from the main brigade to the west. By nightfall Hatch was five miles south of the river and decided it was prudent to go into camp there.[31]

Major Graham's 7th Illinois battalion encountered opposition at New Albany itself, which one of the men described as "a small place composed of a few dry-goods stores, whose stock needed replenishing; also some fine residences; altogether a pleasantly situated country town." The Confederates tried to tear up a bridge over the river to deprive the Union troopers of an easy crossing, but they were unable to finish the job before the battalion approached the structure. Out of time and options, the enemy instead tried to burn the bridge. The Federals braved small-arms fire from the opposite bank and galloped ahead to smother the flames.

---

29 *OR* 24, pt. 1, 522, 529; Grierson, *A Just and Righteous Cause*, 147; Woodward, "Grierson's Raid," 688.

30 *OR* 24, pt. 1, 522; "The Grierson Raid," *Weekly Register* (Canton, IL), September 7, 1863; Curtiss, diary, April 18, 1863.

31 *OR* 24, pt. 1, 522-23, 529; Pierce, *History of the Second Iowa Cavalry*, 49.

"Rising in their stirrups and shouting the battle cry," Graham's cavalry drove the enemy away, repaired the bridge, and crossed the river.[32]

New Albany was in Union hands, but Grierson had no interest in holding towns or territory. The small victory, however, coupled with the easy crossing of the Tallahatchie River, elated the colonel. Taking advantage of his good fortune, he pushed southward toward Tardyville, putting ample distance between his command and the river. The two Illinois regiments, which rejoined south of New Albany, rode on about four more miles along the Pontotoc road. Hatch, meanwhile, was riding to a point roughly the same distance south of the river, parallel to Grierson and about ten miles farther east.[33]

It was about this time the men noticed the darkening western skies. Heavy storms normally moved west to east, as they still do. Grierson wanted nothing to do with moving his men and supplies during a heavy rainstorm, and he ordered the men to halt at a plantation that was likely full of the supplies he needed to continue the journey. It was a wise choice, he later recalled, because "the rain fell in torrents all night." The same process that had played out at Ellis's the night before again took place, although this time with more theatrics from the plantation owner.[34]

William D. Sloan's small plantation was four miles southeast of New Albany and near Tardyville. The 55-year-old was one of the more prominent members of Pontotoc County society (the area later divided into a new Union County). Sloan was not a member of the planter class, as historians later defined it, and he lived in what Samuel Woodward described as "a rude log dwelling." Sloan hailed from South Carolina, owned 18 slaves in 1860, and had a real estate value of $7,000 and a personal estate valued at $20,000. He had collected a large amount of corn and bacon to supply his operation, but he was in no mood to share what he had accumulated with Grierson or the Federal troopers.[35]

32 Surby, *Grierson Raids*, 24; *OR* 24, pt. 1, 522; Abbott, "Heroic Deeds of Heroic Men," 273.

33 *OR* 24, pt. 1, 522; Daniel E. Robbins to Brother, May 7, 1863, Daniel E. Robbins Letters, HC.

34 *OR* 24, pt. 1, 522; Curtiss, diary, April 18, 1863.

35 1860 Pontotoc County Population and Slave Schedules; William D. Sloan, Deed, Book 3, Pontotoc County Chancery Clerk; William D. Sloan, Deed, Book 17, Pontotoc County Chancery Clerk.

Grierson and Woodward, along with their orderlies, approached the cabin. Sloan, Grierson remembered, "wanted in a small way to resist, where effective resistance was of course impossible." Woodward recalled that Sloan "was profuse in his professions of loyalty to the United States government and in protests against our use of his corn and bacon to feed the command." When he refused to turn over the keys and Grierson ordered the locks broken, the Mississippian grudgingly obliged. His mild resistance turned to rage, however, when Union troopers began dividing his hard-earned goods. "When he saw his stores issued out, he was completely beside himself," Grierson related, "alternately going to cut my throat and apparently desirous of having his own throat cut." Sloan's wife, Margaret, described by Grierson as "more self-possessed than her husband," pled with her husband "not to be a fool," and tried to calm him down, as did Grierson, who "tried to reason [with] and pacify him, to cool him off."[36]

Sloan would have none of it, and the confrontation grew more heated and lasted much of the night inside his house while the rain made everyone outside that much more miserable. After Sloan admitted giving some of his provisions to Confederates, Grierson joked, "The least he could do was to contribute to the old Union cause." The Mississippian alternated between periods of calm and bouts of anger—or, as Grierson put it, "He would moderate a little [until] the sight of some new depredation would set him in a tantrum again." The Illinois colonel's explanation that seizing his supplies was a necessity of war or that supporting the Confederacy was treason "would [not] avail to quiet him." At one point Sloan loudly congratulated himself that the enemy had not gotten his horses, which were "safely hidden away where no Yankee in the world could find them." On cue, some of Grierson's troopers rode past, driving those very horses and mules to the Federal camp. "He fairly foamed," Grierson remembered, "rushed towards me, and for the fiftieth time demanded that we should 'take him out and cut his throat and be done with it.'"[37]

"Worn out by his whining," the performer in Grierson decided to have a little fun. The commander's personality—alternately described as "full of vivid, elastic life, overflowing with enthusiasm" and "modest, gentle

---

36   Woodward, "Grierson's Raid," 688; Grierson, *A Just and Righteous Cause*, 148-49.

37   Grierson, *A Just and Righteous Cause*, 149; Woodward, "Grierson's Raid," 688-89.

and genial in his manners"—was soon on full display. He winked at his officers and loudly called upon an orderly to do the deed. "I concluded to take him at his word," Grierson joked, "as nothing I could say or do would suffice to quiet him." Grierson explained to the orderly—"an immense, athletic, heavily bearded man"—that the plantation owner "was very desirous of having his throat cut" and that he had "tried to reason with him out of his strange wish, but that he persisted and that the orderly might take him out into the field nearby and 'cut his throat and be done with it,' according to his oft-repeated and urgent request." The aide played his part perfectly. "The huge orderly never smiled or hesitated," recorded the perpetrator of the prank, "but deliberately taking a large knife in one hand, with the other seized Mr. Sloan and moved off with him as if he had been a kitten."[38]

"Then a general hub-bub began," wrote Grierson. Margaret Sloan, who had been trying to convince her husband that even if the enemy took everything they still had the plantation and that they could not do anything about it anyway, lost her self-composure. "She began to scream in chorus with the servants and beg me not to mind what her husband had said; that he did not know what he was about." Sloan, before exiting the house, "was hollering lustily for the commanding officer and begging for dear life of the strong hand which held him." When the larger orderly roughly ushered the man back into the room where Grierson was waiting, Sloan "avowed that he did not want to have his throat cut—that he did not want to die." Grierson ordered him released. "Thereafter during our stay, he remained comparatively quiet."[39]

The next morning, as the Federal troopers went about their morning routine, Grierson showed the Mississippian all the "tired stock, horses, and mules we would leave in place of the fresh animals we had taken from him." The turn of events surprised Sloan, who was "quite appeased," Grierson concluded, and "he was not so sure but he had the best of the trade with the Yankees after all." In truth, Grierson was not overly concerned about the exhausted livestock he was leaving behind. He was much more worried about the rain that was still coming down and its effects on his troopers and their horses. Colonel Hatch, isolated farther

---

38 "Ben Grierson," n.d., in Henry C. Forbes Papers, CHM; Grierson, *A Just and Righteous Cause*, 149; Woodward, "Grierson's Raid," 689.

39 Grierson, *A Just and Righteous Cause*, 149.

to the east, was also on his mind. That the column had not covered as much ground on the second day of the raid as it had on the first was another fact that weighed heavily on him. Grierson's initial ride had quickly slipped through and beyond the first level of enemy defenses by crossing the Tallahatchie, but on the second day, rain and other factors had forced him to halt much earlier than he would have liked after covering only 25 miles—5 fewer than he had logged the day before.[40]

It was important to make up the lost time. Whether the roads would dry out quickly and the enemy would cooperate remained to be seen.

*   *   *

Deception has been a part of everyday life since the serpent lured Adam and Eve into eating the fruit in the Garden of Eden. Deception in warfare has been practiced nearly as long. The same army manual that today teaches officers about the nine principles of war discusses "deliberately mislead[ing] adversary decision makers as to friendly military capabilities, intentions, and operations, thereby causing the adversary to take specific actions (or inactions) that will contribute to the accomplishment of the friendly mission." Grierson's raid was part of the larger effort by Grant to do exactly that: fool General Pemberton about where the major Union effort was being made. Although he was not trained at West Point like Grant, Grierson used deception on his raid as well, though on a much smaller level. He had gotten off to a good start because of other diversions that had helped open a riding lane through north Mississippi. Now it was time to implement some of his own trickery to make his effort that much more successful.[41]

Despite his need to move quickly, Grierson decided to implement a different plan that morning than simply push south. Confederate camps of organization were operating east and west of his position, and he decided to take the opportunity to break them up while at the same time deceive the locals about his overall intentions. "I thus sought to create the impression that the object of our advance was to break up these parties," Grierson later explained. Lateral moves like this would

---

40 Grierson, *A Just and Righteous Cause*, 149-50.

41 *Field Manual 3-0: Operations*, 6-19; Leckie and Leckie, *Unlikely Warriors*, 312n15; Dinges, "The Making of a Cavalryman," 54-55n32.

also allow more time for the roads to dry. While some of Grierson's men rode out to break up the enemy camps, the rest remained at Sloan's plantation. Their continued presence gave them time to explore and find additional foodstuffs and other valuables, a fact that surely did not sit well with the excitable planter.[42]

The troopers involved in the raids within the raid set off on their assignments. One detachment rode east to find Hatch and the 2nd Iowa Cavalry (which was about ten miles away) and to threaten Chesterville, the location of a reported enemy camp. Grierson also sent troopers back to New Albany under Capt. George W. Trafton and more to the northwest, toward another reported enemy camp at King's Bridge over the Tallahatchie River. The latter camp included Maj. A. H. Chalmers, the brother of James Chalmers, commander of the Confederate cavalry in northwestern Mississippi.[43]

All four of these mini raids ran into Confederates or at least the place where they had encamped. Hatch moved southward, "parallel to us," reported Grierson. He had skirmished lightly with the enemy the previous afternoon, but the fighting increased that morning as he rode toward Chesterville. Hatch reported killing, wounding, and capturing several Confederates, but he soon broke off the chase and rode his Iowans southwest to rejoin the main body for the continued drive south. The troopers sent to threaten the camp at Chesterville never reached it, returning instead with several horses they had discovered en route.[44]

The expedition to King's Bridge was thwarted by quick-acting Confederates. By the time the Union troopers reached the bridge on the Tallahatchie River, the enemy was already gone. When word had reached them that Union cavalry was in the vicinity, they "had suddenly left in the night, going west." Chalmers evidently decided the safety of his brother's larger command made more sense than remaining on the river.[45]

Captain Trafton's cavalrymen, sent north to New Albany to secure the bridge and reconnoiter for any Confederate pursuit, also encountered the enemy. About 20 gray riders slipped in behind them as they drew near

42 *OR* 24, pt. 1, 522.

43 Grierson, *A Just and Righteous Cause*, 147; *OR* 24, pt. 1, 522.

44 *OR* 24, pt. 1, 522-23, 530.

45 Ibid., 522.

the small town. The minor skirmish that followed killed and wounded a few enemy riders. Trafton had the information he needed and wisely returned to inform Grierson of the potential danger in his rear.[46]

Once the various detachments returned and reported, Grierson ordered the entire column south on a wet April 19. Moving out was an imperative, but traversing the route was more difficult than Grierson had hoped. As he soon discovered, "the road being slippery and muddy somewhat retarded our progress and damped our feelings." Progress may have been slower than desired, but this was the third day out and the column was still heading south. The continued ride, observed one trooper, "made the rank and file of our command prick up their ears to find ourselves on the third day still marching south." Grierson headed straight toward Pontotoc, crossed Cherry Creek, and pushed on through the late morning. Welcome news arrived in the form of Hatch's 2nd Iowa Cavalry, which reached the main Pontotoc road after disengaging the enemy and riding southwest to intersect with the main column. Hatch and Grierson spent some time discussing the intelligence gleaned from the Iowan's raid, and all three regiments moved on toward Pontotoc.[47]

Before long, scouts discovered a house full of military provisions, including "United States muskets," gunpowder, and other weaponry. "Unfortunately," wrote one Illinois trooper, this "resulted in the burning of the house and most of its contents." The deed infuriated Grierson, who had issued orders at the raid's outset to avoid destroying civilian property. The scout who helped provide the original operational plan had also recommended leniency. "The officers made every effort to find the guilty party," continued the trooper, "but it occurred mysteriously, no one knew anything about it."[48]

Grierson arrived at Pontotoc around 5:00 p.m. A Federal described the town as "a brisk business place, boasting a population of about three thousand inhabitants, a fine brick court-house, and beautiful residences, denoting wealth." The brigade's advance elements "dashed into the town, came upon some guerillas, killed 1, and wounded and captured several more." According to Adjutant Woodward, "The advance guard,

---

46 Grierson, *A Just and Righteous Cause*, 147; *OR* 24, pt. 1, 522.

47 Surby, *Grierson Raids*, 25; *OR* 24, pt. 1, 522-23, 530; Curtiss, diary, April 19, 1863; "Grierson's Big Raid," n.d., in Thomas W. Lippincott Papers, ALPL.

48 Surby, *Grierson Raids*, 25.

one troop, charged through the town, separating by twos at the different cross-streets." Only one Confederate stood firm and fired at the blue invaders. One historian described him as "a solitary hero," but a Union trooper offered a different reason for his bravery when he accused him of being "one drunk Confederate." Whether a lone hero or simply inebriated, the Rebel was the only fatality of the Pontotoc skirmish. The scene that unfolded after he was killed, confessed an Illinois trooper, was sad: "They laid him by the side of the road. I seen a young woman come up apparently in great distress. I afterwards found out that it was her lover."[49]

Grierson ordered a halt so his troopers could rest and gather supplies and intelligence. As the Illinois and Iowa riders discovered, there was plenty of both in Pontotoc. They found a mill and several hundred bushels of salt, a much-needed commodity in wartime Mississippi. Unable to take it with them, they poured it on the ground. The troopers also found the camp and books of "Captain [John T.] Weatherall's command," which they examined and destroyed. The townspeople were justifiably nervous, but Grierson and his officers kept a close eye on the men and very little was damaged. The Gordon plantation house, known as Lochinvar, just south of Pontotoc, exemplified the care Grierson's men took to preserve private property. Woodward was approaching the house when someone handed him a note explaining that the Gordons' son had shown kindness to a federal officer earlier in the war. Woodward placed a guard at the house until the column passed. Whether any of Grierson's men would have pillaged or damaged the place is unknown, but the Gordons were convinced the note saved their mansion.[50]

It was dark by the time the brigade moved out of Pontotoc. Five miles farther south the head of the column reached a sprawling plantation along Chiwapa Creek, owned by 62-year-old Stephen Daggett, that afforded

49 Ibid., 26; *OR* 24, pt. 1, 523; Grierson, *A Just and Righteous Cause*, 150; Woodward, "Grierson's Raid," 690; Bearss, *The Vicksburg Campaign*, vol. 2, 190; E. T. Winston, "The Story of Pontotoc," April 7, 1932, Pontotoc *Progress*, copy in Grierson's Raid Subject File, MDAH; Daniel E. Robbins to Brother, May 7, 1863; Michael Freyburger, *Letters to Ann* (Shelbyville, IL: Shelby County Historical Society, 1986), 46.

50 Woodward, "Grierson's Raid," 690; Grierson, *A Just and Righteous Cause*, 150; Forrest T. Tutor, *Gordons of Lochinvar* (n.p.: n.p., 2008), 60-61, 81; Mrs. N. D. Deupree, "Some Historic Homes of Mississippi," in Franklin L. Riley, ed., *Publications of the Mississippi Historical Society* (Oxford: Mississippi Historical Society, 1902), vol. 6, 248 (245-64).

ample space to camp and the chance to stock up on supplies. Although Daggett had been born in Connecticut, he had made a fortune in land and slaves in Mississippi. According to the 1860 census, he owned 48 slaves, $18,000 in plantation real estate, and boasted a net worth of $62,000—a substantial sum at that time. Some troopers also camped at the adjacent Weatherall plantation, owned by the brother of the Confederate commander whose papers had been discovered in Pontotoc.[51]

The various side raids dispatched to confuse and disrupt the enemy, coupled with the rain and muddy roads, made it impossible for Grierson to cover as much ground as he had hoped that day. His main body put 15 to 16 miles behind them, about half of what he had covered on each of the two previous days. Whether the side raids, which traded time for diversion, were worth the slowed pace of the raid or would reduce his chances of reaching the Southern Railroad was a question no one could answer.[52]

*   *   *

Grierson had now ridden three full days into Mississippi. Two interconnected events had significantly enhanced his early success. The first was the triumph of the other Union raids designed to draw the enemy's attention away from his larger expedition, which itself was a diversion to focus attention away from Grant's objective of crossing the Mississippi River with the Army of the Tennessee. "Those movements, of course, aided materially in giving me a better opportunity of getting a good start within the rebel lines," Grierson admitted, "and assisted in giving the enemy the impression that my command would, like all others, return again to Tennessee, and had a tendency to hold a larger force of the enemy in northern Mississippi than would have otherwise remained there if not held by the timely advance of troops of XVI Army Corps then under General Hurlbut's command."[53]

The second factor was the tepid Confederate response. The enemy had made little effort to defend northeastern Mississippi, as illustrated

51 *OR* 24, pt. 1, 523; 1860 Pontotoc County Population and Slave Schedules; Surby, *Grierson Raids*, 26; Stephen Daggett, Deed, Pontotoc County Chancery Clerk.

52 Woodward, "Grierson's Raid," 691.

53 Grierson, *A Just and Righteous Cause*, 146.

by Grierson's easy penetration of the Confederate defensive lines around New Albany and Pontotoc. Most of the Confederate cavalry was either in the northwest part of the state, confronting Memphis, or farther south in Gen. Daniel Ruggles's district under Samuel Gholson, who was locked in a custody battle with General Chalmers over the use of state forces in northwestern Mississippi. "General Gholson," complained an outraged Chalmers, "came into my district, and without notice to me, without any communication of any sort whatsoever with me, and without my knowledge or consent, ordered six companies outside the limits of my district, and the first information I ever had of any such order was in the refusal of some of these companies to obey my orders previously issued." Ruggles, who was on an inspection trip during the early days of the raid, was as ill-informed as Chalmers, and his subordinates were corresponding directly with Pemberton at Vicksburg rather than through Ruggles, as military protocol dictated. The defensive lethargy was not surprising. Pemberton himself had yet to demonstrate any real concern about the threat of this raid because his attention was still fixed firmly on Grant's larger southward movement west of the Mississippi River.[54]

The Pennsylvania-born Pemberton had built a solid résumé of service with the U.S. Army that included action during the Seminole and Mexican Wars. In 1848, the artillerist married a woman from Norfolk, Virginia, and her influence on him, together with years of service in the southern states, convinced him to resign his commission at the start of the war and offer himself to the Confederacy. Early service as the commander of the Department of South Carolina and Georgia revealed deficiencies for responsibilities at that level. Instead of finding a position that suited Pemberton's skill set, President Jefferson Davis promoted him to lieutenant general in October 1862 and transferred him west to oversee a new department in Mississippi and defend the fortress of Vicksburg. It was a poor choice for such an important command, and Davis would come to regret his decision.[55]

---

54 *OR* 24, pt. 3, 758; Grabau, *Ninety-Eight Days*, 117; Bearss, *The Vicksburg Campaign*, vol. 2, 192.

55 Michael B. Ballard, *Pemberton: The General Who Lost Vicksburg* (Jackson: University Press of Mississippi, 1991).

John C. Pemberton. As the Confederate commander in the area raided by Grierson, Lieutenant General John C. Pemberton found himself more interested in the raid than Grant's major threat across the Mississippi River in Louisiana. For five critical days Pemberton was so focused on Grierson that he let Grant slip across the river almost unmolested and move inland. *Library of Congress*

By April 19 Pemberton found himself awash in activity that was difficult to understand and even harder to follow. In addition to Steele's Federals, who had just returned from the raid around Greenville, he had to worry about Adm. David Dixon Porter, who ran a few ships past the Vicksburg batteries the night before Grierson departed La Grange. Several Union gunboats and transports were now south of the city—a clear indication that operations were likely to shift in that direction. Pemberton's concern increased when Federals began to arrive and operate out of New Carthage, Louisiana, which was below Vicksburg. "The enemy," he warned theater commander Joseph E. Johnston in Tullahoma, Tennessee, on April 17, "has nine boats between Vicksburg and Port Hudson. He has landed forces at New Carthage from Grant's army, and can re-enforce them to any extent. He can use his nine boats to cross his troops to this side." And now Grierson was moving steadily south during the first three days of his raid. Although Pemberton possessed little knowledge about this cavalry thrust, his emphasis, and rightly so, focused on the most serious threat to Vicksburg. The best he could do, however, was order reinforcements south to John S. Bowen, who was guarding a major crossing point at Grand Gulf.[56]

Additional Federal raids consumed Pemberton's time, energy, and attention, especially Abel Streight's move into the deep rear of the Confederate army in Tennessee. Streight had left Nashville on April 7, riding west to Fort Henry and then due south into the northeast corner of Mississippi and east into Alabama. Under normal circumstances, Pemberton would not have paid as much attention to events unfolding so far away, but General Johnston had ordered him to do so. At that time, Johnston's headquarters were in Middle Tennessee with Braxton Bragg's Army of Tennessee, and he was better situated to ascertain the potential danger posed by Streight's raid. He did not hesitate to order help from Pemberton's command in Mississippi, especially since the threat had emanated from his area of command.[57]

Johnston informed Pemberton on April 18 that a Union force (Streight's) was moving east from Corinth, Mississippi, and, "If you can send troops from Columbus [Ruggles's command] or elsewhere, to aid Colonel [Phillip D.] Roddey, they may do a great service to the two departments. Colonel Roddey and your nearest officer must cooperate against the enemy's raids from Corinth." Johnston followed up that message two days later on April 20: "It is necessary that your northeastern

---

56   OR 24, pt. 3, 751-53, 755, 762.

57   Ibid., 760, 767, 769.

troops and Roddey's force should always act together against raids from Corinth, either south or east. Please instruct your commanding officer. Let him help Roddey now, or as soon as possible. This co-operation will prevent or defeat serious raids." Pemberton, however, had already ordered Ruggles on April 19 to "send all mounted troops, both state and Confederate, toward Corinth." The pace of events, coupled with the micromanagement of his command by a superior hundreds of miles away from Mississippi, exasperated the lieutenant general. "I have not sufficient force to give any efficient assistance to Colonel Roddy," Pemberton explained on April 20 before detailing the various raids into Mississippi, including Grierson's, which he misidentified as moving "from Corinth, via New Albany." He cautioned Johnston, "You are aware I have but feeble cavalry force, but I shall certainly give you all the assistance I can. I have virtually no cavalry from Grand Gulf to Yazoo City," he continued, "while the enemy is threatening to cross the river between Vicksburg and Grand Gulf, having twelve vessels below Vicksburg."[58]

Similar events were unfolding in northwest Mississippi, where Colonel Bryant's and Gen. Sooy Smith's raids attracted his attention. General Chalmers urged Pemberton that "all available cavalry be sent here and one or two sections of artillery." Believing the threat in northwestern Mississippi to be serious, Pemberton sent reinforcements on April 19.[59]

Sifting through all the various intelligence reports, which by their nature were outdated by the time he read them, Pemberton was only slowly learning about the various raids, Grierson's included. It was not until April 20, however, that Pemberton even acknowledged Grierson's raid, once to Joe Johnston and again to Gen. Samuel Cooper in Richmond, both as indirect references. The enemy, he telegraphed Cooper, was "also making strong raids from three points on [the] Memphis and Charleston railroad between Memphis and Corinth. I shall look to them."[60]

Most of whatever he learned about Grierson's activity came from lower-level officers. "I hear from several sources, but not your headquarters, that the enemy is approaching Pontotoc," he reprimanded Ruggles on April 20. "This is a mere raid, but should not be unmolested by you."

58 Ibid.

59 Ibid., 766-67.

60 Ibid., 768.

Grierson had been riding south for three days, but Pemberton had yet to grasp the importance of what was transpiring. That same day he telegraphed Johnston, "Can you not make a heavy demonstration with cavalry on the Tallahatchee toward Abbeville, if only for 50 miles? The enemy are endeavoring to compel a diversion of my troops to Northern Mississippi."[61]

Grierson's main objective was not to draw troops from Pemberton's command at Vicksburg (although that would be a welcomed reaction) but to attract and maintain Pemberton's attention toward north Mississippi. By April 20 the strategy was beginning to bear fruit. Pemberton's primary focus was still on Grant's movement west of the Mississippi River, but his eyes were casting furtive glances in the opposite direction.

Benjamin Grierson, meanwhile, continued to drive deeper into the state toward the Southern Railroad of Mississippi, Pemberton's one and only link to the outside world.

61 Ibid., 769-73.

CHAPTER FIVE

The Detachments

If Benjamin Grierson learned anything during the first few days of the raid, it was how to manage his forces. He had tried marching south in a single column, which necessitated a long line of cavalry, wagons, and artillery, delayed the rear's advance, and extended its march at the end of the day. When that formation became unwieldy, he separated his command, most notably at the crossing of the Tallahatchie River, which provided some useful feedback and proved more flexible and effective. Now that he was deeper into Mississippi, some 60 miles southeast of La Grange and nearly that far inside the state, he had to decide how to array his brigade, manage it on the march, and satisfy his objectives. These major decisions occupied Grierson during the night of April 19 at Daggett's plantation south of Pontotoc.[1]

Grierson weighed his options as he prepared to move south the next morning. On the one hand, he had made 30 miles in one day, his best march thus far, when the brigade utilized the same road together. Sending detachments in various directions, as he had done the previous day, consumed significant time but garnered some worthwhile results that were perhaps more important at that stage of the raid than moving south quickly. Still, these time-consuming sideshows netted little real long-term gain. Were the smaller side raids within a raid worthwhile?[2]

1   *OR* 24, pt. 1, 523.

2   Ibid.

Other factors weighed on Grierson. This deep into Mississippi, some of his men and mounts were beginning to show signs of fatigue and breakdown. His troopers evinced illness and exhaustion, some of which was attributable to their exposure to the elements during the severe rainstorm the night before. His horses showed obvious signs of fatigue and needed proper rest and care after three days of riding, which was a major drawback for any cavalry operation. The growing number of prisoners taken during the minor skirmishing around Pontotoc and New Albany also had to be guarded, fed, and transported on good mounts. Should he take them with him, let them go, or parole them? Letting them go while he was still on the move was a potentially dangerous option, because they could provide valuable information that would pinpoint the Union cavalry brigade for potential pursuers to find and destroy.[3]

Grierson also had to consider his original orders. Hurlbut and Smith expected him to send three regiments in three different directions (east, west, and south). This would potentially confuse the Confederates and perhaps disperse any pursuing bodies of enemy cavalry, making it more likely that one or two of the three regiments would successfully complete the raid. The two that peeled off to the east and west would be moving into well-guarded territory into which the Confederates could transport troops by rail. Getting back to La Grange after their circuitous routes would require them to ride into the arms of their pursuers. The hope was that any damage these regiments could inflict, coupled with the confusion they might sow, would be beneficial to Grierson's lone regiment riding south. The aim of the branch raids was to strike vital railroad lines the Confederates had to defend. Grierson, meanwhile, would be moving into parts of the state that had not yet learned of his raid, making it easier to catch the enemy napping as he passed through.[4]

With these factors weighing on his mind, Grierson plunged ever farther into the Mississippi countryside.

*   *   *

Grierson's first decision was straightforward. "I gave orders to the regimental commanders to cause a close inspection to be made," he wrote,

3   Ibid.

4   Ibid., pt. 3, 207.

"with a view of selecting all men and horses [in] any way disabled or not fit for further hard marching." The inspection at Daggett's during the evening of April 19 made it clear that some of his men and horses could not go any farther. Grierson decided to send them back to La Grange, he explained, to "free . . . the command of any encumbrance or what might become such in our onward movements." It was "absolutely necessary to insure celerity of movements, to reject and separate myself from all but the most serviceable material." The decision was so important to Grierson that he "personally inspected every man as to his fitness for further active duty." The colonel picked about 200 of his 1,700 troopers to make the return journey. The disappointed soldiers, summed up an Illinois man, "could not travel good."[5]

Several of the men ordered back to Tennessee confronted Grierson. "Some of the soldiers who had first been selected to join those returning northward asked permission to speak to me and plead so as not to be sent back," Grierson confessed. After examining them again he relented, stating, "I decided that their disability was only temporary and, satisfying myself that they were of the right kind of stuff to recuperate, consented to their request and permitted them to remain with the main column." Major Hiram Love of the 2nd Iowa Cavalry, who was tasked with commanding the so-called Quinine Brigade back to La Grange, was not among them. According to Grierson, "Although willing to go on, [Love] was not strong or in good health, but was well suited to look closely after the safety of his command." Many of those sent back also had to give up their horses and return north with inferior mounts that could not make the long and dangerous journey that had only just begun.[6]

Grierson had little choice in the matter. Those men and mounts unable to bear their share of responsibilities had to be sent back before the column traveled much deeper into Mississippi. Another few days would put the brigade too far south for the sick to return safely to Tennessee on exhausted or sick horses—especially once the enemy sorted through the intelligence, found out the direction of Grierson's raid, and launched a real pursuit. By that point, the returning sick men

5   Grierson, *A Just and Righteous Cause*, 150; Orange Jackson, *The History of Orange Jackson's War Life: As Related by Himself* (n.p.: n.p., n.d.), 9.

6   "From One of Grierson's Cavalry," *Union Monitor* (Litchfield, IL), June 5, 1863; Grierson, *A Just and Righteous Cause*, 150-51.

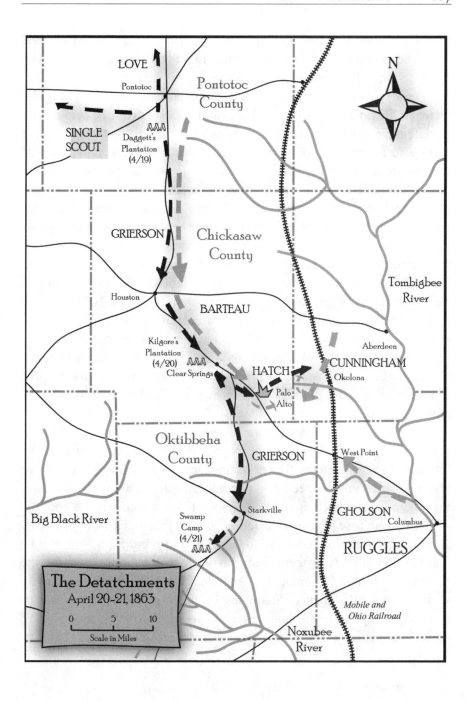

LOVE

Pontotoc   Pontotoc
                County

SINGLE   Daggett's
SCOUT   Plantation
           (4/19)

GRIERSON   Chickasaw
               County

                                        Tombigbee
Houston   River

           BARTEAU

Kilgore's
Plantation   Aberdeen
(4/20)   CUNNINGHAM
Clear Springs HATCH   Okolona

               Palo
               Alto

           Oktibbeha
            County
               GRIERSON West Point

Big Black River   GHOLSON
                                     Columbus
           Swamp   Starkville
           Camp   RUGGLES
           (4/21)

The Detatchments
April 20-21, 1863

0   5   10

Scale in Miles

                         Mobile and
                         Ohio Railroad
                  Noxubee
                  River

would run into the pursuing Confederates. Orders were issued for "the least effective portion of the command" to leave that night. Ultimately, the decision culled some 175 troopers from the brigade.[7]

The departure of the sick and exhausted also solved Grierson's prisoner dilemma, because he sent the captives with them. To help bolster its defensive abilities, Grierson detached one of the guns from Smith's battery to accompany the convalescents and prisoners. It was hoped they would not need the firepower, but the gun might come in handy at the Tallahatchie River if the Confederates tried to block their crossing.[8]

The return of the Quinine Brigade also offered another chance for some chicanery. The large detachment would certainly attract the enemy's attention and perhaps convince the Confederates the entire raiding force had turned back. Retracing the route of the brigade through Pontotoc, New Albany, and Ripley would also focus Confederate attention in that direction and perhaps convince the enemy the raid had been no more than another routine effort to disrupt Confederate camps in the northern counties. Any time the move north gained for the main column was that much more time to move farther south and put more distance between Grierson and any pursuers. Accordingly, Grierson ordered Major Love to attract all the attention he could but also cover his small number as much as possible.[9]

Love's large detachment (about 10 percent of Grierson's total force) was in the saddle early on the morning on April 20 and riding north by 3:00 a.m. toward Pontotoc. The departing men, wrote one witness, "chafed under the order, and turned back with lingering and rebellious looks until the column was out of sight." Love hoped to get as far north as possible before the sun rose and their detection became that much more probable. He carried a note from Grierson to General Smith, informing him that he was sending the "less effective portion of the command, to return by the most direct route." Grierson also explained to Smith that Love's party was to distract the enemy, "marching by fours, obliterating our tracks, and producing the impression that we have all returned." Realizing the precarious nature of his raid, Grierson added, "I may possibly find an

---

7   *OR* 24, pt. 1, 523.

8   Ibid.

9   Ibid.; Grierson, *A Just and Righteous Cause*, 151.

opportunity to communicate with you again in four or five days, but do not wonder if you should not hear from me in thirty days." As it turned out, this would be the last communication from Grierson for weeks.[10]

The most unhappy officer in the brigade was Colonel Hatch, who was less than pleased that most of the invalids were from his Iowa regiment, as was its leader Major Love. The reason so many of the ill and exhausted were from the 2nd Iowa regiment was because the Iowans had had but little rest prior to the launching of the raid. Hatch admitted that he left on the raid "with 250 horses, worn out, which broke down at the end of the second day." His regiment's mounts were so exhausted, he had to mount many on "mules from my train and borrowed mules." Still, the detachment of so many from his regiment, lamented Hatch, cut his numbers "to about 500 men."[11]

Marching loudly in columns of fours, the Quinine Brigade reached Pontotoc a little before daylight. "Sending them by night through Pontotoc was a good ruse," Grierson later boasted. "Making all the spread they could with their led horses, mules, prisoners, and one gun of the battery, the people of that place believed and quickly reported that the whole command had gone back north." Two days later the detachment reached La Grange. Grierson, meanwhile, plunged ever deeper into the Mississippi countryside.[12]

*   *   *

On a "cloudy and damp" April 20, Grierson explained, "two hours after Major Love's departure I proceeded south with the main force on the Houston road." The Federals left Daggett's plantation around daylight with Hatch's reduced 2nd Iowa Cavalry in the lead.[13]

Grierson was not yet finished with the detachments. His orders were to send one regiment west to break the Mississippi Central Railroad, and it was now a good time to do so. The Mississippi Central gradually

---

10 *OR* 24, pt. 1, 521-23; Abbott, "Heroic Deeds of Heroic Men," 274; Woodward, "Grierson's Raid," 691; Davis, diary, April 21, 1863, http://www.rootsweb.ancestry.com/~mscivilw/davis.htm.

11 *OR* 24, pt. 1, 530-31.

12 Ibid., 523.

13 Ibid.; Grierson, *A Just and Righteous Cause*, 151; Surby, *Grierson Raids*, 26.

angled away from Grierson's proposed route, so every mile he moved south would only add distance between his column and the rails. A delay in making the detachment would require the regiment to ride farther to reach the railroad, and it would be that much harder for it to get safely back to La Grange.[14]

Grierson, however, was not in favor of launching the mini-raid against the Mississippi Central. He had earlier operated along the railroad and knew one of the bridges was still out, and there was little prospect of it being rebuilt in the near future. "I have ascertained that the bridges on the Mississippi Central Railroad, over the Yockeney, at Water Valley, have never been repaired," he informed General Smith in the note he had sent north with Major Love. In his view, it was foolish to waste the effort of an entire regiment on the prospect of damaging an already useless railroad, especially when he might need the men later on his own raid. "I thought the forces could be used to better advantage than by sending a regiment to Oxford, as they would be obliged to return to New Albany to recross the Tallahatchie," he freely admitted, even though the statement contradicted his standing orders. Any advantage that might be gained by detaching the regiment, and perhaps further confusing the enemy as to his ultimate direction and goal, was less important at this point than the need to maintain a powerful column. If necessary, he could always detach the regiment later in the raid, although doing so would make it less likely the troopers would reach the railroad and then get back safely to La Grange.[15]

Regardless, Grierson had orders to break the railroad and the telegraph wires running alongside it. The rail line was broken, but the telegraph was not. Since a substantially smaller force could accomplish that task, Grierson opted to send the smallest force possible. As he informed Smith in his letter, "I have ordered a single scout . . . to go from Pontotoc toward Oxford, strike the railroad, and destroy the wires." Grierson was so confident this man could ride the roughly 35 miles west to the

14 For Mississippi's geography, see George B. Davis, Leslie J. Perry, and Joseph W. Kirkley, *Atlas to Accompany the Official Records of the Union and Confederate Armies* (Washington, DC: Government Printing Office, 1891-95), 154.

15 *OR* 24, pt. 1, 522.

telegraph lines and then north to Tennessee that he penned a quick note to Alice for the scout to mail to Jacksonville once he reached La Grange.[16]

With 10 percent of his force heading north and one man moving west, Grierson and the balance of the brigade continued south. "I start at 4 o'clock in the morning," he wrote Smith, "and on the night of the 20th shall be 50 miles below here. Everything looks exceedingly favorable. Rest assured that I shall spare no exertion to make the expedition as effective as possible." Once on the road, the column trudged south toward Houston, which it reached that afternoon. To further confuse the enemy, Grierson moved east around the little town and was beyond it by 4:00 p.m. The move puzzled his troopers. "It was not until I had discovered that we had left the main road," admitted one rider, "and was making a new one through a wheat field of some extent . . . [that] the question arose, what does this mean, and various were the conjectures." There was method to the madness. "The passing around the town of Houston with the main column was for a similar purpose," Grierson explained, "to avoid having our numbers counted. By going through fields and making a wide track, our force was greatly overestimated. And that gave us more time." Later, Grierson claimed his wide sweep created a situation in which "the rebels, before following when they found out the direction we were traveling, waited to amass larger numbers." Little was seen of the small town itself. According to one Illinois trooper, he and his comrades spotted "the house tops and church steeples [which] presented a picturesque appearance to us." After bypassing Houston, the brigade moved southeast down the Pontotoc Ridge toward Starkville, making another 11 or 12 miles before stopping near Clear Springs.[17]

The bypassing of Houston had an ironic result. The people of Chickasaw County had heard of the enemy's pending arrival and many had fled. Some believed the Federals would burn the courthouse, so the county records (including county board of police, deed, and marriage record books) were piled into a wagon and sent southeast of town. Grierson's cavalry, of course, skirted the town and left the courthouse perfectly safe. When the riders spotted the wagon and rode toward it, the men guarding the valuable documents dumped the books on the side

16 Ibid., 522-23.

17 Ibid., 522-23, 530; Grierson, *A Just and Righteous Cause*, 151; Woodward, "Grierson's Raid," 691; Surby, *Grierson Raids*, 226-27.

Houston-Starkville Road. This section of the old Houston-Starkville Road is not much different than when Grierson passed through back in 1863. *Author*

Benjamin Kilgore Grave. Grierson's column spent the fourth night of the raid on Benjamin Kilgore's plantation. While his plantation house is no longer standing, its location is known. Kilgore is buried just across the ridge from his house. *Author*

of the road and set fire to them to keep them out of enemy hands. The county records, which would have been perfectly safe in their original building in Houston, went up in smoke on the road outside town. Even more ironic was that the Federal troopers were not interested in the Chickasaw County civil records and probably would not have damaged them had they seized the wagon, much less the courthouse. The Federals were more interested in finding a lush plantation, and they discovered just what they were looking for near Clear Springs.[18]

Dr. Benjamin Kilgore was something of a legend around Chickasaw County. He was 70 years old in 1863, a well-known plantation owner, postmaster, physician, and politician. Kilgore had served in the War of 1812 in his native South Carolina's militia and later as a member of the Mississippi legislature. His substantial plantation—exclusive of his 32 slaves—was valued in 1860 at more than $6,000. It was situated on the main road running southeast to Starkville and Columbus near the small hamlet of Clear Springs, directly in the path of the Federal raiders.[19]

18 Tim Turpentine, "A History of Chickasaw County," in James R. Atkinson, ed., *Journal of Mississippi History* (November 1979), vol. 41, Issue 4, 319.

19 Surby, *Grierson Raids*, 27; 1850 Chickasaw County Population and Slave Schedules; https://www.findagrave.com/memorial/59333701/benjamin-kilgore.

Other civilians also faced the swarm of arriving Federals, including Sterling G. Ivy, who lived in the nearby Kilgore Hills. When Ivy learned the enemy was at hand, he sent his slaves into the swamps with his food and livestock, but he acted too late and Grierson's troopers captured the entire lot. Ivy, who had a substantial sum of money with him, nonchalantly tossed his purse under a log and sat on it. Feigning surprise at the approach of the Federals, he tried to run and was quickly caught. His captors put the man on a slow mule, but he jumped off the animal and hid under a bridge. When his guards asked about Ivy's whereabouts, a slave replied, "Dat man runned away off yander." The Federals crossed the bridge under which Ivy was hiding but did not search beneath it. The fugitive waited until the raiders left before returning home—and retrieving his money in the process.[20]

Riding more than 13 hours from before sunup to sundown made for a long day. In addition to sending Major Love's detachment north and the lone scout to the west, Grierson had guided his brigade another 35 miles into Mississippi. It was not the full 50 miles he had hoped to achieve, but there were no pursuing Confederates in sight. "We have yet encountered no force except the unorganized cavalry scattered through the country," Grierson informed Smith in his note earlier that day. The intelligence was still true at the end of the long day. But now more than ever, Grierson was in a race against time. The lack of an organized pursuit or mounted interception of the Federal expedition was bound to change, especially behind him. News of his presence was spreading. Still, the less fuss and noise he made as he quietly entered towns and plantations as he picked his way south, the better his chances were of success. Whatever he did, Grierson would have to keep in front of any Confederate pursuit and any news of his daring ride through the heart of Mississippi.[21]

*   *   *

Grierson had no idea what Confederate forces, if any, were gathering in his front, but he knew with certainty some were concentrating behind him. His scouts had picked up enough information to know that the weak

20 Clay County History Book Committee, *History of Clay County, Mississippi* (n.p.: Curtis Media Corporation, 1988), 180.

21 *OR* 24, pt. 1, 522.

outer shell of Confederate resistance around New Albany was not all there was to worry about. The Federal brigade was approaching central Mississippi and the heart of the First Military District commanded by Gen. Daniel Ruggles of Shiloh artillery fame. The Confederate concentration feared by every Federal was beginning to take form.[22]

Ruggles, a native of Massachusetts and an 1833 graduate of West Point, gained extensive prewar experience, including frontier duty and combat against the Seminoles and Mexicans. Unlike state militia leaders, he knew something about the craft of war. The 53-year-old general digested incoming news about the enemy movements from his commanders and subordinates at his headquarters in Columbus in east-central Mississippi. Notice reached him as early as April 20 that a Union column was approaching his district and that it numbered 2,000 to 3,000 men. Its destination was unknown, although Ruggles's scouts passed along that "negroes report hearing them say they were going to the Southern [rail]road or Grenada." The concerned general rode north by rail on April 20 to see firsthand what was transpiring, only to learn of yet another enemy movement. This force, which was estimated to number between 8,000 and 10,000, was reported to be moving east from the Corinth area—a reference to Grenville Dodge's move to support Abel Streight's raid. Ruggles passed the news on to General Pemberton that "there is evidently some formidable movement in that direction." Still, there was little he thought he could do in the way of sending troops, because there were "none to send [to] Colonel [P. D.] Roddey." General Hurlbut had hoped to take some pressure off Grierson by coordinating with General Rosecrans and Streight, and the ruse worked to a point, but not enough to peel away any men or guns from central Mississippi. Ruggles, meanwhile, concentrated his forces in the Tupelo area to combat what he and others guessed was a raid to break the Mobile and Ohio Railroad somewhere near that point. Why else would large bodies of Federals be moving southeast into Mississippi?[23]

The task of running down the Federals fell to Clark R. Barteau of the 2nd Tennessee Cavalry, a lieutenant colonel who had been born in Ohio. At one time, early in their lives, Grierson and Barteau lived within

22   Ibid., 534.

23   James Burton to Daniel Ruggles, April 19, 1863, in Civil War Collection, Loyola Marymount University; *OR* 24, pt. 1, 550-51.

Clark R. Barteau. As the ranking field commander in north Mississippi, Lieutenant Colonel Clark R. Barteau chased Grierson until he was led astray by Hatch's diversion. *Old Guard in Gray*

100 miles of one another (Barteau was from the Cleveland area while Grierson was still in Youngstown). The Buckeye moved south to have a look at slavery in the 1850s and never left, becoming what one historian termed an "ultrasecessionist." Barteau was quick to join the Confederacy when war broke out, even though much of his family remained in Ohio. His brother fought in the Union ranks.[24]

Like other Confederates in the north Mississippi region, Barteau kept a close eye on the several Federal movements, including those to the west as well as Dodge's eastward move into Alabama. The raid that posed the most danger to him was Grierson's thrust, which his scouts had reported on April 18 as a force "variously estimated in strength." When he learned the enemy column was moving south from La Grange toward New Albany, Barteau assumed—as Grierson hoped he would—that the Federal riders were after the Confederate camps at Chesterville. Barteau concentrated his scattered companies and was moving north by the night of April 19. Other Southern cavalry units also concentrating to

---

24 Bruce S. Allardice, *Confederate Colonels: A Biographical Register* (Columbia: University of Missouri Press, 2008), 55; Dave Roth, "Grierson's Raid, April 17-May 2, 1863: A Cavalry Raid at Its Best," *Blue & Gray Magazine* (June 1993), vol. 10, Issue 5, 23.

stop Grierson joined Barteau, including the 2nd Mississippi Cavalry State Troops under Col. J. F. Smith, four companies of the 16th Battalion State Troops under Capt. T. W. Ham, and two companies of partisan rangers from northeast Mississippi under Maj. William M. Inge.[25]

William Inge, a staunch secessionist from a cooperationist county, was a Corinth native who had run for a seat at the Mississippi Secession Convention and lost. When Gen. Albert Sidney Johnston had arrived in Corinth in late March 1862, Inge was home on leave from Virginia and offered the Southern commander the use of his home. Johnston spent his last night in Corinth at the Inge home, planning his attack on the Federal army gathered at Shiloh. He was killed there on April 6 and his body brought back to the same house and cleaned by Mrs. Inge. Johnston's corpse lay in state for a short time and was then shipped to New Orleans for burial. Major Inge witnessed none of this, however, because he was still at the Shiloh battlefield, serving as a volunteer staff officer for Mississippi Brig. Gen. Charles Clark.[26]

One of Barteau's first decisions as he set after Grierson was a serious tactical mistake. By the night of April 19, Grierson had moved south and around Barteau's concentration at Chesterville, through Pontotoc, and on to Daggett's plantation. Colonel Hatch's thrust toward the Confederate training camp had lured Barteau out of the path of the main Federal column, allowing Grierson to slip past Barteau's command and get ahead of it. That put Barteau nearly 15 miles out of position, and it would take him hours to correct his error, even if the Federals dallied, which Grierson was not apt to do. Grierson had made it through the initial line of resistance and had confused the lone large body of cavalry that could have contested his advance. The small triumph bought Grierson several hours to move even deeper into Mississippi.[27]

---

25 John Berrien, *The Military Annals of Tennessee* (Nashville: J. M. Lindsley & Co., 1886), 613; Rowland Dunbar and H. Grady Howell, Jr., *Military History of Mississippi: 1803-1898, Including a Listing of All Known Mississippi Confederate Military Units* (Madison, MS: Chickasaw Bayou Press, 2003), 427, 511, 533-34; *OR* 24, pt. 1, 534; Smith, *The Mississippi Secession Convention*; 226; Smith, Shiloh, 59, 64.

26 Berrien, *Military Annals of Tennessee*, 613; Rowland and Howell, *Military History of Mississippi*, 427, 511, 533-34; *OR* 24, pt. 1, 534; Smith, *Mississippi Secession Convention*; 226; Smith, *Shiloh*, 59, 64.

27 *OR* 24, pt. 1, 534; Bearss, *The Vicksburg Campaign*, vol. 2, 194.

Out of position to block Grierson, Barteau convinced himself the Federals were moving toward the Mobile and Ohio Railroad, and so he tried to reposition his command to get between the enemy and the railroad. He moved through the night, giving his troopers only a couple of hours of rest after an already long day. Barteau rode toward Pontotoc, where he hoped to catch the Federals. By the time he approached the town soon after daylight on April 20, Grierson was already well down the Houston road. Word arrived that a part of the Federal force had moved west toward Oxford. In Pontotoc, Barteau learned the smaller group of Federals (the Quinine Brigade) had not ridden toward Oxford at all but north to New Albany. If Grierson had delayed sending Love's group back north, the ill men would have been gobbled up rather easily by Barteau's force. As it was, the Quinine Brigade barely escaped before the Confederates reached Pontotoc.[28]

Barteau realized his mistake when he learned the main body of Federal raiders were three hours south of him. "I immediately gave pursuit," he remembered, setting out toward Houston and pushing his men hard. That night (April 20), while Grierson camped at the Kilgore plantation, Barteau called a halt north of Houston to allow his famished and exhausted troopers and horses to rest for the night. The Tennesseans and Mississippians had been moving nonstop for a couple of days, "an almost continuous march of 67½ miles." Despite Barteau's best effort, Grierson had managed to maintain a nearly 15-mile lead.[29]

Like Grierson, Barteau was up early the next morning, and the Confederates reached Kilgore's by 11:00 a.m. The Federals had moved out that morning, but Barteau had cut the lead down to only some two hours. They ran up on a rear guard and exchanged several shots. However, the Confederates soon realized something was amiss. When they reached the point where the Starkville and Columbus roads divided, the mystery deepened. The tracks indicated the Federal column had split. Which road had the main force taken? When it became clear the bulk of the tracks pointed east, Barteau followed, hoping this time he was making the right choice.[30]

*   *   *

28 *OR* 24, pt. 1, 534.

29 Ibid.

30 Ibid.

The decision Barteau faced at the crossroads was the result of more deception on Grierson's part. With the Confederates hot on his trail, Grierson gave serious thought on the night of April 20 about how to manage his troops and when to send a regiment to the east. He had already decided not to dispatch a regiment west toward the Mississippi Central, but that was because the line was already broken. There was no such indication about the Mobile and Ohio Railroad. Grierson decided one regiment could do the job, but which regiment and when to send it?[31]

The sooner Grierson dispatched the regiment the better. A quick thrust would allow the detachment to make its way east and hit the railroad, hopefully before the Confederates realized what was happening. It would also give the regiment a better chance of making it safely back to Tennessee. Grierson decided to send Hatch's 2nd Iowa Cavalry to do the work. Whether it was because Hatch was an accomplished warrior in his own right and could handle the job or because the Iowa colonel was already miffed about not getting the command himself and that Grierson had sent a large chunk of his regiment back the day before is unknown. What is known, however, is that it would not be the last time Hatch would be unhappy in Mississippi.[32]

The 7th Illinois Cavalry took the lead when the brigade began marching southeast around 6:00 a.m. on April 21. The column moved a few miles toward Starkville and, at about 8:00 a.m., reached the split in the road just north of Montpelier. The right fork led to Montpelier and Starkville; the left fork pointed toward Columbus and the Mobile and Ohio Railroad. Grierson sent Hatch to the rear with orders to peel off to the left with his Iowans and one of Smith's cannons. Grierson ordered Hatch to strike the railroad somewhere in the vicinity of West Point, tear up the rails and cut the telegraph wires, and ride south along the railroad—if possible as far as Macon—ripping up the line and causing as much confusion as possible. Once that had been accomplished, the Iowans were to ride back along the railroad, hit Columbus if possible, and then break for La Grange "by the most practicable route." It was a tall order for Hatch, but he was more than capable of executing it. Despite the importance of the damage he might inflict, Hatch's effort was little more than a bold decoy. While he was smashing the railroad,

31 Ibid., 523.

32 Ibid.

Grierson would be riding south to success and glory if he succeeded or death and/or capture if he did not. The soldier in Hatch wanted to be part of the main ride, but orders were orders.[33]

Grierson explained to Hatch that, while he had every confidence in him and his men, the logistics for the overall raid were not in their favor. "I looked upon him as a brave, discreet, and capable officer," Grierson said of Hatch, adding, "and, although I regretted to part with him and his gallant regiment of officers and men, yet his horses, on account of the hard and constant work they had been performing, were not in my judgment as suitable as those of the 7th Illinois Cavalry." State pride and familiarity also played a role. There was never any doubt Grierson would take his own 6th Illinois Cavalry with him, and the choice between the other two was not a difficult one. The officers and men of the 2nd Iowa Cavalry, he explained, were not "so well known to me at that time as those of the 7th Illinois, which was from my own state."[34]

Grierson's explanation may have soothed Hatch's hurt feelings, but the pilfering of Dr. Erastus D. Yule of the 2nd Iowa Cavalry (the only surgeon with the brigade) to accompany the main ride south likely did not sit well. More concerning to Hatch was that he would not leave immediately for his objective, but instead follow Grierson's Illinoisans south toward Starkville about four miles and then double back "to obliterate the tracks of Colonel Grierson," explained Hatch. The intent was to confuse any pursuing Confederates as to which way Grierson's main body was heading. Grierson hoped the enemy would pick up Hatch's movement instead of his own. "These detachments were intended as diversions," reported Grierson, "and even should the commanders not have been able to carry out their instructions, yet, by attracting the attention of the enemy in other directions, they assisted us much in the accomplishment of the main object of the expedition."[35]

Hatch expressed concern about the condition of his regiment, the additional eight miles of riding, and what Grierson expected from his

33 Ibid., 523, 530; *OR* 24, pt. 3, 232; Bearss, *The Vicksburg Campaign*, vol. 2, 194; Surby, *Grierson Raids*, 27; B. H. Grierson to Alice, April 21, 1863. The historic Montpelier is not the present-day town, which is west of the historic site.

34 Grierson, *A Just and Righteous Cause*, 151-52; Erastus D. Yule, Compiled Service Record, NARA.

35 *OR* 24, pt. 1, 523, 530.

Iowans. The pair of officers "were bidding each other good-bye," recalled Grierson, when Hatch suggested that, instead of the entire regiment, "the sending of one battalion [toward Starkville and back] would afford more rest for his tired animals, and I assented to the proposition." Major Datus Coon, whom Grierson declared to be a "brave and most gallant officer," was selected to lead the lone Iowa battalion and a single cannon. While Hatch and the rest of the regiment waited, Coon followed Grierson down the Starkville road. Several miles below, at Montpelier, Grierson stopped to bid the Iowans a final adieu. "I well remember the look of regret he [Coon] gave me," Grierson recalled, "as he warmly shook my hand when the column halted to enable him to counter-march his command. I would gladly have taken him and his brave troops with me, if it had been practicable to do so." Hoping the Iowans would return safely, Grierson wrote a quick note to Alice that he had been through Montpelier: "Dear Alice—All well. Apl 21st Tuesday—6 O'clock a.m."[36]

Coon's returning Iowans played their role perfectly, if not gladly. The troopers formed into a column of fours and, together with the lone gun, made wide tracks northward to confuse the enemy. To add a little more trickery, when Coon arrived back at the fork in the road, he ordered the men to make multiple tracks with the artillery piece so it looked as though the column had multiple guns. As one man put it, "The cannon was turned in the road in four different places, thus making their tracks correspond with the four pieces of artillery which Grierson had with the expedition." Hopefully, any pursuing Confederates would think the main force had turned east toward Columbus.[37] Hatch and his regiment, meanwhile, waited for Coon's return. "In this way I was delayed three hours," reported the colonel, "thus enabling the enemy's cavalry, which had been concentrating for some days in anticipation of a movement on Columbus, to fall upon me." And fall upon him they would.[38]

At this point in the raid, Confederate Lieutenant Colonel Barteau made his third serious mistake. Once he reached the fork in the road southeast of Kilgore's plantation, he examined the tracks and concluded,

36 Grierson, *A Just and Righteous Cause*, 152; Pierce, *History of the Second Iowa Cavalry*, 49; B. H. Grierson to Alice, April 21, 1863, Benjamin H. Grierson Papers, ALPL.

37 Pierce, *History of the Second Iowa Cavalry*, 49.

38 *OR* 24, pt. 1, 530; Woodward, "Grierson's Raid," 692.

"The enemy had divided, 200 going to Starkville and 700 continuing their march on the West Point road." In reality, it was exactly the opposite: Grierson's larger force had moved south to Starkville. As a result, Barteau and his men set out in pursuit of what they considered to be the larger of the two Federal forces, spurring their mounts east after Hatch's Iowans, taking Grierson's bait just as he intended.[39]

*   *   *

Colonel Hatch knew the closer he rode to the Mobile and Ohio Railroad the sooner trouble would find him. He had not ridden very far when reports of enemy cavalry on his rear and flanks reached him. When he was within a few miles of the railroad, he learned an Alabama regiment with artillery was between him and West Point. Confederate district commander Ruggles was sending regular Confederate units and Mississippi state troops under former Federal judge Samuel J. Gholson to either catch the enemy cavalry or protect the railroad, which Ruggles concluded was the raid's primary target. Hatch was beginning to feel boxed in, and he abandoned the plans to move south to Macon or Columbus. His primary concern was to get out of the closing enemy trap, for which he blamed his immediate superior: "[The] delay in time . . . was fatal to carrying out Colonel Grierson's order."[40]

The small community of Palo Alto, less than 10 miles from the Mobile and Ohio Railroad, had once been a thriving community. When the railroad route to the east left it behind, however, its population declined along with its economic vitality. Hatch and his Iowans were approaching the small town just as a group of Confederate cavalry under Barteau, including Smith's partisan rangers (whom Hatch had met earlier around Pontotoc), caught up with them. The result was a running affair beyond the Palo Alto church. Barteau's Tennessee regiment and its allies, including Inge's battalion, were overtaking the rear of the Federal column, which had been delayed in its effort to help Grierson get off on a firm footing down the Starkville road. The pursuing Confederates knew the relative strength of the enemy because, as one Iowan reported, "Our column had been inspected at every house we passed by women

39   *OR* 24, pt. 1, 534.

40   Ibid., 530.

Palo Alto Cemetery. Much of the battle at Palo Alto took place near the church and cemetery. The church is no longer standing, but the cemetery is still active. *Author*

and old men," none of whom were bashful about providing information to Barteau. As a result, Hatch could not make it safely through Palo Alto before the Confederate pursuit caught up with him. He had no choice but to deploy and prepare for a fight.[41]

Barteau and company first hit the Union rear guard some two miles northwest of the Palo Alto church and steadily pushed east, "skirmishing for advantage of ground," explained the Confederate officer. The Confederates managed to cut off one company of Iowans trying to hold back the Confederate onslaught. Hatch, meanwhile, one company short,

41 Ibid., 534; Pierce, *History of the Second Iowa Cavalry*, 49; Roth, "Grierson's Raid," 24.

took up a position in a hedge-lined roadbed near the church, deploying his lone cannon to best advantage. Despite being lined with trees, the position offered an open field of fire. Other Confederates were farther east, including the Alabama regiment. Fortunately for the Iowans, a formidable valley and the channel of Tibbee Creek protected them from that direction.[42]

The next two hours were filled with fitful skirmishing while Barteau decided how best to get at the Federals. "Finding that the enemy would not come out from his position," Barteau had to come up with a different scheme. He still thought the Federals were moving to strike the railroad, so its defense played a large role in his thinking. He also did not know whether General Ruggles at Columbus had been able to forward troops into the area. Left to his own devices, Barteau figured out a way to both fight Hatch and protect the railroad. His biggest problem was that the railroad was behind the Federals. Barteau decided to split his force. Colonel Smith's and Captain Ham's units would deploy in Hatch's front to hold the Iowans in place, "dismounted, and, protected by the church, a small number of trees, and the brow of a slight eminence." Meanwhile, Barteau would take his own 2nd Tennessee under Maj. George H. Morton, together with Major Inge's Mississippians, around Hatch's flank to get between the Iowans and the railroad. The move would allow Barteau to protect the Mobile and Ohio and attack Hatch in the rear. "Should the enemy advance on them," he ordered Smith and Ham, they were "to reserve their fire until he should arrive close enough to make it destructive and deadly, and to hold the position until a charge should be made fully in his rear." With that, Barteau took his men and rode off to implement his bold plan.[43]

The Confederates under Smith and Ham implemented some deception of their own, despite Barteau's orders to stand fast and wait for an attack on the rear of the enemy. The holding force used flags of truce to move closer to Hatch's position in order to launch an attack. When the Mississippians edged a little too close for the comfort of the Iowans

42 *OR* 24, pt. 1, 530, 534-35; Pierce, *History of the Second Iowa Cavalry*, 50; R. R. Hancock, *Hancock's Diary: Or, A History of the Second Tennessee Confederate Cavalry, with Sketches of First and Seventh Battalions; also, Portraits and Biographical Sketches* (Nashville: Brandon Printing Company, 1887), 239.

43 *OR* 24, pt. 1, 534-35; Hancock, *Hancock's Diary*, 239; Company C, 2nd Iowa Cavalry, Muster Roll, RG 94, E 57, NARA.

holding the lane, Hatch's "dismounted and well covered" troopers used their Colt revolving rifles to good effect in unison with the small two-pound cannon. Some of the Confederates later bragged that they "wanted but three minutes in which to capture it," but the barking mobile piece turned the tide, with one shot smashing into the nearby Calvert house. The fire routed the Rebels. According to Barteau's report, "The enemy . . . poured a rapid fire upon Colonel's Smith's regiment and Captain Ham's four companies, before which the men retreated in the utmost disorder, although everything was done which could have been by these two officers to make them stand and at least give the enemy one fire."[44]

The rout of the Mississippians prompted Hatch to order a pursuit westward that covered some three miles. The fortuitous counterthrust recovered his lost company and captured several horses and weapons. Barteau knew from the sound of the fading gunfire that his plan had gone awry, but he achieved one important goal by placing part of his command between the enemy and the railroad. With the battle moving away from him, Barteau wheeled his troopers about and followed the running combat as best he could. "Had not the troops given way so soon in front," he complained in his report, "I should have cut to pieces or captured the entire force of the enemy." Colonel Smith and Captain Ham tried to reform their men in the midst of the chaos. Even Barteau admitted that they "acted gallantly, and took the post of danger, endeavoring by their example to inspire confidence and insure success." There was no inspiring the beaten state troops, however, and Hatch now had an open corridor out of the well-conceived trap. Even better, one Iowan remembered, "Not a drop of Yankee blood was shed."[45]

Recriminations for the failure to trap Hatch came thick and fast. One of Barteau's Tennesseans later complained, "Our attack would have been complete, and we would have captured his whole command, had not a battalion of Mississippi State troops, which had joined us on the march, given way in disorder on one side as we charged on the other." A local citizen agreed with that assessment when he informed Governor John J. Pettus, "From the best information I can obtain one Regiment of our

44 OR 24, pt. 1, 530, 534-35; Pierce, *History of the Second Iowa Cavalry*, 50, 54; Ruth White Williams, *On the Map 145 Years: The History of West Point, Mississippi, 1846-1991* (West Point, MS: City of West Point, 1996), 54.

45 OR 24, pt. 1, 530, 534-35; Pierce, *History of the Second Iowa Cavalry*, 50, 54.

newly organized state cavalry (Smith's Regt) behaved very badly in the late skirmishes with the Yankees. Indeed, many of the men shamefully threw away their arms and ran away." In fairness, little could be expected from fresh state troops, but the civilian had little better to say about the regular Confederates when he added, "Barteau's Cavalry is a nuisance."[46]

By this time Hatch knew he was no longer in a position to carry out Grierson's orders. Even though he was miffed at Grierson, Hatch was a patriot and a career officer first. Accordingly, the Maine native fell back to the northeast. "From that time until dark it was a constant skirmish," he reported, "the enemy having taken me for the main column. Believing it was important to divert the enemy's cavalry from Colonel Grierson, I moved slowly northward, fighting by the rear, crossing the Houlka River, and drawing their forces immediately in my rear." When an impediment appeared, the men swiftly vaulted over it. At times, they even lifted the little cannon by hand or took it apart to more easily move it. "The naked gun weighed 140 pounds," recalled an Iowan, "and the carriage could be so taken apart that the gun was heavier than any piece about it."[47]

Captain Henry Forbes of the 7th Illinois was riding with Grierson's column and praised Hatch for his accomplishment, concluding, "The enemy left 25 of their men on the field and Hatch had the right of way." Grierson admitted Hatch had successfully diverted Confederate attention. "It had lately rained considerable throughout that section of the country," he explained, "and the fact that the freshest tracks pointed northward led the rebels, when they examined the trail three hours afterwards, to believe that the whole command had marched eastward." However, the brigade commander was not completely satisfied with Hatch's performance. The regimental commander, he argued, had been taken "somewhat by surprise" at Palo Alto. "The colonel did not follow up his advantage and reach Macon as I had hoped and directed." After recovering from the appearance of the enemy, continued Grierson, "It would appear . . . he might have dashed down to Macon." Ultimately, Grierson gave Hatch the benefit of the doubt, writing that "he, however, no doubt did what he deemed best, considering the condition of his horses and the distance he

---

46 Berrien, *Military Annals of Tennessee*. 613; James H. Rives to John J. Pettus, May 2, 1863, in John J. Pettus Correspondence, MDAH.

47 *OR* 24, pt. 1, 530; Forbes, "Grierson's Raid," 10; Pierce, *History of the Second Iowa Cavalry*, 51.

had to march through the enemy's country." He also praised Hatch for making "a skillful retreat . . . doing what damage he could by the way and drawing the enemy after him as far north as practicable." In fact, Hatch had played his role perfectly and with a willingness to sacrifice his command, if necessary, to further the overall objective. "The Fight at Palo Alto, and diverting the enemy from Colonel Grierson," he wrote as Grierson continued southward, "has undoubtedly given him thirty-six hours' head start." Such selflessness was the mark of a true patriot.[48]

By that evening, Ruggles knew of Barteau's fight and Hatch's escape. The enemy had gotten away, he reported, and the smaller forces that had ridden down the Starkville road had returned and rejoined the troops he had fought earlier in the day. Barteau was ashamed to admit he had not fully taken care of either enemy force, but he assured Ruggles that he hoped to do just that the next day—especially with reinforcements from Lt. Col. James Cunningham's 2nd Alabama Cavalry, which was expected that night from Okolona. Barteau also called on Ruggles to send more mounted troops to West Point. "We will not, if possible, allow the enemy to reach the railroad," he assured the district commander. "I do not know whether we can succeed in gobbling up this force as I desire to do," he added, but he reassured Ruggles that the enemy would not make any farther penetration south, because all of the Federals were riding hard north again. As Barteau wrote these words, Grierson steadily moved south through Starkville and beyond with the bulk of his command.[49]

*   *   *

While Hatch was riding west and fighting for his life around Palo Alto, Grierson was making a swift and unobserved getaway south on April 21. One Illinois man remembered that, despite approaching bad weather, the men "were cheerful and enlivened the march with songs and jokes." Questions, however, coursed through the ranks. Why had an entire regiment broken off the main column? Why were they still

48 Forbes, "Grierson's Raid," 10; Grierson, *A Just and Righteous Cause*, 152; *OR* 24, pt. 1, 531.

49 *OR* 24, pt. 1, 534; "Skirmish in Chickasaw County," *Jackson Daily Mississippian*, April 23, 1863.

moving southward? "Various were the opinions by the men as to our destination," admitted one trooper.[50]

Grierson's main column now consisted of two regiments and the four remaining pieces of Smith's Illinois artillery battery, about 950 men in all. He allowed the troopers half an hour to rest and then rode hard for Starkville. The Illinois soldiers passed through Tampico, where they saw evidence of what trooper Daniel Robbins described as "the R. R. through there [which] is not completed." Next up was Starkville, which Grierson reached late in the afternoon. The column entered without opposition because no one there knew Grierson was coming until just minutes before he and his men arrived. According to one Mississippian at nearby Mayhew Station, the Federals loudly proclaimed that "every citizen caught showing that he was a Combatant would be hung immediately." It is highly unlikely Grierson would have hanged anyone under those circumstances, but the threat surely discouraged opposition. Grierson captured a good deal of mail and "government property," all of which the Illinoisans destroyed.[51]

The troopers made quite a stir in each town they rode through, and the chaos amused the fun-loving colonel. "Upon entering a town," Grierson recalled in reference to their entrance into Starkville, "we were surprised to find ourselves at times ahead of information and were, therefore, often taken for Confederate soldiers going to intercept the Yankees, of whom all had received more or less exaggerated reports. The consternation occasioned by the sudden appearance of our detachments in conjunction with the main column," he continued, "apparently so widely scattered and traveling in opposite directions, caused reports of our force to be greatly overestimated."[52]

The Illinois troopers had what fun they could while abiding by the strict rules Grierson laid down. Generally, they adhered to them. When opportunities arose, the troopers could not resist being kind to the slaves they encountered. One newspaper reported what happened when "Hale

---

50 Curtiss, diary, April 21, 1863, Wisconsin Historical Society; Surby, *Grierson Raids*, 28.

51 *OR* 24, pt. 1, 523; Grierson, *A Just and Righteous Cause*, 152; A. K. Brantley to John J. Pettus, April 24, 1863, in John J. Pettus Correspondence, MDAH; Daniel E. Robbins to Parents, May 5, 1863.

52 Grierson, *A Just and Righteous Cause*, 154.

and Murdock's hat wagon, loaded with wool hats," passed through town at the wrong time. The soldiers confiscated the hats, distributed them to the slaves, "and took the mules." The nearby Columbus *Republic* sarcastically editorialized, "Starkville can boast of better head covering for its Negroes than any other town in the state." In a show of mercy, troopers going through the captured Confederate mail "handed back a letter from a soldier to his wife, containing $50.00, and ordered the postmaster to give it to her." The Federals left almost all property intact because, as the newspaper explained, "They stated that they were not destroying property; that they were gentlemen."[53]

Having no reason to remain in town and an urgent reason to be on his way, Grierson took a doctor as a temporary prisoner and the column moved south on the Louisville Road. The western skies grew dark and foreboding soon after the ride was renewed. A major storm was approaching. By nightfall, the heavens opened, dumping what Grierson described as "a violent rain."[54]

This storm was not the only thing Grierson and his men had to endure. Four or five miles south of Starkville, a series of tributaries threading out from a large river system slowed their progress. The Noxubee River's headwaters were west, on the high ridge dividing the watersheds of the Tombigbee River and its tributaries from the watersheds of the Big Black and Pearl Rivers farther west. The Noxubee River flowed generally southeast between Starkville and Louisville, through Macon, and into Alabama, where it entered the Tombigbee River near Gainesville. Numerous feeder creeks and branches flowed roughly parallel with the main channel, all of which is now a part of the Noxubee National Wildlife Refuge and the Tombigbee National Forest. The road from Starkville to Louisville crossed each ribbon of water. This made it difficult to move quickly, especially during storms and particularly after a heavy rainfall.[55]

Grierson had been fortunate thus far, putting his copy of Colton's pocket map to good use. After crossing the Tallahatchie River rather easily three days earlier on April 18, the brigade had not encountered any significant obstacles. He had ridden his men along the high Pontotoc

---

53 Forbes, "Grierson's Cavalry Raid," 130.

54 *OR* 24, pt. 1, 523.

55 Ibid.

Ridge southeast as it formed the high headwaters region of most of the nearby major streams flowing east and west. This route through Pontotoc, Houston, and nearly to Starkville had allowed Grierson to bypass the headwaters and channel of the Big Black River off to his west and also avoid the lowlands flooded by the tributaries of the Tombigbee River to the east (the same ones Hatch had encountered). Now that Grierson was off the Pontotoc Ridge, he needed to negotiate several waterways, including the Noxubee and the upper reaches of the larger Pearl River, to reach the Southern Railroad of Mississippi nearly 100 miles farther south.[56]

Grierson had little choice but to plunge ahead. Every major raid faced obstacles, but how he and his men and animals managed these challenges would determine success or failure. The Federal commander pushed his men into the Noxubee River swamps, crossing the muddy tributaries before negotiating the main channel the next day. It was a difficult journey. Grierson described the area as "a dismal swamp nearly belly-deep in mud." His men had no choice but to push ahead, "sometimes swimming our horses to cross streams." Somehow the column managed to cover almost 40 miles that day before Grierson finally called a halt to allow his wet and exhausted troopers to find a suitable campsite amid the swamps around Talking Warrior Creek, one of the Noxubee River's major tributaries. "We encamped for the night in the midst of a violent rain," Grierson reported, his column having finally reached "high and suitable ground."[57]

It was a miserable night despite the "high and suitable ground." There was little shelter for man and beast and precious little for either to eat. According to Adjutant Woodward, the men without tents huddled in any outbuildings they could find. This was the first night of the raid the troopers had not encamped at a plantation, where enormous amounts of forage and provisions were always within reach. In a sense, it was the first time Grierson had failed to find his men suitable accommodations. He may have been better off stopping a few miles back, closer to Starkville, but the urgency to keep moving had pressed him on. As Grierson later explained, "I always had rather a remarkable faculty for judging correctly

---

56 George B. Davis, Leslie J. Perry, and Joseph W. Kirkley, *Atlas to Accompany the Official Records of the Union and Confederate Armies* (Washington: Government Printing Office, 1891-1895),154.

57 *OR* 24, pt. 1, 523; Grierson, *A Just and Righteous Cause*, 152.

as to where supplies could be obtained, readily determining from the character of the country where a large plantation or mill ought to be located, and was sure to reach them unerringly." Occasionally, "after a hard day's ride in a desolate looking country," he added, "night would approach with no apparent prospect of supplies or food for men or animals. But, by what seemed to the men an unfailing instinct, orders would be given to flank off some by-road or across a field to an unknown or unsuspected foraging place, till the command learned to trust to my discretion or judgment without complaint." Regardless of Grierson's good instincts, they failed him this night as his tired command huddled on the only high ground discernable in the Noxubee River bottoms.[58]

*   *   *

As it turned out, the miserable day was not over for a few unlucky companies of the 7th Illinois Cavalry. Scouts brought Grierson news of a "tannery and shoe manufactory in the service of the rebels" near Longview, just three miles to the northwest. The place was a novelty in the area because its owners, Roderick Green and Dossey A. Outlaw, operated the first steam engine in the county. The engine powered not only the manufactory but also a saw, grist, and flour mill, which meant grateful farmers no longer had to go all the way to the Noxubee River mills farther to the south to process their harvests. Grierson was more interested in the tannery, and he sent a battalion of the 7th Illinois under Major Graham to destroy it. Graham's troopers caught the tannery workers unaware and "accomplished the work most effectually," Grierson happily reported. The small raid destroyed a large number of shoes, leather, and the machinery needed to make them, "in all amounting, probably, to $50,000, and captured a rebel quartermaster from Port Hudson, who was there laying in a supply for his command." The officer, a member of a Tennessee regiment, had no idea any enemy was operating in the vicinity. The battalion returned without any trouble other than battling heavy rain and tried to get what rest they could before heading out the next morning.[59]

58 Woodward, "Grierson's Raid," 692; Grierson, *A Just and Righteous Cause*, 154.

59 *OR* 24, pt. 1, 523; Thomas Battle Carroll, *Historical Sketches of Oktibbeha County (Mississippi)* (Gulfport: Dixie Press, 1931), 77; Grierson, *A Just and Righteous Cause*,

The mini-raid to destroy the tannery was but one of many raids, scouts, and smaller detachments Grierson dispatched from the main body as he drove deeper into Mississippi. Some were to reconnoiter, some to destroy significant local establishments such as the tannery, and others to gather supplies. By this time, Grierson's men had exhausted the five-day supply of food they had taken with them when they left La Grange. The colonel had opted to spend most of the raid living off the country, and he was fortunate to find sufficient provisions at most of the plantations. "We were getting a long way from our own base of supplies," he admitted, "but managed to live quite well off the products of the country." Still, "living quite well" took work. "Foraging parties became a necessity," he reported, "and besides, when we stopped at a plantation for the night or to feed during the day, a detail for guard was immediately placed at the smokehouses, kitchens, and dwellings, with instructions not to allow anything to be taken without permission of a commissioned officer." Meanwhile, the quartermaster and commissary issued the items evenly to the troops "pro-rate to the various companies," and if there was not enough, squads rode to neighboring plantations to fill in the balance. "Still," Grierson confessed, "the rapid marches made were such that the command seldom got more than one good meal per day."[60]

Grierson also used the scouts and mini-raids as his eyes and ears. "Occasional small detachments sent out as foragers and select scouts for special services managed to obtain all necessary information of the country and the movements of the enemy," he confirmed. Eventually, Grierson decided to institute a more formal scouting effort, one based on the idea of Canadian Richard W. Surby of the 7th Illinois Cavalry. "Possessed of a venturesome disposition I naturally wanted to be in the front," recalled Surby. After thinking on the subject, "It occurred to me I could do so." Surby sought out Lt. Col. William Blackburn, his former captain and now the impetuous 26-year-old lieutenant colonel of the regiment, and told him of his idea of dressing scouts in civilian clothes

---

152-53; "The Grierson Raid," *Weekly Register* (Canton, IL), September 7, 1863; Surby, *Grierson Raids*, 31; Joey Partridge, "Grierson Raided Here 130 Years Ago," *Winston County Journal*, April 21, 1993.

60 Grierson, *A Just and Righteous Cause*, 154.

William D. Blackburn. Lieutenant Colonel William D. Blackburn, who oversaw the selection of the scouts, was a brave but rash officer, second in command of the 7th Illinois Cavalry. His rash action resulted in his mortal wounding at Wall's Bridge. *Steve Hicks*

and sending them out to gather intelligence. An enthusiastic Blackburn carried the idea to Grierson.[61]

The idea of a more muscular group dedicated to the task of scouting appealed to Grierson, especially as "we approached the heart of the rebel country." He discussed the idea with his officers, and a jocular competition to obtain "the most venturesome and daring soldiers" emerged. Grierson stipulated they be chosen "with great care" and that they volunteer for the duty because it was "so hazardous and the difficulties so great." The group needed "men of nerve, untiring energy and steadfast integrity," thought Adjutant Woodward. Some of the first volunteers stepped forward so they could steal for personal gain. "The detachment was thoroughly purged of this class," wrote a disgusted Woodward. Blackburn "entered into the spirit of the thing at once," claiming he knew exactly what

61 Surby, *Grierson Raids*, 29; Roth, "Grierson's Raid," 23, 62. For Surby's accounts, see Richard W. Surby, *Two Great Raids: Col. Grierson's Successful Swoop Through Mississippi, Morgan's Disastrous Raid Through Indiana and Ohio, Vivid Narratives of Both These Great Operations, with Extracts from Official Records, John Morgan's Escape, Last Raid, and Death* (Washington, DC: National Tribune, 1897) and Surby's multi-issue account in the *National Tribune*, starting with "The Grierson Raid," July 12, 1883, *National Tribune*. Surby's Compiled Service Record indicates he was born in Canada according to one document and Kinston, Ohio, in another (Richard W. Surby, Compiled Service Record, NARA).

men to choose. Blackburn, described as a "very energetic and capable officer," recommended the regiment's quartermaster sergeant, Richard W. Surby, to lead the scouts.[62]

Surby took to his new duty with gusto, and soon he had a small group of nine scouts equipped and ready for service. Grierson ordered him to stay "in advance and upon the flanks of the column to gain information as to the movements of the enemy, the character of the country, the different roads, streams, bridges, the products of the country, the whereabouts of forage and other supplies. In short," continued the Federal commander, "anything which would be of interest or importance to know was to be promptly reported." In order to make his task easier, although much more dangerous, Surby acquired civilian and Confederate attire, including butternut uniforms in which the scouts dressed to quickly blend into the countryside. Their appearance, thought Grierson, "was well calculated to deceive. In fact, they were for some days taken for rebels by our own men and presumed to be prisoners, as they would at times pass the column to the rear or front. But the officers and soldiers soon came to know them." Grierson remembered the scouts many years later when he recalled how "their singular appearance always brought forth smiles . . . their quaint citizen's dress, saddles, long rifles, shotguns, pouches, and general make up completing their admirable disguise." Surby and his scouts soon came to be known as the Butternut Guerrillas.[63]

The scouts looked so benign that some were taken to be clergymen. Samuel Nelson, for example, was "slightly deformed," with one leg shorter than the other, "so that he was not suspected of being in any way connected with the army." The scouts carried weapons under their clothes and out of sight until they were needed. If they were discovered dressed in civilian or Confederate clothing, however, they would be treated as spies and likely executed. Surby pondered that possibility. "I began to reflect; what, if we should be detected, our fate was certain death—we would be treated as spies. Then imagination pictured home with all its inducements, and I could see many sad countenances and bitter tears."[64]

---

62 Surby, *Grierson Raids*, 29; Grierson, *A Just and Righteous Cause*, 153.

63 Grierson, *A Just and Righteous Cause*, 153-54; Woodward, "Grierson's Raid," 687.

64 Surby, *Grierson Raids*, 29, 89.

Richard W. Surby. As commander of the scouts, Sergeant Richard W. Surby was instrumental in many of the more delicate and daring events of the raid. His coolness allowed Grierson to slip out of several tight spots. Surby was wounded as a result of Blackburn's rashness at Wall's Bridge and fell into enemy hands as a prisoner. *M. K. Surbey*

To avoid being fired upon by their own men, the scouts worked out a system of signals so the rest of Grierson's troops would recognize them. Unfortunately, this did not always work, and even Surby came under friendly fire, particularly at night when it was hard to distinguish friend from foe. In fact, a ball fired by one of his own comrades in the 7th Illinois Cavalry grazed his hip. The scouts quickly showed their mettle, capturing a Confederate officer just below Starkville even before going into camp during the miserable night of April 21. The enemy soldier was "a lieutenant from Vicksburg with a spanking team of gray horses with which he was cutting a dash with his lady love while home on leave," Grierson explained. He had no sympathy for either the lieutenant or the woman, and "the horses were turned over . . . to the battery."[65]

The scout service provided the small group of volunteers with freedom and flexibility, which was exactly what Surby desired. He was, however, "fully resolved not to abuse the confidence reposed in me." The Canadian-born quartermaster kept his word, and he and his motley band quickly became one of Grierson's most potent weapons.[66]

The Federal brigade commander needed all the weapons he could muster. A quick glance at Colton's map clearly showed that the rest of the way to the Southern Railroad would be more difficult because of the terrain, not counting any enemy they might encounter. It was time to make the final push south to break the railroad. The next few days would be the raid's defining hours and would determine its success, failure, or even the life or death of its participants.

65 Grierson, *A Just and Righteous Cause*, 154; Surby, *Grierson Raids*, 42, 52-53.

66 Surby, *Grierson Raids*, 29-30; *OR* 24, pt. 3, 215; Grierson, *A Just and Righteous Cause*, 151.

Chapter Six

The Push

John Pemberton's attention was being pulled in several directions. While Grant showed signs of a major operation unfolding west of the Mississippi River, the raids taking place elsewhere posed serious challenges for the Confederate general. By April 22 it was obvious that Grierson's incursion into Mississippi, which Pemberton had dismissed just two days earlier as "a mere raid," was something much more substantial.[1]

"Heavy raids are making from Tennessee deep into the State," Pemberton informed theater commander Joe Johnston at Tullahoma, Tennessee, on April 22, "and one is reported now at Starkville, 30 miles west of Columbus." The Vicksburg commander added, "Cavalry [is] indispensable to meet these raids," but "the little I have is in the field there, totally inadequate to prevent them."[2]

Unfortunately for Pemberton, he had no mounted troops south of the Confederate cavalry chasing Colonel Hatch to meet the enemy or defend key points, including the vital Southern Railroad of Mississippi. "I have so little cavalry in this department," he complained, "that I am compelled to direct a portion of my infantry to meet raids in Northern Mississippi," Pemberton informed Richmond. Abraham Buford's infantry, then in motion in Alabama, received word to halt and await further orders while other bodies of infantry were instructed to move north along the

1   *OR* 24, pt. 3, 770.

2   Ibid., 761, 770, 776-78.

rail lines to take positions better suited to meeting or stopping the enemy raid. Eventually, most of the troops in the eastern portion of the state would end up under the command of Maj. Gen. William W. Loring. Meanwhile, additional commands also concentrated on the compromised area, including Brig. Gen. Winfield S. Featherson's brigade, which moved to the Mississippi Central at Winona and Duck Hill, some of Loring's brigades, which moved north along the Mobile and Ohio from Meridian to aid General Ruggles, and Brig. Gen. Lloyd Tilghman's brigade, which moved north along the Mississippi Central from Canton. These infantry maneuvers, however, would be hard pressed to make any difference unless the Federals stumbled into an area they defended.[3]

Despite these hurried activities and his concern for what was unfolding in central Mississippi, Pemberton's main attention remained focused on Grant's operations west of the Mississippi River in Louisiana. Another movement of Federal vessels past the Vicksburg batteries on the night of April 22 was disconcerting, as were the infrequent messages reaching him concerning the Union raid. Pemberton told General Loring, who was moving troops northward from Meridian to meet Grierson, to keep him informed "hourly." The end of his message demonstrated the concern he felt about Grant's operation when he added that Loring's troops may "be required here at any time. Six boats passed Vicksburg last night."[4]

Pemberton's concentration on Vicksburg, his lack of cavalry, and the need to use infantry instead of mounted troops made the Confederate pursuit of Grierson less successful than it might have otherwise been. The fractured Southern command structure also accounts for the chaotic pursuit. Ruggles was in charge of the district when Grierson rode into it, but Gen. Samuel Gholson was in command of the state troops there. These included Col. J. F. Smith's 2nd Mississippi Cavalry State Troops, Capt. T. W. Ham's four companies of the 16th Battalion State Troops, and two companies of partisan rangers under Maj. William M. Inge. In the field, however, these officers and commands reported not to Gholson but to Colonel Barteau. (Regular Confederate cavalry units operated under their regular commanders, such as Barteau.)[5]

---

3   Ibid..

4   Ibid., 779.

5   Ibid., pt. 1, 535, 552; Bearss, *The Vicksburg Campaign*, vol. 2, 197.

The fact that many of the commanders did not get along only made the fluid and dangerous situation that much worse. When the troopers of Lt. Col. James Cunningham's 2nd Alabama Cavalry heard Hatch's small two-pounder firing the day before, the mounted outfit left camp at Okolona and rode toward the fighting. Barteau, however, was none too impressed and blamed much of the previous day's failure on Cunningham's tardiness in reaching the field. "The reinforcement," Barteau reported snappily, "was too late to be of any service. In fact, the tardiness of his movements allowed the enemy to reach Okolona; for had he joined me before reaching Palo Alto, we should have routed and scattered the enemy." Cunningham then made matters worse, Barteau reported, because "upon his late arrival he desired to assume command, which I declined to grant him." Unsure of their relative rank status, Barteau added, "If I committed an error in this respect, I am subject to such remedy as the case may require." With some of the Confederate officers arguing among themselves, and all of them working within a rickety system of command, the hope of actually catching Hatch, much less Grierson, became that much more difficult.[6]

Still, Barteau had done well by staying just a few hours behind Hatch's Iowans. Smith's and Ham's units had rejoined Barteau after the fighting at Palo Alto, when Barteau again divided his forces, this time sending the state troops toward Pontotoc while he moved toward Okolona with his own and Cunningham's regiments. The latter command, however, was blocked by a flooded creek, which Barteau described as having "no bridge, and the water swimming deep," and stopped its advance. Trouble between the lieutenant colonels, meanwhile, continued to fester. When Cunningham informed Barteau that "his command was exhausted and without rations [and] that he could not continue the pursuit," Barteau decided he had had all he could stand of Cunningham. His own men, after all, were at the point of exhaustion and had been in the field longer than Cunningham's troopers. Barteau accepted his explanation and simply continued on with his own command. The Alabamians' departure weakened the pursuing force, and the Confederates left broken-down horses and men all along the road. Barteau, meanwhile, with Ham's, Smith's and Inge's troops, pushed northward, hoping for a chance to catch up with the withdrawing Federal column. What they would do if

6   Ibid., pt. 1, 535, 552; Bearss, *The Vicksburg Campaign*, vol. 2, 197.

they actually caught Hatch's Iowans remained to be seen, because each Confederate had only about ten rounds of ammunition.[7]

*   *   *

The main beneficiaries of the Confederate chaos were Hatch's Iowans, although Grierson also gleaned advantages from it. By the morning of April 22, Grierson was moving south toward Louisville with an extensive set of obstacles to surmount, but not a single hindrance was the result of Confederate defenders or pursuers, primarily because Hatch's bold diversion continued to attract Barteau's attention.[8]

Hatch's Iowans avoided major trouble throughout the afternoon of April 21 and by nightfall were falling back slowly to the northeast, fighting a careful rear-guard action designed to keep the enemy in pursuit. With Barteau's command at bay, Hatch camped for the night east of the formidable Tibbee Creek, not far from the Mobile and Ohio Railroad. It had been a hectic day and evening for the midwesterners, who at one point rode down a large watershed blocked by Confederates to find an alternate crossing point. Bonfires raged on each bank during the night as the soldiers crossed via a makeshift footbridge and the horses swam across. As one Iowan recalled, "Three or four troopers would seize each horse and throw him into the stream, when they would, by the aid of long poles, compel him to swim to the opposite bank." The men took apart the small cannon and used ropes to haul it across.[9]

Hatch continued his diversion the next morning, rousting his Iowans early on April 22 and moving toward the railroad. They soon found the Confederates were still in active pursuit, and the Union cavalrymen fended off the enemy in a series of minor skirmishes that stretched for miles. This time, however, it was not just Gholson's state troops and Barteau's regulars in pursuit but also "citizens in the country, armed with shot-guns and hunting rifles, firing constantly on our flanks."[10]

7   *OR* 24, pt. 1, 535-36.

8   Ibid., 523-24.

9   Pierce, *History of the Second Iowa Cavalry*, 51; Grabau, *Ninety-Eight Days*, 114; Company C, 2nd Iowa Cavalry, Muster Roll, RG 94, E 57, NARA.

10   *OR* 24, pt. 1, 530.

Hatch did his best to bob and weave his way through the danger while still endeavoring to confuse the enemy as to his intent and direction. "Before noon we had marched to all points of the compass," one Iowan declared, "baffling all attempts on the part of the enemy to keep track of us." The Federal column passed through numerous swamps, which the same Iowan declared "everywhere abounds" in central Mississippi, and came across slaves sent out by their owners to hide their horses and mules. By the time Hatch made a dash north for safety, he and his Iowans had gathered as many as 600 horses and mules and around 200 slaves.[11]

Even with the larger Confederate numbers nipping at his column from various directions, Hatch was able to make good time. He was careful not to outrun his pursuers and yet make sure he was far enough ahead to avoid having to wage a pitched fight a second time. If the Confederates discovered that his was not the only Union column in central Mississippi, they might well conclude Hatch was the lesser risk and pursue Grierson. Consequently, Hatch had to make as much fuss as possible, and he reasoned Okolona was as good a place as any to do so. Whatever fuss he intended, however, would be limited, because Hatch's Iowans had only about 21 rounds of ammunition per man themselves.[12]

Around 4:00 p.m. on April 22, the 2nd Iowa Cavalry rode into Okolona, a small town along the Mobile and Ohio Railroad almost midway between West Point and Tupelo. They easily dispersed the few Confederate defenders there, even though some regular cavalry was mixed in with the state troops. Once it was safe to do so, the men went to work destroying the railroad and anything else they could find of military value. A large barracks complex that could house as many as 5,000 men was torched, and a large stash of supplies and ammunition that Hatch's men could not take with them destroyed. Some of the destruction included "about three hundred shot-guns and rifles, mostly Enfield."[13]

11 Ibid., 531; Pierce, *History of the Second Iowa Cavalry*, 52; "The Enemy in Starkville," *Jackson Daily Mississippian*, April 21, 1863; Joe Rollins, "Ex-Slave Autobiography," in West Point, Mississippi, Miscellaneous Papers, Mississippi State University.

12 *OR* 24, pt. 1, 531; Pierce, *History of the Second Iowa Cavalry*, 52; "The Enemy in Starkville," *Jackson Daily Mississippian*, April 21, 1863.

13 *OR* 24, pt. 1, 530-31.

Hatch knew he could not remain in Okolona overnight, for the railroad offered the Confederates a quick means of concentrating against him. With the sun dipping toward the western horizon and the shadows growing longer by the minute, Hatch rode his troopers northwest and camped about five miles outside town. He needed to get away from the railroad, but he still needed to play his role as bait lest his pursuers abandon him and go after bigger game.[14]

The Iowans had covered 20 to 25 miles in their ride north toward Tennessee on April 22 and continued on toward Tupelo on April 23. The longer they lingered along the railroad, however, the greater the danger. Hatch gained information that Confederates from General Chalmers's command in northwestern Mississippi were moving to cut him off. That made sense because the various Union raids sent out of Memphis and La Grange to keep Chalmers occupied were over (unbeknownst to Hatch, Gen. Sooy Smith's and Col. George Bryant's commands had returned to the Memphis vicinity by April 23), and the men and horses were back in their respective camps. Chalmers was free to focus his attention elsewhere, but contrary to Hatch's intelligence, he had not yet moved east to intercept the Iowans.[15]

Hatch, however, was not in a position to risk Chalmers striking him in front and Barteau (and perhaps other Confederates) in the rear. He destroyed the bridges over the formidable Chiwapa Creek between Okolona and Tupelo to keep the pursuing enemy at bay and moved to Tupelo, where his tired Iowans made camp.[16]

As Hatch was dodging his pursuing Confederates while making his way north to Tennessee along the Mobile and Ohio Railroad, Grierson's main body was quickly and quietly moving south. If Hatch regretted playing the role of bait while Grierson continued with the main raid, he said nothing about it to his Iowans. As far as he knew, the overall plan was still operational and working. If the number of Confederates converging on him was any indication, there should be few left to go after Grierson.

*   *   *

14 Ibid., 530.

15 Ibid., 530, 554.

16 Ibid., 530.

While Hatch was luring Confederates northward, Grierson was entering the final phase of his approach to the Southern Railroad of Mississippi. He was 70 miles north of Newton Station when his Illinoisans awoke on April 22. They were almost within striking distance, and the fact that they had made it this far with little to no opposition was nearly miraculous. If Grierson's fortune held, he would reach the railroad and surely surprise whatever enemy he found there. Now was the time to push hard. Perhaps he could make longer, harder rides each day and cover the distance in as little as two days.[17]

Grierson had his men up early on April 22, ready to cross the various watercourses in the Noxubee River bottom on his way to the rail line. Heavy rainfall the night before, however, had swelled the creeks almost to capacity and turned the roads and byways through the swampy terrain into ribbons of mud. The brigade followed the main road through Webster, but the sticky ground and deep water were difficult to traverse. A portion of the column tried to bypass this danger by detouring through Whitefield (present-day Sturgis). The valley was "a dense, overflowed swamp," recalled Adjutant Woodward. "No road was discernable, and the column was simply following the 'blazing' on the trees." Grierson agreed, noting he and his men rode "for miles belly-deep in water." Ammunition was lifted from artillery limbers and distributed to the men to carry above the water. At times, the Illinoisans had no choice but to swim their horses across flooded waterways. After one was crossed, however, another appeared in the distance. The route mandated the crossing of six major streams in addition to numerous swollen tributaries. The Noxubee River channel curved just east of Louisville, forcing the Illinois troopers to cross it twice during their approach to the high ground upon which the town was situated. Their introduction to Winston County, Mississippi, was wet, cold, and miserable.[18]

A fortunate opportunity greeted the exhausted column struggling across the soaked valley, recalled Woodward, when "a young doctor of the neighborhood appeared." Although it took some convincing because he was afraid his neighbors would accuse him of assisting the enemy, the Federals finally convinced him to act as a guide. The local "guided the

17 Ibid., 523-24.

18 Ibid., 523-24; Woodward, "Grierson's Raid," 692; Surby, *Grierson Raids*, 34; Daniel E. Robbins to Brother, May 7, 1863.

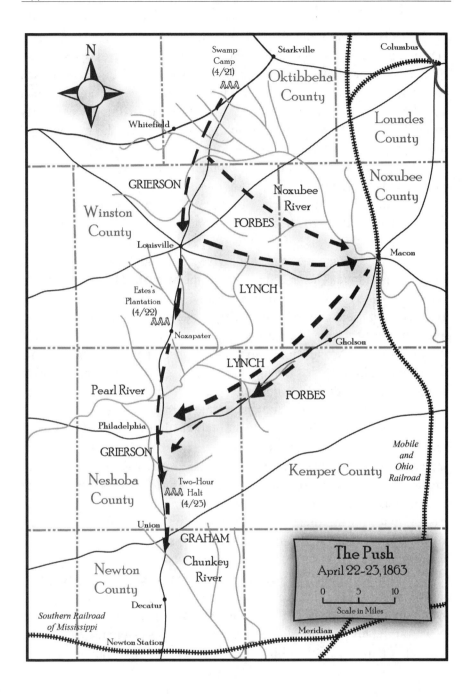

N

Swamp
Camp
(4/21)

Starkville

Columbus

Oktibbeha
County

Whitefield

Loundes
County

GRIERSON

Noxubee
River

Noxubee
County

Winston
County

FORBES

Louisville

Macon

Estes's
Plantation
(4/22)

LYNCH

Noxapater

Gholson

LYNCH

Pearl River

FORBES

Philadelphia

GRIERSON

Mobile
and
Ohio
Railroad

Neshoba
County

Two-Hour
Halt
(4/23)

Kemper County

Union

GRAHAM

Newton
County

Chunkey
River

The Push
April 22–23, 1863

Decatur

0   5   10

Scale in Miles

*Southern Railroad
of Mississippi*

Meridian

Newton Station

column around the heads of some deep sloughs and ravines, into which it would have otherwise marched blindly, and probably have drowned men and horses," admitted the adjutant. Fortunately for everyone involved, the column broke through to higher and drier ground before anyone discovered the doctor helping them. He was sent on his way with a better horse, although it later dawned on Woodward that "the original owner of the mount" might one day find his horse in the doctor's possession and accuse him of theft.[19]

It had been a slow start to a very long couple of days—exactly what Grierson had been hoping to avoid. There was nothing to do about it, however, except to slog onward. It was clear the raiders were still well ahead of any news. The few civilians encountered moving through this area of northern Winston County knew nothing of their pending arrival, and they were surprised when hundreds of Union horsemen suddenly appeared this deep in Mississippi. "The inhabitants through this part of the country generally did not know of our coming," wrote a relieved Grierson, "and could not believe us to be anything but Confederates."[20]

The same phenomenon occurred when the tired troopers finally reached the high ground and approached Louisville. Because of the difficult trek across the river bottoms and the fact that Louisville was nearly 30 miles south of Starkville, it was nearly dark by the time the Illinoisans approached the town. If any of the troopers thought they might rest in Louisville, as they had at other towns, they were sorely disappointed. Grierson intended to keep on moving.[21]

To better facilitate the move through Louisville, Grierson sent ahead a battalion of the 6th Illinois Cavalry under Maj. Matthew Starr "to picket the town and remain until the column had passed." Starr's troopers performed as ordered, although word broke out in Louisville of the pending Federal arrival just minutes before Grierson and his men thundered into the place. "Many had left," observed the brigade commander, "taking only what they could hurriedly move."[22]

---

19 Woodward, "Grierson's Raid," 693-94.

20 *OR* 24, pt. 1, 524.

21 Ibid., 523-24.

22 Ibid., 524.

Matthew Starr. Major Matthew Starr of the 6th Illinois Cavalry was a solid officer who often led detachments on the raid. *Randy Beck*

"The column moved quietly through the town without halting," Grierson reported, "and not a thing was disturbed." Civilians who had stayed put "acknowledged that they were surprised," he continued. "They had expected to be robbed, outraged, and have their houses burned. On the contrary, they were protected in their persons and property." The destruction of personal property was not uncommon in the Civil War, and the practice would become more destructive as the war dragged on. Yet Grierson had made it clear that destroying personal property was against his wishes. Besides, he had other, more important things on his mind than sacking an insignificant Mississippi village.[23]

None of Louisville's civilians knew any of this. Years later a young girl penned her vivid recollections of the day the Yankees came to town. "Louisville had one wide street, with stores and public buildings on either side," she wrote, "and my home was on a side street just off of Main Street, with a road separating it from the Old Masonic Building surrounded by a large oak grove." Many people buried their silver and valuables. "This time my people," she continued, "accompanied by several other families, fled to a small place we owned about a mile from town and off the main road. I still remember how branches of trees were

23 Ibid.

piled over the road after we passed to show no trace of another road. We carried food."[24]

Some Louisville residents resisted any way they could. According to one account, a Union cavalryman, perhaps one of Surby's scouts, demanded the keys to a smokehouse in which Sara Jane Johnston, whose husband was in the Confederate army, had hidden her fine horse. She refused. When the trooper came to take it by force, the brave woman stood in the doorway and wielded a butcher knife until the Federal left without either ham or horse. Another citizen hid his food and horses except for one "old blind mule named Pompey, which was so feeble the men did not want it." Trickery also helped. At the Corley homestead, two fine gray mules had wallowed so long in the mud that they looked haggard. The children yelled to the approaching soldiers that they were simply "broken down stock." The soldiers let them be and passed by.[25]

Other notable Louisville natives fled quickly. William Bolling, one of Winston County's pair of delegates to the secession convention two years earlier, had been extremely vocal about his support for the Confederacy and his intent to fight the enemy. "His voice was heard on nearly all occasions," one county history read, "rallying the patriotic and chivalrous sons of Winston County, to arms. He proclaimed with vehement asseverations that he would be with them in their marches and drink all the blood that was spilt and pay for all the powder that was burnt." Bolling had his opportunity to live up to his words when Grierson's troopers arrived. Instead of bravado, however, he was among the first to flee, "hid[ing] himself among the rocks in the mountains of Alabama." The town doctor, Dr. J. B. Covington, made his getaway in a rather macabre fashion. With a trusty slave in tow, he escaped to an old cemetery outside town, where the slave lifted "one of the box tombs while he crawled in and stayed there until the soldiers passed through Louisville."[26]

24 "The Day the Yankees Came to Town: 1863," *Winston County Journal*, May 1, 2014.

25 Jennie Newson Hoffman, "A History of Winston County Volume 1," in Federal Writer's Project: Works Progress Administration, 1938, Winston County Public Library, 146-47.

26 Ibid., 83, 159; William T. Lewis, *The Centennial History of Winston County, Mississippi* (Pasadena, TX: Globe Publishers, 1972), 107-9; Josie Worthy Holman, in

All the effort and fear went for naught as the Federals simply moved through the town without stopping. While the residents wondered what was happening, Major Starr's battalion of the 6th Illinois Cavalry continued guarding the town until the lengthy column passed through. Once out of town and riding south, Grierson relieved the 6th Illinois provosts with a similar battalion from the 7th Illinois under Major Graham, whose duty it was to remain in town about one hour to keep any citizens from moving south to alert anyone in advance of the Federal column and to make sure no enemy followed. A pursuing enemy from Louisville was unlikely, because Grierson had not seen any Confederates since leaving New Albany. Still, there was much at stake and he was a careful soldier. Graham's orders were to "remain until we should have been gone an hour, to prevent persons leaving with information of the course we were taking, to drive out stragglers, preserve order, and quiet the fears of the people." Once Graham's Illinoisans finished their task, they rejoined their comrades as they continued their ride toward the Southern Railroad of Mississippi.[27]

The same civilian confusion witnessed at Louisville repeated itself as the column advanced farther south. The muddy terrain also played to Grierson's advantage by covering their blue uniforms so thoroughly it was difficult for anyone to recognize them as Federal cavalry. (Grierson was also careful to keep their colors encased most of the time.) After passing through the swamps around Louisville "and reaching the rolling country beyond," recalled Grierson, "the troops were taken for Van Dorn's rebel cavalry and complimented on their appearance."[28]

The confusion was at least partially understandable. The people in this portion of Mississippi never imagined a heavy Union column of cavalry could have ridden this deeply into the state. Even when the blue uniforms were recognizable, many locals assumed they were Confederates wearing captured Union clothing. A good example of how the mind plays such tricks occurred while clattering past a schoolhouse. The teacher allowed the pupils outside to watch the procession. According to Grierson, "They flocked to the roadside, hurrahing for Beauregard, Van Dorn, and the

---

Accounts, Civil War in Winston County Vertical File, Winston County Public Library, 5; Hoffman, "A History of Winston County Volume 1," 150.

27 *OR* 24, pt. 1, 524.

28 Grierson, *A Just and Righteous Cause,* 156.

Confederacy. One little girl thought she recognized one of the men and, running up, asked him how John was, and if her uncle was along with the soldiers." On another occasion, ladies picked roses and presented them to the passing soldiers. As one Illinois man admitted, "We enjoyed ourselves very much at the expense of the deluded citizens."[29]

When the column stopped at a mill to procure grain for the horses, "the old miller grumbled loudly" when told the soldiers would be taking the grain. The fact that he would receive a receipt did not help soothe his disgust. This particular miller, who had been on the short end of Confederate receipts before, knew they were essentially worthless. "Yes, I've met your sort before," he chastised Grierson. "You always say you'll pay and you give receipts, but they ain't worth a damn. I wish the Yankees would come along and clean you out. They might give a fellow something. But you," he continued angrily, "you eat up everything in the country without keeping them out. . . . Yes, I know you. You say you'll pay, but I never got a cent for what I gave you before. The yanks might as well have it as you." The old man was not finished. "Why don't you go after Grierson instead of hanging around here?" he asked. By leaving "the impression that we were Confederates," Grierson noted, "we readily gained much valuable information, besides misleading the enemy into many contradictory reports as to our force and movements." According to Woodward, "The men were instructed that in their intercourse with citizens they should convey the idea that we were Confederates en route to Vicksburg."[30]

Leaving the humorous exchange behind them, Grierson and his troopers continued through the darkness. Unfortunately, wrote a rider, the head of the column struck what he thought was "another swamp." In reality they had come up against Tallahaga Creek, a major tributary and part of the headwaters of the Pearl River system that began in the highlands southeast of Louisville, flowed southwest toward the state capital at Jackson, and then on to the Gulf of Mexico. The Pearl River ran between Louisville and Philadelphia, and Grierson's column would have to cross it and other major tributaries. It would be hard enough to do so in daylight, but Grierson did not have the luxury of waiting hours

29 Ibid.; Surby, *Grierson Raids*, 33, 35.

30 Woodward, "Grierson's Raid," 691; Grierson, *A Just and Righteous Cause,* 156.

for the sun to rise. Instead, he plunged ahead into the boggy land around Tallahaga Creek, where the Federals "lost several animals drowned, and the men narrowly escaped the same fate," Grierson reported. Another observer complained that "the marshes were swamp, and swamps were ponds. The roads, of which they were utterly ignorant, were like rivers, the water being in many places three or four feet in depth." Fortunately for Grierson's men, Surby's scouts directed them along the best route "unmarked by a beacon post or guide" and provided fresh horses captured along their journey. The fresh mounts were especially valuable because they allowed those troopers who had lost a mount in the bottomland to continue. One observer detailed the problems they faced there:

> On each side of the road were enormous trees, and the water was every where from three to four feet deep, with every few hundred yards a mire hole, in which frequently, for a few moments, man and horse were lost to view. The Seventh Illinois being in the rear found these holes impassable, from the action of the large body of cavalry which had preceded them, and they were compelled to leave drowned some twenty noble animals, whose strength was not equal to such an emergency. The men so dismounted removed their saddles, placed them on some other led beasts, and pushed onward cheerfully.

Grierson kept his exhausted men in the saddle until the column reached the Estes plantation just north of Noxapater. There and at the nearby Payne plantation, 10 miles south of Louisville, he finally called a halt and ordered his troopers to go into camp. It was about midnight. After riding at least 30 miles that day (and perhaps as many as 40), the Illinois troopers were tired and sore, and any chance of a respite was welcomed. Only Grierson knew their rest would be brief. He was rapidly approaching his major objective. Lingering in camp would not help them achieve it.[31]

Charner Estes and his son, W. E. W. Estes, were South Carolina natives. In 1857 the 50-year old Charner moved to Mississippi with his children and their families and purchased acreage north of Noxapater and southwest of Tallahaga Creek. By 1860 Charner's land was valued at $12,000 and he owned 15 slaves. His 30-year-old son owned 4. With

31 OR 24, pt. 1, 524; Grierson, *A Just and Righteous Cause,* 156; Abbott, "Heroic Deeds of Heroic Men," 276-77; Surby, *Grierson Raids,* 40; Partridge, "Grierson Raided Here 130 Years Ago"; "Details of Grierson's Great Raid," *Sacramento Daily Union,* June 10, 1863; "From New Orleans," n.d., in Thomas W. Lippincott Papers, ALPL.

many of the Estes men off to war, Charner and his wife remained behind to care for 2 of their grandchildren. Son W. E. W., who served in the 35th Mississippi Infantry, was severely wounded at Corinth in May 1862.[32]

The men dismounted at the small plantations and made sure their horses were well cared for before turning to themselves. The mixture of long rides, unreliable provisions, and potential enemy action was beginning to catch up with the troopers. As an Illinois man in Prince's 7th regiment recalled, "We traveled so much after night that we were so sleepy we could hardly keep our eyes open." The troopers had eaten only one meal that morning at breakfast, so the lack of quality food also affected them. "We some times would mix up dough & bake on boards & very often we would go to bed without supper," grumbled the same Illinoisan. "Twice I went two days without eating any thing except some sugar & raw sweet potatoes."[33]

Rest was what the men wanted and needed, but Grierson disappointed them by calling his troopers back into the saddle after just two or three hours since they had stopped. He wanted to get the column on the road by daybreak on April 23. After securing a carriage from Estes to carry one of the cannons whose carriage had broken down, Grierson and his saddle-sore troopers rode south once more, moving quickly to take advantage of whatever opportunities Hatch was giving them as his Iowans moved along the Mobile and Ohio Railroad some 85 miles to the north.[34]

* * *

Thus far, Grierson had been able to ride deep into Mississippi without having to cross any major rivers except the Tallahatchie, which he crossed easily, and then skirted the head of the Big Black River near Starkville. Ironically, the smaller rivers and streams were giving him the most trouble. Now, however, Grierson was coming up against a major river system, and there was no way to ride around it. If the crossing of one of its tributaries the previous night was any indication, the Pearl River and its deep and swampy tentacles posed a major problem. They were

---

32 1860 Winston County, Mississippi, Population and Slave Schedules; Bearss, *The Vicksburg Campaign*, vol. 2, 203; Louis Taunton and Nancy R. Parkes, *Winston County and Its People: A Collection of Family Histories* (Louisville, MS: Winston County Genealogical and Historical Society, 1980), 79-81.

33 Freyburger, *Letters to Ann*, 46.

34 Partridge, "Grierson Raided Here 130 Years Ago."

now entering bottomland, observed one trooper, and it was "considerably flooded with water, making progress slowly."[35]

Fortunately, Grierson knew a bridge spanned the river on the main road to Philadelphia, a route that jogged west to Pearl Valley. The brigade commander received a steady stream of reports from his scouts about the route and other information from captured Confederate mail. One mail coach taken near Louisville the day before contained, oddly enough, letters written mostly in French. Sergeant Major Augustus LeSeure of the 7th Illinois Cavalry, who was fluent in French, read them for whatever helpful information they might contain, but there was little in the missives of military interest. Unfortunately for the raiders, they had no way of knowing whether the critical bridge was still standing. If word of their presence preceded them, they feared the structure "would be destroyed by the citizens to prevent our crossing." Its destruction would force Grierson to make a difficult crossing of a major waterway. If their presence this deep into Mississippi was still a surprise, as it had been in Louisville, there was a chance the troopers could reach the bridge and cross without incident. Thus, the faster they rode, the better their chances of finding the span intact. Grierson urged his men on, the 7th Illinois Cavalry taking the advance. "We were all well aware of the necessity of gaining the bridge at all hazards, and no time was lost in reaching it," Grierson wrote. The bridge, he continued, "must be captured before it could be set on fire or destroyed, as its destruction would be fatal to our progress."[36]

Heavy rains had saturated the region over the past few days, and the "rushing of the turbulent flood" increased as the Federal troopers approached the river. When the water came into view that morning, it was obvious the river was at flood stage and flowing rapidly. The Pearl was "very high and unfordable," concluded Grierson. The Union commander dispatched scouts to collect information, and before long Surby came upon "an old gentleman" named George P. Woodward, who

---

35 Surby, *Grierson Raids*, 37.

36 *OR* 24, pt. 1, 524; Grierson, *A Just and Righteous Cause,* 156-57; Abbott, "Heroic Deeds of Heroic Men," 277; Woodward, "Grierson's Raid," 695; Surby, *Grierson Raids,* 36; Pearl Valley Location, Historic Neshoba County Maps, Neshoba County Public Library; Reece, *Report of the Adjutant General of the State of Illinois,* vol. 8, 54; Partridge, "Grierson Raided Here 130 Years Ago"; "The Great Cavalry Exploit of the Times," *New Orleans Era,* May 5, 1863.

confessed that a few locals, including his son, were planning to burn the bridge upon word of the enemy's arrival. Though genial and kind by nature, Surby could be harsh when necessary. The news convinced the scout that a different approach was needed, so he threatened to burn down the old man's house if he did not disband the group intent on destroying the bridge. "My object," explained Surby, "was to save life if possible, the bridge at all hazards." Woodward saw the wisdom in cooperating and convinced the defenders of the bridge to leave. The Union scouts moved ahead at a gallop, with Colonel Prince of the 7th Illinois Cavalry accompanying them and the balance of his troopers charging behind them. To everyone's delight, the bridge was intact and the few Southerners visible were fleeing as fast as they could get away. It was a close-run affair, because the men had already stripped a few planks off the structure and were preparing kindling to set fire to the bridge. The Federals were on them "so suddenly and unexpectedly that their well-laid plan was disconcerted, and they all fled without firing a shot or lighting the incendiary match," Grierson proudly reported. Several troopers dismounted and replaced the planks so the column could cross the river and its soggy valley. Grierson was overjoyed when he heard "the tread of the horses feet . . . as the command crossed to the south side of the swollen river." Everyone involved knew they had come within a hair's breadth of potential catastrophe. Just "a few minutes delay or hesitation would have cost us trouble, and that delay might have proved fatal to the success of the expedition," he confessed. As fate would have it, the Pearl was the last major obstacle standing between Grierson and the Southern Railroad of Mississippi.[37]

Grierson, to his wife's chagrin, was not a religious man, although others riding with him attributed their success to God. "Here the shielding Providence of God was manifested," exclaimed Colonel Prince, who agreed with Grierson on the importance of what had just been achieved when he added, "If the bridge had been destroyed it would have been fatal to the expedition." Another man described the crossing of the bridge even more pointedly. "Ten minutes later and all would have been

37 OR 24, pt. 1, 524; Grierson, A Just and Righteous Cause, 156-57; Woodward, "Grierson's Raid," 695-96; "Museum Memories," Neshoba Democrat, April 24, 2013; Surby, Grierson Raids, 38; Jenelle B. Yates and Theresa T. Ridout, Red Clay Hills of Neshoba: Since 1833: Roots—Reflections—Ramblings: The Early History of Neshoba County, Mississippi (Philadelphia, MS: Neshoba County Historical Society, 1992), 223.

lost. But for hours and days back minutes of grace had been, by God's care, accumulating for their rescue. It is a solemn thought, and one which those brave troops did not forget to hold in devout recognition," he continued, "that at any time in the whole course of their six days' marchings, haltings, and startings, a few minutes' tardiness on the part of a commander, a few moments' delay with a restive horse, a few minutes' lingering on a tedious ascent, would have brought them too late to the Pearl River bridge, and have made to all of them the difference between life and death." Although he never wrote about it, Rev. Capt. Jason Smith, the commander of the Illinois battery riding with Grierson, surely said a prayer of thanks.[38]

Securing the bridge over the Pearl River turned out to be much less trouble than Grierson had feared it might be. Riding through the town of Philadelphia just south of the river, however, proved more troublesome. "Our advance caught sight occasionally of a mounted rebel," confirmed Grierson, and the frequency of such sightings increased the closer the Federals came to town. "Finally," continued Grierson, "quite a number of mounted and dismounted men were observed stretched in line across the road, apparently in readiness to dispute our passage." The last thing he wanted was a pitched fight with what looked to be a Confederate force this far from the railroad, but it looked increasingly like he would have no choice. Grierson sent his scouts, along with several regular troopers, forward to test the enemy line. To his surprise and thanks, it dissolved after a few of the enemy fired a handful of wild shots. Riding hard and fast, the scouts captured six of the defenders and their horses. The men were not Confederate soldiers after all, but simply armed citizens of Philadelphia.[39]

The leader of the ragtag defenders was an older man who served as a Neshoba County judge, "under whose fatherly lead it seemed his citizen neighbors had armed for resistance," reported Grierson. "He was no doubt a very worthy man, and one who would naturally be looked to for advice in an emergency, but he was decidedly out of his element in command of those would-be soldiers." The "misguided" citizens of Philadelphia were "greatly agitated and alarmed" because they

---

38 "The Grierson Raid," *Weekly Register* (Canton, IL), September 7, 1863; Abbott, "Heroic Deeds of Heroic Men," 277.

39 Grierson, *A Just and Righteous Cause,* 157.

believed the Federals were going to either shoot or hang them. Grierson quieted their fears, "good-humoredly" explaining they were not there to tamper with civilians, only regular Confederate forces. When one Philadelphian asked if he was going to burn the town, Grierson peered at the dilapidated courthouse and other buildings, smiled, and sheepishly replied, "No Sir. My orders are not to leave the countryside better off." Additional conversation ensued, an informal parole administered, and the men were turned loose, "a wiser if not better lot of men." Surby recalled the odd scene of the Mississippians "standing in line with arms extended perpendicular, and Colonel Prince swearing them not to give any information for a certain length of time."[40]

Grierson bid his captives goodbye and moved through Philadelphia, where, he reported, "nothing was disturbed." There might have been good intelligence to be had or supplies in town waiting to be found, but the Federal leader did not have the time to question civilians or locate and destroy things of military value. He had to keep riding south. "We moved through Philadelphia about 3 p. m. without interruption," he reported. Concerned his column might be discovered and confronted with a credible enemy force, he kept Surby's scouts "well out in every direction with a view to prevent any information as to our whereabouts or movements reaching the enemy."[41]

Night was only a few hours off by the time the tail of the column exited the town. Grierson pushed on another five miles, angling southeast toward Meridian to give any watching Confederates the impression his objective lay in that direction. Once well away, he called a halt to feed his mounts and take stock of the situation. Usually the horses were fed when the column stopped to camp for the night, and where they had stopped was a logical place to camp. The regiments had already covered about 25 miles that day, but this night was different. When darkness arrived, observant troopers who were surprised with the order to stop earlier than usual to feed the mounts began to realize they would not make camp

---

40 Ibid.; Surby, *Grierson Raids*, 39; Steven H. Stubbs, *Neshoba at War: The Story of the Men and Women of Neshoba County in World War II* (Philadelphia: Dancing Rabbit Press, 2003), 10-11.

41 *OR* 24, pt. 1, 524; Grierson, *A Just and Righteous Cause,* 157-58.

at all that night. Grierson was only stopping to feed his horses and rest the men for a couple of hours before taking to the saddle once more.[42]

*   *   *

While Grierson continued south at a rapid pace, he took care to cover his flanks and confuse the enemy. Before arriving at Louisville, he had sent an entire company west toward the Mobile and Ohio Railroad at Macon, south of the West Point–Starkville–Columbus area and north of Meridian. It was the same area he had directed Colonel Hatch to ride toward with his Iowans, although he had no way of knowing Hatch had actually retreated northward. Perhaps Grierson intended to mass a large number of Federal raiders at the small Mississippi town as a further distraction for the Confederates. If Hatch had failed to reach the railroad near Macon, pushing a company in that direction offered another opportunity to damage the line. Grierson talked over the plan with his officers, all of whom agreed it was dangerous but necessary.[43]

According to one Federal, "The detachment to be thrown against this road was used as a forlorn hope, and was expected to be thrown away." Grierson's actions lend some credence to this claim because he asked for volunteers rather than select the men himself. A couple of scouts stepped forward, but they changed their minds once they had time to think about it. Grierson next asked Colonel Prince of the 7th Illinois Cavalry to "pick" the volunteers. The selection fell upon Capt. Henry C. Forbes's Company B when Prince "dropped back to what chanced to be for the day's march his rear Co." When the colonel asked the captain if he would undertake the dangerous journey, Forbes agreed—despite Prince's being unable to tell him much about what he would find or how to get back to the main column. Prince "could give him no intimation of the course the regiments would take, but that it seemed to him highly probable that after they had crossed the Vicksburg road they [Grierson's

---

42   *OR* 24, pt. 1, 524; Woodward, "Grierson's Raid," 696.

43   William D. Lyles to Daniel Ruggles, April 22, 1863, in John J. Pettus Correspondence, MDAH; *OR* 24, pt. 1, 528; Grierson, *A Just and Righteous Cause,* 164; Surby, *Grierson Raids*, 31.

Henry C. Forbes. As commander of Company B, 7th Illinois Cavalry, Captain Henry C. Forbes led his company on a raid within the raid, making a miraculous journey and escape. *University of Illinois*

column] would swing eastward into Alabama, and through it retreat northward to the Federal lines."[44]

Company B was a solid outfit. Under Forbes's leadership, the 30-plus troopers had become a brotherly unit. Forbes often acted as a father figure and even paid for supplies out of his own pocket. His younger brother, Stephen, was also a member of the company. One family member described the pair as "the one, a dashing, sagacious captain of thirty; the other, an impulsive, loyal corporal of nineteen." Ironically, the Forbes brothers also had a cousin who lived in Mississippi and fought for the Confederacy with the Jeff Davis Legion in Lee's Army of Northern Virginia.[45]

44 Forbes, "Grierson's Raid," 13-14; Abbott, "Heroic Deeds of Heroic Men," 274; "From New Orleans," n.d., Thomas W. Lippincott Papers, ALPL. For more on Henry C. Forbes and his poetry, see the Henry Clinton Forbes Collection, University of Arizona.

45 Forbes Edited Letters, 1863, in Stephen A. Forbes Papers, UI, 203; Brown, *Grierson's Raid*, 79-80; J. B. Forbes to S. A. Forbes, November 27, 1908, in Stephen

Stephen, the younger of the Forbes, was a good soldier with a poetic bent. In a letter home, he used colorful prose to describe the April weather. "The woods are green and the sun bright, the sky blue and the birds musical, the peach trees are covered with young fruit, the thunderstorms are getting quite fashionable, and everything bears evidence of the unmistakable presence of spring. Perhaps it seems a little strange to you," he added, "that we should think anything about pleasant weather, we, who have come down here to kill our fellows and carry distress to families, to dislocate the country and destroy life by wholesale." There was no glory in war, he confided to his sister. "If you only knew what a commonplace matter it was to be a soldier . . . we are not at all anxious for a battle . . . what a miserable dressing for a shattered bone or a gunshot wound glory makes! In short," he continued, "for all of the untold honor that is to descend unto our cherished names for unnumbered generations is we shed our blood for our country, it hurts like the deuce to be shot." Stephen went on to describe how he dreamed of "myself riding boldly over the hills and coming suddenly upon the enemy and blazing away at them with my revolver, when at least three men were to tumble down." He also dreamed of "blood running down from my left shoulder, never my right; when, after a few days of graceful bandaging, I would be alright and eager for another one, and have the honor of carrying rebel lead in my body to the grave."[46]

The dreamy youth at the beginning of the war was, by 1863, a grizzled veteran who knew better. Stephen had been captured in the 1862 fighting around Corinth and had spent four months in a Confederate prison before spending a similar stretch in a hospital. In an odd twist of fate, the enemy had shipped him south to a Confederate prison along the same railroad he was now riding toward on horseback, and he had stopped in the same town of Macon that was now the target of his detachment.[47]

Henry Forbes was older, wiser, and more down-to-earth than his artsy younger brother. The realist in him was soon on full display. Before he led his company away from the main column, Forbes pulled a few troopers of questionable health out of the ranks. He also asked that his

A. Forbes Papers, UI.

46   S. A. Forbes to Sister, April 13, 1863.

47   Roth, "Grierson's Raid," 18.

Stephen A. Forbes. The younger brother of
Captain Henry C. Forbes, Stephen A. Forbes
revisited places he knew well from his earlier stint as a prisoner of war in Mississippi.
University of Illinois

men detailed to ride and scout with Surby—William Buffington, Arthur
Wood, and Isaac Robinson—be returned so they could perform similar
duties for his own small column. It did not take long for some of the men
to wonder what they were getting into, or, as one would put it, whether
"this little band would ever rejoin their comrades, unless, indeed, in a
Confederate prison." Captain Forbes put it a different way, writing simply,
"A soldier accepts every challenge to duty." And so the 36 troopers of
Company B rode east with orders from Grierson to, "if possible take the
town, destroy the railroad and telegraph, and rejoin us."[48]

48   William D. Lyles to Daniel Ruggles, April 22, 1863; *OR* 24, pt. 1, 528; Grierson,
A Just and Righteous Cause, 164; Brown, *Grierson's Raid,* 80; Forbes, "Grierson's
Raid," 14; Forbes, "Grierson's Cavalry Raid," 105. See also Forbes, "An Adventure
of Co. B."

The small Federal company rode southeast and soon came upon one of the consequences of the raid into Mississippi. Behind and on either side of the main column was a mad rush of civilians desperately trying to move out of the reach of the roaming Federal cavalry. "We had not been long on our route before we were made ludicrously aware of the tremendous panic which the raid was causing in these parts," explained Captain Forbes. Much like a boat creating a wake through otherwise calm water, Grierson's raid had caused a wave of panic all along the route. Gossip and rumors inflated Federal numbers into the thousands, and the kind treatment meted out along the route evolved and spread into stories of harsh treatment. "The whole region was terrorized," observed Forbes. The Illinois troopers were shocked they had caused such an uproar, because so little alarm had been raised along the main route. After some effort, Company B reached the front of the human wave and overtook it, where, explained the captain, "We found ourselves in the midst of the left hand crest of the panic-stricken overflow from the main march, a stampede wh[ich], as we afterwards learned extended 20 to 30 miles in either direction. As our march cut through this crest diagonally," he continued, "near evening we got outside it and approached Macon."[49]

The key question facing Forbes was whether Macon had been alerted to their approach and then garrisoned. He questioned several local slaves but found them unreliable. "They were exceedingly gullible: they always preferred the biggest story," he explained, and "if the negro could divine what he thought his questioner would wish to hear, he would often say it, although he had to manufacture his statement out of whole cloth." Forbes called a halt at "Madame Augustus' plantation" a couple of miles outside Macon and sent scouts ahead to find out the truth. They returned a few hours later with a prisoner, John Bryson. Unfortunately, as Forbes explained it, Bryson "had that most difficult virtue to contend with, a nice sense of honor. He refused to give information." What happened next is unclear, but Forbes confirmed that "much diplomacy was finally rewarded" with news that a train was expected any minute with troops. The intelligence was supported by a report from the scouts who had heard locomotive whistles. A scout dressed in a Confederate uniform and sent into town returned with confirmation of the news. Forbes wisely

---

49 Forbes, "Grierson's Raid," 14-15.

decided to bypass Macon, which he considered "too large a prize to be captured by 36 men."[50]

Forbes may have failed in taking Macon, but he succeeded in other ways. Exaggerated rumors of his strength increased the value of his diversionary side raid, and the people who had gathered in Macon were not motivated to march out and stop them. "This is a good example of an instance in which the shadow is more important than the substance," Forbes concluded. Meanwhile, he continued, "We had accomplished what we were sent for: we kept all eyes on the Mobile and Ohio Road."[51]

Knowing he had nothing left to accomplish, Forbes released Bryson and gave him "a good horse and . . . a poor pistol," a gesture that prompted the Confederate to part "with many expressions of esteem. . . . He had seen the Yankee Devils at close range and they were not so black as common report had painted them." Forbes turned Company B around and rode back toward the main column.[52]

The troopers of Company B trotted through the night and the following day in an effort to link up with Grierson, passing through the small hamlets of Summerville, Gholson, Pleasant Springs, and Caffadelia in their effort to do so. At Summerville, the small column was taken by surprise when "an ovation from an entire female Seminary, whose lovely members had been temporarily released from their tasks to give us joyful greeting . . . fluttered their dainty kerchiefs and kissed their daintier finger tips to us." As the amazed troopers later learned, the scouts riding ahead of the column "had lied to them, making them suppose us a company of Alabamians in pursuit of the horrid Yankees." A military school for boys in Summerville repeated the mistake when the cadets stepped outside to cheer the passing riders. One overly excited youngster dressed in his uniform performed "a series of hand springs which he turned on the grass." The ruse was soon discovered, however, and the inhabitants realized the riders were Yankees. Once that knowledge sank in, the animated gymnast "strutted away rigid as an icicle," penned one eyewitness, "with the rankling consciousness nevermore to be

50 Ibid.,16; William D. Lyles to Daniel Ruggles, April 22, 1863; *OR* 24, pt. 1, 528; Grierson, *A Just and Righteous Cause,* 164; "The Yankee Raid," *Jackson Daily Mississippian, May* 2, 1863.

51 Forbes, "Grierson's Raid," 17.

52 Ibid.

dismissed, that . . . [he] had been turning somersaults of joy in honor of [the] invaders, who, as he slipped behind a hedge, were roaring with irrepressible laughter."[53]

A similar occurrence unfolded at Gholson, where a fine old gentleman offered everything he had to the supposed Confederates. The man "gloated over the thought that we had the courage to march toward those execrable Yankees whom report placed to the south and west of us in immense numbers," wrote Forbes, "and when we told him that if we could but overtake them we would go through them from end to end if we perished to a man, his ardor knew no bounds." As it had in Summerville, the realization that all was not as it appeared soon dawned on the residents of Gholson, and a proffered supper was enjoyed "with some lack of hospitality, [although] it was eaten with a relish that did not need that fine sauce." The Federals, wrote Forbes, left the old man "a sadder, a wiser and a madder man."[54]

Company B picked up Grierson's trail at Philadelphia, which the main column had ridden through 21 hours earlier. The troopers also came upon "a large number of horses tied near the old-fashioned hotel." Forbes ordered his men to surround the building and learned the citizens were forming a company to resist more enemy raids. "To a man and to a horse and to a shot-gun they were made prisoners," confirmed Forbes, who added that the Federals "sat down to their dinner which was just being spread as we appeared on the scene." He and his men also engaged in "some one-sided swapping of horses, but we left as good as we took, save that ours were less fresh."[55]

Matters took a more serious turn just south of Philadelphia, where the three scouts from the company who had not heard the bugle call to halt had ridden on and met up at a house with straggling Confederate soldiers. The suspicious Southerners accused the scouts of being spies. The accusation triggered an argument that escalated until shots rang out. Forbes's men heard the firing and set their spurs, but they were too late to affect the outcome. When they arrived at the scene, scout William Buffington was "dead on his back in the middle of the road"

---

53 Curtiss, diary, April 23, 1863; Forbes, "Grierson's Raid," 17-18.

54 Forbes, "Grierson's Raid," 18-19.

55 Forbes, "Grierson's Cavalry Raid," 110; Forbes, "Grierson's Raid," 19.

and a wounded Charles E. Martin and the third companion were found hiding nearby in the woods. "We left our dead soldier stretched on a Southern porch, under solemn promise from the householder that he would decently bury him," one Federal reported. The troopers of Company B rode away despondent, "not merely because we had lost a comrade," explained Stephen Forbes, "but because the men who had killed him were ahead of us and now knew who and what we were." The fear of an ambush was "in all our minds as we rode that day through the thickety woods, scanning every cover and watchful of every turn in the road."[56]

*   *   *

Grierson and the main column, meanwhile, had made decent time while Forbes and Company B sidetracked to Macon. The Federal commander remained concerned about Forbes's ability to reach the town and cut the Mobile and Ohio Railroad. When the main column passed through Louisville, Grierson decided to send yet another detachment east to Macon to sever the railroad or at least cut the telegraph lines running along it. As he later explained, he worried that Forbes "might not be able to reach the line of the railroad with so large a force." This time Grierson dispatched a pair of volunteers to make the trip: Capt. John Lynch of Company E, 6th Illinois Cavalry, and a trooper, Cpl. Jonathan W. Ballard. Lynch and Ballard dressed in civilian attire before splitting off from the main column, focused on cutting the telegraph wires "to prevent information of our presence from flying along the railroad to Jackson and other points." After a long ride Lynch and Ballard came up against the same obstacle Forbes's small command had encountered, namely, Confederate forces. The pair managed to make it to the outskirts of town where, Grierson later reported, they "ascertained the whole disposition of their forces and much other valuable information."[57]

Lynch kept a cool head when he ran into Confederates already agitated at the news of Forbes's approach from the north. The enemy was

---

56 Curtiss, diary, April 24, 1863; Forbes, "Grierson's Raid," 20; Forbes, "Grierson's Cavalry Raid," 110; Woodward, "Grierson's Raid," 705; "Museum Memories," *Neshoba Democrat*, April 24, 2013; Surby, *Grierson Raids*, 74; Zenas Applington to Wife, March 4, 1862, in John W. Clinton Papers, ALPL; William Buffington, Compiled Service Record, NARA.

57 *OR* 24, pt. 1, 528; Grierson, *A Just and Righteous Cause*, 155.

contemplating mounting infantry on mules to give chase. Rumors ran wild about Federal numbers, with one Confederate insisting Forbes's 36 men numbered closer to 4,000. After Lynch told the Southerners he had been sent from Enterprise to locate and scout the Federals, a talkative Confederate told him all about his own command around Macon and that the enemy was near the town, just to the north and within a couple of miles. The news was especially welcome because, as Grierson later observed, Lynch was "at once made aware of the movement of Captain Forbes's command." With that valuable information in hand, Lynch told the men that he had to ride back a couple of miles to get two men he had left at a plantation, and he would return with them to camp with the Confederate pickets that night. "The guards thought it alright and allowed him to depart," Grierson reported, adding, "Of course, they were not troubled by another visit from the captain, who made good his escape." Lynch and Ballard rode hard to rejoin the main column on the road to Newton Station. Incredibly, they covered nearly 200 miles in just two days.[58]

By this point Grierson had detachments riding in almost every direction across much of Mississippi. He had earlier sent a lone scout west to the Mississippi Central and Major Love's battalion back north. Colonel Hatch's regiment, meanwhile, was busy luring Confederates north toward Tupelo. Detachments under Captains Lynch and Forbes were moving east toward the Mobile and Ohio, and small numbers of troopers had been dispatched to gather horses and mules to remount troopers whose own animals had broken down during the unrelenting journey. Grierson and the main column, meanwhile, were still riding south.

In addition to the military aspects of the raid, the deep ride through Mississippi exposed the Illinoisans and Iowans to a heavy dose of Mississippi culture and society, including the institution of slavery. Every plantation along the state's meager interior road system allowed the Federals to set eyes on the practice held in such contempt by so many Northerners, including Republican Benjamin Grierson. A few slaves found the opportunity for freedom too powerful to resist and followed

58 William D. Lyles to Daniel Ruggles, April 25, 1863, and D. Lyles to John C. Pemberton, April 22, 1863, in John J. Pettus Correspondence, MDAH; John J. Pettus Correspondence, MDAH; Grierson, *A Just and Righteous Cause,* 158; Woodward, "Grierson's Raid," 695.

the column "of their own accord," recalled an Illinois trooper. Many of Grierson's troopers hailed from the Democrat-stronghold southern counties of Illinois, however, and may not have viewed slavery with the same critical eye Grierson did.[59]

Most of the slaves were fearful of the Federals because, like many of the white children in Mississippi, they had been told the "hated Yankees [were a] kind of beast, had horns, hooves and claws; were like the devil and would eat people up, would run the blacks off to Cuba and sell them, etc.," explained Grierson. Some believed the lies, but Grierson had the distinct idea that the slaves let their white masters try to scare them but believed very little of it. "Among themselves," he elaborated, "they imagined God was sending the Yankees, like angels, on purpose to make them free." The arrival of the God-sent angels, however, added another layer of complexity to their already difficult lives. The slaves were happy to see the Federal troops, but they could not openly express their joy for fear of repercussions from their white owners. Grierson noticed this fear and later wrote, "Not a word could be pumped out of them in the presence of their masters. But out of sight of the manor house, from under bushes or logs or fence corners or tall weeds or swamp grass, a wooly head and shambling figure would crawl slowly out, look carefully about, and then tell with grinning lips or point with dusky finger 'whar massa's horses done be hid,' or 'whar spec de secesh soldiers is.'" And, when it was safe to do so, they would also inquire, "When are you uns gwine to make we uns free?"[60]

* * *

Grierson was doing all he could to keep the enemy off balance by dispatching diversionary detachments, but the ultimate success of the raid depended on his main column. He had to keep moving toward his objective. Word spread among the companies stopped south of Philadelphia that Grierson intended to push on to the Southern Railroad of Mississippi, now only a little more than 20 miles to the south. Like he had the day before, Grierson sent troopers ahead to surprise any enemy at Newton Station while the remainder of the brigade approached the town behind

---

59 Surby, *Grierson Raids*, 32.

60 Grierson, *A Just and Righteous Cause,* 162.

them. At an officers' council, Lieutenant Colonel Blackburn of the 7th Illinois Cavalry offered to take the advance and Grierson agreed, sending him with two battalions to "capture the place and to inflict all the damage possible upon the enemy." Blackburn's command thundered down the road toward Decatur at 10:00 p.m. The 7th Illinois's remaining battalion, together with the 6th Illinois Cavalry and Smith's battery of small guns, rested an hour longer before mounting up and riding off around 11:00 p.m.[61]

For the second day in a row, Grierson refused to allow his men a full night of rest. The troopers had enjoyed only a few hours out of the saddle the night before at the Estes place, halting about midnight and marching once more about 5:00 a.m., with all the attendant duties of feeding and caring for the horses and themselves sandwiched into those five hours. This second night would be even more arduous, with even less time for rest and recuperation.[62]

Grierson had a couple of good reasons for pushing his men so hard. First, he was so close to the target of his raid that he could not take the chance of any word of his pending arrival reaching Newton Station before he and his men arrived. Grierson knew the Confederates could use the railroad and telegraph to concentrate more troops at Newton than he had in his entire command before the Federal column could cover the last 20 miles to the rail line. If he arrived and Newton Station was well defended, one of the main objectives of the dangerous campaign would go unfulfilled. Getting the entire column out of Mississippi safely at that late date would be doubly difficult.[63]

The second reason Grierson pressed so hard was that, if surprise could be achieved, he wanted to enter Newton at the best possible time of day, which was about daylight. The tactic of surprising your enemy around dawn had been around since the beginning of warfare. Johnston had attacked Grant at Shiloh under similar circumstances earlier in the war, and the Japanese would strike America at Pearl Harbor 78 years later in the same manner. Reaching Newton at daylight required an approach under the cover of darkness, with the first glow of dawn providing just

61 *OR* 24, pt. 1, 524; Grierson, *A Just and Righteous Cause,* 158; Surby, *Grierson Raids,* 40.

62 *OR* 24, pt. 1, 524.

63 Ibid., 524.

enough light to see where and how to attack. It would also catch many of the enemy sound asleep.[64]

Grierson and his men had ridden nearly 80 miles in just 48 hours—50 miles in the last 24 hours alone. These difficult miles included crossing three major waterways. It would be worth the effort if everything went according to plan. If Grierson could reach the railroad before the enemy concentrated there against him, he could inflict the significant damage and chaos he had been dispatched to achieve.

---

64 For Pearl Harbor, see Gordon W. Prange, Donald M. Goldstein, and Katherine V. Dillon, *At Dawn We Slept: The Untold Story of Pearl Harbor* (New York: Penguin, 1981).

CHAPTER SEVEN

The Attack

By April 1863 the overworked and undermaintained Southern Railroad of Mississippi was the most important rail line in the state. It was also one of the worst in the entire Confederacy. Since its official charter in 1857 and completion prior to the war, the railroad had experienced economic downturn and stagnation despite increased wartime business. The railroad could barely maintain its locomotives and track under the best of conditions, and the heavy demands of war only increased its burden. Frequent weather-related problems, including the heavy monsoon-like rains that had recently descended upon the area, completely shut down some sections of track.[1]

By the spring of 1863 the rail line was so unreliable it had become the butt of jokes. English traveler and wartime observer Arthur Fremantle, who would soon travel to the Eastern Theater and witness the climactic battle at Gettysburg, experienced it firsthand. The railroad is "in a most dangerous state, and enjoys the reputation of being the very worst of all the bad railroads in the South. It was completely worn out and could not be repaired. Accidents are of almost daily occurrence, and a nasty one had happened the day before." One such calamity took place that February, just a couple of months before Grierson's arrival, when a train derailed and tumbled into the Chunky River between Newton Station

---

1   "The Legislature," *Mississippi Free Trader,* January 22, 1861; "Damage to the Southern Road," *Vicksburg Evening Citizen,* January 17, 1861; Smith, *Mississippi in the Civil War,* 36. For more on the Southern Railroad and its rebuilding after the war, see Southern Rail Road Records, Auburn University.

and Meridian, killing a large number of its passengers. The *Jackson Daily Southern Crisis* engaged in some dark humor about the horrendous events when it asked, "Have you heard of the railroad accident[?]" to which another responded, "No—where was it?" The reply: "The Western Train left Meridian and arrived at Jackson in schedule time." Some found humor in using fatal train accidents to point out how unreliable the rail line had become. John Pemberton was not among them. The Southern Railroad was no laughing matter to the commander in Vicksburg. In fact, it was his lifeline.[2]

The Southern Railroad stretched 135 miles from Meridian in the east all the way to Vicksburg in the west on the Mississippi River. Most of the supplies required for Pemberton's army, as well as the troops at Jackson and Port Hudson, Louisiana, passed over this line, which was also a connecting link for states in the Trans-Mississippi Theater, including Arkansas, Missouri, and Texas. By April 24, 1863, the day Grierson's troopers descended on the Southern Railroad, it remained the one and only connection Vicksburg had to the rest of the Confederacy. Other regional rail lines feeding into the Southern Railroad helped keep the Mississippi River garrison supplied, but earlier Union campaigns had diminished their importance. The Mississippi Central, for example, ran out of west-central Tennessee south through Canton and on to Jackson, where it intersected with the Southern Railroad running west to Vicksburg. Likewise, the New Orleans, Jackson, and Great Northern ran north through eastern Louisiana to Jackson, hauling men and supplies up from that region. Unfortunately for the Confederacy, neither railroad extended to its natural terminus. The Mississippi Central's line was broken just south of Oxford, and not too much farther north the line ran into Union-held territory. As Grierson observed, the line only ran as far north as the damaged Yacona River bridges. The New Orleans, Jackson, and Great Northern ran into Union-held territory before it reached New Orleans.

---

2   Arthur J. L. Fremantle, *Three Months in the Southern States: April-June, 1863* (Edinburgh: W. Blackwood and Sons, 1863), 127; Ben Wynne, *Mississippi's Civil War: A Narrative History* (Macon, GA: Mercer University Press, 2006), 90-91; John K. Bettersworth, *Confederate Mississippi: The People and Policies of a Cotton State in Wartime* (Baton Rouge: Louisiana State University Press,1943), 142; John K. Bettersworth, ed., *Mississippi in the Confederacy: As They Saw It* (Baton Rouge: Louisiana State University Press, 1961), 263; Luther S. Baechtel, diary, May 7, 1863, in MDAH. For more on railroad accidents, see Bettersworth, ed., *Mississippi in the Confederacy*, 261-63.

This fact diminished the railroads' effectiveness and reduced the area from which the Confederacy could draw supplies and transport men.

This was not the case with the Southern Railroad, which ran due east to Confederate-held Meridian. The line connected there with the Mobile and Ohio Railroad, which Union forces had severed farther north, just below Corinth. The line was also broken in other places now that Colonel Hatch's Iowans were temporarily operating along its right of way. But it still ran all the way south to Mobile, Alabama. Large numbers of troops, goods, food stuffs, and ammunition could still reach Vicksburg by way of Mobile and Meridian along the Southern Railroad. And that made it especially vital to John Pemberton.

Striking and severing this major route of supply was the chief objective of Grierson's attack on April 24. His success would also divert attention away from Grant's crossing of the Mississippi River south of Vicksburg. Grierson had no way of knowing when or if that crossing would occur, but if he could move the last 20 miles to Newton Station, he could personally oversee at least one of his objectives: creating as much damage as possible to the railroad. That action would further cripple the Confederate complex of lines, decapitating it at all points of the compass around Jackson. Grant's larger plan to put Grierson in this position had worked to perfection.

*   *   *

By the early morning of April 24, Grant had moved south through Louisiana until he was below Vicksburg, and he established his headquarters at New Carthage. He was pushing General McClernand to cross his corps over the Mississippi River as soon as possible. Grant was also interested in the various diversions. By this time, both Bryant's and Smith's expeditions were back in the Memphis area. These operations had helped pin down Confederates west of Grierson's proposed route, leaving the raiders plenty of room to set off south relatively unopposed. Similarly, Grenville Dodge had moved east from Corinth and was now well into Alabama and approaching Tuscumbia, while Abel Streight's mule-mounted troopers were culling their sickly men and mounts in order to continue their expedition once Dodge completed his eastward trek. Grierson benefited from both.[3]

---

3   *OR* 24, pt. 1, 554; *OR* 23, pt. 1, 255, 287.

Perhaps the most influential and beneficial diversion for Grierson was the one still underway in Mississippi. While Grierson's men were preparing to close the handful of remaining miles to their objective, Colonel Hatch's 500 Iowans continued pulling the Confederates closest to Grierson northward. When dawn broke over his camp at Tupelo, Hatch pointed his regiment northwest in the direction of La Grange, Tennessee. He was worried General Chalmers's Confederates were lurking in the vicinity and might pounce on his vulnerable command. Hatch marched his Hawkeyes through Birmingham toward Molino, where he had earlier encountered the enemy during his ride southward. His plan was to cross the Tallahatchie River there. The waterway was the last major impediment to reaching Tennessee. This route also left Hatch with the alternative of peeling away toward Union-occupied Corinth if he ran into too much trouble trying to cross the Tallahatchie at Molino.[4]

Indeed, trouble found Hatch below the Tallahatchie River. "I was attacked in the rear by what I believe to be Chalmers' forces at 10:00 a.m.," he later reported. In fact, the enemy was not Chalmers but Colonel Barteau's persistent 2nd Tennessee Cavalry, which had ridden most of the night and caught up with Hatch even though the Iowans had burned several bridges in their wake. Hatch fought off the enemy troopers with Companies A and C while the rest of his men guarded prisoners and captured horses. According to Barteau, the fighting consumed more than two hours. Sensing success, Barteau pushed his Tennesseans forward as the Iowans fell back, "driving [them] in confusion across Camp Creek," where the Union troopers burned the bridge. Unbeknownst to Barteau, however, Hatch had not been driven back but had withdrawn. When his ammunition began to run low, he decided to make some mileage by executing another fighting retreat—a running duel between his regiment and his aggressive Tennessean pursuers. Hatch stopped "occasionally to repel their charges, concealing my men at all favorable points with the 2-pounder, which did excellent service." The excellent tactician "waited until the enemy was nearly on me, when I opened fire at short range, the enemy suffering terribly, with small loss to me. In this way the attack was kept up for 6 miles."[5]

---

4   *OR* 24, pt. 1, 531.

5   Ibid., 531, 536; *OR* 24, pt. 3, 237, 789-90; Pierce, *History of the Second Iowa Cavalry*, 54-56; Hancock, *Hancock's Diary*, 241; Company C, 2nd Iowa Cavalry,

Fortunately for the Federal cavalry, the Tennesseans finally had enough and broke off the chase and returned to their pre-raid camps. "The enemy were evidently tired, and, with the exception of annoyance from guerilla parties," explained Hatch, "we were not troubled by the enemy from that point." Hatch moved his Iowans on through Ripley, where Judge Davis noted in his diary that part of the Iowa command "passed through going north in a hurry." Hatch's column made it back to La Grange without further interference. Remarkably, Hatch lost only 10 men on his daring side raid. General Hurlbut had been right when he informed Grant that Hatch and his troopers "are not in yet, and may have some trouble, but Hatch will take care of himself and his men."[6]

The Iowans were immensely proud of their work. "We have just come off a 10 days scout," one crowed, "and we had a good hard time and found plenty of Rebs to keep us in exercise." He added that he and his comrades had been "down 150 miles inside their lines" and deplored the death of one man shot by a guerrilla within 20 miles of La Grange. Still, the Iowan confessed, "I think our Regt is the luckiest one in service."[7]

The Iowans had taken part in most of the major raid and pulled off the important and dangerous diversion Grierson had dropped in Hatch's lap. The daring ride convinced Confederate commanders, including General Pemberton in Jackson, that the Federal cavalry threat in north Mississippi had ended. State commander Samuel Gholson, for example, notified his superior, Governor John J. Pettus, that the "enemy that were here have been driven back." Although he had earlier called Pemberton to send him reinforcements, General Ruggles reported much the same as Gholson, beginning as early as April 23, when he observed that the enemy was "reported falling back before our cavalry." He elaborated on that message: "Reliable information has just been received that the enemy were passing Houston this morning, going toward Pontotoc."

Muster Roll, RG 94, E 57, NARA; Orlando Davis, diary, April 25, 1863, http://www.rootsweb.ancestry.com/~mscivilw/davis.htm.

6   *OR* 24, pt. 1, 531, 536; *OR* 24, pt. 3, 237, 789-90; Pierce, *History of the Second Iowa Cavalry*, 54-56; Hancock, *Hancock's Diary*, 241; Company C, 2nd Iowa Cavalry, Muster Roll, RG 94, E 57, NARA; Orlando Davis, diary, April 25, 1863, http://www.rootsweb.ancestry.com/~mscivilw/davis.htm.

7   John to Jennie, April 28, 1863, John Letter, in Filson Historical Society; Pierce, *History of the Second Iowa Cavalry*, 55.

Ruggles boasted, falsely as it turned out, "The force confronting me has been routed and driven back by my troops."[8]

The surge of Southern confidence sweeping through north Mississippi, however, was misplaced. Unbeknownst to anyone in the upper echelons of the Confederate leadership, the main enemy column had not turned around and skedaddled or been "driven back," as Ruggles claimed, but was riding hard to strike Newton Station and break the vital Southern Railroad of Mississippi.[9]

While these diversions played out in north Mississippi, the main raid—itself a diversion in a much larger scheme—was ready to spring like a coiled snake. Only 20 miles separated Grierson's troopers and the Southern Railroad at Newton Station. As far as he had come and with as much success as he had thus far managed, Grierson knew he had a real chance to surprise the enemy and inflict some major damage. And he intended to do just that on April 24.[10]

*   *   *

Lieutenant Colonel Blackburn and troopers from the 7th Illinois formed the first wave of Grierson's strike force. Blackburn had led his men south at 10:00 p.m. on the evening of April 23, riding through small Mississippi villages dotting the road leading to Newton Station. The Illinois cavalrymen rode through Neshoba Springs (east of the modern-day Neshoba community) and a town called Union. According to local lore, the Federals did not burn Union because they had told the civilians there that "Union" is exactly what they were fighting for. Next came the Newton County seat at Decatur, which was just 10 miles from the railroad. It was there that the first inkling of trouble presented itself when unsuspecting citizens reported to Surby and his scouts that Newton Station was well guarded and that Confederate cavalry had recently passed through. The fast-moving but now considerably more worried Illinoisans moved through Decatur just as the sun began to peek over the

8   *OR* 24, pt. 1, 543-44, 552-53; Grabau, *Ninety-Eight Days*, 119.

9   *OR* 24, pt. 1, 524.

10   Ibid.

horizon. Blackburn kept riding and approached the station about 6:00 a.m. If Newton was garrisoned, no one seemed to be expecting them.[11]

Grierson followed an hour behind Blackburn with the second wave, taking the same route with the rest of the 7th Illinois Cavalry and the entirety of the 6th Illinois Cavalry, along with Captain Smith's four small guns. The column was approaching Decatur with the sun breaking in the east when Captain Lynch and his lone trooper of Company E caught up with Grierson. The pair had finished their dangerous ride to Macon and back to cut the telegraph line. Their arrival astounded the brigade commander, because they had "ridden without interruption for two days and nights without a moment's rest." He added, "All honor to the gallant captain, whose intrepid coolness and daring characterizes him on every occasion." Despite the captain's gallantry and hard riding, there was no rest for the weary. Lynch and his comrade joined the column and continued riding on like everyone else toward the goal awaiting them to the south.[12]

The critical hour of the entire raid was upon them, and much of the responsibility for its success now fell onto the shoulders of the young and often impetuous Blackburn. Cutting the telegraph lines running out of the station might indicate to other operators there was trouble along the line, but if Blackburn could isolate Newton Station before word got out, the Confederates would not be able to send news about the Federal arrival any faster than a horse could gallop. Blackburn also had to disrupt Newton's transportation potential. A train with its steam up could slip away and spread the alarm to a nearby station, which could telegraph the news around the state. If that happened, the Confederates could use the railroad to quickly concentrate troops and trap Grierson's command.[13]

With Grierson about an hour behind him, Blackburn decided to scout the area around the town and sent Surby and a few horsemen to reconnoiter. The scout, who found "an elevated position, from whence

11 Ibid.; Woodward, "Grierson's Raid," 696; Neshoba Springs Location, Historic Neshoba County Maps, Neshoba County Public Library; George Smith, "A History of Union, Mississippi," n.d., 8; A. J. Brown, *History of Newton County from 1834 to 1894* (Jackson: Clarion Ledger Company, 1894), 115; Keith Justice et al., *Newton County and the Civil War* (n.p.: Eseff Press, 1995), 247-51; Daniel E. Robbins to Brother, May 7, 1863.

12 *OR* 24, pt. 1, 528.

13 Surby, *Grierson Raids*, 45-46.

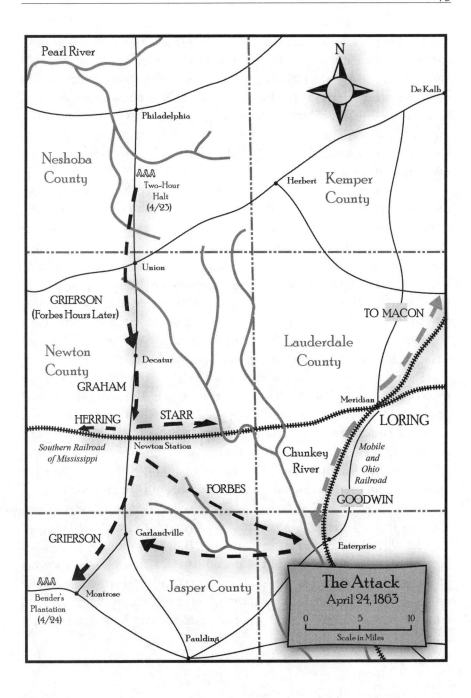

Pearl River

N

De Kalb

Philadelphia

Neshoba
County

⋀⋀⋀
Two-Hour
Halt
(4/23)

Herbert   Kemper
County

Union

GRIERSON
(Forbes Hours Later)

TO MACON

Newton
County
GRAHAM

Decatur

Lauderdale
County

Meridian

HERRING   STARR

LORING

Southern Railroad
of Mississippi

Newton Station

Chunkey
River

Mobile
and
Ohio
Railroad

FORBES

GOODWIN

GRIERSON

Garlandville

Enterprise

⋀⋀⋀
Bender's
Plantation
(4/24)

Montrose

Jasper County

The Attack
April 24, 1863

0   5   10

Scale in Miles

Paulding

I could obtain a pretty good view of the place," reported Surby, also rustled up two important facts from a resident: The town was not garrisoned, and a pair of trains, a freight train from the east and another from the west, were momentarily expected. The news spurred Surby to send word to Blackburn to hurry his men forward. Within minutes, the lieutenant colonel and his Illinois battalions thundered into town. Everything had worked perfectly. The last thing Newton was expecting was Grierson's men.[14]

After issuing orders not to sever the lines, Blackburn swept in and took possession of the telegraph office. Anticipating the arrival of the trains, he hid men at the switches so they could throw them after the trains arrived to prevent their escape. He "barely had time to do this and conceal his men and horses when a freight train of twenty-five cars came rolling in," a staff officer recorded. Several Federal troopers jumped into the cab and took the engineer and fireman prisoner, and the train was moved onto a sidetrack before the second train arrived. Blackburn gave this one the same treatment, also without incident, and ordered his men out into the open to begin their destructive work.[15]

The first captured train was loaded with railroad equipment, including crossties to repair the line. The second train was shorter than the first and carried passengers and military goods, including commissary and ordnance stores, "among the latter several thousand loaded shells." The troopers rounded up about 100 prisoners, most of them convalescing in a hospital. According to an Illinois cavalryman, the Southern men were "ready to join their regiments" when they fell into Union hands.[16]

Blackburn, marveled Grierson, had "succeeded in capturing two trains in less than half an hour after his arrival." By the time Grierson arrived with the balance of the brigade, Blackburn's men were hard at work destroying the cars. It sounded as if "a first-class battle was in progress," thought one Federal officer. With the main column now on hand in Newton, Grierson sent more men out along the rail line to widen the destruction. Other troopers fanned out and found a significant

---

14 Grierson, *A Just and Righteous Cause*, 158; Woodward, "Grierson's Raid," 696; Surby, *Grierson Raids*, 45-46.

15 Woodward, "Grierson's Raid," 697.

16 *OR* 24, pt. 1, 524; Grierson, *A Just and Righteous Cause*, 158; Daniel E. Robbins to Parents, May 5, 1863; Freyburger, *Letters to Ann*, 44.

amount of supplies in town, including "a large quantity of commissary and quartermaster's stores and about five hundred stand of arms."[17]

The haul of 2 locomotives, 40 cars, and commissary and ordnance stores was impressive. Grant had been begging in recent months for more locomotives for his department. Grierson, however, was too deep in Mississippi, and there was no way to get any of this valuable equipment into Union hands. Besides, his orders were to destroy and divert, not capture and confiscate. The brigade commander ordered everything his men could not carry away to be destroyed.[18]

The cavalrymen did their jobs well. Destroying the small arms and military supplies proved easy enough, but the larger railroad equipment was a different matter. Destroying a heavy locomotive beyond repair was extremely difficult, and simple tools were not enough to put them out of use for long. As a last resort, Grierson ordered his men to pack gunpowder around them. "The locomotives were exploded and otherwise rendered completely unserviceable," he stated. Mississippi newspapers, however, reported that the damage inflicted on the engines was negligible and that the Federals had run one of the locomotives off the tracks, where it overturned. To render the line temporarily inoperable, Grierson also had his men tear up the track at Newton Station and destroy a bridge half a mile farther west.[19]

Damaging the locomotives, burning supplies, and destroying a small bridge was a good start, but Grierson had bigger plans in mind. In addition to diverting attention away from Grant's crossing of the river, he wanted to inflict long-term damage to the rail line supplying Vicksburg. The Chunkey River just east of Newton Station flowed in a snakelike course from its headwaters around the town of Union. Both waves of cavalry crossed it that morning before reaching Newton. Because of the river's curvy path, the railroad crossed it three times in just three miles, once west and twice east of the little village of Chunkey. The concentration

17 *OR* 24, pt. 1, 524; Woodward, "Grierson's Raid," 698; Surby, *Grierson Raids*, 48; Daniel E. Robbins to Parents, May 5, 1863.

18 Simon, *PUSG*, vol. 6, 328.

19 *OR* 24, pt. 1, 524; Grierson, *A Just and Righteous Cause*, 158; "The Grierson Raid," *Weekly Register* (Canton, IL), September 7, 1863 ; "The Great Federal Raid," *Natchez Daily Courier,* May 5, 1863.

Newton Station. The tangible goal of the raid was to break the Southern Railroad of Mississippi at Newton Station. This photo shows the modern station on the site of the one Grierson's men destroyed. *Author*

of these large bridges in one small area offered a perfect opportunity to inflict the sort of damage Grierson hoped to achieve.[20]

The Federal brigade commander sent a battalion of the 6th Illinois Cavalry under Maj. Mathew H. Starr to strike the 150-foot-long bridges to the east and a similar body west under Capt. Joseph R. Herring of Company K of the 7th Illinois Cavalry. Once the destruction was complete, reported Colonel Prince, the troopers had "burned the bridges for six miles." The simultaneous cutting of telegraph lines involved a bit more trickery. The saboteurs sought out sections of the line encumbered by brush and cut it there, tying the ends together with leather straps. The action broke the line, but made it exceedingly difficult for repair parties to find the breaks and fix them.[21]

Grierson, meanwhile, kept a watchful eye on the level of destruction. Some private structures in Confederate service were destroyed, such as a storehouse owned by James McGrath, the first postmaster in Newton Station and a Unionist who had already fled town. According to the county history, Grierson's men "did not destroy any private residences, or any private property." Grierson treated civilians well, hoping to garner their support or at least keep them silent for as long as possible. One Mississippi newspaper declared that the raiders took "surgical instruments," which were of military value, but also noted that Grierson stopped other looting. "The safe at the railroad depot was also broken open and the funds abstracted. The money was returned, however, by order of the commanding officer, with the exception of fifteen hundred dollars that it was claimed some of the men had stolen." The paper went on to note, "We can hear of but little outrage having been committed upon the persons of non-combatants or their property except by the seizure of every good horse, and of necessary forage and provisions. They had to depend on the country entirely for these."[22]

---

20 *OR* 24, pt. 3, 197.

21 "The Grierson Raid," *Weekly Register* (Canton, IL), September 7, 1863; Forbes, "Grierson's Cavalry Raid," 106; Woodward, "Grierson's Raid," 698; Surby, *Grierson Raids*, 48.

22 Nancy Catherine Williams, *The History of Newton, Mississippi 1860-1988* (Newton: Newton Record, 1989), 3; Brown, *History of Newton County*, 338; "The Great Federal Raid," *Natchez Daily Courier*, May 5, 1863.

Other cases of lenient treatment emerged. The eastbound train included a passenger car and a couple of boxcars stuffed with private items belonging to civilians fleeing Vicksburg. Once Grierson's men attacked the train and the civilians onboard realized what was happening, they threw their valuables out the windows on the opposite side, hoping they could return later to retrieve them. Once the escapees fell into Union hands, they begged Grierson not to harm or rob them. After the brigade commander calmly explained that he and his men were "not making war upon private citizens or unnecessarily destroying their property," the rattled civilians realized they would not be robbed and were "much chagrined at their own actions." One Union soldier helped a Southern man find a wallet stuffed with $6,000.[23]

Once the Federals had damaged Newton Station's military facilities as thoroughly as they were able, their brigade commander concluded it was time to pull up stakes and get as far away from the place as possible. Grierson knew he could not keep word of his arrival or his day's work secret for long, and that meant every available Confederate soldier would soon be after him. Major Starr and his Illinoisans, however, were still engaged in their bridge-destroying duties at Chunkey and had yet to rejoin the column. Thus, Grierson decided to move several miles in an effort to put some distance between his men and any pursuing Confederates and yet remain within supporting distance of Starr's column. It would also allow him to take some time to feed his bone-tired men and horses who had been enduring lengthy rides (Grierson called them "forced marches") for several days, in addition to their destructive work.[24]

Almost as quickly as the Federals had swept down upon the unsuspecting railroad town, buglers sounded rally and the troopers were gone, riding away, as Daniel Robbins of the 7th Illinois Cavalry described it, "to the music of secesh shells bursting in a yankee bonfire." With their main objective behind them, surely some of Grierson's troopers wondered where in the world they were going next. To their surprise, the head of the column was moving south.[25]

---

23 Woodward, "Grierson's Raid," 697-98.

24 *OR* 24, pt. 1, 524; Surby, *Grierson Raids*, 49; Daniel E. Robbins to Brother, May 7, 1863.

25 *OR* 24, pt. 1, 524; Surby, *Grierson Raids*, 49; Daniel E. Robbins to Brother, May 7, 1863.

*   *   *

The destructive work inflicted upon Newton Station on April 24 accomplished the dual goal of diversion and destruction in just a few hours. For the past week Grierson had ridden south as stealthily as possible, doing as little as he could to call attention to himself. When necessary, he had used detachments to confuse the enemy and achieve other smaller goals. Once he reached the Southern Railroad of Mississippi and Newton Station, however, all bets were off. His destruction of the railroad, cars, locomotives, telegraph, and bridges sent a shock wave through the region and alerted the Confederate high command as to precisely where he was. Now that his work was done, Grierson had to escape his vulnerable position deep behind enemy lines. In order to accomplish that, he would have to disappear once again.[26]

Fortunately for the Federal raiders, the Confederate leaders assumed he would turn north and retrace his steps back to Tennessee by following the same way he had entered the state. The smaller detachments, as well as Hatch's Iowans, had done exactly that. Likely, many of Grierson's troopers thought the same thing. In truth, Grierson had yet to make up his mind on the route he would take to escape what would soon be a closing enemy trap. "Having damaged as much as possible the railroad and telegraph, and destroyed all Government property in the vicinity of Newton," Grierson wrote, "I moved about four miles south of the road and fed men and horses. The forced marches which I was compelled to make in order to reach this point successfully, necessarily very much fatigued and exhausted my command, and rest and food were absolutely necessary for its safety."[27]

There was little time to rest. "From captured mails and information obtained by my scouts," explained the Federal commander, "I knew that large forces had been sent out to intercept our return." The time to make one of the major decisions of the campaign had arrived: Which way should he go? General Hurlbut had counseled riding east and then north to return through Alabama. General Smith, however, left the escape route to Grierson. His last orders to the raider were to "move in any direction from this point which, in my judgment, would be best for the

26 *OR* 24, pt. 1, 524-25.

27 Ibid., 524; Grierson, *A Just and Righteous Cause*, 159.

safety of my command and the success of the expedition." Grierson was in a much better position to determine the best route of escape than any general hundreds of miles away.[28]

Grierson had several options from which to choose. He could follow Hurlbut's advice and move east by northeast in a large circle through Alabama or he could keep his column moving south toward Union-held territory, his most likely objective being Baton Rouge, Louisiana. A third possibility, and one that would give him additional chances to damage the state's infrastructure, was to move west toward Grant's anticipated crossing point of the Mississippi River. At no time, however, did he give serious consideration to returning north along the same route he used to get to Newton Station.[29]

Each choice posed a unique set of problems. Circling through Alabama would entice numerous Confederate commands into action against him, including Nathan Bedford Forrest, whose cavalry was even then chasing Abel Streight's mule-mounted raiders across the northwestern part of the state. Moving south to Baton Rouge was similarly risky. It was a much longer route, and Confederates in and around Port Hudson might take the opportunity to move against him. Riding west toward Grant was perhaps the most dangerous choice of all. There were far more Confederates in the Vicksburg and Jackson areas than anywhere else in the state, so the decision to make for the Mississippi River meant riding into the enemy's strength. Meeting up with Grant's army as quickly as possible was an absolute priority, but there was always the chance that Grant might not cross the Mississippi River at all or that his crossing might be delayed for unforeseen reasons.[30]

Grierson decided to take some time to decide on his proper course of action. His men and horses were tired, and several small detachments were operating apart from the main body, most notably Starr's battalion against the Chunkey River bridges. When Starr and his men returned, they arrived armed with invigorating news. According to the major, he had "destroyed most effectually three bridges and several hundred feet

---

28 *OR* 24, pt. 1, 525.

29 Ibid.

30 Ibid.

of trestle-work, and the telegraph from 8 to 10 miles east of Newton Station."[31]

Grierson spent the next three hours pondering his choices before finally deciding to move south, keeping his options open as to whether he would turn west to connect with Grant or move on to Baton Rouge. Circling through Alabama seemed too difficult, but Grierson did not completely close off that option. If he met too much resistance in the south, he could always turn back east and then north. Accordingly, late on the afternoon of April 24, he put his regiments on the road south toward Garlandville while hinting to the Confederates that he might be heading east.[32]

If Grierson did not expect to meet substantial opposition from the Confederates that day, he was right. If he did not expect to meet any resistance at all, he was greatly mistaken.

*   *   *

The troopers passed throngs of civilians on the road leading south from Newton Station. "We overtook quite a number of citizens who were fleeing from the Yankees," was how Grierson put it, "having with them only such things as they most valued, fearing that they would be robbed." He took special care to assure these people that they would not be harmed and told them to "return to their homes; that they would not be molested. Nothing whatever was taken from them," he pointed out. "Of course, they were greatly astonished at such kind treatment when they had been led to believe that they would be mistreated, insulted, beaten, and even murdered on sight by the so-called villainous Yankees."[33]

Despite the good treatment meted out to the civilians along the route, Garlandville's residents had either not heard of the kind treatment or simply did not believe it. The town was eight miles below Newton, recalled Adjutant Woodward, "a pretty, quiet village, in the midst of a beautiful country." To Grierson's amazement, the citizens were waiting for the Union cavalrymen. Woodward described the scratch force as "old, grey-haired men, beyond the age for conscription." Word of Grierson's attack

31 Ibid.

32 Ibid.

33 Grierson, *A Just and Righteous Cause*, 159.

against Newton had spread, and the townspeople, true citizen-soldiers, were ready to defend their beloved village.[34]

"We found the citizens, many of them venerable with age, armed with shot-guns and organized to resist our approach," reported Grierson. In a bid to test their mettle, he sent an advance group into town and quickly learned they meant business. The Mississippians opened fire on the cautiously advancing troopers, wounding one Illinoisan and a horse. That was enough to convince Grierson they were serious about defending their town with lethal force, but they were still nothing more than armed citizens. He ordered his men to charge, and the Illinois troopers bolted down the main road. As Grierson suspected, the defense evaporated. "We charged upon them and captured several," he confirmed.[35]

In a display of mercy, the Federal brigade commander disarmed them and "showed them the folly of their actions, and, released them." Woodward remembered that the "only house subjected to search was the post office." Many Confederates thought the enemy would burn and pillage the place, with one slave going so far as to beg the soldiers from atop a porch not to burn "Mars Bonner's" house. When it became obvious to the citizens of Garlandville the raiders intended them no harm, "without an exception they acknowledged their mistake, and declared that they had been grossly deceived as to our real character." One resident even volunteered to act as a guide to help extricate the isolated Union brigade from the fix into which it had voluntarily ridden.[36]

The surprising episode at Garlandville would replay itself elsewhere in a phenomenon that was growing in this section of the state. At this point in the war, Mississippi was no longer the bastion of Confederate patriotism it had once been. If the heart of the resistance to the Southern Confederacy was in middle and southern Mississippi (which included Jones County, known as the Free State of Jones), it was no longer confined to that lone county. The Free State of Jones and its supposed secession gets most of the attention, but the movement was taking place farther north

34 Woodward, "Grierson's Raid," 698-99.

35 *OR* 24, pt. 1, 525; "The Great Federal Raid," *Natchez Daily Courier*, May 5, 1863.

36 *OR* 24, pt. 1, 525; Grierson, *A Just and Righteous Cause*, 159; Woodward, "Grierson's Raid," 699-700; Jean Strickland and Patrician N. Edwards, *Records of Jasper Co. Mississippi: W.P.A. Source Materials, Will Abstracts 1855-1914* (n.p.: n.p., 1995), 42.

in the delta region as well as to the south along the Pearl River. It was also evident in the area Grierson was now entering. Exhaustion with the war effort and its accompanying change of heart became evident when, after learning the riders were Federals, a group of women retrieved a hidden United States flag. According to trooper Richard W. Surby, the women "soon displayed to us a good sized flag, representing that good old flag for which we were fighting."[37]

Newton Station was in southern Newton County, so Grierson had crossed into Jasper County by the time he reached Garlandville. Jones County was below Jasper, and Confederate disloyalty had seeped its way northward, as it had to the surrounding counties, such as Smith County just to the west. Grierson later explained that the Union raid through these counties unleashed a groundswell of support that was otherwise lurking just beneath the surface. "Hundreds who are sulking and hiding out to avoid conscription," he explained, "only await the presence of our arms to sustain them, when they will rise up and declare their principles; and thousands who have been deceived, upon the vindication of our cause would ultimately return to loyalty." As it turned out, Grierson's prediction would come true.[38]

Of course, not everyone was a Union sympathizer or had turned their back on the Confederacy. One family near Garlandville wanted nothing to do with the Federals and was perhaps frightened by rumors of destruction and pillage. Grierson's adjutant, Samuel Woodward, came across a "pretty little house almost hidden by foliage," with the lamps burning brightly. When no one replied to his knocks, he entered and found "supper on the table, the corn bread actually steaming hot from the stove, and everything else correspondingly fresh." Woodward called for the owners, but no one appeared, and his quick search failed to turn up anyone. The adjutant knew a good thing when he saw it and called for his commander "to observe the condition of affairs." Grierson agreed with Woodward that there was no use in wasting such delicacies. "Having a very decided relish for such savory food," Grierson remembered, "we

---

37 Surby, *Grierson Raids*, 55-56; Smith, *Mississippi in the Confederacy*, 125-42. For a modern account of Jones County, see Victoria E. Bynum, *The Free State of Jones: Mississippi's Longest Civil War* (Chapel Hill: University of North Carolina Press, 2001).

38 *OR* 24, pt. 1, 525.

could not resist the temptation and sat down to the table and ate the supper at our ease." Perhaps feeling a little guilty, he added, "We never learned for whom it was prepared." Grierson and Woodward left a note "on the table, expressing thanks for the hospitality."[39]

Grierson took only as long as was required in Garlandville and moved on only "after such delay as was deemed advisable." The colonel pointed his troopers west and continued his trek, knowing he would soon have to make camp. April 24 had been yet another exhausting day. The adrenaline-fueled raiders had achieved a major part of the raid's goal by damaging the railroad at Newton Station, but now they needed rest. Grierson rode his men another 10 miles through the small hamlet of Montrose and to a plantation a couple miles farther west.[40]

Griffin M. Bender's plantation ran along Tallahala Creek, and it was there the tired Illinoisans finally unsaddled, took care of their mounts, and rested. One Illinois trooper recalled that it was 11:00 p.m. before they made camp, "and for the first time in forty hours did we take off our saddles from our weary horses." Fortunately, the plantation provided everything the raiders needed. Bender, a 69-year-old native of Georgia, was one of the richest men in the area. The 1860 census estimated the value of his real estate at $93,700 and his personal net worth at $172,800. A large portion of his wealth was tied up in his 41 slaves, which was a large number in this section of Mississippi. One county newspaper, the *Paulding Clarion*, reported that the Illinoisans "took all Mr. Bender's mules and two of his Negroes, and consumed a large amount of his corn and meat." The paper also reported some Federal compassion, noting that Colonel Prince signed a receipt "for three thousand rations of meat and forage."[41]

What they did not get was Bender's gold. The owner watched from his house as the Federals arrived, holding in his hands a bag of gold. When he realized they were going to not only invade his plantation but his house as well, he tossed the bag out the window to a slave, who

---

39 Woodward, "Grierson's Raid," 701; Grierson, *A Just and Righteous Cause*, 160.

40 *OR* 24, pt. 1, 525; Grierson, *A Just and Righteous Cause*, 160.

41 Surby, *Grierson Raids*, 53; *OR* 24, pt. 1, 525; Forbes, "Grierson's Cavalry Raid," 127; 1860 Jasper County, Mississippi, Population and Slave Schedules.

dashed away with it. Once Grierson's men left, the slave returned with the gold, safe and sound.[42]

* * *

There was no corresponding rest for the Confederates, who by this time were abuzz with activity at the alarming news filtering out of Newton Station. Something had to be done to stop the invaders, but the Confederates were slow to respond. Unbeknownst to Grierson, he had penetrated another hollow Confederate defense shield, behind which there was nothing available to prevent further rampages. Grant had discovered as much earlier in the war when the Federals broke through at Forts Henry and Donelson. Once those barriers fell, there were few Confederate forces in place to keep Grant's army from moving all the way down into the cotton states of Mississippi and Alabama. Similarly, Grierson had found that the Confederate defensive veneer in northern Mississippi was thin to the point of worthlessness. He was able to push rapidly through it and on south while most Confederate assets in northern Mississippi chased Hatch's Iowans. The result was an undisputed path straight to the Southern Railroad of Mississippi at Newton Station.[43]

Despite the critical importance of that railroad, the Confederate high command failed to allocate many resources to defend it. Most of the few Confederate units operating in the area were infantry, which was all but useless against a cavalry raid, unless the troopers attacked a garrisoned post. Most of the Confederate defensive effort was on the western flank along the Mississippi River, not the interior of the state, which appeared safe from Union arms. Because of the obvious threat looming from Grant's semiconcentrated army in Louisiana opposite Vicksburg, however, Pemberton had little choice but to keep the bulk of his forces in that area. In fact, four of the five divisions that would eventually join Pemberton to defend Vicksburg manned the Mississippi River line or its extension along the Yazoo River. Divisions under John H. Forney and Martin L. Smith held the northern extremities along the Yazoo River at

---

42 J. M. Kennedy, *History of Jasper County* (Bay Springs, MS: Bay Springs Municipal Library, 1957), 23.

43 York, *Fiction as Fact*, 19; Mary S. Robinson, *A Household Story of the American Conflict: The Great Battle Year* (New York: N. Tibbals & Son, 1871), 52.

Haynes' Bluff and Chickasaw Bayou, which was where Sherman would soon make a feint in a further attempt at operational diversion. Carter Stevenson's large division held the Vicksburg and Warrenton areas, and John S. Bowen's smaller division defended the Mississippi River line south to Grand Gulf. This westward orientation illustrates where Pemberton believed the biggest threat to Vicksburg rested. His bet, however, left much of the rest of Mississippi an empty shell.[44]

With four Confederate divisions watching the Mississippi River line, only one division was available for use elsewhere. The division that would eventually become Maj. Gen. William W. Loring's was strung out along the Southern Railroad of Mississippi at Jackson and Meridian, though not in any major strength at Newton Station. Loring, an experienced soldier who had lost an arm in the war with Mexico, made his headquarters at Meridian. A portion of his force there, including a brigade under Brig. Gen. Abraham Buford, defended the important area north and south of the city, with some elements now as far north as Macon. To the east at Jackson was Brig. Gen. John Adams with several Mississippi regiments. Brigadier General Lloyd Tilghman's brigade, farther north along the Mississippi Central at Canton, had recently played a heavy role in repelling the Yazoo Pass expedition and Frederick Steele's Greenville incursion. The result was that most of the available cavalry was operating with the bulk of the army along the Mississippi River or in northern Mississippi.[45]

As a result, when a heavy force of Union raiders suddenly appeared deep within the state, confusion spread and the Confederate response was understandably slow. "The reports of the enemy's operations are very conflicting," admitted General Loring. The slow pace at which Loring's infantry could react vexed the officer. The best way to utilize their strength was to move them quickly by rail to where they could perform worthwhile service. And the Confederates did just that, shipping infantry units on the Mobile and Ohio Railroad to defend the critical bridges south of Meridian.[46]

The wires went dead early on the morning of April 24, and it was not until well into that day that the Confederates were able to

44 Grabau, *Ninety-Eight Days*, 120.

45 William W. Loring to John C. Pemberton, April 23, 1863, in John J. Pettus Correspondence, MDAH; *OR* 24, pt. 3, 786.

46 William W. Loring to John C. Pemberton, April 23, 1863.

construct a reasonable guess as to what the Union raiders were up to. After sifting through conflicting reports, Pemberton began sending troops toward the obvious crisis area. Most of the reinforcements were infantry, because as he freely admitted, "I have no cavalry of importance to operate against the Newton Station party." He told Governor Pettus the same thing, emphasizing that he had a "very inadequate force of cavalry in this department to successfully repel the heavy raids of the enemy now in operation." Pemberton called on Pettus to form citizens into military units to defend local towns and to supply horses to mount a credible pursuit. "I have the honor to call upon you to exercise the right vested in you by the Legislature of Mississippi," urged Pemberton, "and to seize or impress the requisite number of animals." Doing, so, however, would take time, and that was something Pemberton did not have. Hoping Pettus would act quickly, he shifted what little cavalry he had by ordering James Chalmers to ride his troopers east toward Okolona from northwestern Mississippi, "to intercept force of enemy now at Newton, on Southern Road." Chalmers acknowledged his orders, reported a new Federal threat in his area, and requested permission to leave one regiment in place "until my stores are removed."[47]

For Newton, Pemberton had nothing but infantry to send. A brigade under John Adams at Jackson began the journey late on April 24, but logistical roadblocks hampered the effort. Delayed by the need to issue rations, Adams managed to lead the small 420-man 26th Mississippi from Jackson, along with seven companies of the 373-man 15th Mississippi westward by train around 4:00 p.m. He stopped them at Lake Station, where Pemberton erroneously informed Adams the Union raiders "have certainly been." Adams waited there for the other three companies of the 15th Mississippi (111 men) and the Point Coupee Louisiana Artillery battery of six guns, which were on the way on a later train.[48]

Closer to the scene of action, Adams discovered what he could and relayed the information to Pemberton. The brigadier detected Confederate movement on the far side of Newton Station, which seemed to indicate that General Loring at Meridian was aware of the developments and

47 John C. Pemberton to John J. Pettus, April 25, 1863, and J. H. Campbell to John J. Pettus, May 12, 1863, in John J. Pettus Correspondence, MDAH; *OR* 24, pt. 1, 546; pt. 3, 781-83, 786-87, 789.

48 *OR* 24, pt. 1, 546; pt. 3, 781-83, 786-87, 789.

responding accordingly. Just what Grierson's raiders were up to, however, remained a mystery. Adams learned several waves of Federals had been through Newton, one as recent as 2:00 a.m. on April 25. He estimated the strength of Forbes's Union column at 500, when in reality it was closer to 35. The fact that Grierson had ridden south and Forbes east only added to the brigadier general's confusion.[49]

Adams spent a nervous night at Lake Station. He thought he heard firing off to the east, but most of it was a figment of his imagination. He tried opening a line of communication with Loring at Meridian and even sent a train there, but nothing could get through. Adams also attempted to keep Pemberton advised of his actions by telegraph, but even that proved problematic. At one point the Jackson operator wired Pemberton, "Did you get a dispatch from General Adams, dated 3 o'clock this morning? The courier being absent (delivering a message) at the time of its reception, I left it by his bedside with lighted candle near it." When civilians in the area informed Adams that no enemy had been spotted around Meridian, he moved his infantry toward Morton Station.[50]

Other commanders were also moving troops. Lloyd Tilghman at Canton shifted the 54th Alabama and a pair of artillery pieces east, although that left his position at Canton vulnerable. Winfield S. Featherston and others at Fort Pemberton, near Greenwood on the Yazoo River, were ordered to move east to Grenada to cover the Mississippi Central line. While Tilghman and Featherston shored up the western front, the major activity about to unfold occurred well to the east and south around Meridian. There, brigade commander Abraham Buford informed Pemberton that nothing had happened. "I can hold this place," he added. "Nothing lost or destroyed on the Mobile road." As had other commanders, Buford confirmed that he could not take the offensive without cavalry.[51]

Although Meridian was safe, the next major station down the line was not. Captain Forbes and his small company from the 7th Illinois

---

49 Forbes, "Grierson's Raid," 20; *OR* 24, pt. 1, 531; Forbes, "Grierson's Cavalry Raid," 110. The force riding through Newton early on April 25 was Captain Forbes's Company B, 7th Illinois Cavalry, trying to catch up to Grierson's column.

50 *OR* 24, pt. 1, 532; pt. 3, 785, 789. Henry Forbes related that as he passed through Newton, "The public ruins . . . were still smoking."

51 *OR* 24, pt. 1, 538, 544, 553; pt. 3, 782, 789; Timothy B. Smith, *James Z. George: Mississippi Great Commoner* (Jackson: University Press of Mississippi, 2012), 65-66.

Cavalry had ridden from Macon along Grierson's track. Forbes crossed the railroad at Newton Station after Grierson's Illinoisans had left—the move that resulted in Adams reporting waves of Federals moving through the area. From Newton, Forbes continued southeast, trying to learn anything he could about Grierson's whereabouts. He knew Grierson had ridden south to Garlandville and hoped he would turn east as Colonel Prince had indicated. Thus, Forbes moved directly east to "cut off a large part of their loop [whereby] we could save the day's march which they were in advance." His decision moved his three-dozen riders toward Enterprise, south of Meridian. In actuality, as Grierson later wrote, Forbes "was thrown off at Newton Station by the very success with which he had fooled the rebels. He had to go through swamps, [cross] swollen streams, [and] travel through timber, often regardless of roads, for hours at a time in order to avoid forces that were patrolling the country in quest of the Yankees."[52]

Forbes stopped his company within five miles of Enterprise at the home of a Dr. Hodges. Although the doctor was absent, his daughters were not. The Hodges women failed to appreciate the demand for food or that, as one Mississippi newspaper reported, "the rose bushes and flower beds of the young ladies were . . . sadly despoiled by the unwelcome visitors." All things considered, the Hodge property and occupants got off easy, as the paper admitted: "Beyond this, our informant says they did not damage, nor did they insult the ladies."[53]

Once at Enterprise, Forbes boldly approached the place and, as Grierson later related, "found instead of myself and command, 3,000 rebels." The heavily outnumbered Forbes kept his head. "Quick as thought," Grierson continued, Forbes raised a handkerchief, borrowed from a nearby laundry line, on his sword and rode toward a stockade. Even though at least one Confederate fired a round in their direction, Forbes and his lieutenant continued. Three Confederates appeared with a handkerchief of their own tied on a ramrod and bellowed, "To what are we indebted for the honor of this visit?" Forbes boldly replied, "We came from Maj. Gen. Grierson to demand the surrender of Enterprise." Forbes later observed, "It is unnecessary to remark that Grierson was

---

52 OR 24, pt. 1, 528, 538, 544; Grierson, *A Just and Righteous Cause*, 164; Forbes, "Grierson's Raid," 20.

53 "The Great Federal Raid," *Natchez Daily Courier,* May 5, 1863.

promoted from Col. on the spot." When Grierson learned of Forbes's claim, he acknowledged proudly, "My name was a host on that occasion." The real "host," however, was on the Confederate side of the lines.[54]

When Loring received word via telegraph that the Federals were approaching Enterprise, he responded decisively by moving two regiments (the 7th Kentucky and 12th Louisiana) to the area to reinforce Col. Edward Goodwin and his 35th Alabama. The Alabamians, one remembered, "beat him [Forbes] there, and, leaping instantly from the train, we double-quicked down a dirt road to a bridge near the town." By that time, Loring reported, the Alabamians had "defied them [Forbes]" by sending back a note asking for an hour to consider the surrender. Forbes continued his bold bit of trickery by asking to whom he should address his note. "Col. Goodwin commanding Post," replied a Confederate. The response informed Forbes that Enterprise was garrisoned and that Goodwin was buying time to get his men and perhaps reinforcements in line for defense. Forbes, who knew he was outnumbered, promised to carry the Confederate message back to "Gen. Grierson" and return with an answer. With that, the captain turned his mount and, once out of hearing range, ordered his men, "Attention Company! By twos right; column right; march; trot; gallop march!" Grierson, who had nothing but praise for Forbes's bold effort to gain an hour's head start, could not help but wonder "whether he was pursued, or how long the rebel colonel with his 3,000 men waited for the expected reply or to consider the proposition." Colonel Prince pondered much the same thing, adding, "It is not known whether Enterprise surrendered or not." One Alabamian described Forbes's actions as a "rascally trick on him."[55]

Once out of immediate harm's way, Forbes turned his troopers west and moved quickly to rejoin Grierson's command, having now "lost,

54 Forbes, "Grierson's Raid," 21; *OR* 24, pt. 1, 528, 538, 544; pt. 3, 781; Grierson, *A Just and Righteous Cause*, 164-65; "The Grierson Raid," *Weekly Register* (Canton, IL), September 7, 1863; Fred L. Hatch to S. A. Forbes, December 1, 1908, in Stephen A. Forbes Papers, UI; Henry Elsey, "The Grierson Raid," n.d., in Stephen A. Forbes Papers, UI.

55 *OR* 24, pt. 1, 528, 538, 544; pt. 3, 781; Grierson, *A Just and Righteous Cause*, 164-65; "The Grierson Raid," *Weekly Register* (Canton, IL), September 7, 1863; Forbes, "Grierson's Raid," 21-22; Elsey, "The Grierson Raid"; Forbes, "Grierson's Cavalry Raid," 111-12, 128; Albert Theodore Goodloe, *Confederate Echoes: A Voice from the South in the Days of Secession and the Southern Confederacy* (Nashville: Publishing House of the M.E. Church, South, 1907), 148-50.

by this attempt to shorten our ride, much more than we had gained the preceding day." The Confederates attempted but failed to catch up to the Illinois company. "I have no hope of catching them on foot," Loring admitted to Pemberton. An Alabamian agreed, writing the effort was "a very tiresome expedition in which we were engaged."[56]

In the ensuing hours, with Federals popping up on several points of the compass, Loring took firm command of the situation on his side of Newton Station. The Southern general telegraphed Mobile, Alabama, to send troops north to hold the key bridges, and he dispatched some of Buford's troops to do the same along the critical Southern Railroad. Loring also tried to box Grierson in by destroying bridges farther south between Meridian and Paulding. Thinking the Federal raiders would probably return north by way of Newton, he also called on Pemberton to send cavalry east from Jackson to tighten the noose. "If they get there in time," Loring explained to Pemberton, "and you can send force to intercept them at Newton, it will force them to go in the direction of Baton Rouge. Please order cavalry to intercept them in that direction."[57]

As the hours passed, Loring acquired good intelligence about Grierson's whereabouts. "When last heard from," the Federals were at Garlandville on April 25, reported Loring, and then later at Montrose and even Westville farther west. All indications were "they will attempt to cross the road at Newton, or some point between Meridian and Jackson." Loring promised to do what he could "to prevent their doing so this side of Newton." By this time Grierson had moved west, and Loring informed Pemberton that he "thought they would go that way, striking for Baton Rouge, as we have blocked their return by the way they came." Eventually, Loring was only able to mount some 150 men to pursue Grierson, but it was much too little and far too late. A Confederate brought up from Mobile with his regiment summed up the inability to do much of anything worthwhile:

---

56 OR 24, pt. 1, 528, 538, 544; pt. 3, 781; Grierson, *A Just and Righteous Cause*, 164-65; "The Grierson Raid," *Weekly Register* (Canton, IL), September 7, 1863; Forbes, "Grierson's Raid," 21-22; Elsey, "The Grierson Raid"; Forbes, "Grierson's Cavalry Raid," 111-12, 128; Goodloe, *Confederate Echoes*, 148-50.

57 OR 24, pt. 1, 544.

"For ten days we rushed up and down the roads of Mississippi, ordered around by telegraph, and saw the Yankees but once."[58]

*   *   *

In the state capital at Jackson, meanwhile, a group of high government executives and citizens, presided over by Governor Pettus, met "to devise the best means for repelling the present daring raid of the enemy." Lieutenant Colonel Edward Fontaine, Mississippi's chief of ordnance, offered resolutions for mounting infantry, moving troops quickly, and assigning less-pressing positions to citizens to free up soldiers for more important tasks. The resolutions passed. "I am afraid that the action upon them will be so slow that the Yankees will escape with impunity," Fontaine admitted. "I wish that I could this day be in Genl. Pemberton's place, & have the power to give orders instead of *advice*." The *Jackson Mississippian* took a sarcastic swipe at the ineffective Confederate efforts by observing, "We hope . . . Grierson . . . will not take off the wires of the telegraph as he proceeds—for, as it seems he can't be caught or headed off, we feel some curiosity to be regularly informed of his whereabouts."[59]

John Pemberton was also busy, sending a flurry of messages in several directions in an effort to garner some help to stop Grierson. Like the rail lines themselves, the telegraph wires running through Meridian and beyond ran through Newton Station. Breaking the line there isolated Pemberton, cutting him off from theater commander Joseph E. Johnston and his superiors in Richmond. Pemberton ordered General Adams to move east in an effort to reestablish contact with Loring in Meridian and through him other commanders in order to get word to Johnston at Tullahoma of the debacle unfolding inside Mississippi. The message that made it through to Johnston noted that Pemberton was "sorely pressed on all sides, and urges you to send at once 2,000 cavalry to fall on rear of enemy."[60]

---

58 Ibid., 544-45; Henry Ewell Hord, "Her Little Flag," *Confederate Veteran* (October 1915), vol. 23, no. 10, 474.

59 Bettersworth, *Mississippi in the Confederacy*, 112-14. For Edward Fontaine's diary, see Edward Fontaine Papers, MSU.

60 *OR* 24, pt. 1, 532, 553.

Pemberton hoped also that word would reach Maj. Gen. Simon Bolivar Buckner at Mobile to send more troops north. When Adams notified Buckner, "All is lost unless you can send a regiment or two to Meridian," Pemberton scolded the brigadier, telling him, "I never authorized you to use such an expression." Word reached Loring to move west from Meridian to block the route of the enemy, a course the one-armed general was already pursuing. Pemberton also sent a message south to Maj. Gen. Franklin Gardner at Port Hudson that Grierson had hit Newton Station and "It is possible they are making their way to join [Nathaniel] Banks." The news would have interested Gardner on several levels, especially since Banks was the Union commander trying to capture Port Hudson. Pemberton wanted Gardner to send cavalry east and shift infantry to a position near Tangipahoa, Louisiana, to block Grierson's advance in that direction.[61]

The strike against Newton Station and the Southern Railroad of Mississippi had changed everything. Pemberton's focus had shifted from one of casual interest in Grierson's activity, as evidenced by the paltry number of prior messages, to a sudden realization of its importance and a nearly obsessive preoccupation with pinpointing and capturing the Federal raiders. Thomas Lippincott, an observant Federal trooper, later wrote about how Grant benefited from Grierson's raid. "Thus, already so early in our progress the plans of Grant for the disposal of his enemy's forces had been so perfectly fulfilled, that all dangers of these numerous brigades being sent to confront him was removed," he explained. "Had his own adjutant written these various orders for Pemberton's troops they could not have been more perfectly in accordance with Grant's plans." The job of diverting Pemberton's attention away from Grant and the Mississippi River to Grierson in the interior of the state was complete. The Confederate command played right into Grant's hands, who was now in position and poised to strike across the Mississippi River while Pemberton and his lieutenants were looking in the opposite direction.[62]

61 OR 24, pt. 1, 532, 553; pt. 3, 781, 783-87, 791.

62 OR 24, pt. 1, 532, 553; pt. 3, 781, 783-87, 791; Larry J. Daniel, "Bruinsburg: Missed Opportunity or Postwar Rhetoric?" Civil War History (September 1986), vol. 32, no. 3, 259; "From Mobile and Ohio Railroad," Jackson Daily Mississippian, April 28, 1863; "Grierson's Big Raid," n.d., in Thomas W. Lippincott Papers, ALPL.

In some regard, Pemberton's scattered reaction is understandable. Multiple reports were flooding his desk that phantom Federals were operating across a broad swath of the state. General Tilghman, for example, wrote Pemberton from Canton on April 24 that a messenger from Carthage reported "a regiment of cavalry approaching that place." Other Federal forces were reported at Kosciusko, Bankston, and even Paulding, south of the railroad. In reality, there were no Federal regiments within miles of any of those places.[63]

Pemberton was also justifiably concerned about the state of the vital Southern Railroad. On the last day of April, he expressed perhaps his greatest fear in a message to the president of the Southern Railroad at Jackson. "It is of the utmost importance that the break in your road should be repaired with the greatest expedition," he urged, "and I hope that you will devote your energy and attention to the matter, and employ such a force on the work that the necessary repairs may be completed in the shortest possible time, as a great portion of the supplies for this command must now come over your road."[64]

---

63 *OR* 24, pt. 1, 315-16, 532, 553; pt. 3, 781, 783-87, 791.

64 *OR* 24, pt. 1, 315-16, 532, 553; pt. 3, 781, 783-87, 791.

CHAPTER EIGHT

The Getaway

Mortification engulfed Southern hearts as news of a deep Federal incursion swept across Mississippi during the evening of April 24 and the next morning. The reports from Newton Station traveled quickly along the railroad lines extending east and west from the scene of Grierson's attack and from there north and south where that line crossed other railroads at Jackson and Meridian.

The April 24 evening edition of the *Jackson Daily Mississippian* was the first to report the raid at Newton Station. Subsequent editions added details and noted the enemy was heading east toward Enterprise. The paper described all sorts of depredations. The Federals had robbed "every one about Newton Station supposed to have money," and the people of Garlandville "suffered severely." It also reported the invaders had hanged a doctor who had been a member of the Mississippi senate in Louisville. The news of the Federal incursion moved more slowly into the inner areas of the state not connected by telegraphy, but by that point almost everyone knew of the Union thrust, and they would soon learn the objective of the expedition.[1]

Up until this point of the war, Mississippi had suffered but little from Union invasion. Only peripheral areas along the Mississippi River

---

1   "The Enemy Cavalry on the Southern Railroad," *Jackson Daily Mississippian*, April 24, 1863; "The Cavalry Raid," *Jackson Daily Mississippian*, April 25, 1863; "The Yankee Raid," *Jackson Daily Mississippian*, May 2, 1863.

and the Memphis and Charleston Railroad had been occupied, and only slightly more territory had been raided or temporarily marched through. The enemy had taken up residence along the river by occupying Memphis, Tennessee, Helena, Arkansas, and Greenville, Mississippi, as well as many areas around Vicksburg. None of these efforts included the long-term occupation of any Mississippi land along the river, although brief incursions, such as Sherman's December 1862 Chickasaw Bayou effort, the Yazoo Pass expedition, and Steele's Bayou attempt moved significant numbers of troops into Mississippi. No inland Mississippi cities such as Greenwood, Yazoo City, or especially Vicksburg had been taken or held.[2]

Matters were a bit different along the state's northern border, where a long-term occupation of Corinth at the junction of the Memphis and Charleston and the Mobile and Ohio railroads provided the Federals with a key strategic center. From the Union garrisons at Memphis and Corinth and many points in between, such as La Grange, the Federals had frequently staged raids—some under Grierson—into the state. Each effort was short, temporary, and shallow. The one major campaign into the Magnolia State was Grant's Mississippi Central advance in November and December 1862, but it, too, turned out to be temporary. The majority of the Federal troops in these efforts had penetrated only about 50 miles into the state, with the deepest advance elements reaching perhaps another 20 miles beyond that.[3]

As a result, most Mississippians who did not live along the river or in the northern counties felt relatively safe. The belief in safety and security held by most Mississippians crumbled in April 1863, along with some of their faith in the Confederacy, when Grierson's troopers rode 200 miles into the heart of the state and struck Newton Station. Everyone who heard of the destruction there knew what it meant. "We expect to hear of the destruction of Chunkey Bridge and trestle work, thus cutting us off from Mobile," warned the *Jackson Daily Mississippian* in its April 24 evening edition. In an effort to keep up local morale, the paper trumpeted a silver lining when it declared that "at any rate the blue-bellied rascals will be made to suffer for their boldness."[4]

2   For early Vicksburg efforts, see Ballard, *Vicksburg*.

3   For occupied Corinth, see Smith, *Corinth 1862*.

4   "The Enemy Cavalry on the Southern Railroad," *Jackson Daily Mississippian*, April 24, 1863.

A similar feeling of incredulity engulfed Richmond. "We have bad news from the West," War Department clerk John B. Jones confessed in his diary. "The enemy (cavalry, I suppose) have penetrated Mississippi some 200 miles, down to the railroad between Vicksburg and Meridian. This is in the rear and east of Vicksburg, and intercepts supplies. They destroyed two trains. This dispatch," he continued, "was sent to the Secretary of War by the President without remark."[5]

*   *   *

The troopers of the 6th and 7th Illinois Cavalry driving the widespread chaos in Mississippi woke on the cloudy morning of April 25 feeling exhausted and sore. Prior to stopping at the Bender plantation, the cavalrymen had made "80 miles, without scarcely halting," reported Colonel Prince. The long distance covered in just 40 hours included the lengthy delay to destroy military property and the railroad at Newton. With that station still smoldering and Grierson's objectives of damaging enemy communications and diverting enemy attention fulfilled, there was just one objective left: returning safely to Union lines.[6]

Two competing ideas on how to get his men safely out of Mississippi tore at Grierson. On the one hand, he wanted to move away from the scene quickly. That required speed and trickery. On the other hand, the forced marches and the stress of operating deep within enemy territory had exhausted the troopers. A light day to allow the men and horses to recoup some of their strength would be beneficial. Some men were already "too feeble to travel," observed Colonel Prince. One of them, Sgt. H. C. Allen of Company C, 6th Illinois Cavalry, would be captured and sent to Jackson to be interrogated.[7]

Grierson concluded the best course was to rest for a short time before climbing back into the saddle. "Our men and horses having become gradually exhausted," he wrote, "I determined on making a very easy

5   J. B. Jones, *A Rebel War Clerk's Diary: At the Confederate States Capital*, ed. James I. Robertson Jr., 2 vols. (Lawrence: University Press of Kansas, 2015), vol. 1, 266.

6   Surby, *Grierson Raids*, 53; "The Grierson Raid," *Weekly Register* (Canton, IL), September 7, 1863.

7   "The Great Federal Raid," *Natchez Daily Courier*, May 5, 1863; "The Grierson Raid," *Weekly Register* (Canton, IL), September 7, 1863.

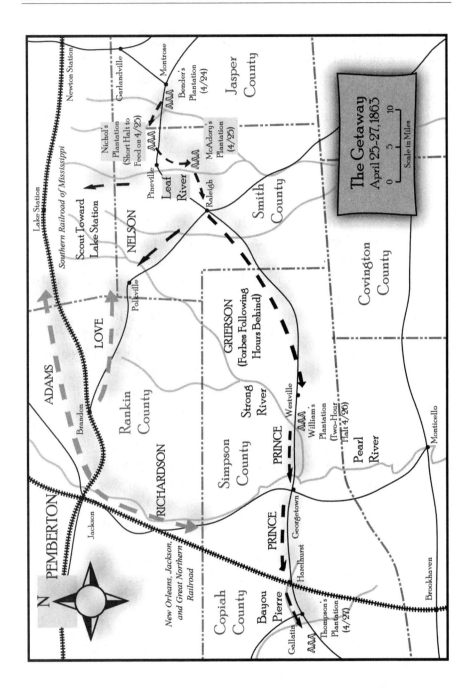

The Getaway
April 25-27, 1863

0   5   10
Scale in Miles

march the next day, looking more to the recruiting of my weary little command than to the accomplishment of any important object." The brigade commander knew the immediate future would include hard and long riding and perhaps even pitched fighting. His men and horses would need all the strength they could muster, and April 25 was as good a time as any to make a short march and allow the troops to rest up. Hopefully, Confederate attention would remain on Newton and the railroad and on the Macon and Meridian areas. If so, Grierson could make his way west at a pace of his choosing while the Confederates looked for him farther to the east. Although he did not know it at the time, the sudden appearance of Captain Forbes's troops at Enterprise aided him in this effort.[8]

After allowing his men to sleep later than their usual dawn departure, Grierson ordered the march to resume at 8:00 a.m. The column spent the next five miles meandering west and northwest before reaching a large plantation in Smith County owned by Elias Nichols. The 39-year-old's sprawling land was valued at $10,000 in 1860, and Nichols had a net worth of $38,867, much of it vested in his 36 slaves. Grierson allowed the men to feed their horses and themselves and rest. According to the *Paulding Clarion*, the Federals "robbed [Nichols] of all his mules, a carriage, several of his Negroes, and a greater part of his corn and meat."[9]

Grierson moved out around 2:00 p.m., riding west and then south. Around Pineville, the Federals received a solid taste of slavery, Mississippi style. Although they had encountered slaves all along the route, they had not yet witnessed the depredations they saw this day. "We came upon a large plantation, the owner of which was in the field with his whip driving the Negroes," recorded Grierson, who sent word for the owner to meet him at the house. By that time the Illinoisans were helping themselves to the man's provisions, including fodder for the horses. The angry planter protested that "he had none to spare. Not[hing] but the Confederate vouchers were good enough, and he was willing to loan his share, but he had fed several squads already and had no more left than he wanted for his own use." Grierson ignored the man's pleas and the soldiers continued their work. In one of the outbuildings, troopers "found and released an imprisoned Negro slave, manacled and chained to a ruin in

8   OR 24, pt. 1, 525.

9   Ibid.; Forbes, "Grierson's Cavalry Raid," 127; 1860 Smith County, Mississippi, Population and Slave Schedules.

Elias Nichols Grave. Grierson's column stopped to rest and eat at Elias Nichols' plantation the day after sacking Newton Station. A modern house sits on the original plantation house site, but Nichols and his family are buried just to the south. *Author*

the floor for trying to run away. The irons, an inch thick, had worn the flesh to the bone, inducing gangrene and almost mortification." Grierson ordered his release, to which the planter made "a very wry face." The unshackled slave made good on this once-in-a-lifetime opportunity and rode out of Pineville with the Federal column. The freed slave "went through with us . . . and never tired of serving his deliverers."[10]

As the Federals suspected, danger increased by the hour. The people of Paulding, a small Jasper County town 15 miles south and east of Pineville, organized a group of 50 men and rode west in search of the raiders. When they realized the enemy cavalry was leaving their area, however, the civilian soldiers returned home. Grierson's new direction was west and a bit southwest into Smith County, toward Raleigh, the county seat. The column made another dozen miles before Grierson called a halt around dark just east of the Leaf River at a plantation owned by Dr. Chambers McAdory.[11]

---

10 Grierson, *A Just and Righteous Cause*, 162.

11 *OR* 24, pt. 1, 525; Forbes, "Grierson's Cavalry Raid," 127; *Smith County, Mississippi, and Its Families*, 2 vols. (Raleigh, MS: Smith County Genealogical Society, 2006),

Grierson's column covered about 17 miles by the time camp was made that evening. That was fewer than usual and significantly fewer than the column had marched the past several few days. The mileage, however, included crossing Otokoochee Creek, one of the major tributaries of the Leaf River, which itself lay ahead. Grierson could have reached it, but he may well have learned his lesson about driving his troopers into swampy areas with darkness approaching, as he had done south of Starkville and again below Louisville.[12]

Despite the short ride that day, Grierson was pleased. By the end of day, arguably his easiest thus far, his men and mounts were once more well-fed and well-stocked. "Having obtained during this day plenty of forage and provisions," he wrote, "and having had one good night's rest, we now again felt ready for any emergency." He knew the Confederates were slowly but surely reacting and concentrating to cut off and destroy the bold band of Federals that had dared to penetrate the inner sanctum of Confederate Mississippi. They had achieved their main objective, but their position remained perilous at best. One Federal described it this way: "We had marched a solid week straight into the heart of the enemy's country—were in the center of a large Confederate state, in which, save at Corinth, there was not a camp or fort over which floated the stars and stripes. We were certainly a week's vigorous march distant from a friendly camp."[13]

Just how concentrated and organized were the Confederates? The precise nature of the dangers facing Grierson was anyone's guess, but he prepared for the worst. The Federal commander kept his scouts well out in every compass direction and sent additional patrols to find out

---

vol. 2, 7, 235; W. D. Moss, Deed, Book 0524, Smith County Chancery Clerk, 631. McAdory's story is worth retelling. He was a native of Alabama, where he graduated from the state university before moving north to study medicine at Jefferson Medical College in Philadelphia. The young doctor then moved south in late 1860 to practice medicine and run a plantation along the Leaf River. When the war began, he joined the Confederate army and served as a lieutenant in the 37th Mississippi Infantry. He was severely wounded and captured at Corinth in October 1862, paroled, and spent much of the rest of the war recovering in central Mississippi (John W. DuBose, *Jefferson County and Birmingham, Alabama* [Birmingham: Caldwell Printing Works, 1887], 511).

12 *OR* 24, pt. 1, 525.

13 "Grierson's Big Raid," n.d., Thomas W. Lippincott Papers, ALPL; *OR* 24, pt. 1, 525.

more information and divert the enemy's attention from his main column. For example, earlier on the morning of April 25, Grierson dispatched a pair of detachments north. One was a small group of troopers bent on wreaking more havoc along the already disrupted Southern Railroad "at Lake Station and other points." The men did exactly as instructed and rejoined the main body a few hours later with news of Confederates moving east along the broken line. Although they did not know it, the enemy they discovered was John Adams's men moving along the rail line to secure the escape route to the north.[14]

Wanting to know more about his surroundings, about midnight while camped at McAdory's plantation, Grierson sent out a scout, Samuel Nelson. Grierson described the man, who dressed in civilian clothes for the mission, as a "medium sized, muscular man [with] sandy complexion [and] redish hair." Sometimes, he continued, the trooper was "as honest and harmless-looking as a Presbyterian deacon"—an image Grierson wanted to play up with Nelson dressed as a civilian. Nelson, who had served as one of Surby's scouts during the long raid, had another quality: "A peculiar impediment, or sort of stutter, in his speech which enabled him to think twice before he answered once any question put to him."[15]

Nelson's speech impediment was a source of amusement for some of the men. After a particularly long ride, Grierson expressed concern that he was so tired he would not wake even if a crisis befell them. Sure enough, when important news arrived, Adjutant Woodward and other troopers were only able to stir him to consciousness by lightly striking him. With difficulty, the sleepy Grierson mounted his horse and began riding, although everyone thought the colonel was fast asleep. When Grierson and his small party reached a gate where Nelson was keeping watch, the scout asked, "Are there any wu-wu-wu-wagons back there?" A trooper responded, "Yes, there's wu-wu-wu-one." Grierson awoke suddenly and roared with laughter, chuckling to himself for the next

---

14 Grierson, *A Just and Righteous Cause*, 160; *OR* 24, pt. 1, 525, 531-32.

15 *OR* 24, pt. 1, 525; Grierson, *A Just and Righteous Cause*, 160; Dinges, "The Making of a Cavalryman," 378n81. Grierson later stated the scout was George Steadman, but virtually all other sources say it was actually Nelson. While there is no way to know for sure, I have yielded to the weight of evidence.

half mile. "By that time I knew he was wide awake," said one Illinois trooper.[16]

When Grierson was sure the scout understood what he wanted, Nelson moved across Leaf River and headed northwest to gain intelligence, cut the telegraph lines, and "if possible, fire a bridge or trestle-work." The colonel later recalled thinking that "the rebels would not get the best of that singular-looking, but bright and sharp, individual." His hope was that the Confederates would think the entire Federal command was moving along the railroad, doing more damage, rather than quietly riding west 25 miles farther south. If the enemy believed the destruction was creeping toward Jackson, perhaps they would worry that the state capital was in danger and act accordingly.[17]

As he moved northwest, Nelson encountered a formation of Confederate cavalry operating out of Brandon. The troops were Capt. R. C. Love's squadron, sent out by Pemberton himself with orders to "get on his [Grierson's] rear, and plant ambush and annoy him. See if something can be done." The civilian-clad Nelson spent several minutes stuttering his way through a conversation with the Confederates. The import of what was transpiring was not lost on Nelson: The enemy was riding on the road leading straight to Grierson's column camped at McAdory's plantation.[18]

Nelson's presence of mind and ingenuity saved Grierson's column from an ugly and potentially deadly surprise. The scout, reported the brigade commander, "conversed with the commanding officer, and answer[ed] all the questions put to him in a satisfactory manner considering the impediment in his speech." Nelson talked as if he knew the area well, shared news that he had seen the Yankees, and pointed the Confederates in a completely different direction. "He succeeded in misdirecting them as to the place where he had last seen us," Grierson explained. Once Love's squadron moved out, Nelson remained behind to make sure they were "well on the wrong road," at which point he "immediately retraced his steps to camp with the news." The scout reached McAdory's on a

16 "Grierson's Raid Recalled by Death," *Decatur Daily Review*, September 9, 1911.

17 *OR* 24, pt. 1, 525; pt. 3, 791; Grierson, *A Just and Righteous Cause*, 160-61; Forbes, "Grierson's Cavalry Raid," 109.

18 *OR* 24, pt. 1, 525; pt. 3, 791; Grierson, *A Just and Righteous Cause*, 160-61; Forbes, "Grierson's Cavalry Raid," 109.

sweat-lathered horse, and he informed Grierson of Love's column and everything else he had learned. Grierson later expressed his gratitude: "When he first met them they were on the direct road to our camp, and had they not been turned from their course would have come up with us before daylight."[19]

With the immediate threat receding by the mile, Grierson planned his next move. As his adjutant later described it, Grierson's orders from Generals Smith and Hurlbut "abandoned him in the heart of the enemy's country." After compiling and sifting through Nelson's information and other reports, Grierson made his decision. Grant was planning to cross the Mississippi River somewhere south of Vicksburg at a point now less than 100 miles west of Grierson's present position. Information gleaned by his scouts confirmed the enemy was worried that just such a thing might take place. "It was seriously contemplated to swing back to the east," Woodward wrote, but "Jackson [Mississippi] and the stations east as far as Lake Station had been re-enforced by infantry and artillery." When he learned "a fight was momentarily expected at Grand Gulf" near the area Grant intended to cross, Grierson recorded, "I decided to make a rapid march, cross Pearl River, and strike the New Orleans, Jackson, and Great Northern Railroad at Hazlehurst, and, after destroying as much of the road as possible, endeavor to get upon the flank of the enemy and co-operate with our forces, should they be successful in the attack upon Grand Gulf and Port Gibson."[20]

The bold plan had to be executed perfectly to succeed. It was also against Hurlbut's orders, which were to circle back through Alabama. Grierson, however, was more worried about timing than Hurlbut's distant directive. If Grierson showed up at Grand Gulf ahead of Grant's crossing, he would do so without support and be exposed to destruction. If he was too late and unable to help Grant, the Confederates would be in a position to concentrate to meet the mounted threat and cut him off from the main army or escape in a different direction. If he timed his ride perfectly, however, he could assist Grant's army and create real havoc for the defending enemy. This plan necessitated more forced marches, but his men were now well rested with two full nights of sleep and a

---

19   *OR* 24, pt. 1, 525; Grierson, *A Just and Righteous Cause*, 161.

20   *OR* 24, pt. 1, 525-26; Woodward, "Grierson's Raid," 687, 701.

relatively leisurely day's ride under their belts. After weighing all his options, Grierson decided it was worth the risk.[21]

*   *   *

The morning of April 26 was like most of the raid's previous mornings. Grierson ordered his troopers out of their slumber early and had them on the road by daylight. He wanted to get a fresh and early start. One of the major obstacles standing in the way of his goal was just west of McAdory's plantation.

With its headwaters to the north around Lake Station and the Southern Railroad, the Leaf River flowed southward to the Pascagoula River and into the Gulf of Mexico. The impediment could be turned into an advantage by putting it behind them and obstructing the crossing for any pursuing Confederates. One of Grierson's troopers summed up their situation: "In entering the state from the north it had in its favor all the advantages of a surprise, and could also count on the enemy's ignorance of the numbers to be met. But surprise was now no longer possible, and the strength of the invading column had by this time been more or less correctly ascertained."[22]

Grierson turned his refreshed column west, with the 6th Illinois Cavalry riding in the lead. To the surprise of many, the Federals reached and crossed the river on a good bridge soon after beginning the march around 6:00 a.m. The unguarded span indicated the Confederates did not expect the Federals to be in the area. Once across, Grierson rode most of his command onto the high ground separating it and the Strong River, the next potential obstacle blocking his route of escape. Other troopers, meanwhile, remained behind to burn the Leaf River bridge by piling brush around its supports and setting fire to the structure "to prevent any enemy who might be in pursuit from following," Grierson explained.[23]

The column continued five miles west and entered Raleigh later that morning. Once again there was no resistance, although three companies

---

21 Forbes, "Grierson's Cavalry Raid," 108.

22 *OR* 24, pt. 1, 526; Forbes, "Grierson's Cavalry Raid," 108.

23 *OR* 24, pt. 1, 526; Surby, *Grierson Raids*, 61; "This Month in Smith County History: 'Grierson's Raid,'" *Smith County Reformer*, April 22, 1998.

Leaf River Crossing. Grierson crossed the Leaf River at the Chambers McAdory plantation and burned the bridge behind him. This photo shows the bridge site. *Author*

of Smith County citizens, two of cavalry and one of infantry, had been raised to defend the town. Fortunately for everyone involved, the Mississippians had neither arms nor ammunition. The scratch militiamen were under the command of John J. Thornton, a disabled former colonel of the 6th Mississippi who had received a crippling blow in the thigh at Shiloh. One Smith County defender boasted a couple of days later that with arms and ammunition, "We would have given them the best fight we had—without regard to consequences." The Union troopers came upon the town so quickly they captured the sheriff of Smith County, with some reports indicating he approached them thinking they were Confederates. The troopers also took "about $3,000 in Government funds." Unwilling to waste precious time dealing with sheriffs and citizens, Grierson departed Raleigh almost as quickly as he arrived, heading west toward the Strong and Pearl Rivers.[24]

Still, an odd episode unfolded in Raleigh, demonstrating once again that the world was indeed a small place. "I stopped at a house for water, and the people received me very kindly," A. N. Shattuck of the 7th Illinois Cavalry wrote home to Litchfield. When a Mississippian learned where he was from, the man responded that he "had an uncle in Illinois." Amazingly, Shattuck knew his uncle. As it turned out, the uncle's brother was in the Raleigh area, although he was not in town when the Federals passed through. The Mississippian introduced Shattuck to the man's wife, who wanted Shattuck to carry a letter for her brother-in-law back in Illinois. Shattuck, however, explained "there was a prospect of fighting in front and I could not wait for them to write." He promised to let the uncle in Illinois know they were all well, or as they put it, "as well as anyone in the Confederacy, that is, they were making a living." Their next objective, added the Mississippi man, "was to escape the Conscript, this they did by getting a Gov. contract for tanning hides."[25]

The route that afternoon carried Grierson and his men through miles of heavy pine thicket until they reached the small hamlet of Westville, nearly 30 miles west of Raleigh. One Illinois trooper remembered the joy when they "emerged from that stretch of pine forest of 30 miles."

24 J. M. Quin to John J. Pettus, April 28, 1863, John J. Pettus Correspondence, MDAH; *OR* 24, pt. 1, 526; Grierson, *A Just and Righteous Cause*, 161; Woodward, "Grierson's Raid," 703.

25 "From One of Grierson's Cavalry," *Union Monitor* (Litchfield, IL), June 5, 1863.

Locals in the area were still irritated decades later at the treatment meted out by Grierson's raiders. "On the march they stole horses, mules and cattle and robbed farm houses and most especially smokehouses and barns and carried off all they could find," grumbled one in a letter. Every word of it was true, as was the added conclusion, "It does not appear that they burned any houses in Simpson County." As usual, the Federals had little time for pillaging. By this time it was well after dark, and Grierson knew he had to move on even though the Strong River was smaller than many others he had easily crossed. As far as obstacles went, it was not much of a concern. The Strong's headwaters were several miles to the northeast, near Morton and Lake, the same area where the much longer Leaf River also began. Unlike the longer Leaf, however, the Strong River's path was cut short because it flowed into the Pearl River just south of Georgetown. A "fine bridge" over the river just west of Westville would make the crossing easier.[26]

Two miles west of Westville was a plantation owned by George W. Williams. Grierson stopped the 6th Illinois Cavalry there along the east bank of the river to feed his men and horses while the 7th Illinois Cavalry rode across the Strong River bridge to the Smith plantation. According to local lore, some of Grierson's men found some whiskey and "got so drunk that he had to strike [stop] at the Williams place." In fact, a heavy rain convinced Grierson to go into camp.[27]

Yet another exchange between raider and plantation owner unfolded. Several issues larger than forage and rest threaded through this particular meeting. George Williams was a Confederate soldier (a major, according to Grierson) who was home on leave. His sprawling plantation was valued at $6,000 in 1860, and his net worth at $19,590—much of which was bound up in 17 slaves. As was his custom, Grierson rode up to the plantation house, this time during a cold, driving rain, to seek out the owner. Like every other landowner in the area, Williams was accustomed to Confederate units occasionally paying a visit in search of

26 George A. Root to S. A. Forbes, November 30, 1908, in Stephen A. Forbes Papers, UI; *OR* 24, pt. 1, 526; "Federal Soldiers Marched in Westville," *Simpson County News*, October 11, 1984; "The Grierson Raid," *Weekly Register* (Canton, IL), September 7, 1863; Surby, *Grierson Raids*, 63; Daniel E. Robbins to Brother, May 7, 1863.

27 George A. Root to S. A. Forbes, November 30, 1908; *OR* 24, pt. 1, 526; "Federal Soldiers Marched in Westville," *Simpson County News*, October 11, 1984; "The Grierson Raid," *Weekly Register* (Canton, IL), September 7, 1863; Surby, *Grierson Raids*, 63.

provisions, and he naturally assumed the dirty column was simply more of the same. According to Grierson, Williams "came quietly to the door and asked whose command it was . . . never dream[ing] of the presence of Yankees." The Confederate officer's demeanor turned to frustration when he could not get a satisfactory answer or even get anyone to pay him any mind. When he discovered soldiers taking his goods—thinking all the while he was being robbed by his own army—Williams "became furious. [He] swore that he would report the commanding officer to General Pemberton; that he would not stand such abuse and insult on his own premises; they were ruining his garden and feeding up his corn and fodder." Grierson let the man rant for a while before finally letting him in on the identity of the mud-covered troops. "He became cooler when to his great surprise he found out with whom he had to deal."[28]

Despite the cold rain and even colder reception, good news arrived. During his return trip after leaving Enterprise, Captain Forbes had sent three couriers (his brother Stephen, John Moulding, and Arthur Woods) ahead to find Grierson. They caught up with him and the rest of the column just past Westville near the Williams plantation. The couriers brought news that Forbes and his small command were on their way to join him. The second part of the message, recalled Colonel Prince, was that "the main column should stop burning bridges, as Captain Forbes was endeavoring to reach the main column." The news of the column's pending arrival pleased at least one other Illinois man: "I well remember what a thrill of joy we experienced when the sharp clear voice of John Moulding announced that your command was struggling with floods and blockaded roads not far in our rear."[29]

While cheered and perhaps a little surprised at the news of Company B's imminent return, Grierson had yet to decide whether to remain in camp or march through the night. His custom was to make camp and remain there until about dawn, especially after the 40-mile day. He had only pushed the men through the night on one occasion, and that was to make the final run to Newton Station at dawn on April 24. Time was of the essence now more than ever. Colonel Prince of the 7th Illinois

---

28 Grierson, *A Just and Righteous Cause*, 162; 1860 Simpson County, Mississippi, Population and Slave Schedules.

29 "The Grierson Raid," *Weekly Register* (Canton, IL), September 7, 1863; Forbes, "Grierson's Cavalry Raid," 113; George A. Root to S. A. Forbes, November 30, 1908.

Cavalry thought so as well. "Notwithstanding . . . a severe rain most of the day," he explained, "as I learned the citizens were arming themselves, and the news of the expedition was flying in every direction, it became to my mind a matter of life and death that the Pearl River should be crossed and the N. O. and Jackson Railroad reached without any delay."[30]

The Pearl was the largest waterway Grierson would face on his trek. Adjutant Woodward described the river as "a wide, deep and rapid stream with precipitous banks, navigable for good sized vessels and unfordable." If the Confederates were going to stop Grierson anywhere, it would be along the Pearl, pinning his men against the unfordable river. The Pearl, declared one writer, "held in its silent grasp the fate of the entire command." The Federals believed that few if any locals realized they were anywhere near the Williams plantation, but the risk of discovery increased with each passing hour. If word reached Georgetown, the residents would disable or destroy the ferry there, making it impossible to cross the river. Grierson's men and horses were rested and fed, and if he was going to move, now was the time.[31]

The decision to move meant that no one would get much sleep on the night of April 26—especially for two unfortunate battalions of the 7th Illinois Cavalry. Colonel Prince convinced Grierson to allow him to lead the advance "with 200 picked men of the 7th Regiment, to secure the ferry across Pearl River before the enemy should destroy it." The action made sense, and Grierson had executed a similar move once before when he dispatched a couple of battalions to Newton Station early on the morning of April 24 before following up with the rest of the command an hour later. The decision to let Prince lead the thrust also made sense. Grierson wanted this done right, and sending the regiment's commanding officer signaled how important he considered the movement to be. "Two hundred of us went in the night to take possession of the ferry boat," recalled a 7th Illinois Cavalry trooper. Whether they would arrive in time to secure the ferry, or even reach the river, remained to be seen.[32]

---

30 "The Grierson Raid," *Weekly Register* (Canton, IL), September 7, 1863; Abbott, "Heroic Deeds of Heroic Men," 277; Woodward, "Grierson's Raid," 705.

31 "The Grierson Raid," *Weekly Register* (Canton, IL), September 7, 1863; Abbott, "Heroic Deeds of Heroic Men," 277; Woodward, "Grierson's Raid," 705.

32 "The Grierson Raid," *Weekly Register* (Canton, IL), September 7, 1863; *OR* 24, pt. 1, 526; Freyburger, *Letters to Ann*, 44.

Prince led his troopers west of the plantation and through the miserable night for nearly 10 miles to reach the Pearl River valley. The riders slipped to within sight of the crossing point, but they remained hidden to reconnoiter the situation. The ferry boat was on the opposite side of the Pearl. Prince mulled the idea of riding to the riverbank and hailing its operators to send it over, but he dismissed the idea as too dangerous. "I thought it not prudent, under the circumstances, to call for the ferryman," Prince explained. If the operators realized he was a Federal, they would keep the ferry out of reach or sink it. Instead, the colonel asked for a volunteer on a "powerful horse" to swim the wide river, capture the ferry, and bring it to the near side at gunpoint, if necessary. Henry Dower of Company I volunteered for the hazardous duty. The recent rains that had flooded the Noxubee River and others had swelled the Pearl into a raging river. Dower eased his mount to the bank and slipped into the dark water to swim across, reported the colonel, but he "was carried far below the landing, and finding quicksand, barely escaped with his life."[33]

To Prince's delight, the ferryman solved his otherwise vexing problem for him when the commotion east of the river snagged his attention. "The proprietor of the ferry soon appeared on the opposite bank and queried, in the broad speech of a North Carolinian, if we wanted over," recalled an incredulous Prince. The Federal officer took the man up on his offer by yelling back in his best Southern drawl, "A few of us would like to cross, but it was harder to wake his nigger ferryman than to catch the conscripts." For good measure, Prince added that they were the 1st Alabama Cavalry—a bold lie, as that outfit was serving with Braxton Bragg's Army of Tennessee around Tullahoma, Tennessee. Hearing enough to convince him that Prince was a Confederate, the Mississippi boat owner "at once woke up the ferryman and sent him over with the boat." It took time, but Prince managed to ferry his two battalions across without any additional trouble: "We took possession of the boat, and received an appreciated breakfast with the proprietor, as the 1st Alabama regiment of Cavalry."[34]

33 Grierson, *A Just and Righteous Cause*, 162-63; "The Grierson Raid," *Weekly Register* (Canton, IL), September 7, 1863; Surby, *Grierson Raids*, 64.

34 Abbott, "Heroic Deeds of Heroic Men," 277; Grierson, *A Just and Righteous Cause*, 163; David A. Powell, *The Maps of Chickamauga* (New York: Savas Beatie, 2009), 267.

Prince's good fortune continued. "Thirty minutes after crossing," he wrote, his men captured a Rebel courier "with dispatches that the Yankees were coming and ordering the destruction of the ferry immediately." He also learned about a steamboat fitted out with cotton bales and cannon that was supposedly lurking upriver. The fact that it had not shifted its position to protect the ferry was a good omen. Grierson sent a troop of horsemen to watch out for the warship, but if it existed, it never made an appearance. This was the second time the Pearl River had nearly tripped up the Federal raid, with the Illinoisan troopers dodging a pending crisis by mere minutes on each occasion.[35]

By the time the Confederate dispatch rider appeared, Prince was over the river, finished with his meal, and Grierson had reached the east bank with the rest of the command. Keeping up the ruse that the riders comprised the 1st Alabama Cavalry, Grierson "receipted to the ferryman for the passage of the command in the name of that regiment." At 24 horses and riders a ferry load, it took 41 separate trips to get the column across, not counting the artillery, forage wagons, and ambulances. The hours-long operation continued until 2:00 p.m. that afternoon. Grierson, Prince, and the rest of the men, meanwhile, did their best to keep up the charade to prevent anyone from discovering their real identity.[36]

While his command was being transported across the Pearl River, Grierson and his staff met a family who lived next to the ferry. Still thinking they were Confederates, the courteous Mississippians invited the officers in for breakfast. "The meal was well served [and] the ladies were all smiles," Grierson remembered. His good fortune, however, ended before the repast could be finished. "Up came some blunder head of a soldier and blurted out to me something about the '6th Illinois Cavalry' and what they were doing," related a mortified Grierson. "The countenances of the host changed, and some persons at once left the room. I knew very well that every effort would be made to give information."[37]

---

35 "The Grierson Raid," *Weekly Register* (Canton, IL), September 7, 1863; *OR* 24, pt. 1, 526; Grierson, *A Just and Righteous Cause*, 162; Woodward, "Grierson's Raid," 706.

36 Grierson, *A Just and Righteous Cause*, 163; Daniel E. Robbins to Brother, May 7, 1863.

37 *OR* 24, pt. 1, 526; Grierson, *A Just and Righteous Cause*, 163; Woodward, "Grierson's Raid," 703-4.

Informants who made it out of Georgetown could ride 10 miles west to the railroad and telegraph across the state the precise news of the invaders' location. Intelligence that Grierson and his command were strung out on both sides of an unfordable river would trigger decisive Confederate action, and the railroad would make it easy to concentrate the resources needed to defeat his column. It was imperative that Grierson minimize the potential damage and at least unify his entire command so it could fight, if necessary, as one brigade. The worst possible scenario would be having to fight piecemeal with a wide and raging river dividing his command.[38]

Grierson acted decisively. He had already sent riders ahead toward the New Orleans, Jackson, and Great Northern Railroad, and when Prince's two battalions fully crossed, pushed them on as well to inflict as much damage as possible. Now it was time to do more. "Bidding the ladies good-bye rather hastily, and without waiting to finish the breakfast," he later wrote, "I instantly dispatched a messenger to hurry up my scouts previously sent to Hazlehurst [and] with a written dispatch in the name of the rebel colonel to General Pemberton at Jackson to say that 'the Yankees had advanced to Pearl River and finding the ferry destroyed they could not cross and had left, taking a north-easterly course.'" Grierson intended to ride his command on a southwesterly course, pushing on toward Grand Gulf.[39]

The Pearl River was the last major obstacle between Grierson's command and Grant's army, which Grierson expected would cross the Mississippi River at any time. The Federal raiders were now on the same side of the Pearl as Grant, and there were few, if any, serious obstacles between them. If, that is, the timing worked out.

*   *   *

The crisis emerging at Georgetown was a grave threaten to Captain Forbes's company, which was making a determined effort to catch up with the main column. If Grierson crossed his entire command and destroyed the ferry, Forbes would be trapped east of the river. Neither Forbes nor his troopers, however, knew anything about what was transpiring at the Pearl River crossing or that Grierson was pushing the column southwest.

38 Grierson, *A Just and Righteous Cause*, 163.

39 Ibid.

Forbes and his men spent days on the diversionary ride to Macon and then Enterprise, confusing the enemy and damaging whatever military property they could find. When he discovered he was heavily outnumbered, Forbes had hurriedly, but in his words, "very cheerfully" left Enterprise and rode hard to catch up to the main force. The troopers were overjoyed at their escape and the "superior game of bluff" that had played out at Enterprise. They also realized they were still in danger, or as Forbes poetically put it, "out of the lion's mouth, but woefully and inextricably entangled in his den." According to the captain, "We rode on towards the sinking sun and—planned. Should we run North? Should we attempt Pensacola, Mobile, Vicksburg?" Forbes decided on "one more despairing effort at a stern chase of the Regiments," despite the fact that his company was many hours behind the column.[40]

Grierson's last known position was Garlandville, so Forbes set out hoping to meet it there. His scouts found the townspeople preparing for resistance, but not a man of Grierson's column was in sight. One of the advance riders befriended the county sheriff. The scout talked the sheriff into riding with him to help warn the townspeople that Alabama cavalry was coming through and not to fire on them. The trick worked, with the hoodwinked sheriff helping the Federal scout clear the way. "We rode undisturbed thro' this town," confirmed Forbes, "which contained nearly twice our number of armed enemies." Hours later, at Raleigh, Forbes's advance found another group of civilians organizing for resistance. The Illinois troopers captured the captain "by a headlong charge" and rode on through the night, eventually cutting the distance between the company and the main column to just seven or eight hours.[41]

Making up those hours was exceedingly difficult, especially since Grierson was burning the bridges behind him. Stephen Forbes described the Leaf River bridge as nothing more than "a wreck of blackened timbers." He later admitted that Grierson had "[given] up Co. B as necessarily lost," and some of the fatigued men began to wonder whether they had been abandoned in enemy territory. Exhausted sentinels, including Stephen, fell asleep at their posts only to be shaken awake by the clattering of

40 *OR* 24, pt. 1, 528; Grierson, *A Just and Righteous Cause*, 165; "The Grierson Raid," *Weekly Register* (Canton, IL), September 7, 1863; Forbes, "Grierson's Raid," 22-23.

41 Forbes, "Grierson's Raid," 23; Forbes, "Grierson's Cavalry Raid," 113.

wooden rails when a restless horse pulled down a fence. Bereft of both sleep and bridges, the company soldiered on, swimming across five creeks and rivers—"all of them difficult, and one of them fairly desperate," recorded one participant. It is little wonder that Captain Forbes described this part of the journey as "the hardest and most discouraging ride of the Raid." At one point Company B had to take "a long detour to find a place where we could get into the water and out again." Unaware of where the main column was heading, "We were now wholly at a loss to understand Grierson's plans." Forbes thought Grierson would turn north, for the "broad, navigable [Pearl] river, lay close in front."[42]

Experiencing all the uncertainly he could stand, Forbes sent three men, including his brother Stephen, on strong horses in a desperate effort to locate the main column. "I never expected to see one of them again," admitted the officer, "feeling sure that they would be picked off by stragglers." When the trio came across the rear of the brigade column near Westville, Grierson's guards shouted, "Halt! Who comes there?" The overjoyed riders ignored the question and yelled, "Company B!" as they rode past the stunned guards. Cheers of "Company B has come back!" ran down the line "from company to company, cheer upon cheer, faster than our horses could run," recalled the younger Forbes. "Captain Forbes presents his compliments," he announced, "and begs to be allowed to burn his bridges for himself." Preparations to burn the Strong River bridge were canceled and a company was left to guard the span for Company B's use.[43]

The three scouts had caught up with the main column, but the rest of Company B was still struggling to reach the Pearl. At one point, Forbes found a man at a small dwelling where the company stopped to feed who informed him that Grierson was eight hours ahead. The man agreed to guide the troopers on their route, but soon lost his way in the darkness. An exasperated Forbes recalled that the man "seemed to fall into confusion, grew excited, chattered incessantly and often incoherently . . . frightened at his responsibility, [he] presented a good case of emotional insanity. He expected momentarily to be shot as the penalty of his blundering." Some of the troopers grew suspicious and wondered aloud whether he

---

42 Forbes, "Grierson's Raid," 24; Forbes, "Grierson's Cavalry Raid," 113; Forbes Letters, 1863, in Stephen A. Forbes Papers, UI, 210.

43 Forbes, "Grierson's Cavalry Raid," 113-14.

was "blundering or treacherous" and sought permission to shoot him. "We were roadless, guideless, and suddenly found ourselves involved in the path of an old tornado, which, two years previously," explained the captain, "had prostrated the pine forest, dashing the trees in every direction." The disoriented troopers, riding under a steady rain, "for an hour or more blundered blindly on through the hideous maze," losing two of their three prisoners in the process. Once they emerged on the far side of the damaged woods, Forbes called a halt for the night, and the men, guards included, did their best to get some sleep.[44]

The arrival of daylight helped the scouts get their bearings, and the company moved on after losing another dozen hours of precious time. Fortunately, although unbeknownst to Forbes and his men, Grierson's column was engaged in the painfully slow process of crossing the Pearl River on a single ferry. Forbes's troopers rode hard and caught up with Grierson just as the last members were being pulled over the swollen river. The return of the lost company, recalled Woodward, "caused as much joy to the officers and men as did that of the biblical 'Prodigal Son' to his father."[45]

Forbes was especially proud of Company B's exceedingly difficult ride within the larger raid. Later, after having time to think about it, he put pen to paper and sketched the adventure for posterity:

> We had been absent five days and four nights. We had marched fully 300 miles, in ten different counties; had captured and paroled 40 prisoners; confronted and evaded several thousand Confed. troops at Macon and Enterprise; slipped through the home guards of six county towns; been twice misled and once lost; had had five bridges burned in our faces; and in all this time had had but 18 hours of sleep, while rations for man and horse had been for the most part conspicuous for their absence. We had not had time to eat.[46]

Grierson agreed. Forbes's ride, as he described it, was a "most exciting and wonderfully successful expedition." In order to catch up with the column, continued Grierson, Forbes "was obliged to march 60 miles per day for several consecutive days. Much honor is due Captain Forbes for the manner in which he conducted this expedition." Despite

---

44 Forbes, "Grierson's Raid," 24-25; Forbes, "Grierson's Cavalry Raid," 114.

45 Forbes, "Grierson's Raid," 25-26; Woodward, "Grierson's Raid," 704.

46 Forbes, "Grierson's Raid," 26.

everything he had experienced, Forbes lost only one man killed and another wounded.[47]

*   *   *

Crossing the Pearl in dramatic fashion was quite an accomplishment, but Grierson had more in mind. The New Orleans, Jackson, and Great Northern Railroad was ripe for destruction at or around Hazlehurst, and he wanted to tear up some of the track before word of his approach tipped off the locals or, more important, Confederate commands in the area. As noted earlier, he sent some scouts and Colonel Prince's two tired battalions out to do just that as soon as they crossed the Pearl and while the rest of the column was still making the agonizingly slow passage via ferry. Prince's orders were to ride west and strike the railroad at Hazlehurst, similar to what he had done at the ferry at Georgetown, and destroy a large section of track before any resistance developed.[48]

Fifteen miles of enemy territory separated the Pearl River from the railroad at Hazlehurst. The chance of surprise diminished as news spread that Federals had descended upon Georgetown, so speed was everything. Surby's scouts led the way, with Prince's battalions riding behind them, and they quickly ran into civilians armed to the teeth. One, who bragged that he was planning to "exterminate the invading Yankees," was taken prisoner. Some of Prince's troopers stopped and destroyed an assortment of weapons at a gunsmith's shop before continuing the ride.[49]

When they reached Hazlehurst, two of the scouts made for the telegraph office, where several Confederate officers were found surrounding the operator. Dressed in dirty civilian garb, the Illinois men calmly handed Grierson's note to the telegrapher. The message, intended for General Pemberton at Jackson, falsely claimed that "Yankees had advanced to Pearl River and finding the ferry destroyed they could not cross and had left, taking a north-easterly course."[50]

---

47 OR 24, pt. 1, 528; Grierson, A Just and Righteous Cause, 165; "The Grierson Raid," Weekly Register (Canton, IL), September 7, 1863; Forbes, "Grierson's Raid," 22.

48 OR 24, pt. 1, 526.

49 Grierson, A Just and Righteous Cause, 163.

50 Ibid.

The message, Grierson later explained, fit perfectly with "the orders already sent to destroy the ferry," which in turn made it completely believable. A frank discussion broke out that satisfied the operator, who dutifully tapped out the message. The telegrapher and Rebel officers "had not the least idea that the Yankees were [on] that side of Pearl River."[51]

The ruse ended when the famished scouts made their way to the hotel for something to eat. On their way there, an escaped prisoner who had fled the night before on one of Grierson's orderly's horses recognized the scouts and sounded the alarm. Several citizens tried to stop them, but the scouts drew their pistols, jumped on their horses, and galloped out of town and into Prince's thundering battalions, which were bearing down on Hazlehurst just as Grierson had ordered. A few locals formed to defend the town, but, as Grierson related, "Here, again, we found the citizens armed to resist us, but they fled precipitously upon our approach."[52]

With the element of surprise now lost, the scouts raced to the telegraph office to prevent word of their arrival from spreading. Their concern was understandable, but the Confederate officers and operator had fled, together with the telegraph instrument, leaving "not a soul . . . but two old men." As it turned out, Grierson had little to worry about on that score. Other scouts had waited until they knew the Confederate clerk had tapped out Grierson's phantom message before cutting the lines.[53]

The Federals had the run of Hazlehurst. Prince's men entered the town first, but Grierson's following column came in at a gallop shortly thereafter because, as had been the case at Newton Station, they heard ammunition blowing up and mistakenly assumed Prince was "hotly engaged." The relieved Federals began destroying military equipment as well as archives and papers stored in the Marx and Loeb store. An owner of a dwelling next door had a pack of bloodhounds to track slaves and Union prisoners, so Grierson's ordered both structures burned. The fire, however, spread to Benjamin R. Neal's store. The Federals were busy destroying the railroad when word arrived that another train was due in from the north. The news prompted the men to take up positions

---

51 Ibid.

52 *OR* 24, pt. 1, 526; Grierson, *A Just and Righteous Cause*, 164; Surby, *Grierson Raids*, 68.

53 Grierson, *A Just and Righteous Cause*, 164.

to capture it. When the train failed to arrive as soon as they expected, the impatient Federals returned to their work of destruction. A short time later, however, the train steamed around the bend and into sight. Some would later claim the cars were laden with troops and carried a large cache of Confederate money. When the eagle-eyed Southern engineer spotted the Federals tearing up the track, he stopped the train and put it hard in reverse, saving the valuable locomotive, cars, and perhaps much more. The temporarily disappointed Federals soon found other railcars on the sidings stocked with "500 loaded shells and a large quantity of commissary and quartermaster's stores, intended for Grand Gulf and Port Gibson," reported Grierson. The troopers moved the cars out of town and set them afire while others cut the telegraph lines in additional places and destroyed as much track as they could.[54]

Unfortunately, the fire engulfing the railroad cars spread to nearby buildings, including a drug store. The Federals "worked energetically and, by great exertion, saved the town from destruction." Citizens who just a few hours earlier were ready to fight the invaders "were greatly astonished at our action," confirmed Grierson, "and complimented us upon our good conduct." Proud of how he had handled his command, the colonel added, "They were not the first nor the last of the citizens of Mississippi who were surprised at our gentlemanly bearing and leniency towards those who might have been treated as foes to the general government and Union cause." Grierson rarely granted leniency toward eatables, however, and "several barrels of eggs, [together with] a lot of sugar, flour, ham, and bacon . . . which with other supplies appropriated proved sufficient for a hearty meal for the entire command."[55]

Lingering in Hazlehurst offered the Confederates an opportunity to catch up with the raiders, and this was something Grierson could not afford. Even though the railroad was broken and the telegraph lines cut, word was surely spreading of their arrival, and the engineer who had saved his train at the last moment was certain to do so. Around sunset, the brigade commander pointed his reunified command west once more

54 *OR* 24, pt. 1, 526; *Senate Report 772*, 52nd Congress, 1st Session, 1-2; Grierson, *A Just and Righteous Cause*, 165; Woodward, "Grierson's Raid," 708; Surby, *Grierson Raids*, 70; "Escape of a Train," *Jackson Daily Mississippian*, April 30, 1863. Neal tried unsuccessfully to recoup his losses.

55 Grierson, *A Just and Righteous Cause*, 165.

and moved out. He intended to ride far enough away from the railroad to allow his men a decent night's sleep, because he had kept them awake the night before.[56]

It was a good thing Grierson moved when he did. News of his presence flashed all along the rail and telegraph lines, especially to Jackson, where those who had been convinced the raid had been turned back north now realized their mistake. One of Pemberton's confidants, reported the editor of the *Jackson Daily Mississippian*, had declared the raiders "were running for dear life—that their horses were jaded and worn down and the men in constant dread of capture." But he added, "Such is just the opposite of the facts." The Federal brigade, continued the newspaper, was a "splendid looking and daring set of men, well equipped and well horsed." According to an informant from Hazlehurst, "The whole force entered the town in squads of fifty and a hundred—several hours interval between the van and rear guards."[57]

Grierson, meanwhile, moved west toward the small village of Gallatin, which was four miles off the railroad. There, he turned the column southwest and rode along the road leading toward Union Church, capturing along the way at Hargroves a large "64-pound artillery piece, a heavy wagon load of ammunition, and machinery for mounting the gun." The large cannon had been destined for the Vicksburg area; Grierson thought the mostly likely destination was Port Gibson.[58]

One trooper in the 6th Illinois Cavalry detailed the destruction of the captured weapon and its wagons. The cannon, he wrote, was one of the largest "I ever saw. . . . They were hauled by cattle." The Illinois men spiked the gun, destroyed the carriage and the ammunition, and killed the oxen pulling it. They next gathered the ammunition wagons, piled boards and fence rails on top, and set them on fire. The ensuing explosions shocked the onlookers, and "the rails flew in the air like birds. There was never such noise. There were some dismounted. We lit running, the horses tore loose from the boys that were dismounted; we

---

56   *OR* 24, pt. 1, 526; Freyburger, *Letters to Ann*, 45.

57   "The Raid at Hazlehurst—From Our Jackson Boys," *Jackson Daily Mississippian,* April 30, 1863.

58   "The Grierson Raid," *Weekly Register* (Canton, IL), September 7, 1863; *OR* 24, pt. 1, 526; Woodward, "Grierson's Raid," 708-9; Daniel E. Robbins to Brother, May 7, 1863.

ran about one hundred and fifty yards before we stopped." The shells, thought another trooper, "made a fine booming."[59]

With the excitement behind them, Grierson urged his column on. The sun was approaching the horizon, but the men could not see it. Another storm system had moved in, and a drenching rain pelted the exhausted Federals. That afternoon, reported Grierson, "It rained in torrents, and the men were completely drenched." The fact that the men had worked hard all day and had not slept the night before, coupled with the terrible weather, convinced Grierson to halt a few miles outside Gallatin. The Federals made camp on the spacious Jesse Thompson plantation along the upper reaches of the same Bayou Pierre that would, closer to its mouth, play a large role in Grant's upcoming Vicksburg operations.[60]

Like several other plantation owners the Federals had met in Mississippi, the 50-year-old Thompson was also a slave owner. His total net worth, including 39 slaves, was placed at $60,000. The weary band of Illinoisans spent the night along Thompson Creek grateful for the provisions and rest. Their commander was thankful they had put 30 miles behind them that day and more than 70 since they had logged their last full night of sleep at McAdory's plantation on April 25.[61]

Grierson knew he was approaching the end of his raid, although how it would end remained to be determined. His column had ridden some 110 miles since leaving Newton Station on April 24. He did not know where Grant was, but the best chance of ending his raid successfully was to link up with his army on this side of the Mississippi River. Perhaps news would arrive with better information to help guide him on his final leg of the journey. If no intelligence on Grant's location reached him, Grierson knew his next best chance to emerge safely from Mississippi was to continue riding south toward Union-held territory and Baton Rouge.[62]

59 Jackson, *The History of Orange Jackson's War Life*, 9; Daniel E. Robbins to Parents, May 5, 1863.

60 *OR* 24, pt. 1, 526; 1860 Copiah County, Mississippi, Population and Slave Schedules, NARA; Jesse Thompson Deed, Book R, Copiah County Chancery Clerk, 289-90.

61 *OR* 24, pt. 1, 526; 1860 Copiah County, Mississippi, Population and Slave Schedules, NARA; Jesse Thompson Deed, Book R, Copiah County Chancery Clerk, 289-90.

62 *OR* 24, pt. 1, 526.

Although he was unsure what direction to ride, one thing Grierson knew with near-certainty was that enemy forces would quickly hem him in if he did not keep moving.

CHAPTER NINE

The Failure

The tangible objective of Benjamin Grierson's long trek through Mississippi was to break the Southern Railroad of Mississippi, Vicksburg's lifeline to the outside Confederacy. His skillful and daring leadership had carried his troopers to the railroad almost unopposed. Once there, his men damaged the line as best they could with the little time and few tools they had in their possession. The extent of the damage he inflicted had yet to be determined.[1]

The second goal of his raid was less tangible and more complicated. Grant intended for Grierson's raid to divert focus away from his army's crossing of the Mississippi River. On that score, Grierson had no idea whether this objective was being achieved. Yet every indication was that his ride was confusing the enemy and thus helping the Army of the Tennessee. The fact that messages were flying out of Pemberton's headquarters in Jackson in an effort to catch and trap Grierson demonstrate the Confederate commander's interest and focus on the Federal raider. Although he was completely unaware of Pemberton's state of mind, Grierson would have been comforted to know his effort had knocked the Confederate gyroscope askew.[2]

---

1 "The Great Federal Raid," *Natchez Daily Courier*, May 5, 1863; "The Yankee Raid in Mississippi," n.d., *Mobile Advertiser and Register*, copy in Stephen A. Forbes Papers, UI.

2 *OR* 24, pt. 3, 781-800.

Now that the road had been damaged, Grierson and his cavalry set off on the last leg of their historic ride in an effort to get out of the Magnolia State as quickly and as safely as possible. This final objective was even more complicated because the situation that would dictate how he would accomplish it remained in flux. Possibilities about how to escape from deep within the state had been tossed about even before the raid left Tennessee. Only Grierson could judge the best route to safety, and even he remained unsure, changing his mind on more than one occasion. He first considered taking a wide swing east and north through Alabama but then decided that continuing south was his best course. While a haven in Baton Rouge offered refuge from Confederate retribution, scouting reports suggested he should move west and break up more railroads in the process and join Grant once he crossed the Army of the Tennessee into Mississippi.[3]

Getting the timing right was the main concern. Grierson's troopers would be exposed and vulnerable to capture or destruction if they reached the Grand Gulf area ahead of Grant's crossing. If he arrived too late, his troopers would be unable to help Grant—if such help was needed—and still be vulnerable because Confederates (already alerted to Grant's presence and likely intent) would be concentrating into the area. An approach to Grand Gulf also risked turning the important diversionary aspect of his raid on its head. If the cavalry brigade were corralled and captured, or just pinpointed, the game of cat and mouse across the Magnolia State would be over, and Pemberton and his generals could shift their focus back to the river and zero in on the real threat looming just across the water in Louisiana.[4]

Because of these timing issues, Grierson approached the Mississippi River counties cautiously and in something of a quandary during the period from April 28 to 30. Adjutant Woodward perhaps summed it up best when he wrote, "The march was resumed . . . without any definite objective, relying on information as to the movements of Grant's army about Vicksburg."[5]

*   *   *

3   Ibid., pt. 1, 527.

4   Grierson, *A Just and Righteous Cause*, 166.

5   Woodward, "Grierson's Raid," 709.

While Grierson made his way west, the larger aspects of the diversionary operation were in full bloom, its various components having either recently concluded or having reached their final stages. Sooy Smith's and Colonel Bryant's forays into northwestern Mississippi were long over, but other efforts were ongoing and new ones just beginning. In Alabama, for example, Abel Streight's raid was well underway, screened initially by Grenville Dodge's expedition until he turned back on April 29 to return to Corinth. Streight, meanwhile, was now moving through the middle part of the state toward Georgia in the face of nothing more than light skirmishing.[6]

Federals in West Tennessee also restarted their efforts to aid Grierson should he decide to return north. After arriving back at La Grange on April 26, Edward Hatch refitted his Iowa regiment and, with fresh orders from Sooy Smith in hand, led a new brigade south three days later with the express purpose of attacking "the forces of the enemy concentrating at New Albany and Pontotoc, to intercept the supposed return of Colonel Grierson." Hatch had with him his own 2nd Iowa Cavalry, the 4th Illinois Cavalry, and the mounted 6th Iowa Infantry, along with some local West Tennessee cavalry and a four-gun battery. The Iowa infantry boys, veterans of Shiloh and other actions, were as skeptical about being mounted on mules as some cavalrymen, with one Hawkeye describing it as "quite an odd looking sight." The Iowan was soon a hearty supporter, writing, "I thought our regiment was good at jayhawking but they can't hold a candle to the 6th." In all, Hatch's force numbered more than 1,200 men, larger than the column Grierson was now pushing toward Grand Gulf and with much more firepower. Worried about Grierson's whereabouts and status, General Hurlbut was more than anxious to get Hatch's command up and moving. On April 29, he informed General Halleck, "I have sent 1,200 men this morning from La Grange to take them in the rear and help Grierson. His orders are to return by Alabama. If accomplished as reported, it is a gallant thing."[7]

Employing scouts in civilian dress or Confederate uniforms, much as Grierson had done, Hatch rode south through Ripley and flanked the Confederates at New Albany by crossing the Tallahatchie River farther

6   OR 23, pt. 1, 248-49, 256-57, 287-89.

7   Ibid., pt. 3, 247; Pierce, *History of the Second Iowa Cavalry*, 56-57; John to Jennie, April 28, 1863.

to the east. Once over, he chased a small Confederate regiment south toward Okolona before discovering the main enemy body under General Chalmers had moved into his rear and crossed north of the Tallahatchie. Confident Grierson was nowhere in the area, Hatch rode back north and reached the cavalry depot at La Grange on May 5. Although Hatch had managed to avoid any serious fighting, he had not found Grierson or any indication that the raid had decided to return north. In fact, Grierson was more than 250 miles south, around Union Church on the morning Hatch left Tennessee to find and assist him. Hatch's ride made little difference at that point, and neither did another cavalry foray under Dodge sent out from Corinth for the same purpose.[8]

Other actions closer to Grierson, however, did make a difference. Sherman, for example, was in the midst of his Haynes' Bluff diversion. Grant made a formal request that he launch the feint on April 27. Sherman took one of his divisions up the Yazoo River and went ashore near where he had been bloodily repulsed the previous December. There, he bluffed and feinted, gathering as much attention as possible while resisting the temptation to avenge his earlier defeat. Historians have debated the operation's effectiveness, but Sherman had no doubt about it. A staff officer, Sherman reported, explained "that our division has had perfect success, great activity being seen in Vicksburg, and troops pushing up this way." He later concluded, "This diversion, made with so much pomp and display . . . completely fulfilled its purpose."[9]

Part of the operation's success came about because Sherman called his effort off as soon as he could. Grant was convinced that crossing the river south of Vicksburg was the only way to successfully attack the enemy bastion, and Sherman wanted to be with the army and his boss when that happened. Therefore, he stayed up the Yazoo River just long enough to buy Grant some additional time while attracting the enemy's attention and no longer. Sherman turned his corps south as soon as he reached the Mississippi River. Even though he did not have much faith in Grant's operation, he was intent on being part of it and would do what he could to make it a success.[10]

8   *OR* 24, pt. 1, 579; Davis, diary, April 29, 1863, http://www.rootsweb.ancestry. com/~mscivilw/davis.htm; John to Jennie, April 28, 1863.

9   *OR* 24, pt. 3, 240, 244, 261; Sherman, *Memoirs*, vol. 1, 319.

10   *OR* 24, pt. 3, 261.

The most critical movement underway while Grierson was hovering just east of Grant's potential crossing point was the crossing itself. General John McClernand's failure to have his corps ready to lead the way across the Mississippi River on April 27 or 28 aggravated Grant, but the political general had his men and materiel in readiness on April 29. Admiral David Dixon Porter's gunboats pummeled Grand Gulf mercilessly for hours that day, but his guns were unable to silence the Confederate batteries. A crossing at Grand Gulf was too risky and now out of the question. Undeterred, Grant moved his army downriver to seek out another crossing point the next day. He found what he was seeking at Bruinsburg, where the Union host crossed undetected and unopposed—in large part because of Grierson's inland diversion, aided also by the other raids previously mentioned.[11]

By this time Grierson was within about 30 miles of the river and the Confederate bastion at Grand Gulf and the ultimate crossing point at Bruinsburg. A junction was entirely feasible with good timing and even better good fortune.

*   *   *

A new threat added another wrinkle of difficulty for Grierson and his men. According to the *Jackson Daily Mississippian*, Confederate leaders had pinpointed "Grierson and his jolly raiders" by April 28 and were doing all they could to track them down and destroy or capture "these vile raiders who had created such havoc in the state." The newspaper was sure the raiders who hit Hazlehurst were "no doubt the same party" that had sacked Newton Station four days earlier, and it printed a remarkably accurate order of battle of the Federal units involved and the names of their officers, down to the artillery's two pounders. A courier who had escaped from Grierson aided the Confederate high command with many of the details.[12]

Pemberton was adamant about catching Grierson. The bold enemy raider had entered an area overflowing with Confederate troops, including

11 Smith, *The Decision Was Always My Own*, 94-101.

12 "The Yankee on the N. O. and Jackson Railroad," *Jackson Daily Mississippian*, April 28, 1863; Grierson, *A Just and Righteous Cause*, 166; "The Yankees at Brookhaven," *Jackson Daily Mississippian*, April 30, 1863.

almost the entire army defending Vicksburg as well as the troops stationed in and around nearby Port Hudson. The general area was smaller than the expansive interior through which the Federals had ridden, and a major railroad made it relatively easy for Pemberton to rapidly combine troops at a given point. By this time, the Confederate commander had almost exclusively focused his attention on catching Grierson. Pemberton had remained attuned to Grant's activity up through April 23, but when Grierson hit Newton Station the next day, he swiveled his focus toward the raider. Although Pemberton's division commanders were still watching and warning him about the threat posed by Grant's army, Pemberton had his sights set on bagging Grierson. The long Federal ride south through Mississippi made it clear to many in and out of the army that Pemberton was not doing his job particularly well. One Smith County citizen went so far as to ask Governor Pettus, "Is Pemberton asleep?"[13]

Pemberton was not asleep, but he was woefully lacking in the cavalry he needed to stop Grierson. He complained loudly to anyone who would listen, especially his superior Joseph E. Johnston in Middle Tennessee. His messages betrayed his mind-set during the last days of April. Nearly every missive, including those discussing the basic threat posed by Grant's army in Louisiana, dwelled to one degree or another on Grierson's raid. "However necessary cavalry may be to Army of Tennessee, it is indispensable to me to keep my communications," he lectured Johnston on April 27. "The enemy are to-day at Hazlehurst on New Orleans and Jackson Railroad. I cannot defend every station on the road with infantry. Am compelled to bring down cavalry from Northern Mississippi here," he continued, "and the whole of that section is consequently left open. Further, these raids endanger my vital positions." The cavalry he brought down was Colonel Barteau's Tennessee troopers; Pemberton advised Barteau to mount the state troops in north Mississippi to replace his regiment. The Vicksburg commander also shifted infantry units under General Loring farther south now that the threat had moved into that part of the state. Pemberton wrote President Davis the next day, "A demonstration is now being made in large force at Hard Times." He also pleaded, "It is indispensable that I have more cavalry. The approaches

13   J. M. Quin to John J. Pettus, April 28, 1863.

William Wirt Adams. As part of the Vicksburg army watching the Mississippi River crossings, Colonel Adams and his cavalry regiment were called east from along the river to intercept Grierson. His departure left Grant easy access to landing spots on the east bank of the Mississippi. *Photographic History of the Civil War*

to Northern Mississippi are almost unprotected, and it is impossible to prevent these raids with infantry."[14]

Off in distant Tennessee, meanwhile, Johnston remained out of touch with what was unfolding on the ground in Mississippi. "I am sorry that you did not sooner report raid in Southern Mississippi," he wrote his subordinate. An incredulous Pemberton responded, "This expression of your regret may seem to imply censure, which I feel is undeserved." He reminded Johnston that he had informed the theater commander of the raid nine days earlier, on April 20.[15]

Pemberton believed the major threat posed by Grierson was his ability to move into the rear of his Vicksburg army. He informed Gen. John Bowen at Grand Gulf on April 27 of this threat and made a special effort to reinforce the garrison guarding the Big Black River railroad bridge east of Vicksburg, which he believed was Grierson's next target. "A guard of a company should be kept at each end of this bridge and trestle

14   *OR* 24, pt. 3, 791, 794, 797.

15   Ibid., 791, 802.

work," he ordered, though it was unclear what he expected a company or two could do against a large force of veteran cavalry with artillery.[16]

Pemberton continued working the wires during the final days of April, sending a flurry of messages to small unit commanders (including captains and majors) to move to the scene of the raid, "harassing his rear and flank." By this time, two main contingents of cavalry were on Grierson's trail. One was Wirt Adams's Mississippi cavalry regiment, which included companies of Alabamians. Adams had been deployed south of Vicksburg with John Bowen before his command was broken up to cover more territory along the Mississippi River to better prevent a surprise crossing. When a new threat appeared from the east in the form of the Federal raiders, Pemberton ordered Bowen to "collect Wirt Adams' cavalry and send them out to meet the enemy. . . . Follow them up without delay. Annoy and ambush them if possible." An incredulous Bowen did as ordered, even though stripping away Adams's cavalry uncovered the river crossings Grant was even then threatening. Adams gathered his scattered companies and concentrated his command near Fayette, between Vicksburg and Natchez, with a view to moving east to meet Grierson. Adams already had a contingent of two cavalry companies under Capt. S. B. Cleveland farther east around Union Church, which had ridden there from Natchez. The companies waited around the small hamlet in Jefferson County for the balance of the command to arrive.[17]

A second force under Col. Robert V. Richardson gathered in Jackson. Richardson, who led the 1st Tennessee Partisan Rangers, was an odd choice to lead the effort. Just a few days earlier, Pemberton and Johnston had sought his arrest for illegal partisan conscription activity. As a result, he was no longer with his Tennessee unit because he had traveled to Pemberton's headquarters in Jackson. Richardson had fought Grierson in Tennessee, and since Pemberton was short of riders and experienced officers, he tasked him with catching the elusive Federals. Richardson, however, only had available a few companies of Maj. Walter A. Rorer's newly mounted 20th Mississippi Infantry. Pemberton had ordered the Magnolia troops mounted and told the regiment's colonel, William N. Brown, that he should "take command of [the] cavalry." Despite

---

16 Ibid., 792-94.

17 Ibid., pt. 1, 533, 538; pt. 3, 792, 798-99; R. R. Hutchinson to Wirt Adams, April 17 and 27, 1863, in Wirt Adams Collection, University of Mississippi.

Robert V. Richardson. Although under legal trouble, Colonel Robert V. Richardson was available and thus placed in command of the effort to capture Grierson in south Mississippi. *Photographic History of the Civil War*

Pemberton's efforts, only Major Rorer's small and uninspired battalion received mounts. The major later confided to a cousin, "At first I disliked very much to be mounted, but after being mounted awhile, I liked the service much better than infantry."[18]

Moving south from Jackson by train on April 28 was more difficult than anyone expected. Colonel Richardson arrived at the Jackson station, "supposing the train of troops to accompany me was ready to start." Instead, he discovered the Mississippians were only then just beginning the loading process. The effort consumed several precious hours. The clock was approaching three in the morning before everyone was aboard and ready to move. The fiasco continued when someone realized the conductor had gone to bed "at his chamber." The aggravated colonel sent word for the conductor to get out of bed and conduct the train or "I would send for him a file of men." The conductor did as instructed, but after consulting with the engineer, he protested that too many cars were on the train and

18 W. A. Rorer to Susan, June 13, 1863, in W. A. Rorer Letters, Duke University, copy in MDAH; *OR* 24, pt. 1, 547, 550, 757; pt. 3, 798-99; Waldon Loving, *Coming Like Hell: The Story of the 12th Tennessee Cavalry, Richardson's Brigade, Forrest's Cavalry Corps, Confederate States Army, 1862-1865* (Lincoln, NE: Writer's Club Press, 2002), 21-22.

the locomotive could not pull such a load. Three cars were uncoupled, but the engineer and conductor discovered another problem: There was not enough wood aboard to make it to the next station, and no lamps were available for night travel. "These men [the conductor and engineer] were churlish, and seemed to be laboring to defeat as far as possible the movement of troops," complained an aggravated Richardson. "They claim their privilege of exemption from military service as employees of the railroad company. It should not be granted to men who are so unmindful of the public interests." Axes were distributed so the men could cut wood, but it was daybreak by the time the train finally departed.[19]

The train lumbered south toward Hazlehurst, where word reached Richardson that "1,000 Yankees were within a quarter of a mile of the place, approaching it." Grierson had already passed through hours earlier and was well west of the railroad, but Richardson had no way of knowing that. He rightfully ordered the train to stop and back up. A scout left the train and returned a short time later with the welcome report that there were no Federals in the area. The train continued to Hazlehurst, where Richardson found out the latest on Grierson's whereabouts.[20]

While Richardson fumed over transportation issues, Pemberton continued to fixate on catching Grierson—to the aggravation of his division commanders, particularly John Bowen at Grand Gulf. Bowen, an outstanding and alert commander, knew he was facing the largest threat confronting Vicksburg and informed Pemberton as much. "Reports indicate an immense force opposite me," he wrote on April 28. "Harrison is fighting them now." Pemberton's reply revealed his mind-set: "Have you force enough to hold your position? If not, give me the smallest additional force with which you can. My small cavalry force necessitates the use of infantry to protect important points."[21]

*   *   *

The commotion within the Confederate ranks redounded to the benefit of Grierson's troopers. While Adams concentrated his command and

19 *OR* 24, pt. 1, 547.

20 Ibid.

21 Ibid., pt. 3, 797.

Richardson struggled to squeeze some efficiency out of the railroad, the Illinois riders moved against but little Confederate resistance.

The Federal cavalrymen awoke southwest of Gallatin on the morning of April 28 ready to continue their ride. Grierson had his troopers in the saddle by 6:00 a.m. and, with the 6th Illinois Cavalry in advance, rode southwest toward the small Jefferson County hamlet of Union Church. By 2:00 p.m. the column had made nearly 20 miles since leaving their camp at Thompson's plantation along Bayou Pierre and crossed into the first tier of counties lining the Mississippi River. Grierson stopped to feed his men and mounts about two miles northeast of Union Church on the modest plantation along Hurricane Creek owned by Adam C. Snyder. The native 47-year-old New Yorker had five slaves and a net worth of $6,875, his real estate accounting for most of the wealth. He also had provisions, which the troopers and horses desperately needed.[22]

Snyder's was not the only plantation in the area visited by the raiders. Grierson's horses and mules were close to breaking down, and their Northern owners had little choice but to exchange them for stock found on almost every plantation and farm they encountered. Former slaves provided statements after the war for the Southern Claims Commission about what they witnessed when Grierson and his men made their appearance. According to one slave near Union Church:

> A large lot of the Yankee soldiers who were riding horses and mules came to Mrs. McLean's place and some of them rode through our front yard and there into the side gate of the pasture where we kept our horses and mules, and took them off with them. I was on the edge of the woods—and had a plain view of the pasture where I first heard that the Yankees were coming. I went out towards the woods—I was afraid that they would harm me—and I watched them I stopped in the woods all night—some of them stopped at the place and in the house all night—and some of them down to Union Church. When they left the next day they took off the mules—they left one broken down horse he died shortly afterwards we never worked him.[23]

22 Ibid., pt. 1, 526; Grierson, *A Just and Righteous Cause*, 166; "The Grierson Raid," *Weekly Register* (Canton, IL), September 7, 1863; 1860 Jefferson County, Mississippi, Population and Slave Schedules.

23 Milly McLean, Deposition, October 29, 1873, Southern Claim File of Mariah McLean Buie, Case #2723, NARA RG 123, U.S. Court of Claims, http://www.angelfire. com/folk/gljmr/McLeanMilly.html. For additional descriptions by a slave, see T. H. Bowman, *Reminiscences of an Ex-Confederate Soldier, or Forty Years on Crutches* (Austin, TX: Gammel Statesman Publishing Company, 1904), 12.

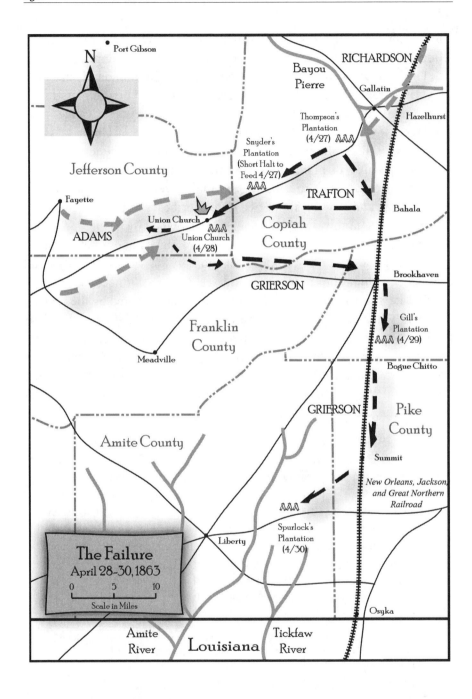

N

Port Gibson

Jefferson County

Fayette

RICHARDSON

Bayou
Pierre

Gallatin

Hazelhurst

Thompson's
Plantation
(4/27) ΛΛΛ

Snyder's
Plantation
(Short Halt to
Feed 4/27)
ΛΛΛ

TRAFTON

Bahala

Union Church
ΛΛΛ
Union Church
(4/28)

ADAMS

Copiah
County

GRIERSON

Brookhaven

Gill's
Plantation
ΛΛΛ (4/29)

Franklin
County

Meadville

Bogue Chitto

GRIERSON

Pike
County

Amite County

Summit

New Orleans, Jackson,
and Great Northern
Railroad

ΛΛΛ

The Failure
April 28-30, 1863

0   5   10

Scale in Miles

Liberty

Spurlock's
Plantation
(4/30)

Osyka

Amite
River

Louisiana

Tickfaw
River

Others slaves left similar accounts. "A large lot of Yankee soldiers came to our place and stopped in the road," one remembered, "and a lot of the soldiers went into the field where the hands were ploughing and bedding up land for corn and told them to stop their work and get the mules out—they did so and they put their saddles upon them, that they took off from the horses and mules that they were riding. They rode them off and led off the stock that they took the saddles off from." Another slave indicated, "The soldiers rode by the house between 10 and 11 o'clock—they were driving a large lot of horses and mules with them. They got our stock out of the field where they were ploughing." Still another recalled, "I had been down to the horse lot and had just fed the stock and was on the point of returning when my attention was called to a body of cavalrymen who were coming up the road. They rode up to where I was and on by. Some of them in the mean time," he continued, "stopped and went into the horse pasture they opened the big gate as they went in, they caught the two mules that were in the lot and a blaze-faced sorrel horse changed their saddle and bridles from some worn out mules that they were riding to Mr. Cato's and immediately rode out and joined the main body."[24]

Grierson contemplated his next move now that he was in the eastern reaches of a county bordering the Mississippi River. He knew the Confederates would have significantly more resources along the waterway watching for Grant than they had chasing the raiders, regardless of the diversion's effectiveness. The Federals were within a box of strong Confederate garrisons, with Vicksburg to the north, Port Hudson to the south, the Mississippi River to the west, and the New Orleans, Jackson, and Great Northern Railroad to the east. Confederate troops could be quickly concentrated against him either by river or, more likely, railroad. It is no wonder he later wrote, "After leaving Hazlehurst, the greatest

---

24 Charles Roundtree, Deposition, October 1873, Southern Claim File of Mary Buie, Case #2568, NARA RG 123, U.S. Court of Claims, http://www.angelfire.com/folk/gljmr/RoundtreeC.html; Alex Roundtree, Deposition, October 1873, Southern Claim File of Mary Buie, Case #2568, NARA RG 123, U.S. Court of Claims, http://www.angelfire.com/folk/gljmr/RoundtreeA.html; and Levi Adams, quoted in "Between the Gate Posts," April 30, 2013, http://betweenthegateposts.blogspot.com/2013/04/a-body-of-cavalrymen-coming-up-road.html.

generalship [and] the utmost care and vigilance was necessary for the safety of my command."[25]

Because of the threat posed by the railroad, Grierson decided to send yet another detachment east to inflict additional damage to the line. After counseling with his officers on the road to Snyder's plantation, he dispatched a battalion of the 7th Illinois Cavalry under Capt. George W. Trafton, along with Surby and another scout, east to Bahala (modern-day Wesson), just 10 miles south of Hazlehurst, to break the line once more and disrupt communications. Trafton, a man Adjutant Woodward described as "an officer of extraordinary good judgment and nerve," had orders to destroy any other government supplies he ran across." Trafton's detachment would damage the railroad as well as a coal-firing operation, a steam engine for pumping water and powering a sawmill, and water tanks. "We chopped down some trestle work, [and] burnt up the tank & some machinery belonging to the Confederates," related one of the Illinoisans.[26]

While Trafton's troopers performed their duties, which included the capture of a Port Hudson officer who worked on Gen. Frank Gardner's staff, Grierson remained at Snyder's plantation. While he and his men were resting there, Captain Cleveland's two companies of Wirt Adams's Mississippi cavalry appeared from the southwest between Grierson's men and Union Church.[27] "While feeding," Grierson reported, "our pickets were fired upon by a considerable force." The colonel immediately turned out both regiments (minus the battalion with Trafton at Bahala) and moved forward, skirmishing with the Confederate horsemen. It did not take Grierson long to discover that he was not facing ill-trained state militia but veteran Mississippi cavalry. What he did not know was that he was only facing two companies and that many more, complete with mountain howitzers, were on the way under Colonel Adams himself. This was the first serious Confederate resistance faced by the main column,

---

25　Grierson, *A Just and Righteous Cause*, 166.

26　*OR* 24, pt. 1, 526; Woodward, "Grierson's Raid," 709; S. L. Woodward, "Grierson's Raid, April 17th to May 2d, 1863," *Journal of the United States Cavalry Association* (July 1904), vol. 15, no 53, 95; Surby, *Grierson Raids*, 78-80; Freyburger, *Letters to Ann*, 45.

27　*OR* 24, pt. 1, 526; Grierson, *A Just and Righteous Cause*, 167; Woodward, "Grierson's Raid," 95; Surby, *Grierson Raids*, 80.

Hatch's diversion excluded, since Grierson had passed through the New Albany-Pontotoc area nine days earlier on April 19. Thus far, the raiders had been extremely fortunate to make it this deep into Mississippi mostly unopposed. The appearance of Adams's Mississippians suggested Grierson's good fortune had turned against him.[28]

The skirmishing caught everyone's attention, including civilians who took shelter wherever they could find it. Twelve-year-old Inez Torrey remembered those frightening hours and how a rider had notified her that the "Yankees were coming." Just a mile or so west of Union Church, she continued, "We were scared to death that they would kill us all. I grabbed my little brother and we hid under the dining room table, which was covered with a long table cloth that reached the floor. I don't know how long we stayed there, but it seemed forever. We could plainly hear the cannon-fire," she added, "just like thunder."[29]

Grierson did not mention utilizing Smith's two pounders, as Inez Torrey remembered, but he certainly did fight. In fact, he pushed his troopers southwest and forced the roughly 100 Mississippians back to and through Union Church. The check suffered by Captain Cleveland was of little concern to the Confederate officer, who sent a report back to Colonel Adams, Franklin Gardner at Port Hudson, and his division commander, Carter Stevenson, at Vicksburg: Grierson's raiders had finally been found. The elusive enemy was near Union Church, reported the captain, and he had "been skirmishing with them for some hours this evening." Although he could not ascertain Grierson's strength, Cleveland informed his superiors that the raiders had four pieces of artillery (which indicates that Grierson had, in fact, used the guns during the skirmishing). The important information pinpointing the enemy moved up the chain of command to Pemberton himself. Even though the Vicksburg commander was not listed as a recipient, an alert telegraph operator forwarded the message to him in the wee hours of the night. Even the *Jackson Daily Mississippian* reported on the fighting in its April 29 evening edition, writing that "quite a lively skirmish ensued."[30]

28 *OR* 24, pt. 1, 526; Roth, "Grierson's Raid," 60.

29 Roth, "Grierson's Raid," 60.

30 *OR* 24, pt. 1, 538-39; "Skirmish at Union Church in Jefferson County," *Jackson Daily Mississippian*, April 29, 1863.

While Cleveland was falling back and sending his report, Grierson refused to let up in his push against what he had now determined to be a relatively small number of enemy cavalry. The Federal advance through the small village was a masterful display of force. The cavalry, explained Grierson, "went through the village of Union Church by sheer might. Whole lines of picket fences were torn up and overturned by mere rush. Right and left went everything that came in their way, scarcely breaking their onward step." The Illinoisans learned the identity of the enemy command by interrogating the wounded and captured Mississippians. Despite the length of the running skirmish, possible use of artillery, hard riding, and flying lead, the affair produced surprisingly few casualties. One of the injured Federal troopers was Sgt. G. M. Vaughn of Company F, 7th Illinois Cavalry, who "was accidentally wounded in the hip while breaking a shot gun" against a tree. The discharge sent buckshot into his thigh, and he had to be left with civilians along the way. With Captain Cleveland's companies dispersed, Grierson ordered his cavalrymen to bivouac for the night at Union Church, where he erected a strong picket line to watch for any renewed Confederate activity.[31]

"We camped at night in Union Town [Church.] Small place," scribbled one 7th Illinois soldier. The village may have been unimpressive, but it was a magnet that pulled Confederates in from afar. While the Federal troopers were "resting and getting into true fighting trim and mood," reported Grierson, scouts concluded that Adams's Mississippians were forming for a joint attack, likely at dawn, against their position at Union Church. Cleveland's pair of Mississippi companies still lurked ahead of Grierson in proximity to the village, but Wirt Adams had arrived with two more companies of his regiment and artillery, and his remaining companies were riding to join him. Adams had moved around the Federal position and was now behind Union Church on the road from Gallatin that Grierson had just traversed. The unsettling news that the enemy had artillery with them increased the odds against Grierson, because just about any size of gun could easily overwhelm Smith's small two pounders. It was, explained Stephen Forbes, "a dangerously complicated situation."[32]

---

31 *OR* 24, pt. 1, 526; Grierson, *A Just and Righteous Cause*, 167; "The Grierson Raid," *Weekly Register* (Canton, IL), September 7, 1863; Surby, *Grierson Raids*, 84.

32 Curtiss, diary, April 28, 1863; *OR* 24, pt. 1, 526, 533; Grierson, *A Just and Righteous Cause*, 167; Forbes, "Grierson's Cavalry Raid," 115.

Fortunately for Grierson, help was on the way. Trafton's 7th Illinois battalion had made its way to Bahala on the morning of April 28, where it damaged the railroad and telegraph before retracing the 20 miles back to Union Church. Because of the distance, the battalion did not arrive in the area until about 3 a.m. Reconnecting with Grierson, however, proved to be quite an adventure.[33]

With Confederates between them and Grierson, Trafton's troopers advanced with Surby's scouts fanned out ahead of them. News that "a large force of the enemy had passed about five hours before" infused the column with caution, and the men continued picking their way forward through the darkness. The scouts played their old tricks when they came upon enemy soldiers by claiming they, too, were Confederates. One of Surby's common ruses involved asking to examine their guns before taking them prisoners. He played one Confederate particularly well. While chatting with the man, Trafton rode up and announced, "This man may be a Yankee." The Confederate "most emphatically denied the soft impeachment, saying: 'No, gentlemen; you are mistaken. I am a lieutenant from Port Hudson, and can tell you all about the post and who commands it, so that you can tell if I am all right." Another Southerner, this one a planter named Mosby, was so convinced Trafton and his men were Confederates that he guided them to Adams's command near Union Church. Almost everything Surby recommended garnered the reply, "A capital idea," and the scouts dealing with Mosby soon took to referring to the planter as "A Capital Idea." Eventually, when the civilian learned the truth about who he was guiding, he protested that it had been "a d—d Yankee trick." Surby admitted as much when he replied, "Mr. Mosby, you are sold, but it is all fair in war times, and do you not think 'a capital idea?'" Adjutant Woodward recalled that the planter was "very much mollified when given a horse and equipments to carry him back to his home." Surby joked that he could keep the horse "in remembrance of the Yankees."[34]

Surby continued disarming and capturing Confederates in front of the column. "I thought of the delay I had occasioned the column so many times, knowing how tired and sleepy the men were, how they must

---

33 Surby, *Grierson Raids*, 82-84, 95-96; Woodward, "Grierson's Raid," 96-98.

34 Surby, *Grierson Raids*, 82-84, 95-96; Woodward," Grierson's Raid," 96-98.

have cursed me," Surby later admitted. "But they were ignorant of the proceeding in front, and as the prisoners continued to be sent back they began to realize the importance of the scouts." When Trafton's column finally eased into the rear of the Confederates northeast of Union Church, the enemy quickly realized their position had been compromised. As one participant described it, "Both Federal and Confederate, were thus cut in two, each by the other."[35]

Even though still separated from Grierson's main command, Trafton's appearance unnerved the Confederates. Adams blinked first. The last thing he had expected was the enemy showing up behind him. The Confederate colonel ordered those of his companies that had reached him to ride west with haste to escape the sudden threat of Federals in both his front and rear. "Turning to the right," Grierson later reported with much relief, "he flanked off and took the direct road towards Port Gibson." Captain Trafton's appearance "with a force in his rear changed his [Adams's] purpose," he added. The rank and file remained mostly unaware of what was transpiring. In an effort to describe what happened, one trooper related, "For reasons better known to themselves they turn off of the road & did not give us a fight."[36]

The arrival of Trafton's battalion shook Grierson from his sleep, and he called in Colonel Prince and Lieutenant Colonel Loomis to consult about the latest intelligence Trafton had gleaned during his perilous ride to and from the railroad. The council also included Adjutant Woodward, who, Surby confirmed, "He consulted on all such occasions." It was time for the officers to ponder their next move.[37]

*   *   *

Trafton's timely arrival and the resulting Confederate stampede meant Grierson did not have to fight his way out of a desperate place at Union Church when daylight appeared on April 29. The "dangerously complicated situation," however, gave him pause and taught him a

35 *OR* 24, pt. 1, 526, 533; Grierson, *A Just and Righteous Cause*, 166; Woodward, "Grierson's Raid," 95; Surby, *Grierson Raids*, 80-81, 92.

36 *OR* 24, pt. 1, 526, 533; Grierson, *A Just and Righteous Cause*, 166; Freyburger, *Letters to Ann*, 45.

37 Surby, *Grierson Raids*, 93-94.

lesson. Why was he moving west toward the river and Grant's supposed crossing point when he had heard nothing from or about that general's status? Serious fighting would have erupted by April 28 if the Army of the Tennessee had crossed the river and marched inland. Grierson would have heard about it from his scouts.[38]

In fact, Grant was not yet on Mississippi soil. "I had hurried forward fearing that I might be too late," Grierson later wrote, "but unfortunately had traveled a little too fast and was a few days ahead of time." Grant had scheduled an April 29 crossing once the navy silenced the Grand Gulf batteries to allow his army a safe passage and a zone in which to land troops. Admiral Porter's lengthy bombardment opened that day about 8 a.m. and lasted for more than five hours. It failed to knock out the enemy guns, however, leaving Grant no choice but to delay the crossing. By this time fewer than 30 miles separated the Army of the Tennessee from Grierson's raiders, so when Porter's guns opened fire, the faint thunder of the guns reached their ears. But what did the firing mean?[39]

"It was impossible to wait or remain quietly there," Grierson explained, "for the rebels were all round us." The Confederates had many advantages by this point in the raid, including "a knowledge of the country; of every road, public or private, every stream of water, large or small, with its fords and bridges," added the Federal commander. "They had forces above and below on the railroad, in front from Port Hudson to Vicksburg on the river, and in rear everywhere in all directions. Their scouts were watching; their couriers flying; their troops concentrating to capture us." What, Grierson wondered, "should hinder them from annihilating myself and small command[?]" He replied to his own rhetorical question: "Only one thing was in the way, and that was there were two parties to that little transaction. I, too, understood the runways and the shortest route to reach them. I also knew the rebels, their whereabouts, and the surest ways to blind and lead them astray."[40]

38 *OR* 24, pt. 1, 526.

39 Grierson, *A Just and Righteous Cause*, 166; "Grierson's Big Raid," n.d., in Thomas W. Lippincott Papers, ALPL; B. H. Grierson to T. W. Lippincott, March 13, 1886; Daniel E. Robbins to Parents, May 5, 1863.

40 B. H. Grierson to T. W. Lippincott, March 13, 1886; Grierson, *A Just and Righteous Cause*, 166.

Grierson thought long and hard as he considered what "Generals Gardner and Pemberton and other rebel commanders would do as capable military men, and what they would expect me to do." He had been riding toward the Mississippi River, and the Confederates in the area surely expected him to continue moving in that direction. Wirt Adams's Mississippians, after all, had fallen back in that direction after Trafton's appearance in order to defend against further Union incursion. Grierson had no firm information about Grant. Unless circumstances changed and he received proof of his crossing soon, moving his command closer to the river was not worth the risk. Grierson finally decided "not do what was expected of me." Instead, he intended to feint west toward Fayette and Natchez and then move east in a direction the Confederates would least expect. Even his own men "supposed we were going to the Mississippi," Grierson later revealed, though "none but myself and my adjutant were in [on] the secret."[41]

The Federal raiders moved out on the morning of April 29, twisting and turning to confuse the enemy. "I do not think we missed traveling toward any point on the compass," concluded Surby, who used some trickery to help improve their chances. A "prominent citizen who had been taken prisoner" rode with the colonel's entourage. Grierson did not let on that he knew "how great a rebel he was or how much he was devoted to the Southern cause." Once they stopped for a rest, Grierson placed the man "rather carelessly" in a room next to where he and Woodward discussed plans a little more loudly than they otherwise would have, the colonel "clearly articulat[ing] the remark that I was determined to go to Natchez and then across the Mississippi." With the fake intelligence seed firmly planted, the civilian was allowed to "slyly" escape without having to give his oath of parole so he could carry the information to the closest Confederate officials.[42]

Grierson employed additional deceit by sending "a strong demonstration toward Fayette, with a view of creating the impression that we were going toward Port Gibson or Natchez." The decision made sense. Other similar detachments had been effective, and there was every indication

41 T. W. Lippincott to S. A. Forbes, December 20, 1908; Grierson, *A Just and Righteous Cause*, 166-67; Woodward, "Grierson's Raid," 98.

42 Forbes, "Grierson's Cavalry Raid," 115; Grierson, *A Just and Righteous Cause*, 167-68; Surby, *Grierson Raids*, 96.

that this one would work just as well. While a small portion of the column moved toward Fayette 15 miles to the west, gobbling up some of Adams's pickets along the way posted to help facilitate a Confederate ambush, Grierson "quietly took the opposite direction, taking the road leading southeast to Brookhaven, on the railroad." In an effort to remain unseen, the column occasionally moved off the road. Grierson later boasted that while Adams's men waited in vain to spring an ambush on the Federals, his own pickets "were riding along with our column [as] prisoners of war." Adams's game, he added, "was 'over the hills and far away.'"[43]

Grierson's new feint worked to perfection. Colonel Richardson at Hazlehurst received reports of Trafton's attack at Bahala as well as the fighting at Union Church and, with three companies of Confederate mounted infantry, drove west. "So far as I could judge," Richardson later reported, "he was leaving the line of the railroad and was going to Natchez." Captain Cleveland had also assumed the raiders would continue toward Natchez and had so warned everyone who would listen. "Tell the operator at Natchez they may look out for them there," he had written while skirmishing with Grierson's Illinoisans on April 28. Adams, who had moved his command toward Fayette to reorganize and hit the Federals the next morning in an ambush, assumed the same thing. "Thinking it was his intention to reach Rodney or Natchez," Adams wrote from Fayette, "I marched my command to this point, where I have been joined by five companies." When Adams realized his error the next morning, he admitted his mistake by writing, "Found he had marched rapidly in direction of Brookhaven."[44]

While every Confederate in the area waited for the westward Union thrust, the column made good time trotting east toward the New Orleans, Jackson, and Great Northern Railroad. One trooper marveled at Grierson's ability to fool the enemy. "Many times," he later recalled, "he came in contact with two or three times his number and when he could not whip the Johnnies he seemed to know how to get out of the snap and was able to outgeneral the rebels at every point." With the 7th Illinois Cavalry in the lead, the column met wagons loaded with goods rolling in their direction, removed from idle railcars or stockpiles to keep it from

---

43 *OR* 24, pt. 1, 526-27; Grierson, *A Just and Righteous Cause*, 167-68; Woodward, "Grierson's Raid," 99.

44 *OR* 24, pt. 1, 533, 538, 547.

falling into Federal hands. One wagon was filled with "hogsheads of sugar . . . of course it was destroyed but not before the men replenished their haversacks." Grierson viewed the affair as a good sign of just how "bewildered were the people of the country."[45]

The trek to the New Orleans, Jackson, and Great Northern Railroad was more than 20 miles, so Grierson kept up the pace as best he could, because he had no time to spare. When he drew close to Brookhaven, he learned its citizens, like those at Garlandville and elsewhere, were organized and prepared to fight him. Rumor had it that an armed mob of 500 men was willing to defend the town. If true, this news was rather surprising. Southwest Mississippi was populated with a large percentage of Union sympathizers, similar to the counties in the northeast corner of the state and some along the Mississippi River. Adams, Franklin, and Amite Counties had all sent cooperationist delegates to the state secession convention, and all of them had voted against secession. Although Brookhaven was in neighboring Lawrence County, which had toed the secessionist line the entire way, there was good reason to expect at least some Confederate disloyalty inhabited the area.[46]

Grierson was in no mood to take any chances, and he could not afford to waste time outside the town deciding what to do. As the column approached Brookhaven, Grierson ordered his leading units to form in a column of fours and charge directly into the village. Someone fired a warning shot, but one Illinois trooper later reported that "'ere the echo of the report dies away we were in and among them." It was all "terror and confusion," confirmed Grierson. The civilians, armed and otherwise, were "running and yelling as our cavalry dashed into the place," with the 7th Illinois Cavalry troopers bursting into town at a full gallop. The defenders were "citizens and conscripts," and thus no match for the hardy Illinoisans bearing down on them. Grierson likely expected as much because the same thing had happened elsewhere, although these defenders did not disperse quite as peacefully as the others had done. At Garlandville, for example, Grierson made friends and left the

---

45 Augustus Hurff Memoirs, n.d., ALPL; "The Grierson Raid," *Weekly Register* (Canton, IL), September 7, 1863; *OR* 24, pt. 1, 527; Surby, *Grierson Raids*, 97.

46 Surby, *Grierson Raids*, 97.

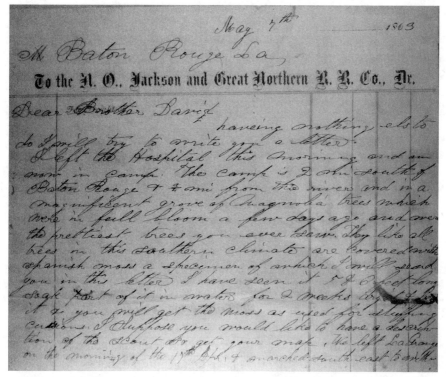

Soldier Letter. One of Grierson's raiders, Daniel Robbins, took letterhead from a New Orleans, Jackson, and Great Northern Railroad train station and wrote a letter home on it after reaching Baton Rouge. *Steve Hicks*

townspeople in peace. At Brookhaven, the Illinois troopers captured about 200 conscripts who had stood their ground a bit too long.[47]

Once the Federals took control of the town, a palpable relief spread through the citizenry when it became obvious the blue enemy did not intend to destroy the settlement. Grierson described their demeanor as "almost a welcome." As they had at Garlandville, the Federals made a few friends, often via dollar diplomacy. When the raiders paid the hotel owner for his food in large amounts of Confederate money gathered along the way, he became quite friendly and remarked that it would be fine with him if "the Yanks would come every day, if they paid like

47 *OR* 24, pt. 1, 527; Grierson, *A Just and Righteous Cause*, 168; "The Grierson Raid," *Weekly Register* (Canton, IL), September 7, 1863; Woodward, "Grierson's Raid," 100; Surby, *Grierson Raids*, 97.

you uns do." Grierson installed guards to protect homes and made sure nothing but military stores were confiscated or burned. When a fire began to spread, troopers used buckets and pails to keep it from burning other buildings. According to Surby, "The saving of the property was personally superintended by Colonel Grierson."[48]

With the possibility of linking up with Grant still in the back of his mind, Grierson ordered his troopers to destroy Brookhaven as a rail and Confederate concentration center. The railroad was the top priority, and the men destroyed a long stretch of track at Brookhaven to add to the destruction already done at Hazlehurst and again at Bahala. The telegraph wire was severed, and government property was destroyed. The latter proved quite extensive, because the state used Brookhaven as an induction center for conscripted troops. The 6th Illinois troopers, Grierson reported, found "a large and beautiful camp of instruction, comprising several hundred tents." The site also held large quantities of quartermaster and commissary supplies as well as arms and ammunition. It was a good haul in the midst of a quiet day of escape.[49]

Although the camp of instruction was basically empty, there was still hundreds of prisoners to parole. Pemberton had instructed officers to scatter their conscripts rather than have them captured, but as the Federals approached and offered paroles that would get the conscripts out of the war for a while, Confederates emerged from the woods to take advantage of the offer. "It was surprising to see the eagerness with which every man liable for military duty, sought one of the papers which exempted him until exchanged. Many who had escaped and were hiding out were brought in by their friends to obtain one of the valuable documents," confirmed Grierson. All this made a long day for staff officer Woodward, who had to write hundreds of paroles by hand. One of them was for "a newly fledged lieutenant in a bright new uniform bedizened with gold." The officer was home, visiting the ladies, and was less than pleased to be apprehended.[50]

Once finished with Brookhaven, Grierson left the paroled prisoners and mostly thankful citizens and moved on. "No private property was

---

48 Grierson, *A Just and Righteous Cause*, 168; Surby, *Grierson Raids*, 99.

49 *OR* 24, pt. 1, 527; "The Grierson Raid," *Weekly Register* (Canton, IL), September 7, 1863.

50 Woodward, "Grierson's Raid," 101.

disturbed," confirmed Colonel Prince, "leaving the inhabitants with a much more favorable opinion of us than they formerly had." It was nearly dark by the time the troopers finished their work. Grierson had little interest in another night march, but he needed to get away from the scene of destruction. The colonel marched his column south about eight miles along the railroad "over the worst kind of road" to a small plantation on Gill's Creek owned by 60-year-old Uriah T. Gill. The native South Carolinian's real estate was valued at only $1,500, but his nine slaves, who made up the bulk of his wealth, were worth $20,000. Grierson's men camped there for the night, satisfied with their work of destruction and escape from watching Confederates closer to Port Gibson. In a day full of trickery and destruction, the brigade had still managed to cover nearly 30 miles.[51]

*   *   *

As daylight spread across the Mississippi Valley on April 30, one of the climactic moments of the Vicksburg campaign and, in fact, of the entire war arrived: Grant's army began crossing the Mississippi River below Vicksburg. The failure to silence the Grand Gulf batteries the day before had forced Grant to push farther south along the river to Disharoon's Plantation, where he ordered a crossing below Bayou Pierre at Bruinsburg. The first Federal soldiers plunged ashore around dawn without opposition. Grant wasted no time shoving one division after another into the Magnolia State. Five divisions from two different corps would be marching inland by nightfall to occupy the hills overlooking the valley, and the vanguard of the Army of the Tennessee would not meet a single Confederate soldier until deep in the night, when troops approached the A. K. Shaifer house near Port Gibson. At that time, Grierson was 50 miles to the southeast. In all likelihood, Grant gave some thought about Grierson's efforts and their positive effect on the conditions of his crossing.[52]

---

51 1860 Lawrence County, Mississippi, Population and Slave Schedules, NARA; "The Grierson Raid," *Weekly Register* (Canton, IL), September 7, 1863; *OR* 24, pt. 1, 527; Freyburger, *Letters to Ann*, 45.

52 Smith, *The Decision Was Always My Own*, 100-103.

While Grant's troops hustled across the river and organized for invasion, Grierson woke his men at the Gill plantation. He still held out a faint hope of hearing something from Grant. That fact that he remained in the dark about the crossing was, in large part, due to his own success. A serious Confederate defensive effort to stop Grant would have triggered fighting and alerted Grierson to the crossing. The Army of the Tennessee spent all of April 30 moving inland without any serious opposition, something Grierson did not learn until after his raid.[53]

Grierson's order to mount up interrupted breakfast. Orange Jackson of the 6th Illinois Cavalry had just put his dough into a pan borrowed from a comrade when "the regimental bugle blew to mount. I just knocked the dough out of the skillet and cleaned it as best I could and gave it back," explained the aggravated and hungry trooper. With the 6th Illinois Cavalry riding in advance, the column set off south along the New Orleans, Jackson, and Great Northern Railroad. Grierson wanted to inflict more damage to the railroad while remaining fairly close to the Mississippi River. The troopers destroyed every bridge they came across as they approached Bogue Chitto, especially where the line crossed the Bogue Chitto River just north of the village, which consisted, wrote one Illinoisan, "of not more than a dozen houses." More destruction took place as the column entered Bogue Chitto itself early that morning. When the Illinois troopers came across a train with 15 cars, they sent it down a slight grade and torched it for good measure. They also burned the depot and, as Grierson described it, "captured a very large secession flag" emblazoned with "God and our rights" and the names Fort Donelson and Shiloh stitched on it. Captain Joseph R. Herring took his company of the 7th Illinois Cavalry farther south along the track to destroy more bridges, but he soon sent word that he needed help because there were too many to destroy and not enough time to do it. Grierson sent Lieutenant Colonel Loomis and 100 men to help finish the job.[54]

53 *OR* 24, pt. 1, 527; "The Grierson Raid," *Weekly Register* (Canton, IL), September 7, 1863.

54 *OR* 24, pt. 1, 527; Woodward, "Grierson's Raid," 102; Surby, *Grierson Raids*, 100-101; Jackson, *The History of Orange Jackson's War Life*, 11. The troopers destroyed all the bridges they came across as they approached Bogue Chitto (which should not be confused with the incorporated Bogue Chitto farther north in Neshoba and Kemper Counties), especially where the railroad crossed the Bogue Chitto River just north of its namesake town.

With the destruction complete at Bogue Chitto, Grierson moved farther south, keeping to the railroad so the troopers could burn every bridge they came across as well as any logistical support structures such as water tanks. A little after noon, the column approached Summit, described by an Illinois man as showing "many signs of once having done considerable business; of a neat, lively appearance, a pretty location." To the delight of the Federals, the citizenry welcomed the raiders, which illustrated the anti-Confederate attitude held by most folks in that area. Grierson chalked the greeting up to news from other locales such as Brookhaven "of our kind and considerate action towards the people." The Federals "found much Union sentiment in this town, and were kindly welcomed and fed by many of the citizens." To his surprise, Grierson was something of a celebrity: "I suddenly found myself an object of special interest, and it seemed as if the inhabitants of that section of the country, as a rule, could not do too much for us. I became as great a favorite as General Pemberton."[55]

The people of Summit welcomed the Illinoisans, but that did not spare any assets that could assist the Confederate war machine. Feats of destruction included a train of 25 cars and a large cache of Confederate sugar. Unlike at Bogue Chitto, however, the troopers spared the depot. Summit also contained 40 barrels of Louisiana rum, which Grierson described as "an enemy more dangerous just then than Wirt Adams' Cavalry and other rebel troops." Surby thought the rum "the meanest stuff in existence, warranted to kill further than any rifle in Uncle Sam's service." Much to his troopers' chagrin, Grierson "emptied the vile stuff" before they could touch a drop.[56]

Grierson's decision to dump the rum was a clear indication he was unwilling to take any risk that might disrupt his column and overturn all his good work. He was also laboring under significant stress because he had a major decision to make. The column was moving rapidly south along the railroad, which meant he was increasing the distance between Grant's army and his command. Grierson, who did not know Grant was over the river, could either hover in the area and await news of Grant's

---

55 OR 24, pt. 1, 527; Grierson, *A Just and Righteous Cause*, 169; Surby, *Grierson Raids*, 102; Freyburger, *Letters to Ann*, 45.

56 Surby, *Grierson Raids*, 101; OR 24, pt. 1, 527; Grierson, *A Just and Righteous Cause*, 169; Surby, *Grierson Raids*, 101.

activities or call the raid a success and ride to Union-held territory in Louisiana. The Federal raider had already accomplished more than anyone had expected. The danger for his regiments would only increase the longer he stayed put. After weighing his options, he decided to ride south for Baton Rouge as rapidly as his men and mounts would allow. From that point, he could always sweep east into Alabama and then north to Tennessee or even cross the Mississippi River and move north through Louisiana. "Hearing nothing more of our forces at Grand Gulf," he explained, "I concluded to make for Baton Rouge to recruit my command, after which I could return." By midafternoon on April 30, Grierson had no choice but to put the interests of his command ahead of everything else.[57]

After a short two-hour rest at Summit, Grierson had his men back in the saddle. This time, however, he left the railroad to begin the trek toward safety. He left in his wake a railroad even more torn up than the Southern Railroad at Newton Station, "a distance of twenty-one miles [about as badly wrecked] as any road could well have been in so short a time." Years later Grierson remembered both the playing of "Boots and Saddles" and a startling encounter with the wife of a Confederate officer just as they were leaving Summit. Grierson was leading the way out of town when word arrived that a lady wished to see him. He guided his horse to her gate and greeted her, dismounting to "listen in a most respectful manner to what she had to say." Grierson described the woman as "very ladylike, polite and courteous, and her civility met a suitable response from me as she apologized for occupying a few moments of my time." She admitted to being a Confederate officer's wife and that "her whole soul . . . was enlisted in the Confederate cause," but that she was "amazed at my great success; that the whole thing from beginning beat anything she had ever heard of or read in history." She even told the raider that if the Union was successful in this war and Grierson ever ran for president, her husband would vote for him or "she would certainly endeavor to get a divorce from him." A startled Grierson thanked her and said his goodbyes, no doubt wondering as he trotted back to the head of the column about the show of respect from a die-hard Confederate.[58]

57 *OR* 24, pt. 1, 527.

58 Forbes, "Grierson's Cavalry Raid," 116; Grierson, *A Just and Righteous Cause*, 170.

Plaudits aside, Grierson had larger issues on his mind as he led the brigade south. He realized his thus-far successful raid could meet a miserable end if he did not push ahead and finish it. Nerves, stretched tight by two weeks of stress and exhaustion, were beginning to fray. One Illinoisan remembered fighting with a fellow trooper he accused of eating his bread. "We got into a racket," he admitted. "I grabbed for my pistol and he caught my hand." The trooper drew his blade and chased his comrade on horseback, "cutting at him with my saber." The pursuit galloped past two companies until the other soldier drew his pistol, which prompted the aggrieved trooper to reverse course as fast as his horse could run. By this time both men seemed to realize the foolishness of their actions, and a captain brought the two together. As Orange Jackson put it, "You can see what a fellow will do when he is hungry." The famished trooper would have scoffed in disgust had he read the *Jackson Mississippian*, which informed its readers that Grierson's raiders were "eating fried ham and eggs and broiled spring chickens every morning for breakfast, at the expense of the planters whom they choose to honor with a visit—luxuriating on fat mutton, green peas and (of course) strawberries and cream for dinner."[59]

Grierson's route took him south to throw off any pursuers and then southwest on the road toward Liberty in Amite County, where anti-Confederate feelings were rampant. The column rode another 15 miles before stopping late in the day at a plantation owned by Thomas J. Spurlock, a 33-year-old doctor and a native Tennessean. The raiders had put another 30 miles behind them.[60]

Spurlock himself was away, serving in the army, leaving his wife, Amanda, to care for their infant son and oversee the plantation. Almost certainly, a deep feeling of dread and apprehension coursed through her when the Federal cavalrymen appeared. She had used her inheritance from a grandfather to buy the house and land a few years earlier in 1859.

59 Jackson, *The History of Orange Jackson's War Life*, 11; Bettersworth, *Mississippi in the Confederacy*, 113.

60 *OR* 24, pt. 1, 527; 1860 Amite County, Mississippi, Population and Slave Schedules; Thomas J. Spurlock, Deed, Book 63, Amite County Chancery Clerk, 393-94, 513-14.

Was her investment about to go up in smoke? At least she had the moral support of her sister, who was visiting from Atlanta.[61]

Fortunately for the Spurlocks, the Federals had little interest in anything other than rest and any available foodstuffs. The men were settling into their bivouacs that evening when Grierson decided he wanted chicken for dinner. He placed the normal guards around the smokehouses and other outbuildings and a special guard at the hen house (the latter to reserve the chickens for himself and staff officer Woodward). To his dismay, when he went to get a few birds, he "saw the last chicken and a hand grasping for it." The Federal commander, who was as enervated as the rest of his men, drew his saber and went after the soldier. "I jumped clean over the hen coop, around the pig sty, through the stable, behind the smokehouse, between the horses and under the horses," Grierson remembered. "Dodging trees and shrubbery, hopping over briars [and] up and down steps, smashing the trellis, and vociferating in language more forcible than polite." He chased the man and the "squeaking hen" all around the plantation while other officers laughed at the ludicrous scene. The colonel finally got what he was after when the terrified soldier dropped the bird while crossing a rail fence. "I grasped the fluttering, cackling thing with a firm hand and held it up in triumph," boasted Grierson, adding, "It did not need much picking by that time."[62]

The humorous event flushed out some of Grierson's stress, but it did not change the strategic situation. He had failed in his attempt to join up with Grant's army, and that left him and his men on their own. "That night," he recalled, "we held the forks of several important roads, on all of which the rebels were closing in on us. Besides myself and [my] adjutant and a few of the scouts, our dangerous situation was unknown to the command."[63]

61   Robert Glen Huff and Hattie Pearl Nunnery, *Amite County & Liberty, Mississippi: Celebrating 200 Years* (Virginia Beach: Donning Co., 2009), 123.

62   Grierson, *A Just and Righteous Cause*, 170-71.

63   Ibid., 171.

CHAPTER TEN

The Escape

"The sun arose in all his glory, not one cloud visible in the sky to obscure its dazzling brightness," wrote an Illinois trooper early on May 1. "A gentle breeze floated through the trees, causing a rustling among the green leaves of the oaks. Perched among the branches was the mocking bird," he continued, "singing a variety of notes, the whole impressing the beholder with a sense of a Creator of all this beauty." The beautiful May Day morning belied the horror of the long and deadly war.[1]

In Virginia, Joseph Hooker pushed part of his Army of the Potomac past a small crossroads and encountered the first enemy resistance from Robert E. Lee's Army of Northern Virginia, triggering the battle of Chancellorsville. The long and bloody combat would witness the mortal wounding of Stonewall Jackson, the defeat and retreat of Hooker's army, and a stunning victory that turned the strategic momentum in the east over to Lee, who would invade the North once more in June and end up at Gettysburg in early July.[2]

Closer to Grierson's camp at Spurlock's plantation in Amite County, Mississippi, Grant was also engaged in battle. The Army of the Tennessee had made an uncontested crossing of the Mississippi River the day

---

1 Surby, *Grierson Raids*, 103-4.

2 For Chancellorsville, see Ernest B. Ferguson, *Chancellorsville 1863: The Souls of the Brave* (New York: Knopf, 1993).

before, and with no enemy force of any strength to his front, Grant pushed his divisions inland from Bruinsburg. He found the enemy just west of Port Gibson, around the Shaifer house and Magnolia Church. Grant's leading corps under John A. McClernand fought throughout May 1, pushing weaker Confederate forces under John Bowen back toward Port Gibson. By the end of the day the town was in Union hands and Grant was more than a dozen miles inland. He now had a firm foothold in Mississippi, and only a decisive defeat in a pitched battle could derail his plans.[3]

When Grierson awoke that morning, he decided the time had come to affect his escape. He had performed his duty well, diverting Confederate attention and breaking up Southern railroads. Meeting up with Grant was no longer feasible, but riding to Union-controlled Baton Rouge remained a viable option. His part of the grand scheme appeared over; certainly the headline-grabbing aspects of his ride were now a thing of the past. The Confederates, however, had finally concentrated large numbers to hem in the raiders, and they were coming after the Union column from almost every direction.

"I knew just where the rebel forces were, and decided just how to avoid them and outwit them," he would later boast, albeit with the benefit of hindsight. His troopers knew much less of what was going on, with one Illinoisan remarking, "Various were the conjectures as to what point on the Mississippi River we would make." Perhaps it was best they did not know what was happening or just how dangerous their situation was that May Day morning.[4]

Avoiding and outwitting the enemy was a tall order, not because of the excellent capabilities of Grierson's pursuers, but because of the large number of small commands closing in on the Union raiders. Once the Federals appeared west of the Pearl River, especially along the railroad, they were easily pinpointed and reported. This intelligence was precisely what Pemberton needed, and he ordered every man who could be spared in the bastion area of Jackson-Vicksburg and Franklin Gardner's Port Hudson to move and trap the raiders. Most of these troops were cavalry, but only in small numbers organized as companies or battalions. Larger

---

3   Winschel, *Triumph and Defeat*, 1-12.

4   Grierson, *A Just and Righteous Cause*, 171; Surby, *Grierson Raids*, 104.

infantry columns were moved to the major bridges on the Amite River, including Williams's bridge near Grangeville and another several miles north, in an effort to block access to the Union territory around Baton Rouge. Grierson's corridor of operations was narrowing by the hour, as were his choices.[5]

Grierson's situation was dangerous but perhaps not quite as desperate as some may have imagined. Ironically, Grant's large-scale thrust into Mississippi and its threat to Vicksburg provided a diversion of sorts in Grierson's favor, soaking up enemy troops that would have otherwise moved to trap the raiders. Pemberton had almost ignored Grierson until the Federals hit Newton Station on April 24, after which he concentrated his efforts between April 24 and April 29 on catching him. Grant's attack at Grand Gulf and crossing of the Mississippi shook Pemberton back to reality. The substance of his barrage of messages changed from a focus on catching Grierson to how best to deal with Grant.[6]

Still, many Confederate units had set out after Grierson. Wirt Adams's regiment had already tangled with the Federals at Union Church before extricating itself by riding west. He had spent the previous night near Fayette while Grierson moved east. Once the reinforced Mississippian (whose remaining five companies had arrived) realized he had been tricked, Adams moved southeast toward Liberty to hem in the elusive Grierson.[7]

Similarly, Colonel Richardson's command of three mounted Mississippi infantry companies rode roughly parallel to Adams's advance toward Louisiana, mainly along the railroad itself. Richardson's numbers substantially increased when he met the squadron under Capt. Hiram Love, the same officer Union scout Nelson had misdirected several days before. Thinking he had finally caught up with Grierson, Richardson made elaborate plans for a night attack near Summit, but the Federals had departed nine hours earlier. "I could find no one in Summit who could tell me anything more than that the enemy had left the previous evening," Richardson complained. Once again the colonel assumed the enemy would follow the railroad and thus he moved south toward

5   OR 24, pt. 3, 793; Grabau, *Ninety-Eight Days*, 120; "The Grierson Raid: What the People Think of It," *Jackson Daily Mississippian*, May 9, 1863.

6   OR 24, pt. 3, 801-18.

7   Ibid., pt. 1, 533.

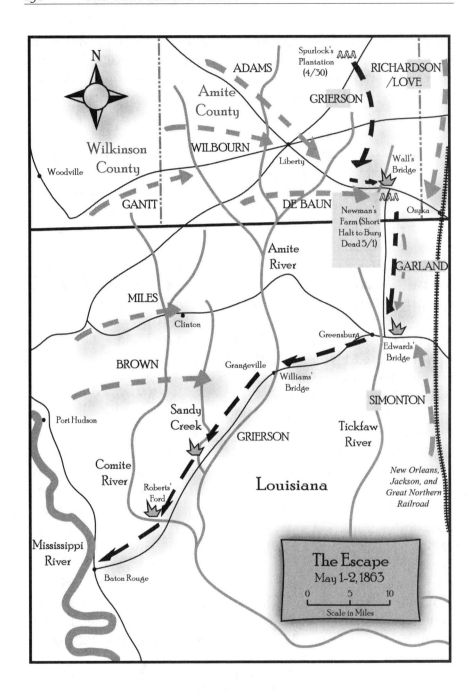

Franklin Gardner. As Confederate commander at Port Hudson in Louisiana, Major General Franklin Gardner sent forces out to hem in Grierson, but failed to trap the elusive cavalryman. *Library of Congress*

Magnolia and Osyka, where valuable Confederate supplies were stored. Richardson believed the rich storehouses would be more than Grierson could ignore, "which pointed to the conclusion that he was then on his way to that place."[8]

Franklin Gardner at Port Hudson also issued orders "to send out all the available spare cavalry." Lieutenant Colonel George Gantt of the 9th Tennessee Cavalry Battalion sent companies toward Tangipahoa and Clinton, Louisiana, and Woodville, Mississippi. Gantt moved northeast with the balance of the command toward Woodville and stopped there, ready to move in any direction "as circumstances might require." When he received word Grierson had gone to Brookhaven, Gantt moved to Liberty, but word soon arrived the previous news was wrong and the Federals had actually moved toward Natchez. Gantt admitted he was unable "to determine from the contradictory statements what was the enemy's direction." Scouts finally determined the enemy had indeed ridden to Brookhaven. Gantt moved his command east toward the railroad and Osyka.[9]

8   Ibid., 547-48.

9   Ibid., 540-41; Berrien, *The Military Annals of Tennessee*, 748-53.

A parallel column under Col. W. R. Miles of the Louisiana Legion also moved east in direct response to Gardner's call for men. Miles moved from Clinton to Osyka, crossing the flooded Amite River on a newly constructed bridge that cost the legion five hours to erect. Thereafter they came upon Grierson's trail, but the Federals were rapidly pushing on. Eventually, Miles met up with Adams's and Gantt's pursuing commands.[10]

Yet another Southern column moved north from the Camp Moore area near Tangiapahoa, Louisiana. Col. C. C. Wilbourn's battalion had ridden east to Tangiapahoa in response to the earliest call for cavalry and then up to Osyka when everyone assumed Grierson was moving on that place. When he did not find the Federals there, Wilbourn rode west to Woodville, never realizing he was moving behind Grierson, where conflicting reports kept him moving in circles. Wilbourn admitted he and his men did "much traveling for nothing" and that Grierson's efforts kept him "so perplexed as [they] greatly retarded his movements." Confederate infantry, meanwhile, followed at a much slower pace. Fresh from the prison camps they had endured as a result of the surrender at Fort Donelson in February 1862, Col. John Simonton's 1st Mississippi Infantry tramped their way north along the railroad to Osyka, intent on defending supplies Grierson had no intention of capturing or destroying.[11]

Despite all this activity, the Confederates were grasping at the wind. None of these commands caught up with Grierson's raiders, who continued moving steadily south.

*   *   *

With the Confederates concentrating against them, the Illinoisans awoke early on May 1, ready to move south to Baton Rouge. Grierson, who knew his best bet was to move quickly and quietly, continued to employ well-proven feints and stealth. He first moved east toward the New Orleans, Jackson, and Great Northern Railroad once more, hoping the Confederates would think he was intent on spending another day wrecking tracks. He had made a run for that railroad after leaving Newton Station and had hit it again two more times, the last strike producing significant damage as the column moved along the road itself. Grierson's move east

10   *OR* 24, pt. 1, 545.

11   Ibid., 541, 553.

toward Magnolia and Osyka, just above the Mississippi-Louisiana state line, convinced the Confederates to focus their attention on those two points just as Grierson intended.[12]

After feinting toward Magnolia, however, Grierson left the main road leading to the railroad and took a southerly route along what Grierson described as "woods, lanes, and by-roads." "It was a poor, pine country," recalled one of his Illinois troopers. "About every five miles there was a farm house." Colonel Prince, riding in the lead with his 7th Illinois Cavalry, described the route as "through the woods without roads." Grierson's aim was to connect with the main road from Osyka that ran southwest to Clinton, nearly 10 miles inside Louisiana. The Federal leader hoped the column could move rapidly in the opposite direction than most of the Confederates thought he was headed. There was a good chance the enemy might not even know he was in the area. If unchallenged, he could move east and cross the southerly flowing Tickfaw River at Wall's bridge and continue on to Greensburg, recrossing the river to the west side at Edward's bridge. The zigzag course would serve to further confuse the Confederates and put Grierson farther south, carefully bypassing the Port Hudson bastion, which Union Gen. Nathaniel Banks had not yet enveloped.[13]

Grierson moved through a heavily timbered region peppered with a maze of fallen trees atop the ridge between the Tickfaw River and the East Fork of the Amite River. Horses could easily navigate such terrain, but it was hard on the artillery, which had two horses tethered together. According to Adjutant Woodward, "It was necessary to lift, by hand, the little artillery over them." Worse, all four guns had already broken down before they reached this leg of the raid. The original wheels had not made it very far before they needed to be replaced. Their primary defect, observed Woodward, was "a peculiarly short hub." The artillerists could only replace the wheels with what they found on the march, so they concocted all sorts of wagon and carriage wheels, sawing off the hubs so they would fit onto the smaller carriages. Unfortunately, Woodward continued, "There were scarcely any two wheels of the same size, so that the guns had an odd, wobbly motion, giving one the idea of a huge bug

12 Ibid., 527.

13 Ibid., 527; Jackson, *The History of Orange Jackson's War Life*, 11; "The Grierson Raid," *Weekly Register* (Canton, IL), September 7, 1863.

ambling along." On occasion, the men hauled the guns by placing them in wagons captured for that purpose. As Woodward put it, "Such was the affection of the command for this battery that the idea of abandoning any part of it because it was disabled could not be thought of."[14]

Moving south cross-country, wobbly guns and all, the head of the column came upon what Grierson described as "an old but well-defined ridge road." No one was in sight, and the path led south with few apparent obstacles. The column soon came upon an old Mississippian who, like so many others, took Grierson's force to be Confederates. The man told them they were on the "old Kentucky trail," a route Kentuckians used before the age of steamboats to get back home after making a trip downriver. The road was so little used that the man admitted "he thought nobody knew [of it] but himself" and boasted he knew "every inch within ten miles." The Federals needed a guide like that, but the old man was reluctant to go with them, claiming "he'd enough of that work; that the fellows had taken him before and never given him a cent for his trouble." He had enough to do, he added, "without fooling his time away with us," explained Grierson. Oblivious as to the real identity of the riders, the old man inquired, "Why we didn't go to fight the Yankees instead of riding around the country in that way." Their uniforms impressed the rural civilian, who asked where the soldiers got their first-rate clothing, adding, "They were better than any clothes he had seen us fellows wear before." The quick-thinking Grierson responded, "We got our clothes from the Yankees at Holly Springs," an excuse his soldiers had been using for much of the trip and one that "always excited great laughter among the secessionists." Sorely in need of a guide, Grierson upped the ante and offered the man a horse for his use, which he could keep when his work was finished, together with a substantial sum of Confederate money. The Mississippian, wrote an amused Grierson, "concluded that he would go along with us for a while." True to his word, he led the column south to the Osyka road Grierson wanted so badly to reach.[15]

When the Union riders hit the main road, however, Surby, riding well in advance of the column, discovered the tracks of what appeared

14 Woodward, "Grierson's Raid," 102, 111; Bearss, *The Vicksburg Campaign*, vol. 2, 229.

15 "Incidents of the Raid," Memphis Daily Bulletin, May 23, 1863; Grierson, *A Just and Righteous Cause*, 171.

to be a mounted unit. The hoof marks were fresh, and the riders were heading east directly toward Wall's bridge, a span named after the Wall family who lived at a nearby plantation named Oak Grove. Surby knew a potential crisis when he saw one and sent word back to Grierson, who spurred his mount ahead to look over the situation in person. "Scarcely had we touched this road," Grierson reported, "when we came upon the Ninth Tennessee Cavalry [battalion], posted in a strong defile, guarding the bridges over Tickfaw River." The grim proposition loomed that Grierson and his men would have to fight their way across the bridge.[16]

Unbeknownst to Grierson, the Confederates were a motley band of hurriedly organized troopers led by James De Baun, a six-foot 40-something Creole major from New Orleans, of the 9th Louisiana Partisan Rangers. When it appeared Grierson was heading for Osyka, De Baun received orders to move there with two companies to protect it. At Woodville, he picked up George Gantt's under-strength 9th Tennessee Cavalry Battalion. The three companies, scarcely 115 men, rode east. "At 11:30 a.m., the men and horses being fatigued, I stopped to rest at Wall's Bridge," De Baun later reported. Grierson's column popped out on the same road just minutes later.[17]

With his route blocked, Grierson ordered Surby to move ahead and, "if I saw any object that I could not satisfy myself about, to report at once to him, and not get more than half a mile from the advance." Although he was heading south, he could not leave an enemy of undetermined size so close and make a run for it, especially with the vast bottomlands of the wide Amite River looming just ahead. In order to reach Greensburg, he would have to cross the Tickfaw River at Wall's bridge, a "narrow plank bridge some fifty feet in length" and the river's only viable crossing point. The Tickfaw, recalled Woodward, was "a deep, abrupt, rapid stream, not fordable, and completely hidden by a dense growth of vines and bushes." Grierson decided his best course of action was to outfox the enemy while they were still concentrating.[18]

The Federal brigade commander stopped the head of his column around the bend of the road out of sight of the nearest Confederate

16 OR 24, pt. 1, 527; Surby, *Grierson Raids*, 104; Roth, "Grierson's Raid," 62.

17 OR 24, pt. 1, 539, Brown, *Grierson's Raid*, 192.

18 OR 24, pt. 1, 527; "The Grierson Raid," *Weekly Register* (Canton, IL), September 7, 1863; Woodward, "Grierson's Raid," 103; Surby, *Grierson Raids*, 104, 110.

pickets around the bridge and sent scouts ahead to feel out the enemy. "Hello, boys, on picket?" Surby called out. "Yes," responded one of the soldiers. "Been on about an hour and feel devlish tired. Been traveling night and day after the damned Yanks, and I'll bet my horse that they'll get away yet." One of Surby's scouts empathized by responding, "That is just our case."[19]

Before Grierson could decide on a specific plan, the actions of others decided his course for him. A few of the soldiers in the rear of the column under Lt. James M. Gaston of Company G, 7th Illinois Cavalry, came upon several Confederates at a nearby farmhouse. The surprised opponents stared at each other a few moments before the shooting began, the shots reverberating loudly up and down the river valley. The Illinois troopers captured two Confederates and four horses, but the damage was done. The gunfire had alerted the enemy pickets near the bridge that something was amiss. Surby's scouts quickly apprehended the closest picket, but others approached, including Capt. E. A. Scott and his orderly. "What in hell does all that firing mean?" demanded the captain. The quick-thinking Surby replied that the pickets had accidentally fired on approaching reinforcements. A relieved Scott laughed and replied, "Is that all?" before riding west and right into the hands of Surby's scouts. Surby told a comrade to let the officer ride between them and "I would manage him." Back at the bridge, meanwhile, the more alert Major De Baun "ordered the bridge to be dismantled . . . posting men at the bridge to destroy it as soon as the rear guard would have reported." By that time, the rear guard was mostly in Union custody.[20]

The exchange of fire also set some of the Union men on edge, including young Lieutenant Colonel Blackburn, who was at the front of the column with the 7th Illinois Cavalry. Colonel Prince described the officer as having "too much daring." Grierson knew Blackburn to be a bold and brave officer, but he worried about the young man's rashness, especially when near the enemy. He had already warned Blackburn to

19 Surby, *Grierson Raids*, 105; Grierson, *A Just and Righteous Cause*, 171.

20 *OR* 24, pt. 1, 539; Grierson, *A Just and Righteous Cause*, 171-72; Surby, *Grierson Raids*, 106; Surby, *Grierson Raids*, 108.

"make a cautious approach." Blackburn's blood was up, however, and he intended to finish the business quickly and decisively.[21]

Determined to take the bridge before the Confederates realized what was transpiring, Blackburn galloped past Surby and called out, "Sergeant, bring along your scouts and follow me, and I'll see where those rebels are!" The stunned scout recalled, "This was a rash movement on the part of Colonel Blackburn, but he had ordered me to follow him, and it was my duty to obey." The small squad took fire while still west of the bridge, but it "did not check our speed, but rather increased it." When the troopers clattered across the wooden structure, however, the now fully alert Confederates on the far side delivered a withering fire. "It seemed as though a flame of fire burst forth from every tree," confirmed the scout. Unfortunately for the Federals, many of the rounds struck home.[22]

Three balls struck Blackburn. The most serious injury was in his thigh. The other two rounds grazed his head and struck his hip. The wounds were serious and perhaps mortal. One of his troopers observed that "his horse [was also] filled full of bullet holes." Another round struck Sergeant Surby, Grierson's gallant scout who had provided outstanding leadership and judgment throughout the raid. The bullet, he later wrote, "struck me on my right thigh, passing through it into my saddle, just grazing my horse's back. I often think that it was a miracle that any of us escaped the first volley," Surby added, "but the ways of Divine Providence are very mysterious, and I have every reason to be thankful that my fate was no worse."[23]

Grierson, who had neither ordered nor expected the mounted charge, was less than pleased by Blackburn's brash action: "The little squad that made the gallant dash with Colonel Blackburn were, of course, quickly repulsed and compelled to retreat and wait for reinforcements to dislodge

---

21 "The Grierson Raid," *Weekly Register* (Canton, IL), September 7, 1863; Grierson, *A Just and Righteous Cause*, 172; Woodward, "Grierson's Raid," 104.

22 *OR* 24, pt. 1, 540; Grierson, *A Just and Righteous Cause*, 172; Abbott, "Heroic Deeds of Heroic Men," 280; "The Grierson Raid," *Weekly Register* (Canton, IL), September 7, 1863; Surby, *Grierson Raids*, 110, 112, 114; "Camp Correspondence," *Fulton City Register* (Canton, IL), May 26, 1863; "From New Orleans," n.d., Thomas W. Lippincott Papers, ALPL.

23 *OR* 24, pt. 1, 540; Grierson, *A Just and Righteous Cause*, 172; Abbott, "Heroic Deeds of Heroic Men," 280; "The Grierson Raid," *Weekly Register* (Canton, IL), September 7, 1863; Surby, *Grierson Raids*, 110, 112, 114; "Camp Correspondence," May 26, 1863; "From New Orleans," n.d., Thomas W. Lippincott Papers, ALPL.

Wall's Bridge. Grierson fought his heaviest action at Wall's Bridge. This photo shows the Tickfaw River at the bridge site. *Author*

the enemy from his strong position." If Blackburn had "been as discreet and wary as he was brave," Grierson added, "it is very probable that not a man would have been wounded, and very likely most of the rebels would have been captured, as our approach was not expected from that direction."[24]

Knowing he had no time to lose, Grierson ordered up more troopers and another attack. A squadron under Lt. William Styles charged with reckless abandon across the span, but a heavy fire drove the cavalrymen back with multiple casualties. Private George Rheinholdt of Styles's Company G was killed instantly and Sgt. S. Record and Pvts. W. Roy and Ruse M. Hughes were wounded. After suffering a pair of repulses, Grierson sent in heavier numbers to complete the job. When the first two companies of the 7th Illinois reached the front, Grierson sent them forward as dismounted skirmishers. The troopers reached the bank of the river and outflanked the bridge and its Confederate defenders. Smith's guns, meanwhile, dropped trail and added some heavier firepower. The small tubes unlimbered and opened fire while the rest of the column launched a thunderous advance, overwhelming the Confederates and driving them eastward. As the Federal troopers rushed past, Blackburn, who was lying partially under his dead horse, yelled to Grierson, "Onward, Colonel. Onward, men. Whip the rebels. Onward and save your command. Don't mind me." The 6th Illinois Cavalry rode after the Louisiana and Tennessee defenders for some distance to make sure the enemy was actually withdrawing. "I skirmished the rebels out of the bushes," was how Colonel Prince described his role in the action. According to Major De Baun of the 9th Louisiana Partisan Rangers, the stout defensive effort consisted of only some 90 men.[25]

The old Mississippi guide accompanying Grierson's column watched as the action unfolded. "It was all accomplished so quickly," recalled Grierson, "that the old man citizen, who had not yet discovered his first mistake, was in high glee. [He] turned round to our men and exclaimed: 'Why you can fight. I thought you were a lot of dandies in your fine

24 Surby, *Grierson Raids*, 109-10; Grierson, *A Just and Righteous Cause*, 172.

25 *OR* 24, pt. 1, 540; George C. Reinholdt, Compiled Service Record, NARA; Grierson, *A Just and Righteous Cause*, 172; Abbott, "Heroic Deeds of Heroic Men," 280; "The Grierson Raid," *Weekly Register* (Canton, IL), September 7, 1863; "Camp Correspondence," May 26, 1863; "From New Orleans," n.d., Thomas W. Lippincott Papers, ALPL; Surby, *Grierson Raids*, 110, 112, 114.

clothes. But, Moses, didn't you clean those Yanks out nicely." Worried that the man might discover the truth, Grierson gave him the promised horse and Confederate money and sent him away "in blissful ignorance as to who we really were. . . . [I]n due time, it is safe to presume, he found that he had been for a time in the clutches of the dreadful Yankees."[26]

Grierson had his bridge, but the manner in which he captured it created other problems beyond what one Mississippi newspaper described as "some punishment" inflicted by the Confederates. The escaping Confederates were spreading the word of Grierson's presence, so the Federal commander had to keep his men riding. However, he also had a dead trooper and five wounded men who needed attention as well as several Confederate dead and wounded. The small affair was the first serious combat most of these troopers had experienced since leaving Tennessee, the skirmishing at Union Church notwithstanding, and the heaviest losses Grierson had endured to date. He especially felt the loss of Blackburn. "I cannot speak too highly of the bravery of the men upon this occasion," Grierson wrote, "and particularly of Lieutenant Colonel Blackburn, who, at the head of his men, charged upon the bridge, dashed over, and, by undaunted courage, dislodged the enemy from his strong position."[27]

Grierson spent as little time as possible overseeing the wounded and the dead. The troopers of the 7th Illinois Cavalry buried Private Reinhold, a sad but relatively quick endeavor. The wounded presented more immediate and complex problems. Unable to care properly for them, Grierson had the injured of both sides transported to a nearby farmhouse owned by James M. Newman about a mile east of the river. The 28-year-old Newman lived in a modest but comfortable house with Caroline, his young wife of 22, and their three children ages three to six. It must have been a chaotic time for the small farmer's family. Newman, whose net worth in real estate was only about $1,200, depended on his

---

26 *OR* 24, pt. 1, 540; Grierson, *A Just and Righteous Cause*, 172-73; "The Grierson Raid," *Weekly Register* (Canton, IL), September 7, 1863; Surby, *Grierson Raids*, 111.

27 "The Great Federal Raid," *Natchez Daily Courier,* May 5, 1863; *OR* 24, pt. 1, 527; George C. Reinholdt, Compiled Service Record, NARA. The small affair at Wall's bridge was also known at the time as the battle at Tickfaw bridge.

crops to survive. With the war now at his doorstep, everything was in jeopardy.[28]

Grierson faced a heartrending decision because he could not take the wounded with him, and leaving men behind to protect them was not a viable option. The seriously wounded Blackburn "could not ride," explained a 7th Illinois trooper and would have to be left with the other wounded and hope for clemency from the enemy. Colonel Prince initially protested the decision to leave the men behind, arguing the column should simply camp there. His emotional plea soon saw the light of logic when Grierson explained that they had "three more rivers . . . yet to be crossed," the enemy was "gathering thick and fast behind" them, and the column was "near their strongholds, and delay would have been fatal to success." The Federal commander did all he could to ensure those he left were well cared for. The 2nd Iowa's surgeon, Erastus D. Yule, who had remained with the column after Colonel Hatch's regiment turned back, together with two nurses, Sgt. Maj. Augustus Leseure and Pvt. George W. Douglass, remained behind to care for the injured. "Everything possible was done for the comfort of those left behind," explained Grierson, including changing Surby back into his Union uniform to keep the Confederates from hanging or shooting him as a spy. After threatening the farmer Newman with reprisals if any of his injured were ill-treated, Grierson bid Blackburn a final farewell, knowing he might never see him again. "We all deeply regretted the loss met with at the Tickfaw, which might have been avoided," Grierson lamented. Ironically, it was a regret borne of Blackburn's own hasty actions.[29]

Newman, who had assured Grierson he would help look after his wounded men, was good to his word and cared for Blackburn and the others despite his modest means. One account claims Newman "was a small farmer with a small but comfortable house. He and his wife gave their best bedroom and best bed to Col. Blackburn." Blackburn

---

28 "Camp Correspondence," *Fulton City Register* (Canton, IL), May 26, 1863; Grierson, *A Just and Righteous Cause*, 173; Woodward, "Grierson's Raid," 105; 1860 Amite County Population and Slave Schedules; James M. Newman, Deed, Book 66, Amite County Chancery Clerk, 356-58.

29 "Camp Correspondence," *Fulton City Register* (Canton, IL), May 26, 1863; Grierson, *A Just and Righteous Cause*, 173; Woodward, "Grierson's Raid," 105; Bearss, *The Vicksburg Campaign*, vol. 2, 230; Dinges, "The Making of a Cavalryman," 334, 386-87n144; Erastus D. Yule, Compiled Service Record, NARA.

appreciated the farmer's efforts and later wrote out a note to protect him: "Newman Farm, Miss., May 5, 1863. This is to certify that I have been very kindly treated by Mr. J. M. Newman and family, and I desire all Union soldiers to respect his family and property. Said Newman has been a friend indeed. William D. Blackburn, Lieutenant Colonel, 7th Illinois Cavalry."[30]

*   *   *

With the way open across the Tickfaw River and the dead and wounded taken care of, Grierson guided his column east some distance before turning south. The Federals made good time on the Greensburg Road and soon "crossed into Louisiana," confirmed a hungry trooper in the 7th Illinois Cavalry. "Had nothing to eat all day." Unfortunately for the raiders, scouts spotted Confederate riders east of the Tickfaw. The brigade was approaching the next crossing point at Edward's bridge on the way to Greensburg when scouts spotted more Confederates riding hard to reach the span before they did. "The Johnnies were hard to keep back," admitted a member of the rear guard. Grierson agreed: "We had a race with about fifty rebels, but our men got to the bridge first." Stopping would only give the enemy more time to concentrate in larger numbers, so Grierson decided to make a running fight of it near Crittendon's Creek as he moved toward and then across Edward's bridge near Greensburg. "At this point, we met Garland's rebel cavalry," he reported, "and, with one battalion of the Sixth Illinois and two guns of the battery, engaged and drove them off without halting the column." Major W. H. Garland of the Mississippi Battalion reported much the same when he informed his superior at Port Hudson that he was unable to stop the enemy. Locals, however, informed the Confederate officer that the Northern raiders were heading for Baton Rouge. Major Garland informed anyone who would listen that the enemy would cross the Amite River. He recommended troops be sent "to stop them at Williams' Bridge," which, he added, "is the last chance."[31]

30 House Report 650, 53rd Congress, 2nd Session, 1-2.

31 Curtiss, diary, May 1, 1863; *OR* 24, pt. 1, 527, 543; Jackson, *The History of Orange Jackson's War Life*, 12; Grierson, *A Just and Righteous Cause*, 173; Woodward, "Grierson's Raid," 107; Grabau, *Ninety-Eight Days*, 116; Freyburger, *Letters to Ann*, 45; Daniel E. Robbins to Brother, May 7, 1863.

The battalion of Illinois cavalry easily drove the enemy away from Edward's bridge, but some Federals ran into problems of their own. One group became embroiled in a small firefight in the creek bottom and eventually ended up in the creek itself. They were not overly concerned, explained one man, because it was likely "only malitia." The squadron stopped at a nearby farmhouse for refreshments but ran into Confederates there—and another unexpected enemy. One of the Union troopers "left his pistol where he was drinking buttermilk," recalled another Illinoisan, but when he made a run back to get it, "a woman beat him back to it; she began shooting at him and he whirled to run out." Whether the trooper ever recovered his pistol was not reported.[32]

Larger issues than buttermilk and pistols were on Grierson's mind. The climax of this stage of the raid was quickly approaching in the form of Williams's bridge, the only place the column could cross the "wide, deep and rapid" Amite River. If it were blocked or destroyed—and there was a reasonable chance it was in enemy hands—the game was up. Word arrived that more Confederates were moving into the area. "We were in the vicinity of their stronghold," wrote a worried Grierson, "and, from couriers and dispatches which we captured, it was evident that they were sending forces in all directions to intercept us." The Confederates, he concluded, "were now on our track in earnest." When Grierson made the decision to ride for Baton Rouge, we were "twice as far from the Amite River bridge as was Gardner at Port Hudson," recalled Stephen Forbes of Company B. "The flying column sped on its way unmolested, and almost unseen, by its swarming enemies." The column's speed, observed Forbes, was set "at the highest pace which they [the horses] were likely to be able to keep to the end."[33]

The Illinois troopers passed through Greensburg about sunset, capturing the county clerk who, Grierson noted, "armed with a shotgun, was waiting at the crossroads for a courier with information." Scout Samuel Nelson, who had taken over for the wounded Surby, secured the clerk's shotgun and explained he was "talking to a live Yankee," though he also gave the stranger a slug of "Yankee whisky." The scout turned the clerk over to other troopers as a prisoner, but not before the Southerner

32 Jackson, *The History of Orange Jackson's War Life*, 12-13.

33 Forbes, "Grierson's Cavalry Raid," 117, 119; Woodward, "Grierson's Raid," 108; Surby, *Grierson Raids*, 117.

asked for "another nip of that Yankee whisky." It was about this time that Lt. George W. Newell, a scout sent out earlier that morning to find horses and provisions, rejoined the column. Newell had stumbled upon the fight earlier in the day at Wall's bridge, where he discovered his route blocked by a swarm of Confederates. His was a dashing escape from the enemy and a roundabout ride to get back to his comrades in blue.[34]

Thankfully, wrote one Illinois man, Grierson's push west in an effort to escape the Confederates on his trail and reach Williams's bridge was assisted by good roads, "level as a floor, beautifully shaded on both sides by tall forest pines, interspersed with a small growth of other kinds of timber, now and then passing a small plantation." The looming valley of the Amite River, however, worried Grierson, who knew the only good crossing point was uncomfortably close to Port Hudson. Knowledge of his route would make it easy for the Confederates to send more than enough men to the choke point to stop him. If the Federals were trapped east of the Amite, deep in Rebel territory, there would be nowhere safe to go.[35]

Fortunately for the Federals, Grierson believed he was "ahead of information." In order to remain so, he did something he had done only twice before during the long raid: Push his men in a forced march through the entire night. He later explained that he "calculated the time" it would take for a courier to reach Port Hudson and for a column to organize and reach Williams's bridge, and that if he kept moving through the night he might just make it. "That a large force would be sent there was very evident to my mind," Grierson reported, "and we must reach that important point before them." By this stage, the troopers were close enough to a safe harbor that a third forced march would not overly tax them. They could rest once they reached Baton Rouge or they would rest when they reached a Confederate prison camp. The stark choice made the strenuous riding a bit more bearable and increased endurance. Grierson had ordered his first forced march on April 23 when he had pushed ahead all night to reach and destroy Newton Station, and his second was three nights later, on April 26, when he had to cross the

---

34 Surby, *Grierson Raids*, 115-16; Grierson, *A Just and Righteous Cause*, 173; Winschel, *Triumph and Defeat*, 54; Daniel E. Robbins to Brother, May 7, 1863.

35 *OR* 24, pt. 1, 527; Surby, *Grierson Raids*, 116; Freyburger, *Letters to Ann*, 45.

Pearl River at Georgetown, the other substantial watercourse that could have hemmed them in.[36]

Making another all-night run this late in the raid, however, was more problematic than the prior two. The men were fresher and better able to endure such hardships earlier in the raid. By this date Grierson's troopers had been in the saddle for 15 days. Every man and most of the mounts were exhausted and sore. Another grueling night ride and lack of sleep would be harder to recover from, and more riding would be needed thereafter to reach Baton Rouge.[37] Fortunately for the raiders, the moon made a stunning appearance about 11:00 p.m. The Mississippi River city of Baton Rouge was only 40 miles from Greensburg as the crow flies, and a handful of miles more along the route the cavalry would ride. "On, then," Grierson recounted, "by moonlight over the level roads and through the beautiful pine forests, when the enemy was sleeping and tarrying by the way."[38]

Grierson rode west intent on securing Williams's bridge at Grangeville "before I halted," his trusty scouts out front doing their work. He had confidence in Nelson, but he may well have wished Surby was still in charge now that the climax of the raid was upon them. After a 12-mile ride, the column slowed as it entered the river valley, where the roads turned "very muddy and rough" in the dark bottomland. The scouts delivered the news Grierson needed: There was only a company of Confederates near the bridge, and they were inexplicably camped a mile away. A detachment of just 10 men guarded the bridge during the day, a paltry number reduced to just 2 men at night. The news surely surprised the brigade leader. Only 2 Confederates were guarding what was arguably the most important bridge in Louisiana at that time?[39]

The scouts cautiously approached the span by quietly announcing to the pair of pickets that they were couriers on the way to Port Hudson. Once upon them, "a cocked revolver [was] quickly placed at the heads of the guards. No words were spoken above a whisper, and both Confederates

36 Grierson, *A Just and Righteous Cause*, 173-74.

37 *OR* 24, pt. 1, 524-526; Surby, *Grierson Raids*, 116; Surby, *Grierson Raids*, 116.

38 Grierson, *A Just and Righteous Cause*, 174.

39 *OR* 24, pt. 1, 527; Grierson, *A Just and Righteous Cause*, 174; Woodward, "Grierson's Raid," 108; Surby, *Grierson Raids*, 117; Daniel E. Robbins to Parents, May 5, 1863.

William's Bridge. The Amite River was the last major obstacle Grierson had to cross to reach safety. He did so at Williams' Bridge, somewhere in the vicinity of the modern view shown here. *Author*

were readily captured." No other enemy soldiers were in sight. The satisfying realization that the Federals had beaten the Port Hudson defenders to the bridge swept down the length of the Union column. A satisfied Grierson recalled the "welcome sound of our horses' hooves . . . reverberating as we went gaily marching on over the raging torrent." Years later he was still amazed about how his men were able to ride across the long bridge at midnight while its "watchers were sleeping a half mile and mile away."[40]

The aggressive Grierson could not resist breaking up the nearby enemy camp once his column was safely across the river. Once the bulk of his command moved on, he sent a company of the 6th Illinois Cavalry "to fire into the camp of the bridge guard." The safer (and perhaps wiser) choice would have been to move on and put six or eight hours between his men and the Confederates before they realized the bridge had been crossed. The company nevertheless hit the camp without warning, scattering the enemy in every direction. "If an earthquake had occurred, or lightening struck them from the cloudless, starlight heaven above," he boasted, "they could not have been more surprised or more bewildered." Grierson joked that "those who could get away, it was thought, never would stop running." The company of Illinois cavalry captured a few Rebels and killed a few others before returning to the westward-riding column.[41]

Grierson's decision to ride all night allowed him to cross the Amite River a few hours before a large force of Confederates dispatched from Port Hudson reached the bridge. In addition to sending cavalry to find Grierson, General Gardner had also sent infantry and artillery, including the 55th Tennessee, 4th Louisiana, and Fenner's Louisiana Battery, all under the command of Col. Alexander J. Brown of the 55th Tennessee. By the time they reached the general area, Grierson was long gone. Brown reported back to Gardner at 9:30 a.m. that he was still six miles from the bridge, but he had already received word the Federal raiders had passed over it during the night. "Starting at the late hour we did," lamented the colonel, "it was impossible to have intercepted the enemy at William's Bridge." There was more to the story than Colonel Brown was willing to admit. The Confederates were passing through Clinton, Louisiana, on the way to reach the bridge when the town's citizens "tendered a complimentary dance to the officers of the rebel command." According to Capt. Henry Forbes, "The [Confederate] officers had carefully estimated the time of our possible arrival near the bridge, and accepted the complement as an incident too pleasant to be needlessly rejected. . . . [W]hile, therefore, we were stretching our legs for the bridge [by riding all night] these gentlemen who had been sent to catch us were

---

40 *OR* 24, pt. 1, 527; Grierson, *A Just and Righteous Cause*, 174; Woodward, "Grierson's Raid," 108; Surby, *Grierson Raids*, 117; Daniel E. Robbins to Parents, May 5, 1863.

41 Grierson, *A Just and Righteous Cause*, 174.

stretching theirs in the cotillion." One of the embarrassed soldiers of the 55th Tennessee summed up the situation by writing, "We made a forced march from Port Hudson to intercept Grierson at Williams' bridge on Amite River, but were an hour or so late and missed our game."[42]

Grierson moved his men through the balance of the night toward Baton Rouge, the 6th Illinois Cavalry in the advance, confident after having made it across the last major obstacle. There were additional waterways to cross, mostly small tributaries of the Amite River, including Sandy Creek and the Comite River, but they could be easily waded across almost anywhere. A quiet wave of excitement infused the exhausted Federals as they plunged along through the moonlight.[43]

*   *   *

Once Grierson passed Williams's bridge, there was little if anything the Confederates who had flooded the area east of the Amite River could do, and they realized it. Wirt Adams's Mississippi Cavalry pursued the raiders southward nearly to Greensburg and eventually linked up with Gantt's Tennesseans and the force under Colonel Wilbourn. None of them could catch the elusive Federals. Several Confederate units passed the scene of the fighting at Wall's bridge and interrogated the wounded Lieutenant Colonel Blackburn, who lied when he told them Grierson's target was Natchez, but that the "check they received at Union Church" changed their plans. Adams was doubly chagrined when he heard the enemy had escaped the closing gray noose. Not only had he been unable to catch them himself, but the force he had sent out under Lt. W. S. Wren to destroy Williams's bridge failed to make it there in time. "I marched over 50 miles per day, and moved during day and night," wrote the disgusted Confederate colonel, "yet the distance I had to traverse from west to east to reach the line of their march, and owing to their use of

---

42 Forbes, "Grierson's Raid," 28; *OR* 24, pt. 1, 527, 537, 543; "The Grierson Raid," *Weekly Register* (Canton, IL), September 7, 1863; Lewis Cole, "Served in the Army and then in the Navy," *Confederate Veteran* (March 1913), vol. 21, no. 3, 112; Fannie A. Beers, *Memories: A Record of Personal Experience and Adventure During Four Years of War* (Philadelphia: J. B. Lippincott Company, 1889), 233; Bearss, *The Vicksburg Campaign*, vol. 2, 231.

43 *OR* 24, pt. 1, 527, 537, 543; "The Grierson Raid," *Weekly Register* (Canton, IL), September 7, 1863.

the most skillful guides and unfrequented roads, I found it impossible, to my great mortification and regret, to overhaul them."[44]

Colonel Richardson's three mounted Mississippi infantry companies also found it impossible to nab Grierson. Richardson had maintained contact with the parallel-riding Adams by courier and reached Osyka, where he learned "the enemy had not approached Osyka nearer than Wall's Bridge." At Osyka, Richardson joined his command with De Braun's troops, fresh from Wall's bridge, a company of the 1st Mississippi Cavalry under Capt. G. Herren and 30 men provided by Osyka's local commander. With this conglomeration of troops, Richardson moved south toward Greensburg, which he reached on the morning of May 2 only to find that the enemy had passed through hours earlier on the way to Williams's bridge. Realizing the futility of the chase, Richardson called off the pursuit and returned to his previous post.[45]

With most of the Confederate cavalry now east of the Amite River, there were few Confederates operating west of the waterway to stop Grierson, and none of them had any idea they were within miles of a much larger Union force. In fact, most were spread out in company-sized detachments and guarding fords and other crossing points. Their attention was mainly focused to the south and west toward the Federals along the Mississippi River and Baton Rouge than north and east in the direction from which Grierson was approaching. Grierson had threaded the needle of Confederate forces aiming to capture him.[46]

*   *   *

Few Confederates were now in a position to stop Grierson, but a new enemy made its appearance. The long and miserable night march had taken its toll. The men were now 16 days into their long and tiring journey and completely exhausted. "All night we rode and made good speed," explained Grierson, "although nearly the entire command was much of the time asleep on their horses." When no longer spurred along by their riders, the horses often stopped to feed on the grass growing beside the road. "The shock given by the occasion of the inaction or

44 *OR* 24, pt. 1, 533, 542; Woodward, "Grierson's Raid," 106.

45 *OR* 24, pt. 1, 548-50.

46 Ibid., 537.

momentum would wake up the rider," continued the brigade leader, at which time "the horse and man would re-enter the column." To keep the men moving, he posted several troopers "who believed they could keep awake" on the flanks, though he later admitted that, "besides myself, few of the command were awake that night."[47]

Captain Forbes's Company B, 7th Illinois Cavalry, took station in the rear to keep the column moving. These men had endured similar hardships on their mini-expedition. Forbes left a detailed account of what was transpiring:

> Men by the score, and I think by fifties, were riding sound asleep in their saddles. The horses excessively tired and hungry, would stray out of the road and thrust their noses to the earth in hopes of finding something to eat. The men, when addressed, would remain silent and motionless until a blow across the thigh or the shoulder should awaken them, when it would be found that each supposed himself still riding with his company, which might perhaps be a mile ahead. We found several men who had either fallen from their horses, or dismounted and dropped on the ground, dead with sleep. Nothing short of a beating with the flat of a saber would awaken some of them. In several instances they begged to be allowed to sleep, saying that they would run all risk of capture on the morrow. Two or three did escape our vigilance, and were captured the next afternoon.[48]

The Amite River crossing unfolded rather smoothly, but the crossing of the waterways that followed did not. The sleepy column plodded southwest to Sandy Creek near Greenwell Springs, described by one rider as "a pretty, rushing stream," where scouts ran up on a Confederate camp guarding the roadway. Grierson marveled at the effect the news of another potential fight had on the men. "At the time this news reached us," he wrote, "nearly the entire command of officers and soldiers were asleep on their horses. The prospect of a fight, however, quickly awakened all the sleepers, who began to tighten up their reins, grasp their carbines and revolvers, and prepare for a charge. . . . It was wonderful to observe what life and vigor was stirred up as the order went back to the rear to prepare for a rapid advance upon a foe which, to judge from the size of the camp, must be a considerable force."[49]

---

47 Grierson, A *Just and Righteous Cause*, 174.

48 Forbes, "Grierson's Cavalry Raid," 120.

49 Grierson, *A Just and Righteous Cause*, 175; Woodward, "Grierson's Raid," 108.

The enemy camp, situated along the main road at the crossing near Burlington's Ferry, belonged to Hughes's cavalry battalion under Lt. Col. C. C. Wilbourn. The troopers, however, were off to the northeast and hunting for Grierson. Grierson was unaware the enemy was gone when he used the same tactic he employed at Newton Station nine days earlier and struck the camp about dawn on May 2. A company of the leading 6th Illinois Cavalry moved out at a trot, followed by a second company from the same regiment. The trot turned into a gallop that developed into a charge as the men rode between the tents, firing into them "with a tremendous yell." The Confederates were so confident that no danger was within striking distance that they had not even posted pickets or skirmishers. "We reached this point at first dawn of day," reported Grierson, "[and] completely surprised and captured the camp, with a number of prisoners." Only one Rebel, dressed only in his underwear, managed to escape by leaping onto a horse and galloping bareback out of harm's way. The camp, explained Grierson, protected only by a small guard, consisted of "about one hundred and fifty tents, a large quantity of ammunition, guns, public and private stores, books, papers, and public documents." The 6th Illinois troopers remained behind to destroy everything they could find, but the 7th Illinois men pushed on with the rest of the column on the road to Baton Rouge. Not far out of camp the Federals came across a lieutenant colonel drawn in their direction by the firing. When he realized his mistake the officer yelled, "Get like hell boys, the road is full of Yanks in our rear!" By that time Grierson's scouts were behind the officer, and one of them replied. "Yes, [and] here you are among them" as the Rebel fell into Union hands.[50]

The column moved on, riding over additional creeks and streams flowing into the Amite River. The only watercourse likely to pose a problem if it was defended was the Comite River, whose headwaters were far north in Mississippi east of Woodville. Unfortunately for the raiders, several companies of Miles's Louisiana Legion were patrolling its banks, watching the crossing points at Haw's, Robert's, Bogan's, and

50 OR 24, pt. 1, 527-28; Grierson, A Just and Righteous Cause, 175; "The Grierson Raid," Weekly Register (Canton, IL), September 7, 1863; Surby, Grierson Raids, 118; Grabau, Ninety-Eight Days, 116.

Strickland's fords. The Federals were heading toward Robert's Ford, which was guarded by a company led by Capt. B. F. Bryan.[51]

Despite the long hours and hard riding, Grierson's men remained awake and alert. "The country hereabout, with its beautiful groves, the trees laden with the grey moss characteristic of Louisiana, was very attractive," explained Woodward. "And as the day dawned, it seemed to inspire the men with renewed life and spirits." The head of the column approached the river around noon, where Bryan's company was discovered blocking the road near modern-day Monticello. As scouts dressed as civilians approached the Confederates, one of the defenders asked, "How are you, gentlemen? Have you come to relieve us?" One of the scouts replied in the affirmative, adding that the main command would be up soon. "It's about time," grumbled the Southerner, "for we have been here four days and are nearly out of rations."[52]

While the scouts were deceiving the enemy, Grierson—who had no intention of slowing down—ordered another attack. Riding in the van, the men of the 7th Illinois Cavalry set their spurs and drove forward, one battalion moving to the left and another to the right, the gap between them filled with the balance of the column. The attack was handsomely delivered even though the men had been in the saddle since daylight the previous day and had ridden some 60 miles in a little more than 24 hours.[53]

The sudden appearance of the raiders bearing down on them from three directions surprised Bryan, who had "only about 30 [men] immediately in camp." The Confederates had been paying more attention to the Federals holding Baton Rouge to the southwest than Grierson's Federals arriving behind them from the northeast, and they had "no possible chance of . . . making a stand." Grierson's cavalry, which Captain Bryan estimated at 1,000 strong, "made a dash and surrounded me on all sides before I was aware that they were other than our own troops, their advanced guard being dressed in citizens' garb. Indeed, I could not think it possible that an enemy could approach my camp without my being notified in ample

51 *OR* 24, pt. 1, 537.

52 Ibid., 528, 536-38; Grierson, *A Just and Righteous Cause*, 176; "The Grierson Raid," *Weekly Register* (Canton, IL), September 7, 1863; Woodward, "Grierson's Raid," 109.

53 Woodward, "Grierson's Raid," 109.

time to be prepared to meet them." The enemy, noted Grierson, was "in happy ignorance of the fact that the Yankees were in their rear and near at hand." Thus surprised and mostly surrounded, the only man to escape was a captain, who hid behind clumps of Spanish moss in a tree. One Illinois trooper corralled at least a dozen Confederates hiding in a hole along the riverbank. In his report, dated May 10, Bryan detailed a list of his losses that included 38 men and as many horses, wagons, small arms, ammunition, and more. "I would state that I have 6 horses left by the enemy at the Comite Bridge," he added, as if that would in some way ameliorate the wholesale embarrassment. The other Confederate units guarding nearby fords quickly figured out what was happening, reporting that Bryan's capture left "our left and rear . . . entirely exposed."[54]

The only problem now was to get across the wide river, which Grierson ordered the troopers to do as quickly as possible. The Comite, observed the brigade leader, was "deep enough to swim many of the horses." Once the scouts found a suitable ford half a mile away, the entire column crossed, with the 6th Illinois Cavalry riding in advance. A large throng of some 500 slaves who had flocked to the column during the last few miles crossed with them. "I tried at first to prevent them," explained Grierson, "knowing how rapidly we would have to march and fearing that they would not be able to keep up, and that they would be made to suffer if caught by their masters, but it was no use." The slaves saw the appearance of the column as perhaps their one chance at freedom, and a motley collection of wagons, carts, horses, and mules followed the begrimed Federal raiders. Once across the Comite River, the slaves burst out in "alternate shouts of rejoicing and prayers." Grierson admitted, "I never before during my life saw such a medley or motley crowd. To describe it would be an impossibility." But it was "the most wonderful appearance imaginable."[55]

With nothing between him and the safety that Baton Rouge afforded, Grierson allowed the exhausted men to stop about four miles from the city to feed their horses and rest a short time. The opportunity was welcomed by everyone, explained Colonel Prince, because it was "the

54 Ibid.

55 "The Grierson Raid," *Weekly Register* (Canton, IL), September 7, 1863; Grierson, *A Just and Righteous Cause*, 176-78; Abbott, "Heroic Deeds of Heroic Men," 281; Surby, *Grierson Raids*, 123.

first [time] that man or beast had eaten for 30 hours." As "hungry and jaded as these men and horses were," he added, "not a murmur was heard from the lips of a soldier." Some of the men were tasked with guarding the substantial number of prisoners with the column, but the rest grabbed what little sleep they could. Soon, declared Grierson, all but "myself, Lieutenant Woodward, and the guard were enjoying a sound and refreshing sleep." He later proudly observed, "The last twenty-eight hours, we marched 76 miles, had four engagements with the enemy, and forded the Comite River. . . . During this time the men and horses were without food or rest."[56]

While many of his troopers slept, Grierson relaxed in a very different way. The brigade commander rode to a nearby plantation house in search of his first love and what he needed most. "I astonished the occupants by sitting down and playing upon a piano which I found in the parlor," he recalled with deep satisfaction. "In that manner, I managed to keep awake while my soldiers were enjoying themselves by relaxation, sleep, and quiet rest." Reaching the outskirts of Baton Rouge after all he had accomplished and being able to play the piano were, he elaborated, a "great relief to the overtaxed mind and nerves. I felt that we had nobly accomplished the work assigned to us, and no wonder that I felt musical. Who would not under like circumstances?"[57]

Benjamin Grierson had just turned in the most renowned performance of his life—a nonmusical recital of epic proportions.

* * *

The Federals in Baton Rouge were as surprised at Grierson's sudden appearance as had been the Confederates at the Comite River. "Judge of the general astonishment and delight," one newspaper said, "when we learned that the brigade was no other than the cavalry force that has for weeks been the terror of Central Mississippi, heard from occasionally in rebel prints, as destroying a train here, a bridge there, terrifying a town in the morning and burning a camp forty miles away in the evening." A Federal in Tennessee had not directly predicted Grierson would end up

---

56 "The Grierson Raid," *Weekly Register* (Canton, IL), September 7, 1863; *OR* 24, pt. 1, 528-29; Grierson, *A Just and Righteous Cause*, 176.

57 Forbes, "Grierson's Cavalry Raid," 120; Grierson, *A Just and Righteous Cause*, 176; Henry C. Forbes to His Sister, May 23, 1863, in Henry Forbes Papers, CHM.

in Baton Rouge, but he made it clear that if he did so, it would surely shock his comrades there: "It would be rather surprising to the Federal soldiers in Louisiana, to see 1200 or 1500 blue coats emerging from the brush some fine morning." A. N. Shattuck of Company E, 7th Illinois Cavalry, wrote home, "We had a grand reception here, the people could hardly believe that we were really troops from the North."[58]

Major General Christopher C. Augur, commanding at Baton Rouge, heard the raiders were approaching in a most unusual way. One of Grierson's orderlies was asleep when the halt was called a handful of miles outside of town. The exhausted man "did not hear the order, went moping on, nodding to the motion of his horse," which kept walking until it reached the Federal lines, where pickets shook the man awake and thoroughly questioned him. "He rubbed his eyes in astonishment and answered all the questions put to him in a sort of a dazed manner," Grierson remembered. The guards found it hard to believe the 6th and 7th Illinois Cavalries operating out of La Grange, Tennessee, had suddenly appeared on the outskirts of Baton Rouge, Louisiana. "They thought it was some sort of a trap to draw their troops out to ambush," wrote the thoroughly amused Grierson.[59]

With no other news about Grierson's position, the logical explanation was that Confederate cavalry had crossed the Comite River to attack Baton Rouge. General Augur sent cavalry troops under Capt. John F. Godfrey to investigate, and a couple of Grierson's orderlies who had remained awake to guard the camp reported the enemy attacking from the west. "Feeling confident that there must be some mistake about the matter and that no enemy could possibly come against us from that direction," Grierson explained, "I rode out alone to meet the troops, without waking up my command." Grierson approached Godfrey's cavalry, who by this time had dismounted and taken cover wherever they could, their weapons pointed at the approaching rider. Grierson did some fast talking to convince the Federal commander of his identity, admitting that Godfrey was "not at all satisfied with the looks of things," nor did he believe "we were really and truly 'bona fide' Illinois troops from

---

58 "The Great Cavalry Exploit of the Times," *New Orleans Era*, May 5, 1863, copy in Thomas W. Lippincott Papers, ALPL; "Army Correspondence," *Weekly Register* (Canton, IL), May 11, 1863; "From One of Grierson's Cavalry," *Union Monitor* (Litchfield, IL), June 5, 1863.

59 Grierson, *A Just and Righteous Cause*, 176.

Grierson's Brigade Column. One of the few contemporary photos of Grierson's raiders. This one shows the brigade after it reached Baton Rouge. *Photographic History of the Civil War*

Tennessee." According to Henry Forbes, Grierson "had to <u>negotiate for admission</u> within the Federal lines." Once Grierson convinced Godfrey he was indeed a Federal officer, the captain popped from behind his fence and shook Grierson's hand, and his soldiers followed suit. Grierson had finally reached Union-held territory after spending 16 days behind enemy lines and riding at least 600 miles since leaving La Grange.[60]

60 *OR* 24, pt. 1, 528; Forbes, "Grierson's Raid," 27; Grierson, *A Just and Righteous Cause*, 177-78. For Godfrey, see John Franklin Godfrey, *The Civil War Letters of Capt.*

Word coursed back east to roust the Illinoisans out of their slumber so the column could formally enter Baton Rouge. General Auger insisted on a parade, including the column's prisoners, most of whom had been captured at the Comite River. The Rebels, recalled Grierson with no little pride, "twitted [teased] the Baton Rouge soldiers, saying that they never could have captured them; that the United States government had to send Illinois soldiers clear from Tennessee into their rear before they could be taken." According to a newspaperman, the prisoners were "only distinguishable from their capturers by being less travel stained and riding in fatigue dress without arms." Grierson gave the honor of leading the final ride into Baton Rouge to his own 6th Illinois Cavalry, followed by Smith's guns, the prisoners, the 7th Illinois Cavalry, and the large throng of slaves moving toward freedom. Word spread and "for nearly a mile before entering the city, the road was lined with wondering spectators—old and young, male and female, rich and poor, white and black, citizens and soldiers—all mixed up indiscriminately." Colonel Prince recalled how he and his comrades "found the people ready to receive us with open arms—Every courtesy was extended to us." Another trooper remembered that "their band played & they gave us three rousing cheers."[61]

Grierson's troopers made their triumphal entry in a column of fours with sabers drawn:

Amid the wildest shouts and cheers and waving of banners and flags, heralded by bands of music, the [tired] and travel-stained troops marched in triumph through the city, around the public square, down to the river to water their horses, and then out to Magnolia Grove, the trees of which were in full bloom and deliciously fragrant, situated two miles south of the city, where at sunset, scarcely waiting to partake of the refreshment provided for us by the kind-hearted soldiers of the 116th New York and 48th Massachusetts infantry regiments, we laid down to sleep amid flowers and perfume, beside the deep waters of the great Mississippi River, without guard and without danger.[62]

John Franklin Godfrey, Candace Sawyer and Laura Orcutt, eds. (South Freeport, ME: Ascensius Press, 1993).

61 *OR* 24, pt. 1, 528; Grierson, *A Just and Righteous Cause*, 177-78, 180; "The Grierson Raid," *Weekly Register* (Canton, IL), September 7, 1863; Freyburger, *Letters to Ann*, 45; Woodward, "Grierson's Raid," 111; Daniel E. Robbins to Parents, May 5, 1863; Daniel E. Robbins to Brother, May 7, 1863.

62 Grierson, *A Just and Righteous Cause*, 178.

CHAPTER ELEVEN

The Results

"Isn't the Grierson 'raid' glorious?" asked Edward Havens of the 103rd Illinois in a letter to his parents from La Grange. Two other expeditions, he added, "started from this point and were gone respectively five and 10 days each. Although they made good long marches and took about 40 prisoners and 500 animals, still we forget them in looking after Grierson." Others compared the raid to more famous expeditions. "The account of Grierson's raid in the South is as cheering as that of [George] Stoneman's and is its equal if not superior," argued another soldier. Other raids achieved important results, but Grierson's thrust through Mississippi consumed so much attention and drew heavy praise because of its length and audaciousness.[1]

Northern newspapers had done their best to keep up with the column, usually reporting what Mississippi newspapers had already printed, such as the sudden attack at Newton Station. "I remember with what interest I watched its progress," explained a newspaperman in Illinois who knew Grierson and Colonel Prince personally. Major media outlets back east, such as the *New York Times* and the *New York Herald*, ran long, detailed stories with multiple illustrations. The *Times*, for example, declared

---

1 Edwin R. Havens to Parents, May 13, 1863, in Havens Family Papers, Michigan State University; Paul Selby to S. A. Forbes, November 24, 1908, in Stephen A. Forbes Papers, UI; Charles W. Wills, *Army Life of an Illinois Soldier: Including a Day by Day Record of Sherman's March to the Sea* (Washington, DC: Globe Printing Company, 1906), 174; "Vicksburg 75 Years Ago," *Vicksburg Evening Post*, April 22, 1938.

that Grierson made a wonderful raid "through the length and breadth of the very long and quite broad State of Mississippi." The reports were reprinted in papers across the continent as far away as Sacramento in its *Daily Union. Frank Leslie's Illustrated Newspaper* reported that "till very lately our military men have been content to leave all the dashing cavalry raids in the hands of [Jeb] Stuart, Fitzhugh Lee and other daring rebels," but now raids by Federal units were soaking up the limelight, "to crown all, that of Col. Grierson's." One *Harper's* writer exclaimed that "the exploits of [John] Morgan, Stuart, and [Joseph] Wheeler, boasted as they have been, are as child's play in comparison with such a raid as this."[2]

One correspondent wondered at the enormity of the raid. More than "20,000 rebel troops were sent out from various points with a view to intercept or capture the bold raider," he marveled, "but they always fell in the rear." Left unwritten was the question of what those 20,000 troops could have done if they had concentrated not against Grierson but against Grant, as he was attempting to cross the Mississippi River south of Vicksburg.[3]

Others were watching as well. General Hurlbut in Memphis provided his superiors with information as reports of Grierson's whereabouts dribbled in. "I learn from two independent sources that Colonel Grierson has passed below Jackson, Miss.; cut the railroad at Hazlehurst, and destroyed 50,000 pounds of bacon and an ammunition train, and is on his way down to Baton Rouge to join General Banks," Hurlbut wired President Lincoln at noon on May 2. "I believe it to be true," he added, "as my orders were to push south if safer than to come north." A response to Grierson's raid from inside the Federal war machine in Washington was bureaucratic in nature. The adjutant general's office, for example,

---

2   "The Romance of the War," *New York Times*, May 18, 1863; "Colonel Grierson's Cavalry Raid," *New York Times*, May 10, 1863; "Details of Grierson's Great Raid," *Sacramento Daily Union*, June 10, 1863; "The Great Raid of the War," *Chicago Tribune*, May 20, 1863; "Colonel Grierson at New Orleans—What He Learned by His Raid," *Cleveland Morning Leader*, May 20, 1863; "The Great Raid of the War," *Times* (Goshen, IN), May 28, 1863; "The Rebellion to Be Crushed with Cavalry," *Advertiser* (Edgefield, SC), June 10, 1863; "Col. Grierson," *Frank Leslie's Illustrated Newspaper*, June 6, 1863; Abbott, "Heroic Deeds of Heroic Men," 281.

3   Grierson, *A Just and Righteous Cause*, 180.

complained about not having received muster rolls and other paperwork from the 6th and 7th Illinois Cavalry on time.[4]

The raiders themselves knew they had done something remarkable, if just not all the details. Captain Henry Forbes joked with his sister in a letter from Louisiana, "You don't need an introduction I trust to a gentleman writing you from this remote spot in Uncle Sam's domain, to save him from the charge of impertinence. If you do, though, it is I." Forbes had much to be gleeful about, having felt as much pressure as anyone except the colonel himself. Forbes described himself to his sister as "a wanderer by flood and waste. I have at last found a resting place, and a refuge out of the wilderness." He went on to describe their "dare devil expedition—our neck or nothing ride through the heart of Dixie" as "the greatest march, in a given time, on record." Forbes was especially proud of his company's six-day detachment, during which "we were the blind used to obscure the real movements." He enumerated how for those six days the company had only 4 meals, 12 "feeds," and 14 hours' sleep, all while being "given . . . up for lost." Yet the company managed to provide "employment to one Maj. Gen. (Loring) and no less than 4000 rebel troops with artillery." His sister also learned that he had gone 48 hours without food and ridden 52 miles without feeding the horses. To another acquaintance, Forbes kidded that they should come "ride out with me a few hundred miles a week for your health," and he recommended they "sleep in the cow pasture without a blanket, eating little or nothing for breakfast, crackers and water for dinner, and tea for tea, which may result in making you as healthy as it has me." Forbes noted that he had lost 22 pounds on the perilous journey, and he wished he had a daguerreotype of "the seat of my unmentionables as viewed before and after the 'great raid.'" The captain was quick to give credit for the success elsewhere, writing that Company B's feat was doing "pretty well for one little company," but that "with *such* men you can accomplish what you will." In a nod to a higher power, he insisted "there was One who covered our defenseless heads."[5]

Other Federals echoed Forbes. Henry Heald of Company K, 7th Illinois Cavalry, boasted that the troops had "performed the greatest feat of the

---

4   *OR* 24, pt. 3, 264; Muster Roll for Company L, 6th Illinois Cavalry, RG 94, E 57, NARA.

5   Henry C. Forbes to His Sister, May 23 and June 24, 1863.

war," and he revealed his own surprise: "The end finds us in Louisiana instead of Tennessee." Another penned that he "stood it tip top, but was very tired, as was every one of us, and glad when we got through." Still another described the brigade "having made the journey through the State of Mississippi on horseback," arrived at Baton Rouge "tired and worn out thinking we had done a big thing." An exhausted trooper informed his hometown newspaper, "We think we have accomplished a great deal in this trip. How we are to get back we do not yet know. We certainly cannot go back the way we came. Perhaps we will not go back at all, but I hope we will, for it is too hot here."[6]

Many echoed the wondrousness of the entire thing. Forbes's brother Stephen described "the rapid march, the subtle ruse, the gallant dash, the sudden surprise, and the quick and cunning retreat which leaves an opponent miles in the rear before he knows that the fight is over." Daniel Robbins embellished a bit when he declared that "not a bridge was destroyed before us not a ford disputed we marched as we pleased when we pleased & where we pleased as far as resistance was concerned." Another described the "panic stricken people through whose country it passed like a tornado. Like a tornado, too, it was in its work of destruction." One Illinoisan recalled the losses of "two men killed and several wounded through bad management," though most of the troopers stood in awe at the lack of casualties and general good health enjoyed by the men. "It is remarkable that so few were left on the expedition from sickness, and so few were killed and wounded," marveled one trooper. "It was the most successful raid of history, or of this war, and attended with the smallest loss. Surely, God was their protection and shield." Once in Baton Rouge, observed yet another participant, "the General here remarked that he thought he had seen cavalry before, but he had not."[7]

Not only were the soldiers praised but so, too, were their horses and mules. Many of the cavalrymen acknowledged the important role the animals played in the success of the raid, even as they were traded out

6   "Camp Correspondence," *Fulton City Register* (Canton, IL), May 26, 1863; Daniel E. Robbins to Parents, May 5, 1863.

7   Forbes, "Grierson's Cavalry Raid," 103; "Ben Grierson," n.d., in Henry C. Forbes Papers, CHM; "Ben Grierson," *St. Landry Democrat*, June 23, 1888; William Dunaway to Wife, May 8, 1863, in William E. Dunaway Papers, UI; "The Grierson Raid," *Weekly Register* (Canton, IL), September 7, 1863; "Camp Correspondence," May 26, 1863; Daniel E. Robbins to Parents, May 5, 1863.

for new animals, which were in turn traded for fresher mounts. "Of the horses that started not more than one hundred come through," recalled one Illinois trooper, "but we captured the finest that there were in Miss., and La." Scout Richard Surby explained "many troopers had to change four or five times." According to one man, "Only a very few of the horses we started with came through. I have the same one I started with, but he is run down so that he is hardly fit for anything—will have to trade him off or buy new, I expect. But I would not have missed the trip for more than the value of 2 horses." Trooper William Dunaway wrote his wife from Baton Rouge, "We had a long, weary-some trip of it. It was trying on man and horse. We traveled almost day and night. A many a night we traveled all night through rain and mud. We wore out one set of horses," he continued, "but we captured another set just as good as the old ones, if not better. I have got as fine a young mare as ever traveled and she did not cost me anything."[8]

Some men found it hard to leave their beloved horses behind in a trade that even the animal found hard to understand, as one owner discovered. "It would sometimes arouse a feeling of regret to witness the attachment displayed by the faithful old horse," admitted Sergeant Surby, "who, on being turned loose by the road-side, to wander where he pleased, would be seen following up the column, and when it stopped he would lay down in the road to rest, and as we started again could be seen occupying a place in the ranks, where he would remain from morning to night, faithful in the discharge of his duty."[9]

The high command was just as impressed. Generals Hurlbut and Sooy Smith were giddy over Grierson's success, with the latter officer erroneously boasting, "The conception and general plan of the raid were mine. Its masterly execution belonged to Grierson and to his able and gallant subordinate officers and brave men, and to them and him I have always gladly given the praise they deserved." Smith was liberal with his praise for Grierson, whom he described as "an ideal cavalry officer—brave and dashing, cunning and resourceful—and his troops were excellent and well worthy of such a commander." Hurlbut was also

---

8   "From One of Grierson's Cavalry," June 5, 1863; Surby, *Grierson Raids*, 103, 128; "Camp Correspondence," *Fulton City Register* (Canton, IL), May 26, 1863; Freyburger, *Letters to Ann*, 45; William Dunaway to Wife, May 8, 1863.

9   Surby, *Grierson Raids*, 103, 128.

effusive in his praise for the manner in which the raid was conducted. "By referring to my previous communications," he wrote Grant,

> you will perceive that the several movements indicated in them to be carried on by this command have been performed with a reasonable degree of accuracy, and with a very brilliant success in the main attempt to pierce the enemy's country. The movement on Tuscumbia on the one side drew attention and gathered their cavalry in that direction, while the movement on Coldwater and Panola drew Chalmers and his band in the other. Thus our gallant soldier, Grierson, proceeded with his command unchallenged, and has splendidly performed the duty he was sent upon. I very earnestly support his claim for promotion, earned by long and meritorious service, and now crowned by this last achievement.[10]

The success of the raid prompted both Hurlbut and Smith to lay claim to its planning and execution—assertions that did not sit well with either officer. According to Smith, Hurlbut changed his story once Grierson arrived safely in Baton Rouge. Hurlbut maintained that Grierson had discretionary orders to go to Baton Rouge if need be, a point Smith took exception to, given his strong arguments prior to the raid. Smith even claimed Hurlbut changed his story "*ex post facto* to the outcome of a successful expedition and I am sorry to feel that he may have been guilty of such reprehensible conduct."[11]

Others in the high command also appreciated Grierson's success. "There is lots of high officers here at this place say that they would rather been a private in the rear rank on this trip," noted one trooper, "than to have been an officer in command." General Nathaniel Banks, who suddenly found himself with a brigade of veteran cavalry in his department, hailed the raid as "the most brilliant expedition of the war. . . . The moral effect of that remarkable expedition upon a wavering and astonished enemy, and the assistance rendered us in breaking up the enemy's communications, in establishing our own, and in covering the concentration of our forces against this place, can hardly be overestimated. Their timely presence has supplied a want which you will remember I have frequently represented was crippling all our operations." The loquacious officer continued: "I trust the services of Colonel Grierson

---

10 Forbes, "Grierson's Cavalry Raid," 125; W. S. Smith to S. A. Forbes, May 4, 1907; Smith, "The Mississippi Raid," 381; *OR* 24, pt. 3, 276.

11 W. S. Smith to S. A. Forbes, May 4, 1907; S. A. Forbes to W. S. Smith, March 3, 1907, in Stephen A. Forbes Papers, UI.

and his command will receive at the hands of the Government that acknowledgment which they so eminently deserve." Sherman praised the raid and its leader with a nod toward the wider strategic importance of the mounted thrust, writing on May 5 to a fellow general, "It was Grierson who made the cavalry raid down to Meridian, and he is supposed to be traveling toward Baton Rouge or Dixie. It has produced a sort of panic South, and Grant's movements will complete it, some say."[12]

No one was more pleased than Grant himself, who received the first indication of Grierson's success on May 1 while moving inland toward Port Gibson. In a quick note to Admiral Porter, Grant observed, "Grierson of the cavalry, has taken the heart out of Mississippi." He later added, "Colonel Grierson's raid from La Grange through Mississippi has been the most successful thing of the kind since the breaking out of the rebellion." He also sang the raider's praises to General Halleck in Washington in a report by explaining the course of Grierson's raid: "[He] was 5 miles south of Pontotoc on April 19. The next place he turned up was at Newton, about 30 miles east of Jackson. From there he has gone south, touching Hazlehurst, Byhalia [Bahala], and various other places. The Southern papers and Southern people regard it as one of the most daring exploits of the war. I am told the whole State is filled with men paroled by Grierson." The general borrowed "the expression of my informant" to offer perhaps the most succinct summation of the raid when he added, "Grierson has knocked the heart out of the State."[13]

All in all, summed up an Illinois newspaper, "It is one of the most daring feats of the war; and the best feature of it all is, that the Jackson papers compliment them highly for the polite manners they have displayed among the citizens."[14]

*   *   *

Newspapers across the Confederacy offered outright praise for Grierson's bold accomplishment. While it was still underway, the *Appeal*

---

12 William Dunaway to Wife, May 8, 1863; *OR* 24, pt. 3, 273, 367.

13 Simon, *PUSG*, vol. 8, 139, 144; "Colonel Grierson's Brilliant Raid in Mississippi," *Union* (Urbana, OH), May 13, 1863; Grant Letter, *Chicago Tribune*, May 17, 1863; *OR* 24, pt. 1, 33-34.

14 *OR* 24, pt. 3, 308-9; "Army Correspondence," *Weekly Register* (Canton, IL), May 11, 1863.

in Jackson, Mississippi, editorialized that the raid "will be recorded as one of the gallant feats of the war, no matter whether the actors escape or are captured." The Magnolia State's *Columbus Republic* admitted that "the boldest, and we may say one of the most successful, raids of cavalry that has been known since the war began, has been made (we say it with shame) through the very center of Mississippi." The editor added, as if surprised: "We can learn no serious damage done or any ill treatment to the inhabitants personally." The *Jackson Mississippian* agreed: "It is stated that they committed no depredation, but on the contrary were particularly polite and compliant to all the people on their route." Still, the raid did not sit well with the editor, who used the word *humiliation* several times in his column. Even the *Augusta (Georgia) Constitutionalist* expressed embarrassment for its sister state when it described the raiders riding through Mississippi "as leisurely and with as much nonchalance as our country people would ride into town on a gala day."[15]

Other Mississippians also admitted Grierson's obvious success. A Federal spy near Yazoo City wrote that the "people were greatly troubled about Grierson's raid on the Jackson and New Orleans Railroad, and thought it surpassed anything done by Morgan or Forrest." A Smith County resident summed it up well when he stated, "Tis a bold move certainly for the enemy."[16]

Some people blamed their fellow Mississippians, especially those who had guided the enemy. A newspaper reported that a man named Hammond had guided Grierson to Newton Station. The man had grown up in the area, explained the paper, but had vanished for 18 months before turning up after the attack. Citizens captured him and "he confessed to having acted as pilot to the Grierson expedition." The man was in a dire situation, continued the paper, "his fate had not been determined on when our informant left Saturday afternoon, but the general voice

15 Forbes, "Grierson's Cavalry Raid," 128-29; "From Mobile and Ohio Railroad," *Jackson Daily Mississippian*, April 28, 1863; "Grierson," *Jackson Daily Mississippian*, May 8, 1863; Frank Moore, ed., *The Rebellion Record: A Diary of American Events, with Documents, Narratives Illustrative Incidents, Poetry, etc.*, 11 vols. (New York: D. Vann Nostrand and Co., 1861-68), 7, 24-25.

16 *OR* 24, pt. 3, 302; J. M. Quin to John J. Pettus, April 28, 1863.

very properly called for his summary execution, and it was expected to take place that evening."[17]

The Confederate response to what had just transpired within Mississippi was no different. Most knew the raid had been enormously successful, and they could only tip their hats to the bold and daring Union raiders. One planter who stood watching as his stores were ravaged remarked: "Well, boys, I can't say I have anything against you. I don't know but on the whole I rather like you. You have not taken anything of mine except a little corn and fodder for your horses and that you are welcome to. You are doing the boldest thing ever undertaken. But you'll be trapped though. Yes you'll be caught yet, mark me." Grierson thought the planter then contemplated what he was saying and added, perhaps for his own protection, "but I really trust that no harm will come to you in any event."[18]

Confederate military personnel from generals to privates knew a military success when they saw one, even if it was at their expense. An enlisted man in Vicksburg took pen in hand to scribble in his journal, "Our regiment was greatly excited over reports of a Federal raid led by Col. Grierson, which passed nearly through the entire state." The raid fascinated Port Hudson commander Franklin Gardner. When his bastion surrendered on July 9, Gardner wanted to meet Grierson to ask him about the details of the operation, and he later wrote of the "extraordinary march from Summit to Baton Rouge." Colonel Wirt Adams praised the logistics employed during the operation by noting that, "during the last twenty-four hours of their march in this State, they traveled at a sweeping gallop, the numerous stolen horses previously collected furnishing them fresh relays."[19]

Other Confederates made similar observations. Colonel (and future general) Robert V. Richardson admitted that Grierson "has made a most

---

17 "Traitor Caught," *Natchez Daily Courier*, May 5, 1863. Further research could not determine Hammond's fate.

18 "Incidents of the Raid," *Memphis Daily Bulletin*, May 23, 1863, copy in Benjamin H. Grierson Papers, ALPL; Grierson, *A Just and Righteous Cause*, 181.

19 William P. Chambers, "My Journal," *Publications of the Mississippi Historical Society, Centenary Series*, 5 vols. (Jackson: Mississippi Historical Society, 1925), 5, 262; W. A. Rorer to Susan, June 13, 1863; *OR* 24, pt. 1, 255, 533, 541, 543, 550; Brown, *Grierson's Raid*, 236; Fremantle, *Three Months in the Southern States*, 53-54; *OR* 24, pt. 3, 803.

successful raid through the length of the State of Mississippi and a part of Louisiana, one which will exhilarate for a short time the fainting spirits of the Northern war party." George Gantt of the 9th Tennessee Cavalry Battalion, who had done his best to catch the Federal raiders, praised Grierson's ability to trick civilians and others as he made his way to Louisiana. The officer, he wrote, "managed so as to completely deceive citizens and our scouts as to his purpose, and by a march of almost unprecedented rapidity moved off by the Greensburg road to Baton Rouge." Lieutenant Colonel W. A. Rorer of the 20th Mississippi described it as "the celebrated raid through our State."[20]

Such praise would never flow from the lips or the pen of John Pemberton. Instead, the Vicksburg commander who had turned his eyes away from Grant's river crossing in an effort to stop Grierson, simply noted in his official correspondence that the Federals "has studiously avoided meeting our infantry." His official report includes a laundry list of things he did to stop Grierson, which was nothing more than an attempt to justify his actions and provide his version of events. In the end, he blamed a lack of cavalry while giving little praise to the "celebrated raid."[21]

While those who had chased Grierson through the southwestern portion of Mississippi expressed their admiration, many turned to the inevitable issue of who was to blame for letting such a thing occur. "The highest accomplishment which graces the Yankee is his skill in stealing," sneered an editorial in the *Jackson Daily Mississippian*. The Federals, it continued, "pushed their way with quite ease and patience, stopping wherever they pleased to feed their horses from cribs, and their soldiers from the larders of Mississippi planters." The editor could not fathom how the raid could have accomplished all it did. "Fifteen hundred Yankees leisurely traversed the hitherto proud State of Mississippi, insulting

20 William P. Chambers, "My Journal," *Publications of the Mississippi Historical Society, Centenary Series*, 5 vols. (Jackson: Mississippi Historical Society, 1925), 5, 262; W. A. Rorer to Susan, June 13, 1863; *OR* 24, pt. 1, 255, 533, 541, 543, 550; Brown, *Grierson's Raid*, 236; Fremantle, *Three Months in the Southern States*, 53-54; *OR* 24, pt. 3, 803.

21 William P. Chambers, "My Journal," *Publications of the Mississippi Historical Society, Centenary Series*, 5 vols. (Jackson: Mississippi Historical Society, 1925), 5, 262; W. A. Rorer to Susan, June 13, 1863; *OR* 24, pt. 1, 255, 533, 541, 543, 550; Brown, *Grierson's Raid*, 236; Fremantle, *Three Months in the Southern States*, 53-54; *OR* 24, pt. 3, 803.

and destroying as they went without having a gun fired at them!" he exaggerated. "We deserve to bow our heads in lasting shame if we do not wipe out this stinging blot upon our fair escutcheon."[22]

Most of the blame for the disaster settled onto Confederate officers. "Governor," fumed one citizen, "I have great reason to believe that in the recent raid through the state our Genl Officers on this road [Mobile and Ohio] are greatly to blame for the want of information at head quarters as to the movements of the Federals. Mississippi," he added, "has been outraged by this raid and the citizens charge its success to the *willful inattention* or *gross* inability of the officers sent here to protect them." A diarist in Jackson agreed, noting that "nothing proves more fully the incompetency of our generals than the miserable disposition of the forces appointed to defend the State." One Vicksburg artillerist went so far as to ask, "Where are our authorities? 'Asleep?'"[23]

The *Columbus (Mississippi) Republic* mocked the military: "We do not know where the responsibility rests, but wherever it is, if it is not a fit and proper subject for court martial, we are afraid there are none." The editor confessed, "We have always doubted the ability of Gen. Pemberton to command this department," but then argued on the general's behalf by claiming he could not handle situations beyond his "eye." There was also some interarmy rivalry among the branches. W. A. Rorer complained about the cavalry, saying that his mounted infantry had done "more fighting in six weeks than most of the cavalry in this state have done since the war commenced."[24]

Out of the raid came a call for better defense of the interior. The *Natchez Daily Courier* decried the march and rightly called upon citizens to organize companies for defense, but then the newspaper demonstrated its own ineptitude by claiming "two hundred men, with shotguns, sand in their gizzards, taking advantage of position, could have arrested Grierson's march, and saved us this humiliation, and the disasters that

---

22 "Grierson's Raid," *Jackson Daily Mississippian*, May 7, 1863.

23 James H. Rives to John J. Pettus, May 2, 1863; Bettersworth, *Mississippi in the Confederacy*, 112; E. T. Eggleston, diary, April 25, 1863, 1st Mississippi Light Artillery File, Vicksburg National Military Park.

24 *OR* 24, pt. 3, 787; "The Yankee Raid in Mississippi," *Republic* (Columbus, MS), n.d., copy in Stephen A. Forbes Papers, UI; W. A. Rorer to Susan, June 13, 1863; Bearss, *The Vicksburg Campaign*, 2, 235.

may follow." In reality, those who had attempted to mount a defense had failed rather spectacularly. Still, the *Jackson Mississippian* lauded the people of Garlandville for their initial defense and called on others to take a stand, arguing "the raid is waking up its people."[25]

Civilians all over the state began forming home defense companies to ward off another crisis. Residents, particularly those left in Grierson's wake, formed militia companies, explained a Palo Alto man to Governor Pettus, "to resist in future any other raids of the Yankees in our midst." He continued: "We want no pay. We will furnish ourselves with every thing we need—We only ask the privilege of fighting the enemy in our own way." The civilian also asked Pettus for commissions for the volunteer officers to protect them in case of capture, thus throwing "the protecting Mantle of the State over us, so we could claim all the privileges of prisoners of war."[26]

In the end, most of the blame fell on the top tier of Confederate commanders, including Pemberton and to a lesser degree theater commander Johnston. Pemberton had no real answer for why the Federal raiders had been able to accomplish what they did, while at the same time passing along some of the blame to his superior: "I confess I did not expect them to penetrate the department to its southern limits, nor, I presume, did you." In truth, Grierson's pluck rather than Confederate blame explains the success of the surprise raid. The enemy, concluded the Federal commander,

> became so excited, bewildered, and amazed that they could not judge what was best to do, being so mixed [up] and perplexed by the apparently reliable but false and contradictory reports received by them that they went blundering along in a haphazard sort of fashion, without gaining any satisfactory advantage or results. We were reported at so many different places at the same time, and our forces so greatly overestimated, that really but little correct information reached the enemy at all in regard to us until it was too late to be of any service.[27]

*   *   *

25 "Grierson," *Natchez Daily Courier*, May 12, 1863; "Proceedings of a Meeting to Organize a Cavalry Company," *Jackson Daily Mississippian*, April 25, 1863; "The Raid in Mississippi," May 7, 1863.

26 A. K. Brantley to John J. Pettus, April 24, 1863.

27 *OR* 24, pt. 3, 802; Grierson, *A Just and Righteous Cause*, 186.

Opinions mattered much less than the actual results. "During the expedition," wrote Grierson in his report just three days after reaching Baton Rouge, "we killed and wounded about 100 of the enemy, captured and paroled over 500 prisoners, many of them officers, destroyed between 50 and 60 miles of railroad and telegraph, captured and destroyed over 3,000 stand of arms, and other army stores and Government property to an immense amount." Grierson added, "We also captured 1,000 horses and mules. Our loss during the entire journey was three killed, seven wounded, five left on the route sick; the sergeant-major and surgeon . . . left with Lieutenant Colonel Blackburn, and nine men missing, supposed to have straggled. We marched over 600 miles in less than 16 days. The last 28 hours we marched 76 miles, had four engagements with the enemy, and forded the Comite River, which was deep enough to swim many of the horses. During this time the men and horses were without food or rest." Later, he explained why he was able to do so much: "by the capture of their couriers, dispatches, and mails, and the invaluable aid of my scouts, we were always able by rapid marches to evade the enemy when they were too strong and whip them when not too large."[28]

The significance of the raid was much greater than Grierson imagined just a few days after safely reaching Louisiana. His report took a narrow view of its importance and focused on the destruction his troops had inflicted across Mississippi. The damage to the railroads in general, and especially to the bridges and trestles, was indeed significant. One newspaper reported that several bridges near Newton Station, 250 feet long each, suffered at the hands of the raiders, as did "seven culverts and one cattle gap." The damage to the Southern Railroad, however, was not as serious as initially believed. The newspaper declared that the culverts would be easily fixed and that the bridges would be repaired and the road running "in four days or less." Fixing the telegraph was more problematic. Although the poles had not been damaged, the wire had been "cut in pieces," and in some cases rolled up and thrown into ditches. Despite the best efforts of the Federal troopers, it, too, was soon repaired and operable.[29]

28 *OR* 24, pt. 1, 528-29; Grierson, *A Just and Righteous Cause*, 179.

29 "The Great Federal Raid," May 5, 1863; Grabau, *Ninety-Eight Days*, 119; "The Yankee Raid in Mississippi," *Mobile Advertiser and Register*, n.d., copy in Stephen A. Forbes Papers, UI.

As the days and weeks passed, Confederate authorities breathed a collective sigh of relief when the realization sunk in that there was not as much damage as had been feared, especially to the all-important Southern Railroad. The line opened in early May, with one newspaper happily reporting on May 5 that the "superintendent of the Southern Express Company . . . came over the road." Numerous trains carrying the state government's archives, treasury, and officials made their way eastward in mid-May when the Mississippi state government fled Jackson in front of Grant's invading army. Arthur Fremantle, a member of the British army visiting the Confederate states, took a perilous journey along the line on May 23 and 24 and recorded his impressions in his memoir, *Three Months in the Southern Confederacy*. There were breaks in the railroad around Jackson, and at one point the engine derailed, forcing the men on the train to push the cars for a while. The line around Newton and the Chunkey River bridges damaged by Grierson, however, were intact. Ironically, the injury to the New Orleans, Jackson, and Great Northern Railroad, a line Grierson's troops had spent much time damaging, was more extensive than the target railroad at Newton Station. It would not be fully repaired until after the war.[30]

Damage to outlying areas, such as the many road bridges Grierson burned in his wake, proved more difficult to repair. They were less significant in terms of military and supply transportation, and in some cases it was months—and even years—before they received any real attention. One Mississippian wrote about riding from Garlandville to Newton Station in January 1864 and the need to go "out of our way to cross a creek called Jarlow, the Grierson raid having burnt the bridge last spring."[31]

Yet the damage Grierson managed to inflict was mostly irrelevant when compared to the real repercussion of the deep cavalry raid: diverting attention away from Grant's crossing of the Mississippi River.

---

30 *OR* 24, pt. 3, 796; "The Great Federal Raid," *Natchez Daily Courier*, May 5, 1863; Fremantle, *Three Months in the Southern States*, 127; Carlton J. Corliss, *Main Line of Mid-America: The Story of the Illinois Central* (New York: Creative Age Press, 1950), 197-99; James Wilford Garner, *Reconstruction in Mississippi* (New York: Macmillan, 1902), 144; Smith, *Mississippi in the Civil War*, 38-39; Michael B. Ballard, *The Civil War in Mississippi: Major Campaigns and Battles* (Jackson: University Press of Mississippi, 2011), 144.

31 Jason Niles, diary, January 11, 1864, University of North Carolina.

It is abundantly clear that Grant intended for Grierson's and the other raids and diversions to help mask his own major operation, even if fully coordinating them was out of the question, given geographical and communication constraints. But the raid was not a lucky shot in the dark launched at exactly the right time and place. One veteran decades later railed against the notion that "our raid was simply a lucky incident—that Gen Hurlbut happened to send us down through Mississippi just at this opportune time."[32]

Grierson's raid was a coordinated effort, and it succeeded beyond anyone's highest hopes. The correspondence among the Confederate high command clearly related the impact of the operation. Pemberton was acutely aware of Grant's movements to the south in Louisiana, and he was watching the effort when it reached New Carthage and concentrated toward Grand Gulf. The passing of the Vicksburg batteries by the Federal navy (twice) also indicated a significant movement was underway, and intelligence received by Confederate troops stationed across the river south of New Carthage indicated the same thing. In fact, there was some concern that Grant would move farther below Grand Gulf; Pemberton warned of enemy efforts as far south as Bayou Pierre (something that was, in fact, undertaken at a later date) as late as April 21.[33]

Pemberton was keeping his eye on Grant even while Grierson was making his way south in the days after April 17. The Vicksburg commander believed his subordinates in northern Mississippi were in the best position to take care of the raiding threat, and he believed Grierson had turned back just as General Ruggles had informed him. Pemberton's false sense of security vanished when the Federals appeared without warning at Newton Station and broke his one connection to the outside world. Naturally enough, he swiveled his attention to the east for the next five days, until Grant and Porter attacked Grand Gulf on April 29, in an effort to trap and destroy Grierson. That event swung his attention back west to Grant.[34]

Pemberton's correspondence in the *Official Records* between April 24 and 28 includes a heavy concentration of communications regarding

---

32 T. W. Lippincott to S. A. Forbes, April 7, 1907 and November 25, 1908.

33 *OR* 24, pt. 3, 775.

34 Ibid., 781-800; Bearss, *The Vicksburg Campaign*, vol. 2, 236.

Grierson's raid. Sixty-four of the 69 messages during that brief period dealt with Grierson. One of the five non-Grierson messages referred to the Yazoo River defenses, while another dealt with the Vicksburg river defenses. Only three messages demonstrated any concern for Grant near Grand Gulf, and two of those, one to Jefferson Davis and the other to Joseph E. Johnston, contained warnings that the enemy was active at Hard Times across the river and might be massing to attack Grand Gulf. Significantly, however, both messages ended with some variation of "the approaches to Northern Mississippi are almost unprotected, and it is impossible to prevent these raids with infantry." Only one message during those April days solely discussed the threat that Grant and the Army of the Tennessee posed across the river. On April 28, Pemberton wrote to division commander Carter Stevenson at Vicksburg with orders to prepare to send reinforcements to John Bowen at Grand Gulf. Other messages during this time were sent to Bowen directly, each of them an attempt to warn him of Grierson's threat to his rear and to activate Wirt Adams's cavalry and send it after the raiding Federals. Based on this evidence, Pemberton almost completely ignored Grant for five full days, but the sudden jolt of news that Grant had crossed the river at Bruinsburg shook Pemberton from his obsession with Grierson. Only then did he turn his attention back to Grant. By that time it was too late.[35]

The bulk of the Confederate forces in the Vicksburg and Jackson areas were also focused on Grierson's raid. The operation kept Loring's brigades occupied in east Mississippi, and once the Federals reached the area south of Jackson, Pemberton sent almost all the cavalry, together with infantry he ordered mounted, to chase the raiders. This included the commands watching the Mississippi River crossings for Bowen south of Grand Gulf, most notably Wirt Adams's Mississippi Cavalry. The result, explained Grierson's adjutant Samuel Woodward, was that the Confederate cavalry "were drawn into wild goose chases and scattered to the four winds in futile attempts to circumvent and capture Grierson." More than four decades after the event, Union infantryman F. T. Demingway recalled the reaction of the soldiers of the Army of the Tennessee to news of Grierson's raid: "We who marched with Grant

---

35 *OR* 24, pt. 3, 781-800; Bearss, *The Vicksburg Campaign*, vol. 2, 236; Edwin C. Bearss, "Grierson's Raid," April 17-May 2, 1863, Vicksburg National Military Park.

to the rear of Vicksburg (I was in the 72nd Ill. Infty.), realized as never before the help your raid was in keeping the enemy away from us."[36]

For five critical days Grierson held Pemberton's almost undivided attention, arguably the five most critical days of Grant's operation. Grierson's nearly unopposed ride through south-central Mississippi was enough to tip the scales in Grant's favor and allow him to gain a crucial foothold east of the Mississippi River.[37]

Grant admitted as much. Years later, when he and Grierson were together listening to several other officers talk about the Vicksburg campaign, Grant leaned over to the former cavalry commander and whispered, "Grierson, when I got that paper at Port Gibson and saw what you had done I would not have given that (snapping his fingers) to have my success assured."[38]

*   *   *

While word spread of the success of the raid, Grierson's troopers embarked on a few days of well-deserved rest. They needed it. "If it does not cover us with glory [it] did cover us with <u>mud</u>," Daniel Robbins declared. Many letters flew out of Baton Rouge informing loved ones that they were safe and in Louisiana. Robbins wrote his brother on New Orleans, Jackson, and Great Northern Railroad Company letterhead, which he had picked up at the depot in Brookhaven. Grierson wrote to Alice: "I arrived at Baton Rouge La. Friday all O.K. with my command. I had a very successful expedition—beyond my own most sanguine expectations."[39]

Unfortunately, some of the troopers were in no condition to live up their newly gained fame and popularity. Most, one Illinoisan described, "suffered from swelling of the legs and erysipelas, from sitting so long in the saddle, but it was only temporary." A few suffered more serious issues, and 12 had to be hospitalized. According to Illinoisan Thomas

---

36 Woodward, "Grierson's Raid," 112-13; F. T. Demingway to S. A. Forbes, May 7, 1910, in Stephen A. Forbes Papers, UI.

37 Grabau, *Ninety-Eight Days*, 121.

38 T. W. Lippincott to S. A. Forbes, January 3, 1908; "Letter to the Editor," n.d., in Stephen A. Forbes Papers, UI.

39 Daniel E. Robbins to Brother, May 7, 1863; B. H. Grierson to Alice, May 6, 1863.

Grierson's Brigade Camp. Another contemporary photo showing Grierson's cavalry camp after the brigade reached Baton Rouge. *Photographic History of the Civil War*

W. Lippincott, "Some of our men whose helpless feet hung numb and useless by their stirrups, were taken to the hospital, helped from their horses to cots, where their boots, which had not been off since leaving Tennessee, were cut from their swollen feet, and were told by the surgeons that, had our raid lasted two or three days longer, their feet would have had to be amputated."[40]

Others suffered different maladies. Henry Forbes, who had done perhaps more planning than anyone else on the raid except for Grierson, became "suddenly delirious . . . as he lay resting by his camp fire," explained an eyewitness, "and [he] was taken with cautious violence to the post hospital, tearing the curtains from the ambulance on the way, and swearing that we might kill him if we would but we could never take him prisoner." Another Illinoisan had a different kind of problem. His family had sent him a care package of "apples, fried cakes & cookies"

40 "Incidents of the Raid," *Memphis Daily Bulletin*, May 23, 1863; "Grierson's Big Raid," n.d., Thomas W. Lippincott Papers, ALPL; Daniel E. Robbins to Parents, May 5, 1863.

to La Grange. "I am afraid . . . [they] will spoil before I get them," he sadly reported.[41]

The troopers of the 6th and 7th Illinois Cavalry regiments who were not suffering any lasting maladies from the raid had the run of Baton Rouge. Many spent their hours in saloons, where fights broke out, often between the Illinoisans themselves. Still, if a comrade found himself in trouble, they were all there to help. Fisticuffs aside, the members of the two regiments became very close. "A better understanding and feeling never existed between two regiments than between these two so linked together," confirmed one of the men. The appearance of the raiders in Baton Rouge not only surprised the local residents but pleased them. In fact, they were so joyous that they rarely allowed the Illinoisans to pay for anything. Most chalked up the rowdy behavior to the stress they had experienced and simply looked the other way. Not all the men participated in hard drinking and fighting, however. One of the troopers recalled spending his free time quietly playing "billiards."[42]

Several members of the regiments experienced a different form of excitement in Louisiana. Four troopers from the 7th Illinois Cavalry who had been captured on the raid were freed when Port Hudson surrendered. Days earlier, another captured 7th Illinois trooper escaped Port Hudson by jumping into the river. The Confederates fired at him, but with one arm over a plank and only his head above water, he managed to swim "two miles upstream to our fleet." Sadly, one of Grierson's orderlies, Billy Post of the 2nd Iowa Cavalry, was killed in the Port Hudson fighting.[43]

For his part, Grierson was startled by the attention lavished upon him. "I woke from my tired sleep and weariness to suddenly and unexpectedly find myself famous," he wrote Alice. "I did not know and could not realize the extent of my success. In fact, I did not then think we had accomplished anything wonderful. I hope to be able to do more

41 Forbes, "Grierson's Cavalry Raid," 120; Grierson, *A Just and Righteous Cause*, 176; Henry C. Forbes to His Sister, May 23, 1863; Daniel E. Robbins to Parents, May 5, 1863.

42 Surby, *Grierson Raids*, 103; Curtiss, diary, May 5 and 7, 1863; Grierson, *A Just and Righteous Cause*, 181.

43 "The Grierson Raid," *Weekly Register* (Canton, IL), September 7, 1863; Soldier Letter, *Fulton City Ledger* (Canton, IL), July 21, 1863; Death of Wm. Post," *Evening Argus* (Rock Island, IL), July 8, 1863.

for the Cause before the close of the War." In some small way, however, the performer in Grierson surely enjoyed the praise heaped upon him.[44]

Grierson's troopers certainly thought he deserved the praise. Daniel Robbins, for example, showed remarkable insight just a few days after reaching Baton Rouge when he wrote that Grierson had "fooled & outwitted the Confederates in fact showed them a new rinkle in the art of war." He added that "probably many a poor soldier at Vicksburg & Port Hudson will go hungry in consequence of this trip." Another example of Grierson's newfound fame occurred in New Orleans. Officially, he and Colonel Prince were there on business to get new wheels for the cannon, but in reality they looked forward to some downtime. There, Grierson was bombarded with attention and even felt the need, "as ugly as I am," to get a photograph made. The locals in New Orleans went wild when he appeared in public. The city, explained one eyewitness, "was thrown into a great excitement when the news of Col. Griersons Cav. Raid through Mississippi and when he came to the city there was given him quite a reception at the St. Charles Hotel. To wit a number of patriotic speeches were made also a lot of fireworks were set off." The people of the city gifted him a "splendid horse" and equipment.[45]

Regardless of their behavior, the hardy brigade of Illinois cavalry was too valuable to be left loitering for long in Baton Rouge. Before long they drew tents, cooking utensils, and other equipment to replace what was left behind in Tennessee or lost along the way in Mississippi and returned to the war. More than one commander wanted the brigade. Grant asked Nathaniel Banks on numerous occasions to send Grierson back into the Department of the Tennessee. Banks balked at the request, arguing that Grierson's horse soldiers was the only major body of cavalry under his command. A disgusted Grierson, who wanted to return to Grant's command, wrote, "General Banks seemed to think that he could not get

---

44   B. H. Grierson to Alice, May 6 and 9, 1863; Grierson, *A Just and Righteous Cause*, 181.

45   Daniel E. Robbins to Brother, May 7, 1863; B. H. Grierson to Alice, May 6, 1863; Horace P. Milton to John, May 8, 1862, Horace P. Milton Letters, Louisiana State University; Grierson, *A Just and Righteous Cause*, 182-83; George H. Hepworth, *The Whip, Hoe, and Sword: Or, the Gulf-Department in '63* (Boston: Walker, Wise and Company, 1864), 285.

along without the cavalry which arrived so suddenly and opportunely within his department."[46]

Eventually, Grierson and his two Illinois cavalry regiments reentered the real war. They fought under Banks around Port Hudson during the early weeks of the summer, making raids into the area near where the column had ridden earlier in May. Once Vicksburg fell and Port Hudson followed suit, the brigade was sent back to Grant and thence northward to La Grange, where the troopers were warmly welcomed. Grierson toured Vicksburg on the way to Tennessee, where his knee was injured by another kick from his horse. He took a leave of absence because of the injury and made his way to Illinois to see Alice and the boys. Grierson's fame followed him, and his return to Springfield and Jacksonville, where he was feted in high fashion, was no doubt welcome to the failed store owner and musician who had left Jacksonville two years earlier in debt and a virtual nobody.[47]

Like it had for so many, the war had given Grierson a unique opportunity he would take advantage of fully. For the musician-turned-warrior, it was the performance of a lifetime.

46 Daniel E. Robbins to Brother, May 7, 1863; *OR* 24, pt. 3, 289, 347, 360, 493; Grierson, *A Just and Righteous Cause*, 184.

47 A. B. Archer to Jennie, June 5, 1863, in Archer Family Papers, MDAH; Soldier Letter, *Fulton City Ledger* (Canton, IL), July 21, 1863; A. Curl, "The Fight at Clinton, La.," *Confederate Veteran* (March 1905), vol. 13, no. 3, 122; Charles W. Gallentine to Sister, June 12, 1863, in Charles W. Gallentine Letter, Navarro College; Charles W. Gallentine to Sister, August 18, 1863, in Charles W. Gallentine Letters, Newberry Library; "Jacksonville Letter," *Telegraph* (Alton, IL), October 16, 1863.

Epilogue

Just because Grierson had made a name for himself and his brigade was now safe again within Union lines did not mean the war was over for them or for anyone else. The fighting would continue for two more years, into April 1865. Many of the raid's participants went on to greater glory. Others went to their graves. Most faded into oblivion, such as the elderly Rev. Capt. Jason B. Smith who had commanded the battery of small guns hauled through Mississippi. He was already in his 60s when the raid began, and the expedition used up whatever energy he had left. Smith resigned from the service in 1864 due to what his surgeon described as "chronic inflammation of the Liver, and advancement in age." Another surgeon's certificate mentioned "malarial fever, and unusually severe fatigue and exposure."[1]

Sadly, many did not survive the war. Lieutenant Colonel Blackburn died on May 17 from the wounds he received at Wall's bridge. Grierson had left the wounded officer at the Newman plantation, where he "suffered greatly and lay for . . . days during which time he had to be waited upon constantly day and night." Blackburn's body was eventually buried behind Federal lines at Port Hudson, Louisiana. "He was a good officer, looked out for his men well, and he was a brave man, perhaps a little too rash at the time he was wounded, or he might have saved himself

---

1 Surgeon's Certificate, June 24, 1863, and John N. Niglas Statement, August 19, 1864, in Jason B. Smith, Compiled Service Record, NARA.

and others," one Illinoisan wrote of their courageous but ill-fated young leader. Fortunately, his widow was able to apply for a pension.[2]

Lieutenant Colonel Reuben Loomis, who had commanded the 6th Illinois Cavalry, did not fare much better. Soon after the raid he took an extended leave of absence because of hemorrhoids, which a surgeon described as "very much aggravated by his uninterrupted service during Gen Grierson's Raid through Mississippi." Just seven months later Loomis became embroiled with Maj. T. G. S. Herrod in a matter of honor after he reprimanded his subordinate for "unwarranted assumption of power." Herrod took exception to the charge and told Loomis to take back his accusation "or I'll kill you." Loomis foolishly replied, "Maj. Herrod, you have got a pistol in your hand and I am unarmed. If you want to kill me, kill me." Herrod did just that by firing five shots, two of which struck Loomis, the fatal ball striking him in the chest. Herrod was court-martialed and imprisoned but then pardoned after the war. Less criminal but just as fatal, Maj. Matthew Starr rose to the rank of colonel and commanded the 6th Illinois Cavalry, but he died of wounds in October 1864.[3]

Others fared better. Edward Hatch continued to serve under Grierson but was wounded in the chest in fighting near Memphis. He recovered and was promoted to brigadier general in April 1864. After the war Hatch was made a colonel in the regular army, given command of the 9th U.S. Cavalry, and once again served with Grierson in the far west. He died in 1889. Colonel Prince, jealous of Grierson's sudden fame, maneuvered to be out from under his command. He never gained further promotion but lived a long life after the war before dying in 1908.[4]

---

2   House Report 650, 53rd Congress, 2nd Session, 1-2; "The Grierson Raid," *Weekly Register* (Canton, IL), September 7, 1863; Soldier Letter, *Fulton City Ledger* (Canton, IL), July 21, 1863; "Camp Correspondence," *Fulton City Register* (Canton, IL), May 26, 1863; Reece, *Report of the Adjutant General of the State of Illinois*, vol. 8, 3; John W. Blackburn to Edward Prince, January 22, 1864, and other death documents in William D. Blackburn, Compiled Service Record, NARA.

3   David W. Lusk, *Politics and Politicians: A Succinct History of the Politics of Illinois, from 1856 to 1884, with Anecdotes and Incidents, and Appendix from 1809 to 1856* (Springfield: H. W. Rokker, 1884), 419; Reece, *Report of the Adjutant General of the State of Illinois*, vol. 8, 3; John N. Niglas, Statement, August 28, 1863, in Reuben Loomis, Compiled Service Record, NARA.

4   Ezra J. Warner, *Generals in Blue: Lives of the Union Commanders* (Baton Rouge: Louisiana State University Press, 1964), 216; Grierson, *A Just and Righteous Cause*, 197; Edward Hatch, Compiled Service Record, NARA.

Many lower-level officers likewise rose in the ranks. Captain John Lynch, who had led the two-man detachment to Macon, became the last colonel of the 6th Illinois Cavalry in 1865. Major John Graham, who had led so many of the battalion-level detachments during the raid, also rose to command his own regiment in 1865, becoming colonel of the 7th Illinois Cavalry. Captain George Trafton, who had also led detachments, rose to lieutenant colonel of the regiment in 1863.[5]

Others went on to illustrious nonmilitary careers, although they always considered the raid to be the center point of their existence. Adjutant Woodward followed Grierson out west after the war. He served as his aide until Grierson retired and then rose in rank to lieutenant colonel in the 7th Cavalry. Woodward retired in 1903 and died in 1924, but not before writing a detailed two-part history of the great raid. Intrepid scout Richard Surby survived his wound and subsequent captivity in Richmond, Virginia, was exchanged by the end of the year, and fought through the remainder of the war. Afterward he became one the major historians of the raid, writing numerous books and accounts of his service. He died in 1897. Captain Henry C. Forbes recovered from his mental fatigue and rose through the ranks to ultimately become lieutenant colonel of the 7th Illinois Cavalry. After the war he became a businessman and librarian. Forbes took an interest in the raid's history and wrote a very personal account of it that was never published. He died in 1903. Henry's younger brother, Stephen, also became one of the major historians of the raid. The teenager grew to manhood and became a successful science professor at the University of Illinois. He wrote extensively on the raid and corresponded with many veterans of the two Illinois regiments. He died in 1930.[6]

Many of the Confederates who pursued Grierson survived the war and went on to live interesting lives. Clark Barteau was promoted to colonel and fought through the remainder of the war, during which he was twice wounded. He survived, practiced law for decades, and died in 1900. William Wirt Adams became a Confederate brigadier general, serving under Nathan Bedford Forrest for the remainder of the war.

5   Reece, *Report of the Adjutant General of the State of Illinois*, vol. 8, 3, 53.

6   Grierson, *A Just and Righteous Cause*, 387n3; Dinges, "The Making of a Cavalryman," 386-87n144; Richard W. Surby, Find a Grave Memorial 24359889, February 3, 2008, https://www.findagrave.com/cgi-bin/fg.cgi?page=gr&GRid=24359889; Richard W. Surby, Compiled Service Record, NARA; "Finding Aid," in Henry C. Forbes Papers, UI; "Finding Aid," in Stephen A. Forbes Papers, UI.

Once the fighting ended, he became a Mississippi state government employee and postmaster. He was walking through Jackson in 1888 when he exchanged heated words with local editor John Martin, who had criticized Adams in his paper. Both men drew weapons and fired. Both were killed. Colonel Edward Goodwin, who defended Enterprise from the "horde" of Yankees numbering all of 35 horsemen, died five months later. Some surmised he lost his command because of the ruse he fell for. Henry C. Forbes, who performed that ruse, later recalled, "We afterwards learned from the Mobile papers that the effrontery of our game seemed so unendurable to those in authority that the Rebel Col. commanding lost his commission because he had lost his hand."[7]

The lives of the two general officers who had the greatest stake in the raid's success or failure could not have been more different. John C. Pemberton was captured and paroled at Vicksburg and exchanged a few months later. Unable to find a suitable command, the disgraced lieutenant general resigned his commission and continued fighting with the Confederacy as a lieutenant colonel of artillery and an inspector of ordnance. The financially strapped officer lived on a small farm in Virginia from 1866 to 1875 before moving to Philadelphia to live with family. He died in 1881. Grant, on the other hand, captured Vicksburg, saved Chattanooga, went east to defeat Robert E. Lee and accept his surrender at Appomattox, and became president of the United States. He died in 1885.[8]

The people of Mississippi never forgot the raid that swept through their state, especially the planters who lived in Grierson's path. William D. Sloan survived his request to have his throat slit but lived only four more years before dying in 1867. Stephen Daggett lived much longer, until 1880, and is buried in the city cemetery in Pontotoc on the route Grierson's troops took through the town. Dr. Benjamin Kilgore lived only a little more than a year after the raid before dying in late 1864 and being buried near his plantation where Grierson's troops had camped.

---

7   Ezra J. Warner, *Generals in Gray: Lives of the Confederate Commanders* (Baton Rouge: Louisiana State University Press, 1959), 3; Bruce S. Allardice, *Confederate Colonels: A Biographical Register* (Columbia: University of Missouri Press, 2008), 55, 168; Forbes, "Grierson's Raid," 22.

8   Ezra J. Warner, *Generals in Gray: Lives of the Confederate Commanders* (Baton Rouge: Louisiana State University Press, 1959), 233; For Grant, see White, *American Ulysses.*

Charner Estes in Winston County lived until 1875; his son, W. E. W. Estes, lived into the next century and died in 1906.[9] The planters in southern Mississippi, south of Grierson's target at Newton Station, likewise mostly lived beyond the war. One of the oldest men in the state, Griffin M. Bender, died in his 90s in 1880. Elias Nichols lived until 1882. Chambers McAdory went back to Alabama after the war and eventually served in the Alabama legislature, dying in 1908. George W. Williams survived until 1877, went by the title "colonel," and is buried near his plantation on the east bank of the Strong River. Jesse Thompson lived until 1900, dying at 87. A. C. Snyder lived until 1876, Uriah T. Gill until 1872, and Dr. Spurlock near Liberty, Mississippi, until 1915, when he died at the age of 85.[10]

James Newman and his wife, Caroline, were true to their word and cared for the wounded Federals for weeks. In fact, they gave of their own means doing so and petitioned congress in the 1890s for $412. A House of Representatives committee investigated their claim. The Newmans "are now poor and old," explained the report, "the bed and all the articles belonging to it were rendered utterly worthless by the use of it for Col. Blackburn, as well as many other articles used to replenish it during the eighteen days that Col. Blackburn lay at his house; and for his use and the other soldiers', for bandages and other purposes, nearly all the bedding,

9   William David Sloan, Find a Grave Memorial 15206302, August 10, 2006, https://www.findagrave.com/memorial/15206302/william-sloan; Stephen Daggett, Find a Grave Memorial 14631957, June 17, 2006, https://www.findagrave.com/memorial/14631957/daggett; Benjamin Kilgore, Find a Grave Memorial 59333701, September 28, 2010, https://www.findagrave.com/memorial/59333701/benjamin-kilgore; Charner Estes, Find a Grave Memorial 22479366, October 27, 2007, https://www.findagrave.com/memorial/22479366/estes

10   DuBose, *Jefferson County and Birmingham, Alabama*, 511; Griffin M. Bender, Find a Grave Memorial 9121577, July 19, 2004, https://www.findagrave.com/memorial/9121577/bender; Elias Nichols, Find a Grave Memorial 122137181, December 25, 2013, https://www.findagrave.com/memorial/122137181/elias-nichols; George Washington Williams, Find a Grave Memorial 18083560, February 26, 2007, https://www.findagrave.com/memorial/18083560/george-w-williams; Jesse Thompson Jr., Find a Grave Memorial 137537073, October 20, 2014, https://www.findagrave.com/memorial/137537073/jesse-thompson; A. C. Snyder, Find a Grave Memorial 37477734, May 25, 2009, https://www.findagrave.com/memorial/37477734/a-c-snyder; Chambers McAdory, Find a Grave Memorial 38840788, June 28, 2009, https://www.findagrave.com/memorial/38840788; Thomas Jefferson Spurlock Sr., Find a Grave Memorial 104073536, January 23, 2013, https://www.findagrave.com/memorial/104073536/thomas-j-spurlock; Uriah Thomas Gill, Find a Grave Memorial 34483133, March 5, 2009, https://www.findagrave.com/memorial/34483133/uriah-gill

bed covering, and linen owned and possessed by claimant were destroyed for use or used up." The report added, "Claimant and his wife spent their whole time during those eighteen days waiting upon and working for the said wounded soldiers." It was also planting season, which meant even more work for James. At the same time, Caroline cooked and washed for the entire party, including Surgeon Yule and others who had stayed behind. The committee report acknowledged that "provisions were scarce and very high in that country." Newman also buried Blackburn and another soldier who died in addition to reburying Private Reinhold properly after the hasty burial by the soldiers on May 1.[11]

Of course, it was Grierson himself who received the most notoriety for the raid that bears his name. Southerners reviled him for the "great suffering" he had caused and all the jewelry and money he had allegedly stolen. One man openly hoped that "the Colonel has long since, by confession, repentance, and prayer, appeased the wrath of Him who said, 'Inasmuch as ye have done it unto the least of these, ye have done it unto me." The federal government was more appreciative of the way he conducted himself and, in large part because of the raid, promoted him to brigadier general in June 1863. As a general he commanded larger cavalry organizations, sometimes including his old 6th and 7th Illinois Cavalries. He even conducted a reprise of his Mississippi raid in December 1864 and January 1865, marching through the heart of the state once more, tearing up railroads and inflicting war on the people of Mississippi a second time. Grierson was promoted to major general after the war. Although mustered out of the volunteer service, he went back into the regular army as a colonel of the black Buffalo Soldiers of the 10th U.S. Cavalry, serving the rest of his career mainly in Texas. He was appointed a brigadier general in the regular army just before his retirement in 1890.[12]

---

11 House Report 650, 53rd Congress, 2nd Session, 1-2.

12 Edwin C. Bearss, *Forrest at Brice's Cross Roads and in North Mississippi in 1864* (Dayton, OH: Morningside, 1994), 354; Thomas E. Parson, *Work for Giants: The Campaign and Battle of Tupelo/Harrisburg, Mississippi, June-July 1864* (Kent, OH: Kent State University Press, 2014), 306; Paul Selby to Jessie Palmer, January 3, 1912, in Paul Selby Papers, ALPL; Edwin C. Bearss, "Grierson's Winter Raid on the Mobile and Ohio Railroad," *Military Affairs* (Spring 1960), vol. 24, no. 2, 20-37; George W. Baskett, "Incidents of Grierson's Raid," *Confederate Veteran* (June 1914), vol. 22, no. 6, 268; "Brief Record of General Grierson's Services During and Since the War, with Special Testimonials and Recommendations from General Officers,

Grierson's wife, Alice, died in 1888, and he remarried soon thereafter, but by this time he was suffering from a variety of health problems. He died in 1911, beloved by many Americans and especially his fellow soldiers. His death was remarked upon across the country. The Society of the Army of the Tennessee passed a resolution upon his passing.[13]

Despite all his other achievements, the 1863 raid remained his major claim to fame, and what Benjamin Grierson is still remembered for to this day, although the memory of the event has changed over time. Many books and articles have been written about the raid, although the writers did not always agree on everything. Richard Surby, Samuel Woodward, and Stephen Forbes wrote accounts for publication, while many others never appeared in print. Writing when Surby's was the only account available, T. W. Lippincott, one of the soldiers on the raid riding with the 7th Illinois Cavalry, bemoaned the fact that it was the only account available, "poor as it is." He advised Grierson to write a *Century Magazine* article about what he called "the greatest feat performed by cavalry *in any war*," but Grierson never did. He did, however, pen his autobiography, which he never dreamed would be published.[14]

In addition to works by amateur historians, novelists, and moviemakers, the raid has been remembered in anniversary commemorations. Even the town of Newton celebrated the raid and attack on the 125th anniversary in 1988, complete with a visit by reenactors of the 7th Illinois Cavalry, who

Senators, Representatives, and Other Officials, 1861-1882," 1882, in Benjamin Henry Grierson Papers, Newberry Library; "Synopsis of Services Rendered to Government During the War," n.d., in Benjamin H. Grierson Papers, ALPL. For Grierson's later commands, see the Benjamin H. Grierson Papers, Texas Tech University.

13   Leckie and Leckie, *Unlikely Warriors*, 298; "Letter to the Editor," *Chicago Inter Ocean*, June 16, 1909; "Ben Grierson," *Rockford Daily Gazette*, April 17, 1888; "Major T. W. Lippincott," *Rockford Weekly Gazette*, April 28, 1886; "Colonel Grierson's Military Achievements," *Chicago Inter Ocean*, March 29, 1890; "A Music Master Goes for a Ride," *Mt. Vernon Register News*, April 6, 1961; "Noted Civil War General Dead," *Daily Review* (Decatur, IL), September 1, 1911; Society of the Army of the Tennessee, *Report of the Proceedings of the Society of the Army of the Tennessee Meetings Held at Columbus, Ohio, November 3-4, 1909, Toledo, Ohio, November 16-17, 1910, Council Bluffs, Iowa, November 10-11, 1911* (Cincinnati: Charles O. Ebel Printing Company, 1913), 278.

14   T. W. Lippincott to B. H. Grierson, June 1889, in Thomas W. Lippincott Papers, ALPL. For the memory of the raid, see York, *Fiction as Fact*, and Charles D. Grear, "'Through the Heart of Rebel Country': The History and Memory of Grierson's Raid," in Steven E. Woodworth and Charles D. Grear, eds., *The Vicksburg Campaign: March 29-May 18, 1863* (Carbondale: Southern Illinois University Press, 2013), 24-42.

Benjamin H. Grierson Grave. After a long and notable career in the United States Army, Grierson died in 1911 and was buried in his native Jacksonville, Illinois. *Author*

demonstrated how to make Sherman bow ties (the heating and bending of rails). Headlines from local newspapers shouted "Newton Welcomes Cavalry Troop" and "Grierson's Raid Commemoration Scheduled in Newton for April 13." Historic signage commemorating the raid also went up in the ensuing years, although it was anything but comprehensive.[15]

Grierson's Raid was an adventure of the first order that helped change the course of the Civil War. The fictionalized version does not do any justice to the true story of Benjamin Grierson and *The Real Horse Soldiers*.

15 "Newton Welcomes Cavalry Troop," *Newton Record,* April 20, 1988; "Grierson's Raid Commemoration Scheduled in Newton for April 13," *Newton Record*, April 6, 1988; "'Grierson's Raid' Historical Marker Ceremony Held," in Grierson's Raid Subject File, MDAH.

Bibliography

Manuscripts

Amite County, MS, Chancery Clerk
    Deed Book 63
    Deed Book 66

Auburn University, Auburn, AL
    Southern Rail Road Records

Author's Collection
    George Smith, "A History of Union, Mississippi"

Chicago History Museum (CHM), Chicago, IL
    Henry C. Forbes Papers
    J. W. Vance Papers

Copiah County, MS, Chancery Clerk
    Deed Book R

Duke University, Durham, NC
    W. A. Rorer Letters

The Filson Historical Society, Louisville, KY
    John Letter

Gettysburg College, Gettysburg, PA
    Benjamin Henry Grierson Vertical File

Steve Hicks Collection (HC)
    Daniel E. Robbins Letters

Huntington Library, San Marino, CA
    Obadiah Ethelbert Baker Papers

Abraham Lincoln Presidential Library, Springfield, IL
    John W. Clinton Papers
    James M. Cole Papers
    Benjamin H. Grierson Papers
    Augustus Hurff Memoirs
    Thomas W. Lippincott Papers
    Marguerite Rawalt Papers
    Rawlinson Family Papers
    Paul Selby Papers

Louisiana State University, Baton Rouge, LA
    Horace P. Milton Letters

Loyola Marymount University, Los Angeles, CA
    Civil War Collection

Michigan State University, East Lansing, MI
    Havens Family Papers

Mississippi Department of Archives and History (MDAH), Jackson, MS
    Archer Family Papers
    Luther S. Baechtel Diary
    John J. Pettus, Correspondence and Papers, 1859-63
    W. A. Rorer Letters
    William T. Sherman Letters
    Subject Files
        Benjamin H. Grierson
        Grierson's Raid

Mississippi State University, Starkville, MS
    Edward Fontaine Papers
    Miscellaneous Papers
        "Ex-Slave Autobiography," Joe Rollins, West Point, Mississippi

National Archives and Records Administration, College Park, MD
    RG 29, Records of the Bureau of the Census, 1790-2007

Entry 293, Census

    1850 Chickasaw County (MS), Population and Slave Schedules

    1850 Tippah County (MS), Population Census

    1860 Amite County (MS), Population and Slave Schedules

    1860 Copiah County (MS), Population and Slave Schedules

    1860 Jasper County (MS), Population and Slave Schedules

    1860 Jefferson County (MS), Population and Slave Schedules

    1860 Lawrence County (MS), Population and Slave Schedules

    1860 Pontotoc County (MS), Population and Slave Schedules

    1860 Simpson County (MS), Population and Slave Schedules

    1860 Smith County (MS), Population and Slave Schedules

    1860 Winston County (MS), Population and Slave Schedules

RG 94, Records of the Adjutant General's Office

    E 57, Muster Rolls of Volunteer Organizations

        6th Illinois Cavalry

        7th Illinois Cavalry

        2nd Iowa Cavalry

        Battery K, 1st Illinois Artillery

    Compiled Service Records

        William D. Blackburn

        William D. Buffington

        Benjamin H. Grierson

        Edward Hatch

        Reuben Loomis

        Edward Prince

        George C. Reinholdt

        Jason B. Smith

        Richard W. Surby

        Samuel L. Woodward

        Erastus D. Yule

Navarro College, Corsicana, TX

    Charles W. Galentine Letter

Neshoba County Public Library, Philadelphia, MS

    Historic Neshoba County Maps

Newberry Library, Chicago, IL

    Charles W. Galentine Letters

Benjamin Henry Grierson Papers

Pontotoc County, Chancery Clerk, Pontotoc, MS
    Deed Book 3
    Deed Book 17

Ripley Public Library, Ripley, MS
    Land Deed Index

Smith County Chancery Clerk, Raleigh, MS
    Deed Book 0524

Southeast Missouri State University, Cape Girardeau, MO
    Ellen Waddle McCoy Papers
        William H. Dennis Letters

State Historical Society of Iowa, Des Moines, IA
    Franklin Hammond Collection
    A.B. Rush Letters

Texas Tech University, Lubbock, TX
    Benjamin H. Grierson Papers

Tippah County Chancery Clerk, Ripley, MS
    Deed Index

United States Army Heritage Education Center (USAHEC), Carlisle, PA
    Civil War Documents
        Collier Family Papers

University of Arizona, Tucson, AZ
    Henry Clinton Forbes Collection

University of Illinois (UI), Champaign, IL
    William E. Dunaway Papers
    Henry C. Forbes Papers
    Stephen A. Forbes Papers

University of Mississippi, Oxford, MS
    Wirt Adams Collection

University of North Carolina, Chapel Hill, NC
    Jason Niles Diary

University of Wisconsin-River Falls, River Falls, WI
Edwin D. Levings Papers

Vicksburg National Military Park, Vicksburg, MS
Edwin C. Bearss, "Grierson's Raid (April 17-May 2, 1863)"
E. T. Eggleston Diary, 1st Mississippi Light Artillery File
"Grierson's Cavalry Raid: Eastern Mississippi Invaded," 1937
Handwritten Notes on Grierson's Raid
"Vicksburg 75 Years Ago," *Vicksburg Evening Post*, April 22, 1938

Winston County Public Library, Louisville, MS
Jennie Newson Hoffman, "A History of Winston County Volume 1," Federal Writer's
Project: Works Progress Administration, 1938
Civil War in Winston County Vertical File
Josie Worthy Holman Accounts

Wisconsin Historical Society, Madison, WI
H. R. Curtiss Diary

Newspapers

Alton (IL) Telegraph
Canton (IL) Fulton City Register
Canton (IL) Weekly Register
Chicago Inter Ocean
Chicago Tribune
Cleveland Morning Leader
Columbus (MS) Republic
Decatur (IL) Daily Review
Edgefield (SC) Advertiser
Frank Leslie's Illustrated Newspaper
Goshen (IN) Times
Jackson Daily Mississippian
Litchfield (IL) Union Monitor
Memphis Daily Bulletin
Mississippi Free Trader
Mobile Advertiser and Register
Mount Vernon (IL) Register News

Natchez Daily Courier

Neshoba (MS) Democrat

New Orleans Era

New York Times

Newton (MS) Record

Pontotoc (MS) Progress

Rock Island (IL) Evening Argus

Rockford Daily Gazette

Rockford Weekly Gazette

Sacramento Daily Union

Simpson County (MS) News

Smith County (MS) Reformer

St. Landry (LA) Democrat

Urbana (OH) Union

Verdan (OK) News

Vicksburg Evening Citizen

Vicksburg Evening Post

Winston County (MS) Journal

Primary and Secondary Sources

Abbott, John S.C. "Heroic Deeds of Heroic Men." *Harper's New Monthly Magazine* 30, no. 77 (February 1865): 273-81.

Allardice, Bruce S. *Confederate Colonels: A Biographical Register*. Columbia: University of Missouri Press, 2008.

Badeau, Adam. *Military History of Ulysses S. Grant, From April, 1861, to April, 1865*. 2 vols. New York: D. Appleton & Co., 1881.

Ballard, Michael B. *The Civil War in Mississippi: Major Campaigns and Battles*. Jackson: University Press of Mississippi, 2011.

_____. *Pemberton: The General Who Lost Vicksburg*. Jackson: University Press of Mississippi, 1991.

_____. *Vicksburg: The Campaign That Opened the Mississippi* (Chapel Hill: University of North Carolina Press, 2004.

Barnet, James. *The Martyrs and Heroes of Illinois in the Great Rebellion: Biographical Sketches*. Chicago: J. Barnet, 1865.

Bearss, Edwin C. "Colonel Streight Drives for the Western and Atlantic Railroad." *Alabama Historical Quarterly* 26 (Summer 1964):133-86.

_____. *Forrest at Brice's Cross Roads and in North Mississippi in 1864*. Dayton, OH: Morningside, 1994.

_____. "Grierson's Winter Raid on the Mobile and Ohio Railroad." *Military Affairs* 24, no. 2 (Spring 1960): 20-37.

_____. *Rebel Victory at Vicksburg*. Vicksburg: Vicksburg Centennial Commission, 1963.

_____. *The Vicksburg Campaign*. 3 vols. Dayton, OH: Morningside, 1985.

Baskett, George W. "Incidents of Grierson's Raid." *Confederate Veteran* 22, no. 6 (June 1914): 267-68.

Beers, Fannie A. *Memories: A Record of Personal Experience and Adventure During Four Years of War*. Philadelphia: J. B. Lippincott Company, 1889.

Berrien, John. *The Military Annals of Tennessee*. Nashville: J. M. Lindsley & Co., 1886.

Bettersworth, John K. *Confederate Mississippi: The People and Policies of a Cotton State in Wartime*. Baton Rouge: Louisiana State University Press, 1943.

_____, ed. *Mississippi in the Confederacy: As They Saw It*. Baton Rouge: Louisiana State University Press, 1961.

Black, Robert C., III. *The Railroads of the Confederacy*. Chapel Hill: University of North Carolina Press, 1952.

Bowman, T. H. *Reminiscences of an Ex-Confederate Soldier, or Forty Years on Crutches*. Austin, TX: Gammel Statesman Publishing Company, 1904.

Brackett, Albert G. *History of the United States Cavalry, From the Formation of the Federal Government to the 1st of June, 1863, To Which Is Added a List of All of the Cavalry Regiments, with the Names of Their Commanders, Which Have Been in the United States Service Since the Breaking Out of the Rebellion*. New York: Harper and Brothers, 1865.

Brown, A. J. *History of Newton County from 1834 to 1894*. Jackson: Clarion Ledger Company, 1894.

Brown, Andrew. "The First Mississippi Partisan Rangers, C.S.A." *Civil War History*, 1, no. 4 (December 1955): 371-99.

_____. *Story of Tippah County, Mississippi: The First Century*. Ripley, MS: Tippah County Historical and Genealogical Society, 1998.

Brown, D. Alexander. *Grierson's Raid*. Urbana: University of Illinois Press, 1954.

_____. "Grierson's Raid, 'Most Brilliant' of the War." *Civil War Times Illustrated* 3, no. 9 (June 1965): 4-11, 25-32.

Bynum, Victoria E. *The Free State of Jones: Mississippi's Longest Civil War*. Chapel Hill: University of North Carolina Press, 2001.

Carroll, Thomas Battle. *Historical Sketches of Oktibbeha County (Mississippi)*. Gulfport: Dixie Press, 1931.

Catton, Bruce. *Grant Moves South*. Boston: Little, Brown, and Company, 1960.

_____. *U. S. Grant and the American Military Tradition*. Boston: Little, Brown and Co., 1954.

Carwardine, Richard. *Lincoln: A Life of Purpose and Power*. New York: Knopf, 2003.

Chambers, William P. "My Journal." In *Publications of the Mississippi Historical Society, Centenary Series*. 5 vols. Jackson: Mississippi Historical Society, 1925.

Chandler, David G. *The Campaigns of Napoleon: The Mind and Method of History's Greatest Soldier*. New York: Scribner, 1966.

Chapman, Mrs. P. T. *A History of Johnson County, Illinois*. N.p.: Press of the Herron News, 1925.

Cobb, James C. *The Most Southern Place on Earth: The Mississippi Delta and the Roots of Regional Identity*. New York: Oxford University Press, 1994.

Coggins, Jack. *Arms and Equipment of the Civil War*. New York: Fairfax Press, 1983.

Cole, Lewis. "Served in the Army and Then in the Navy." *Confederate Veteran* 21, no. 3 (March 1913): 112.

Corliss, Carlton J. *Main Line of Mid-America: The Story of the Illinois Central*. New York: Creative Age Press, 1950.

Curl, A. "The Fight at Clinton, La." *Confederate Veteran* 13, no. 3 (March 1905): 122-23.

Daniel, Larry J. "Bruinsburg: Missed Opportunity or Postwar Rhetoric?" *Civil War History*, 32, no. 3 (September 1986): 256-67.

_____, and Lynn N. Bock. *Island No. 10: Struggle for the Mississippi Valley*. Tuscaloosa: University of Alabama Press, 1996.

Davis, George B., Leslie J. Perry, and Joseph W. Kirkley. *Atlas to Accompany the Official Records of the Union and Confederate Armies*. Washington, DC: Government Printing Office, 1891-95.

Dinges, Bruce J. "Grierson's Raid." *Civil War Times Illustrated* 34, no. 6 (Feb. 1996): 50-60, 62, 64.

_____. "The Making of a Cavalryman: Benjamin H. Grierson and the Civil War Along the Mississippi, 1861-1865." PhD diss., Rice University, 1978.

DeForest, Tim. "Grierson's Raid During the Vicksburg Campaign." *America's Civil War* (September 2000).

Deupree, Mrs. N. D. "Some Historic Homes of Mississippi." In *Publications of the Mississippi Historical Society*, ed. Franklin L. Riley. Oxford: Mississippi Historical Society, 1902.

Donald, David Herbert. *Lincoln*. New York: Simon and Shuster, 1995.

Dubay, Robert W. *John Jones Pettus, Mississippi Fire-Eater: His Life and Times, 1813-1867*. Jackson: University Press of Mississippi, 1975.

DuBose, John W. *Jefferson County and Birmingham, Alabama*. Birmingham: Caldwell Printing Works, 1887.

Eby, Henry H. *Observations of an Illinois Boy in Battle, Camp and Prisons—1861 to 1865*. N.p.: n.p., 1910.

Eddy, T. M. *The Patriotism of Illinois: A Record of the Civil and Military History of the State in the War for the Union*. 2 vols. Chicago: Clarke and Co., 1866.

Ferguson, Ernest B. *Chancellorsville 1863: The Souls of the Brave*. New York: Knopf, 1993.

Field Manual 3-0: Operations. Washington, DC: Department of the Army, 2008.

Forbes, S. A. "Grierson's Cavalry Raid." *Transactions of the Illinois State Historical Society* (Springfield: Phillips Bros. State Printers, 1908), 99-130.

Fremantle, Arthur J. L. *Three Months in the Southern States: April-June, 1863*. Edinburgh: W. Blackwood and Sons, 1863.

Freyburger, Michael. *Letters to Ann*. Shelbyville, IL: Shelby County Historical Society, 1986.

Garner, James Wilford. *Reconstruction in Mississippi*. New York: MacMillan, 1902.

Godfrey, John Franklin. *The Civil War Letters of Capt. John Franklin Godfrey*. Edited by Candace Sawyer and Laura Orcutt. South Freeport, ME: Ascensius Press, 1993.

Goodloe, Albert Theodore. *Confederate Echoes: A Voice from the South in the Days of Secession and the Southern Confederacy*. Nashville: Publishing House of the M.E. Church, South, 1907.

Grabau, Warren E. *Ninety-Eight Days: A Geographer's View of the Vicksburg Campaign*. Knoxville: University of Tennessee Press, 2000.

Grant, U. S. *Personal Memoirs of U.S. Grant*. 2 vols. New York: Charles L. Webster and Co., 1885.

Grear, Charles D. "'Through the Heart of Rebel Country': The History and Memory of Grierson's Raid." In *The Vicksburg Campaign: March 29-May 18, 1863*, ed. Steven E. Woodworth and Charles D. Grear. Carbondale: Southern Illinois University Press, 2013.

Grierson, Benjamin H. *A Just and Righteous Cause: Benjamin H. Grierson's Civil War Memoir*. Edited by Bruce J. Dinges and Shirley A. Leckie. Carbondale: Southern Illinois University Press, 2008.

Griffith, Paddy. *Battle Tactics of the Civil War*. New Haven: Yale University Press, 1987.

Hancock, R. R. *Hancock's Diary: Or, A History of the Second Tennessee Confederate Cavalry, with Sketches of First and Seventh Battalions; Also, Portraits and Biographical Sketches*. Nashville: Brandon Printing Company, 1887.

Heidler, David S. and Jeanne T. Heidler, eds. *Encyclopedia of the American Civil War: A Political, Social, and Military History*. 5 vols. Santa Barbara, CA: ABC-CLIO, 2000.

Hepworth, George H. *The Whip, Hoe, and Sword: Or, the Gulf-Department in '63*. Boston: Walker, Wise and Company, 1864.

Herndon, D. T. *Centennial History of Arkansas.* 3 vols. Little Rock: S. J. Clarke Publishing Company, 1922.

Hicken, Victor. *Illinois in the Civil War.* Urbana: University of Illinois Press, 1966.

History of Clay County, Mississippi. N.p.: Curtis Media Corporation, 1988.

History of Kossuth, Hancock and Winnebego Counties, Iowa. Springfield, IL: Union Publishing Company, 1884.

Hord, Henry Ewell. "Her Little Flag." *Confederate Veteran* 23, no. 10 (October 1915): 473-74.

House Report 650, 53rd Congress, 2nd Session, 1-2.

Huff, Robert Glen, and Hattie Pearl Nunnery. *Amite County & Liberty, Mississippi: Celebrating 200 Years.* Virginia Beach, VA: Donning Company Publishers, 2009.

Jackson, Orange. *The History of Orange Jackson's War Life: As Related by Himself.* N.p.: n.p., n.d.

Joiner, Gary D. *Mr. Lincoln's Brown Water Navy: The Mississippi Squadron.* New York: Rowman and Littlefield, 2007.

Jones, J. B. *A Rebel War Clerk's Diary: At the Confederate States* Capital. 2 vols. Edited by James I. Robertson Jr. Lawrence: University Press of Kansas, 2015.

Jones, James Pickett. *Black Jack: John A. Logan and Southern Illinois in the Civil War Era.* Carbondale: Southern Illinois University Press, 1995.

Journal of the State Convention and Ordinances and Resolutions Adopted in January, 1861, With an Appendix. Jackson: E. Barksdale, 1861.

Justice, Keith, et al. *Newton County and the Civil War.* N.p.: Eseff Press, 1995.

Kelley, Arthell. "The Geography." In *A History of Mississippi,* ed. Richard A. McLemore. 2 vols. Hattiesburg: University & College Press of Mississippi, 1973.

Kennedy, J. M. *History of Jasper County.* Bay Springs, MS: Bay Springs Municipal Library, 1957.

Kennedy, Joseph C. G. *Population of the United States in 1860: Compiled from the Original Returns of the Eighth Census Under the Direction of the Secretary of the Interior.* Washington, DC: Government Printing Office, 1864.

Kiper, Richard L. *Major General John Alexander McClernand: Politician in Uniform.* Kent, OH: Kent State University Press, 1999.

Lalicki, Tom. *Grierson's Raid: A Daring Cavalry Strike Through the Heart of the Confederacy.* New York: Farrar, Straus and Giroux, 2004.

Lardas, Mark. *Roughshod Through Dixie: Grierson's Raid 1863.* New York: Osprey, 2010.

Lash, Jeffrey N. *A Politician Turned General: The Civil War Career of Stephen Augustus Hurlbut.* Kent: Kent State University Press, 2003.

Leckie, William H., and Shirley A. Leckie. *Unlikely Warriors: General Benjamin Grierson and His Family.* Norman: University of Oklahoma Press, 1984.

Lewis, William T. *The Centennial History of Winston County, Mississippi.* Pasadena, TX: Globe Publishers, 1972.

Longacre, Edward G. *Mounted Raids of the Civil War.* New York: A. S. Barnes, 1975.

Loving, Waldon. *Coming Like Hell: The Story of the 12th Tennessee Cavalry, Richardson's Brigade, Forrest's Cavalry Corps, Confederate States Army, 1862-1865.* Lincoln, NE: Writer's Club Press, 2002.

Lusk, David W. *Politics and Politicians: A Succinct History of the Politics of Illinois, From 1856 to 1884, With Anecdotes and Incidents, and Appendix from 1809 to 1856.* Springfield: H. W. Rokker, 1884.

Mackey, Robert B. *The Uncivil War: Irregular Warfare in the Upper South, 1861-1865.* Norman: University of Oklahoma Press, 2004.

Mahin, John Lee, and Martin Rackin. "The Horse Soldiers or Grierson's Raid." *Civil War History* 5, no. 2 (June 1959): 183-87.

Marszalek, John F. *Commander of All Lincoln's Armies: A Life of General Henry W. Halleck.* Cambridge: Harvard University Press, 2004.

_____. "'A Full Share of All the Credit': Sherman and Grant to the Fall of Vicksburg." In *Grant's Lieutenants: From Cairo to Vicksburg,* ed. Steven E. Woodworth. Lawrence: University Press of Kansas, 2001, 5-20.

McPherson, James M. *Battle Cry of Freedom: The Civil War Era.* New York: Oxford University Press, 1988.

McWhiney, Grady, and Perry D. Jamieson. *Attack and Die: Civil War Military Tactics and the Southern Heritage.* Tuscaloosa: University of Alabama Press, 1982.

Moore, Frank, ed. *The Rebellion Record: A Diary of American Events, with Documents, Narratives Illustrative Incidents, Poetry, etc.* 11 vols. New York: D. Vann Nostrand and Co. 1861-68.

Oaks, Elizabeth K. "Benjamin H. Grierson: Reluctant Horse Soldier and Gentle Raider." MA thesis, Mississippi State University, 1981.

Official Journal of the Proceedings of the Convention of the State of Louisiana. New Orleans: J. O. Nixon, 1861.

Parson, Thomas E. *Work for Giants: The Campaign and Battle of Tupelo/Harrisburg, Mississippi, June-July 1864.* Kent, OH: Kent State University Press, 2014.

Pierce, Lyman B. *History of the Second Iowa Cavalry; Containing a Detailed Account of Its Organization, Marches, and the Battles in Which It Has Participated; Also, a Complete Roster of Each Company.* Burlington, IA: Hawk-Eye Steam Book and Job Printing Establishment, 1865.

Powell, David A. *The Maps of Chickamauga.* New York: Savas Beatie, 2009.

Prange, Gordon W., Donald M. Goldstein, and Katherine V. Dillon. *At Dawn We Slept: The Untold Story of Pearl Harbor.* New York: Penguin, 1981.

Reece, J. N. *Report of the Adjutant General of the State of Illinois*. 9 vols. Springfield, IL: Journal Company, 1901.

Richardson, Albert D. *A Personal History of Ulysses S. Grant*. Hartford, CT: American Publishing Company, 1868.

Robinson, Mary S. *A Household Story of the American Conflict: The Great Battle Year*. New York: N. Tibbals & Son, 1871.

Roster and Record of Iowa Soldiers in the War of the Rebellion, Together with Historical Sketches of Volunteer Organizations, 1861-1866. 6 vols. Des Moines, Emory H. English, State Printer, 1910.

Roth, Dave. "Grierson's Raid, April 17-May 2, 1863: A Cavalry Raid at Its Best." *Blue & Gray Magazine* 10, no 5 (June 1993): 12-24, 48-65.

Rowland, Dunbar. *Mississippi; Comprising Sketches of Counties, Towns, Events, Institutions and Persons, Arranged in Cyclopedic Form*. 3 vols. Atlanta: Southern Historical Printing Association, 1907.

_____, and H. Grady Howell Jr. *Military History of Mississippi: 1803-1898, Including a Listing of All Known Mississippi Confederate Military Units*. Madison, MS: Chickasaw Bayou Press, 2003.

Scott, James M. *Target Tokyo: Jimmy Doolittle and the Raid That Avenged Pearl Harbor*. New York: W. W. Norton & Company, 2015.

Senate Report 772, 52nd Congress, 1st Session, 1-2.

Shea, William L., and Terrence J. Winschel. *Vicksburg Is the Key: The Struggle for the Mississippi River*. Lincoln: University of Nebraska Press, 2003.

Sherman, William T. *Memoirs of General William T. Sherman: Written by Himself*. 2 vols. New York: D. Appleton and Co., 1875.

Schiller, Laurence D. *Of Sabres and Carbines: The Emergence of the Federal Dragoon*. Danville, VA: Blue Gray Education Society, 2001.

Simon, John Y., and John F. Marszalek, eds. *The Papers of Ulysses S. Grant*. 32 vols. to date. Carbondale: Southern Illinois University Press, 1967- .

Simpson, Brooks D. *Ulysses S. Grant: Triumph over Adversity, 1822-1865*. Boston: Houghton Mifflin, 2000.

Smith County Genealogical Society. *Smith County, Mississippi, and Its Families*. 2 vols. Raleigh, MS: Smith County Genealogical Society, 2006.

Smith, Timothy B. *Corinth 1862: Siege, Battle, Occupation*. Lawrence: University Press of Kansas, 2012.

_____. *"The Decision Was Always My Own": Ulysses S. Grant and the Vicksburg Campaign*. Carbondale: Southern Illinois University Press, 2018.

_____. *Grant Invades Tennessee: The 1862 Battles for Forts Henry and Donelson*. Lawrence: University Press of Kansas, 2016.

_____. *James Z. George: Mississippi Great Commoner.* Jackson: University Press of Mississippi, 2012.

_____. *Mississippi in the Civil War: The Home Front.* Mississippi Heritage Series. Jackson: University Press of Mississippi, 2010.

_____. The *Mississippi Secession Convention: Delegates and Deliberations in Politics and War, 1861-1865.* Jackson: University Press of Mississippi, 2014.

_____. *Shiloh: Conquer or Perish.* Lawrence: University Press of Kansas, 2014.

_____. "Victory at Any Cost: The Yazoo Pass Expedition." *Journal of Mississippi History,* vol. 67, no. 2 (Summer 2007): 147-66.

Smith, William Sooy. "The Mississippi Raid." *Military Essays and Recollections: Essays and Papers Read Before the Illinois Commandery.* 4 vols. (Chicago: Order of the Commandery, 1907), 4: 379-91.

The Society of the Army of the Tennessee. *Report of the Proceedings of the Society of the Army of the Tennessee Meetings Held at Columbus, Ohio, November 3-4, 1909, Toledo, Ohio, November 16-17, 1910, Council Bluffs, Iowa, November 10-11, 1911.* Cincinnati: Charles O. Ebel Printing Company, 1913.

Starr, Stephen Z. "Hawkeyes on Horseback: The Second Iowa Volunteer Cavalry." *Civil War History,* 23, 3 (September 1977): 212-27.

_____. *The Union Cavalry in the Civil War.* 3 vols. Baton Rouge: Louisiana State University Press, 1979-85.

Strickland, Jean, and Patricia N. Edwards. *Records of Jasper Co. Mississippi: W.P.A. Source Materials, Will Abstracts, 1855-1914.* N.p.: n.p., 1995.

Stuart, A. A. *Iowa Colonels and Regiments: Being a History of Iowa Regiments in the War of the Rebellion.* Des Moines: Mills and Co., 1865.

Stubbs, Steven H. *Neshoba at War: The Story of the Men and Women of Neshoba County in World War II.* Philadelphia MS: Dancing Rabbit Press, 2003.

Surby, R. W. "The Grierson Raid," *National Tribune,* July 12, 1883.

_____. *Grierson Raids, and Hatch's Sixty-Four Days March, with Biographical Sketches, also, the Life and Adventures of Chickasaw, the Scout.* Chicago: Rounds and James, 1865.

_____. *Two Great Raids: Col. Grierson's Successful Swoop Through Mississippi, Morgan's Disastrous Raid Through Indiana and Ohio, Vivid Narratives of Both These Great Operations, with Extracts from Official Records, John Morgan's Escape, Last Raid, and Death.* Washington, DC: National Tribune, 1897.

Talkington, N. Dale. *A Time Remembered: The Verdan, Oklahoma Cemetery.* N.p.: n.p., 1999.

Taunton, Louis, and Nancy R. Parkes. *Winston County and Its People: A Collection of Family Histories.* Louisville, MS: Winston County Genealogical and Historical Society, 1980.

Toll, Ian W. *The Conquering Tide: War in the Pacific Islands, 1942-1944.* New York: W. W. Norton & Company, 2015.

Turpentine, Tim. "A History of Chickasaw County." Edited by James R. Atkinson. *Journal of Mississippi History* 41, no. 4 (November 1979): 319-33.

Tutor, Forrest T. *Gordons of Lochinvar.* N.p.: n.p., 2008.

U.S. War Department. *War of the Rebellion: A Compilation of the Official Records of the Union and Confederate Armies.* Washington, DC: U.S. Government Printing Office, 1880-1901.

Warner, Ezra J. *Generals in Blue: Lives of the Union Commanders.* Baton Rouge: Louisiana State University Press, 1964.

_____. *Generals in Gray: Lives of the Confederate Commanders.* Baton Rouge: Louisiana State University Press, 1959.

White, Ronald C. *American Ulysses: A Life of Ulysses S. Grant.* New York: Random House, 2016.

Williams, Nancy Catherine. *The History of Newton, Mississippi 1860-1988.* Newton: Newton Record, 1989.

Williams, Ruth White. *On the Map 145 Years: The History of West Point, Mississippi, 1846-1991.* West Point, MS: City of West Point, 1996.

Wills, Charles W. *Army Life of an Illinois Soldier: Including a Day by Day Record of Sherman's March to the Sea.* Washington, DC: Globe Printing Company, 1906.

Winschel, Terrence J. *Triumph and Defeat: The Vicksburg Campaign.* 2 vols. Mason City, IA: Savas Publishing Company, 1999-2006.

Wood, Gordon S. *Empire of Liberty: A History of the Early Republic, 1789-1815.* New York: Oxford University Press, 2009.

Woodward, S. L. "Grierson's Raid, April 17th to May 2d, 1863." *Journal of the United States Cavalry Association* 14, no. 52 (April 1904): 685-710.

_____. "Grierson's Raid, April 17th to May 2d, 1863," *Journal of the United States Cavalry Association* 15, no. 53 (July 1904): 94-123.

Woodworth, Steven E., and Charles D. Grear, eds. *The Vicksburg Campaign: March 29-May 18, 1863.* Carbondale: Southern Illinois University Press, 2013.

Wynne, Ben. *Mississippi's Civil War: A Narrative History.* Macon, GA: Mercer University Press, 2006.

Yates, Jenelle B., and Theresa T. Ridout. *Red Clay Hills of Neshoba: Since 1833: Roots–Reflections–Ramblings: The Early History of Neshoba County, Mississippi.* Philadelphia, MS: Neshoba County Historical Society, 1992.

York, Neil Longley. *Fiction as Fact: The Horse Soldiers and Popular Memory.* Kent, OH: Kent State University Press, 2001.

Web Sources

6th Illinois Cavalry, https://civilwar.illinoisgenweb.org/reg_html/cav_006.html

7th Illinois Cavalry, https://civilwar.illinoisgenweb.org/reg_html/cav_007.html

2nd Iowa Cavalry, https://familysearch.org/wiki/en/2nd_Regiment,_Iowa_Cavalry

"A Body of Cavalrymen Coming Up the Road, April 30, 2013, http://betweenthegateposts.
   blogspot.com/2013/04/a-body-of-cavalrymen-coming-up-road.html

Orlando Davis Diary, http://www.rootsweb.ancestry.com/~mscivilw/davis.htm

Find a Grave:

Griffin M. Bender, Find a Grave Memorial 9121577, July 19, 2004, https://www.
   findagrave.com/cgi-bin/fg.cgi?

Stephen Daggett, Find a Grave Memorial 14631957, June 17, 2006, https://www.
   findagrave.com/cgi-bin/fg.cgi?

Charner Estes, Find a Grave Memorial 22479366, October 27, 2007, https://www.
   findagrave.com/cgi-bin/fg.cgi?

Uriah Thomas Gill, Find a Grave Memorial 34483133, March 5, 2009, https://www.
   findagrave.com/cgi-bin/fg.cgi?

Benjamin Kilgore, Find a Grave Memorial 59666701, September 28, 2010, https://www.
   findagrave.com/cgi-bin/fg.cgi?page=gr&GRid=59333701

Chambers McAdory, Find a Grave Memorial 38840788, June 28, 2009, https://www.
   findagrave.com/cgi-bin/fg.cgi?page=gr&GRid=38840788

Elias Nichols, Find a Grave Memorial 122137181, December 25, 2013, https://www.
   findagrave.com/cgi-bin/fg.cgi?

William David Sloan, Find a Grave Memorial 15206302, August 10, 2006, https://www.
   findagrave.com/cgi-bin/fg.cgi?

A. C. Snyder, Find a Grave Memorial 37477734, May 25, 2009, https://www.findagrave.
   com/cgi-bin/fg.cgi?

Thomas Jefferson Spurlock Sr., Find a Grave Memorial 104073536, January 23, 2013,
   https://www.findagrave.com/cgi-bin/fg.cgi?

Richard W. Surby, Find a Grave Memorial 24359889, February 3, 2008, https://https://
   www.findagrave.com/memorial/24359889

Jesse Thompson Jr., Find a Grave Memorial 137537073, October 20, 2014, https://www.
   findagrave.com/cgi-bin/fg.cgi?

George Washington Williams, Find a Grave Memorial 18083560, February 26, 2007,
   https://www.findagrave.com/cgi-bin/fg.cgi?

Ulysses S. Grant Presidential Library, http://www.usgrantlibrary.org

Gerhard Peters and John T. Woolley, *The American Presidency Project*, http://www.
   presidency.ucsb.edu/ws/?pid=69891

Southern Claims Commission Depositions:

Milly McLean, Deposition, October 29, 1873, http://www.angelfire.com/folk/gljmr/ McLeanMilly.html

Alex Roundtree, Deposition, October 1873, http://www.angelfire.com/folk/gljmr/ RoundtreeA.html

Charles Roundtree, Deposition, October 1873, http://www.angelfire.com/folk/gljmr/ RoundtreeC.html

Index

Acknowledgments

Many people across the United States have aided me in this book, and I am most grateful to them for their work on my behalf. My parents, George and Miriam Smith, have always been my biggest cheerleaders, and although it was not a conscious decision on their part, I was fortunate enough to be raised by them amid the very area where much of Grierson's Raid took place. I currently live in West Tennessee, just east of La Grange. I lived for 10 years along Grierson's route near Cherry Creek, between New Albany and Pontotoc. My grandparents lived in Neshoba and Newton Counties, in Philadelphia and Union, both of which Grierson passed through. Our travels to grandparents necessarily followed much of Grierson's route southward down Highway 15 through Pontotoc, Houston, and eventually to Louisville and Noxapater. Grierson's slight detour to the east to Starkville was amply covered when I spent four years gaining a PhD at Mississippi State University. My family also has connections even beyond Newton, such as around Enterprise and Meridian, where I was born. Another branch of my family came from Smith County farther south, through which Grierson also passed. I count it a privilege and an honor to have been born and raised in Mississippi for many reasons, including, specifically for this book, providing an intimate knowledge of much of the area involved in Grierson's Raid.

Many people along this route and in other places aided my research. The many staff at the various national, state, and local libraries and archives were most helpful, particularly those at the Abraham Lincoln Presidential Library, the University of Illinois, the Mississippi Department of Archives and History, and in the many county libraries and historical societies in both Mississippi and Illinois. In particular, Debbie Hamm, Roberta Fairburn, Bill Manhart, John Heiner, Sara Strickland, Libby Thornton, Jessica Perkins Smith, Krista Gray, Johna Picco, Denise Dickerson, and Jeff Giambrone were of immense help.

Several went above and beyond and deserve particular mention. Greg Biggs, Christopher Slocombe, Bjorn Skaptason, Michele Surbey, Randy Beck, and Steve Hicks graciously shared material from their collections. Jim Woodrick of the Mississippi Department of Archives and History helped locate several sites, and Terry Winschel, Tom Parson, Laurie Schiller, Dave Roth, Shirley Leckie, and Bruce Dinges aided in background context. John F. Marszalek and Terry Winschel read the manuscript and provided plenty of good feedback. Ted Savas and his staff at Savas Beatie did a wonderful job on the finished product.

Several people helped me find sites and plantations where Grierson's troops camped. Jill Smith of New Albany helped locate several locations around that area. Jack Elliott of Palo Alto showed me the battle sites as well as Benjamin Kilgore's plantation and burial place. Joe Gibbon, who happens to be a 13-year veteran of the major leagues and a member of the 1960 World Series champion Pittsburgh Pirates) showed me old Garlandville. Rudy Burnett showed me the Elias Nichols plantation house site and his grave. Joe Moss provided detail on the Chambers McAdory plantation just east of the Leaf River, which his family owns. Mark Tullos, who is an attorney and a member of the Mississippi state legislature, provided access to his family's Leaf River property where Grierson crossed and burned the bridge. Steve Amos, chancery clerk of Copiah County, helped pinpoint the Jesse Thompson plantation.

All of these had a big hand in this book and discovering the exact route of Grierson's travels. But my most special thanks go to my wife, Kelly, and girls, Mary Kate and Leah Grace, who continue to be my best friends. I thank God daily for them as I do for His eternal love and watch care.

Timothy B. Smith
Adamsville, Tennessee

About the Author

Timothy B. Smith (Ph.D. Mississippi State University, 2001) is a veteran of the National Park Service and currently teaches history at the University of Tennessee at Martin.

In addition to many articles and essays, he is the author, editor, or co-editor of eighteen books, including *Champion Hill: Decisive Battle for Vicksburg* (2004), which won the nonfiction book award from the Mississippi Institute of Arts and Letters, *Corinth 1862: Siege, Battle, Occupation* (2012), which won the Fletcher Pratt Award and the McLemore Prize, *Shiloh: Conquer or Perish* (2014), which won the Richard B. Harwell Award, the Tennessee History Book Award, and the Douglas Southall Freeman Award, and *Grant Invades Tennessee: The 1862 Battles for Forts Henry and Donelson* (2016), which won the Tennessee History Book Award, the Emerging Civil War Book Award, and the Douglas Southall Freeman Award. He is currently writing a book on the May 19 and 22 Vicksburg assaults.

He lives with his wife Kelly and children Mary Kate and Leah Grace in Adamsville, Tennessee.